ACCOUNTING AND THE ENTERPRISE

Written from a sociological perspective, this book is concerned with ways in which social theories and analyses can inform our understanding of accounting in modern enterprises. Despite its importance in UK and US enterprises, accounting has largely been ignored by sociologists, and until recently accounting research has been dominated by economic perspectives. This has been changing through 'critical accounting' studies which adopt a wide range of social analysis. The book locates these new developments in social science debates on the enterprise in modern society and brings them to a broader audience.

In relating social science debates to accounting four aspects are explored: the influence of social theories of the enterprise on accounting theory; the way changes in enterprises have affected accounting practice; the way in which accounting practice has influenced business practice; and how a study of accounting theory and practice may lead us to revise broader social science theories of the enterprise.

By challenging the view that accounting should be left for accountants to study, the author asserts that an exploration of accounting is an important element in understanding the ways in which modern enterprises and societies operate.

T. Colwyn Jones is a lecturer at the School of Sociology, University of the West of England, Bristol.

ACCOUNTING AND THE ENTERPRISE

A social analysis

T. Colwyn Jones

London and New York

First published 1995
by Routledge
11 New Fetter Lane, London EC4P 4EE

Simultaneously published in the USA and Canada
by Routledge
29 West 35th Street, New York, NY 10001

© 1995 T. Colwyn Jones

Typeset in Times by LaserScript, Mitcham, Surrey
Printed and bound in Great Britain by
Mackays of Chatham PLC, Chatham, Kent

British Library Cataloguing in Publication Data
A catalogue record for this book is available from the British Library

Library of Congress Cataloguing in Publication Data
A catalogue record for this book has been requested

ISBN 0–415–07207–7 (hbk)
ISBN 0–415–07208–5 (pbk)

For Myra, Hilary, Amy and Lauren

CONTENTS

LIST OF BOXES

ACKNOWLEDGEMENTS

I have many people to thank.

I am grateful to friends and colleagues at UWE and other institutions who gave comments and encouragement as I struggled with this book. In particular to those from elsewhere: Pete Armstrong, Rob Gray, Trevor Hopper, Keith Hoskin, Theo Nichols, Prem Sikka and Hugh Willmott; and at Bristol, Arthur Baxter, David Bence, Peter Glasner, Ursula Lucas, Jem Thomas and Peter Wardley. Special thanks go to my research companion over recent years, Dave Dugdale. Most of all I thank Alastair Neilson who made detailed, extremely useful and amazingly speedy comments on every chapter despite his many responsibilities in the Bristol Business School. All these people have helped me to write this book but none is responsible for its failure to live up to their hopes for it – the blame rests with me.

I am also grateful to my students here at Bristol, especially those on the BA Accounting and Finance course (1975–94) who have grappled along with me in attempts to create a social analysis of accounting, and have shown me where I go wrong, where things are too difficult and confused, and (occasionally) where things make sense. They have had a lot to cope with and I thank them for their tolerance of the bothersome bits and their enthusiasm for the more successful topics. Recently I have been joined in teaching this course by Hugh Kirkbride and Bill Lee who have helped me clarify some of the issues involved in applying sociology to accounting.

The staff of the Economics and Social Science Faculty office have been outstandingly helpful and my thanks go especially to Ena Briers and Chris Hunt, and to Helen Robbins who suffered my handwritten scrawl and converted it into pristine text.

The people at Routledge – Elisabeth Tribe, Rosemary Nixon and Gabi Woolgar – I never met, but they gave me space to complete this book with just the occasional encouraging letter. This was very helpful as were the comments of their three anonymous reviewers.

Finally, a word of thanks and apology to my family. They have had to put up with my preoccupations, desperations and celebrations over this book for three years, and with my filling bedroom, dining room and kitchen with manuscripts, books, notes, photocopies, and all the other paraphernalia I seem to gather about me when I am working. It is nearly over now and I will tidy everything up soon, I promise.

Colwyn Jones
University of the West of England
Bristol

Introduction

STUDYING SOCIAL ANALYSES OF ACCOUNTING

In introducing this book I hope to communicate directly as writer to reader. The problem is that we do not know each other – indeed as I write there are no readers and only optimism keeps my pen moving in the hope that one day there will be.

As for me, I am a sociologist who has spent much of the last twenty years teaching sociology to undergraduate students of accounting, grappling with accounting academic literature, and researching accounting practitioners in enterprises. In doing this I have gained some hazy understanding of what accounting is about. This is an unusual thing for a sociologist to do – as my colleagues frequently point out – and this book emerges from that experience. Writing such a book is a foolhardy exercise, since 'the conventional wisdom of sociology teaching is that: *a* Nobody has ever written a decent sociology textbook. *b* Nobody ever will' (Lee and Newby, 1983: 10). However, having recognized the impossibility of their task, they carried on anyway. Writing a text on the sociology of accounting often seemed to me to be an even more ludicrous project – but I pursued it nevertheless.

As for you, I have various conceptions of who you (in the future) might be. You might be male or female; young or old; with different knowledges, experiences, and skills; and from different societies and cultures. I have directed my writing at undergraduates on accounting courses, basing my images on the thousand or so accounting students I have met at the University of the West of England, Bristol. However, I have also tried to keep a more general readership in mind – business studies and social science undergraduates with an interest in accounting topics; trainee accountants on professional courses; postgraduate students of accounting and business; and accounting practitioners and others in business who are interested in exploring the changing role of accounting in enterprises. Other potential readers I have tried to dismiss from my mind whilst writing – my academic colleagues as lecturers and researchers in educational institutions. Of course I hope that they will read this book but it is not directed specifically at them. Too much academic work is addressed to a small, select audience of those who are already knowledgeable about the topics to be discussed. I worried that if I wrote with them in mind I would constantly be anticipating their objections, modifications, and extensions so that my pages

1

might be littered with hesitancies, prevarications, obscure asides, and defensive ambiguities. This might help fend off their critical attacks, but it would make the book unreadable for others. Instead I have tried to write as clearly as I am able, assuming that readers will have some knowledge of accounting but little of social analysis.

Debates

The book is concerned with enterprises – business organizations, privately owned, employing people to produce goods and services to be traded in markets – and their relationship with accounting. It focuses on debates and so is interested in the ways in which academics and others discuss accounting and enterprises. By presenting this in terms of debates I wish to highlight the disagreements, arguments, and controversies which characterize the discussion. This book does not provide a single answer to any of the issues it raises; it attempts to clarify questions and explore how and why different people in different places at different times came to pose particular questions and give their different answers to them. In doing this I hope to help you to understand, and then take part in, contemporary debates.

Structure of the book

The book begins with a brief, and very sketchy, history of the emergence of modern enterprises which is intended to set the scene for the later discussions. Parts I, II, and III each review social science theories of aspects of the enterprise – in relation to capital, management, and labour – and then relate these to accounting. Most of the material refers to the UK and US, with some international comparisons, especially with Germany and Japan. In relating the general (social science) theories to the specific (accounting) case four aspects are covered. First, the influence of social theories on accounting theory. Second, the way that changes in enterprises have affected accounting practice. Third, the way in which accounting practice has influenced enterprises. And fourth (but briefly) how a study of accounting theory and practice may lead us to revise the social science theories with which we began. Although these aspects may be logically separate, when we begin to look at particular issues the discussion (unfortunately but inescapably) becomes more muddled. Part IV draws these themes together in an attempt to delineate what it is that a social analysis of accounting can address, and the social theory which has informed those analyses which have been conducted. It is more usual to define the territory to be covered at the outset of study. In my experience this has more meaning for the expert (who proposes the definitions) than for the newcomer (who has not yet even encountered the terrain to be defined). I have chosen to postpone delineation of the subject matter of this book until the end. If you find this unsatisfactory then I suggest you begin with Chapter 8.

Other than this, I have intended the book to be read from the front. It is sequential, since later chapters assume knowledge of topics dealt with earlier. It is also cumulative in that the early discussions deal with issues more simply than the later chapters. I have tried to match the introduction of analyses to my expectation of the developing knowledge and skill of the reader. That is another reason for leaving the 'Theory' chapter until the end; I find Theory difficult and so have most of my students (two phenomena which may be related!).

Writer bias – reader beware!

In introducing debates you will become aware that I am not a disinterested observer of the scene – indeed if I said I was you should suspect me of deceit or, if I was genuine, conclude that I had nothing of importance to say. The book deals with issues of the world we live in and neither you nor I can pretend to stand apart from this. I have tried to report accurately and clearly theories with which I do not agree, but can never totally escape my biases – those things which make me a human being, not a writing machine. Some recommend that the solution is to strive for impartiality and disguise one's own views. I find this unsatisfactory because so much is inescapably partisan, and to pretend otherwise would be dishonest. I have had to choose some theories and analyses to include, and others to leave out. I have had to make certain interpretations of those things included – there could have been others. The structure of the book – dealing with capital, management, and labour – stems from particular ways of viewing enterprises. Even had I been able to present impartial reports on the various views expressed in the book, my selection and editing of them would be bound to reflect my own perceptions and values. Rather than pretending to you that this is not so, I prefer to warn you in advance that you should read warily. In particular I found that in Part IV my own views on debates in accounting were becoming more intrusive in driving my words. Perhaps I am not the best person to judge this. Since I hope to encourage a critical understanding, I must rely on you to read this book with appropriate caution.

Some words about language

In social analysis our tools are words and we should be careful which are used and how. The reader will become sensitive to this point as the book develops, but some early comments may be helpful. I have tried to be consistent in using *accounting* to refer to theories, techniques and activities; *accountants* for individuals or groups of people who carry this out as their main occupation; and *accountancy* as the organization of the first two as a profession. This is not the only way of using these words, which may each be defined more broadly or more narrowly. I have also preferred to talk of *enterprises* rather than *organizations*, which is more common in business studies texts. This is partly to highlight the focus on businesses and indicates that I shall not be dealing with accounting in schools, universities, hospitals, prisons, and other kinds of organization. More importantly, it reflects my suspicion about organization theory which assumes that all these organizations have essential similarity and that we can create universal theories about how they are to be constructed 'efficiently'. Of course many business theories and methods have been exported into other settings – a notable feature of accounting in recent years. I think we should be surprised and curious about this, rather than seeing it as natural or inevitable. I have also used *social* rather than *behavioural* as a focus. For me, 'behaviour' carries implications of a study of the observed activities of individuals. I am also interested in non-observable thinking processes involving ideas and reasoning; and also in the broader economic, political, and cultural context in which these take place. Thus I prefer the term 'social', but I shall not attempt to define it here; by the end of the book you may have developed many ways of doing so.

In other cases I have made uneasy compromises over words – especially in relation to gender and race. Much discussion of accounting and enterprises assumes a male actor – the accountant and the business*man he* advises. The terms 'black' or 'person of colour' or 'Afro-American' provoke different reactions from different people. To use 'Anglo-Saxon society' pains me (because I regard myself as Celtic); and 'the English-speaking nations' is also inappropriate (especially in the case of the US). Since words reflect their authors I have decided not to adopt a common solution by inserting '[sic]' into quotations to highlight dubious language. Since they also reflect the time and place of their use I have continued to use 'putting-out master' and 'the foreman's empire' in discussion of early enterprises. I shall trust the reader to be aware, and wary of, the words that are used – having raised the issue here. Language itself must be part of social analysis.

Finally, a note on jargon. One of the most frequent complaints about sociology is that it uses a complex, specialized, and obscure terminology which excludes people from debates. There is some truth in this, though when accountants protest about it I sometimes smile – surely their own language is not entirely transparent? I cannot promise that jargon has been eliminated from this book – it would be difficult (impossible?) to do so. I have either defined key concepts as they become central in discussions; or have thrown scare quotes around terms which will later be discussed as problematic. In this introduction I have already referred to 'efficiency' (warning: dangerous notion, not yet defined) and later will talk of 'correct answers' (warning: dubious assumption, probably not capable of agreed definition). I realize that this can be an irritating habit, and have tried to restrict it. Perhaps readers should add their own, mental, inverted commas to any word which appears important but ill-defined or contestable. Language is a crucial part of the ways we understand (and misunderstand) the world and each other.

Studying debates

To those encountering social analysis for the first time its study is often perplexing. In my experience, many accounting students bring with them the expectation that where there are questions there must be answers and that (with diligence) they will be able to learn the correct answers. This view is often encouraged by their early experiences on accounting courses, where emphasis on the bookkeeping aspects gives the impression of a neatly ordered world which is capable of resolution in a proper balance – if only we can distinguish our credits from our debits. Only later in their courses do many students discover that accounting is not entirely like this and that there are many areas of uncertainty, ambiguity, subjectivity, contested interpretation, and disagreement. In studying social analysis this discovery comes much earlier – indeed, in this book the contested nature of discussions will be emphasized from the outset. Students are immediately confronted with a potentially bewildering range of different answers to the same question, with different questions, and sometimes with questions to which there are no answers. Some react by assuming this means anything goes – that if there are no 'correct answers' then there are only opinions, each as valid as any other. If so, they see no point in studying. Others, hoping they are being cynically pragmatic, think that the game must be to detect the opinion preferred by the lecturer/examiner and to adopt it in order to gain high marks. In my experience both approaches are spectacularly unsuccessful as ways of tackling social analysis.

Becoming informed

Coming to terms with the nature of social analysis, and being able not only to understand debates but also to enter into them, can be a long and difficult process. I can suggest some simple first steps. Even if, to begin with, you regard the theories you encounter as merely opinions, then you may recognize that some are more informed than others. To reassure yourself that you are becoming informed about debates a simple checklist will help you keep track of your knowledge – argument, authors, evidence. By *argument* I mean a chain of propositions, or line of reasoning which leads to certain statements being made. You also need to know the *authors* of this. This is not merely because academics like you to remember their names (although they do): it is important as a constant reminder that we are dealing with particular people's theories rather than 'hard fact'. Further, as you read on, you will find that you meet the same authors dealing with different topics. Now your knowledge of what else they said will help evaluation of the new material. You also need to know about *evidence*. This can include observation of people's activities, interviews with them, questionnaire surveys, official statistics, or corporate documents. You need to know the kind of evidence being used and some of the key findings. As a means of tracking your knowledge of debates I have included a review section at the end of the early chapters with short questions picking out some of the main points.

Thinking critically

These first steps do not yet enable you to enter debates – they merely indicate what is the knowledge base for this. Social analysis requires students to think critically about the material which is covered. Many students find this disconcerting. Having only recently come to the subject, how can they be expected to criticize those expert at it? Again I have a few simple suggestions. First, *evidence* can be evaluated against the methods of its collection and presentation. Direct observation studies may be rich in detail but may not be representative of other people/places: large-scale surveys produce large numbers which can be analysed statistically but lack depth. Contemporary studies of enterprises may have access to much material but lack an historical perspective: histories of accounting may be dynamic but rely upon dubious evidence of the past. Evidence may be limited because it only deals with men or manufacturing or manual workers or one country. Once you begin to look at both what the evidence covers and what it does not, then criticism becomes easier. Second, *arguments* may be evaluated by how they use evidence to contribute to debates. In my experience, many students see the task of evaluation as one of assigning the labels 'good' or 'bad' to a piece of work. Whatever these terms are taken to mean, they are clearly big concepts. As a first step it is easier to deal with other evaluations – is the argument important or trivial, central or peripheral, broad or narrow, a short or long term view, adding to existing arguments or overturning them? Third, the *authors* may be evaluated. I have suggested that it is impossible to eradicate bias in social analysis, so identifying this hardly counts as criticism. However, authors may be assessed for their consistency, completeness, the compatibility of some statements with others, or the way they deal with (or ignore) alternative points of view. In the end you should be concerned with whether you find the work convincing – are you prepared to accept this view of the world or not?

Thinking and acting positively

The next issue for many students is that now thinking critically is no longer difficult it becomes far too easy. Any study can be attacked through negative points. This one is old, this only deals with the UK, this has no men in it, this is large-scale so lacks detail whilst that is small-scale and so unrepresentative. This may lead to every study being dismissed for its failings: which ends up as an uncritical rejection of everything. We need to identify the strengths of studies as well as their weaknesses. If a study deals with female office workers in the UK this is not a problem if that is the specific interest of the author. Only if generalizations are made (about all workers or all countries) is there cause for concern. Of more usual importance in thinking critically is the way we treat two similar studies which generate quite different theories. All small-scale studies share certain characteristics – but some may be more convincing than others. Here, I am afraid, I cannot offer any simple suggestions. As you move deeper into debates you will develop ways of evaluating social analyses which are more powerful than the first steps I have outlined. This, I suspect, happens simultaneously with your own construction of informed opinions. Most of my students have felt their views of the social world were very different at the end of their course than at the start. However, the nature of their views has differed very considerably and discussions can become quite heated. They have entered the debates.

In order to prompt you in doing this I have included some general discussion points in the review sections to complement the more mechanistic short questions. I will see this book as a failure if you regard these as merely issues for academic study – relevant only to classrooms, courses and books. For me, the importance of social analysis has always been that it affects the way I make sense of the social world in which I live. I hope you will also be able to apply it in this way. As the most optimistic ambition, I hope you will link informed opinion to reasoned action. If so the book will have helped you not only to enter debates, but also to participate in shaping accounting, enterprises, and the wider social world.

Regrets, apologies and comforting thoughts

I am keenly aware of many limitations in this book. I regret that so many important authors and arguments are missing or under-represented together with the evidence they bring to debates. Indeed many important debates are absent. My excuses are well prepared but, perhaps, not altogether convincing. I cannot cover everything in one book (or ever); debates moved faster than I could keep up with them; this book is intended as an introduction to the social analysis of accounting, not as a definitive or comprehensive statement of it. None of this worries me very much. It is all part of the ludicrous project of writing such a book. Of more concern is that, despite my ambition to achieve clarity, I have found this very difficult and have often (perhaps entirely) failed. I do not share the view, attributed to one famous sociologist, that there was no reason why readers should find it any easier to read his words than he had found it to write them. My apologies to readers who find the book impossibly dense and obscure. But finally, a word of comfort. In my experience, many students aspire to understand everything they read (often at the first attempt) and regard it as failure when they do not. I have been studying social analyses and theories for some thirty years and now expect to understand about 80 per cent of what I encounter. This has been sufficient for me to make a living from it. You are not required or expected to understand everything. If you learn what you can, rather than worrying about what you have not, you may – as I have – find that social analysis can be fun . . . yes, fun! I wish you well with your studies.

1

ACCOUNTING AND THE
RISE OF THE ENTERPRISE

This chapter is concerned with the origins of business enterprises and their development up to the end of the nineteenth century. Business enterprises of many kinds – agricultural, mining, manufacturing, trading, financial, and so on – have a centuries-long history. The chapter cannot deal with all of this. Instead it will focus upon certain key developments, especially in Britain and the US, in the period known as the Industrial Revolution. The aim is twofold. First, to outline some typical forms of organization from which the modern enterprise developed. Second, to identify different kinds of explanation of this development, to introduce a number of concepts and theories relevant to the analysis of enterprises, and so to set the scene for the debates about the nature of modern enterprises.

THE RISE OF THE ENTERPRISE

Much interest in the Industrial Revolution has centred around the rise of the factory. We can begin to analyse this in terms of a simple model of development from cottage, to putting-out, to factory forms of production. There are some dangers in adopting such a simplified approach. Not all industries began with a cottage form, nor did they all go through a putting-out stage. Different industries experienced different changes at different times. There were also important developments in businesses which were not based on factories, such as the railways. Nevertheless, even this stylized model of change does open up a number of different ways of analysing industrial development.

Cottage, putting-out and factory systems

The *cottage system* of domestic production, most clearly exemplified in textiles, rested upon individual families producing goods in their own homes. Here all family members, from an early age, were responsible for undertaking production within the same social and physical environment that they lived their non-work lives. The head of household was also the head of production, and cottages bought-in raw materials (or part-finished goods) from the market and sold on in another market place. Thus the 'family' – which might include a broad range of relatives, friends, and helpers – was both a household and a unit of production.

After about 1700 in the UK, this form of production declined and, in some places, was replaced with a *putting-out system*. In this system the cottages were linked together into an extended production chain mediated by a putting-out master. This person would buy the raw materials, send them out to the first cottage to be worked upon, have them returned, send them to the second cottage for further work, have them returned, and so on. The putter-out paid cottagers on a piece-rate (i.e. payment per item completed) for each stage of this minutely divided process, and at the end sold the finished product in the market. Each cottage was no longer an independent producer but interdependent with other cottages and tied to the putter-out through his organization of the collective process. In some cases the cottages were grouped together on sites with small workshops forming 'manufactories'.

In the second half of the eighteenth century these putting-out systems were increasingly replaced with a *factory system* in which production was transferred to the premises of an owner where workers were brought together under one roof to undertake the conversion of raw materials into products. These factories were not an entirely new form of organization – workers in breweries and iron found-ries, for example, already worked on their employers' premises. They also had some resemblance to the 'workhouses' (which had been created from the earlier 'poorhouses' and which spread in the mid-eighteenth century) as well as to manufactories. As the factory system, at first an important feature of the woollen and cotton industries, was adopted by other manufacturers in the late eighteenth and early nineteenth centuries it became the dominant form of production in the UK and the US (see Box 1.1)

The origins of the factory

How can we explain the rise of factory production during the period of the Industrial Revolution? Although a number of factors were no doubt involved, theories of the factory tend to emphasize one or other of three main concepts – *technological innovation*, *economic efficiency*, and *social control*.

Technology

The most usual way of looking at the Industrial Revolution is as a period of intense technological innovation. In the UK it was a time of rapid change: in transport (with the development of turnpikes, canals, and railways); in sources of power; and in production machinery. Not surprisingly, many explanations of the rise of the factory give pride of place to such technological developments. Thus factory production is associated with the use of water power and the development of Newcomen's and Watt's steam engines, Darby's new methods of smelting iron, the invention of Hargreaves's spinning jenny, Arkwright's water frame, and

Box 1.1

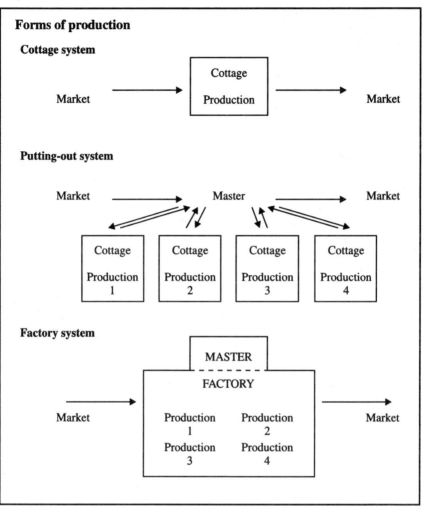

Crompton's mule. This approach to the history of the Industrial Revolution is probably so familiar that it now appears common sense – the obvious cause of the changes which took place. The explanation is that certain key inventors and developers created new technological conditions which impelled a massive change in production systems.

However ingrained such an account of the Industrial Revolution is, there are some difficulties in applying it to the rise of factories. Marglin argued that the link between technologies and factories was not as close as the technology approach assumed. Many of the early factories did not use the new forms of power, but came into existence and continued to operate without them. 'Benjamin Gott, called . . . the "first of the great Yorkshire spinners", never used power in his spinning (or weaving) rooms during his quarter-century career as a factory master and nevertheless appears to have made a satisfactory profit' (1974: 241). Nor did factories necessarily use new production technology. Weaving, for example, took quite a long while to mechanize and in Gott's case 'there is no evidence that the handloom in the capitalist's factory was any different from the one in the weaver's house' (p. 242). Thus, whatever the reason for Gott's decision to set up factory production, it cannot have been the outcome of new power sources or production machinery. Marglin reinforced this argument by re-examining the achievements of Arkwright – one of the archetypical inventors in the conventional (technology-based) explanation. He argued that Arkwright's machine was only a minor technical advance on the Wyatt–Paul design, from which it differed only in detail, and which had been invented some ninety years earlier. Yet Arkwright's factory was successful whereas that of Wyatt and Paul failed. The difference lay in Arkwright's ability to organize and administer his factory 'whose success had little or nothing to do with the technological superiority of large-scale machinery' (p. 239).

This downgrading of the importance of technology in the early factories flies in the face of another commonly held image of the Industrial Revolution – that it was a period of struggle by workers against the new technology. This view is dramatically illustrated in the case of the Luddites – a nickname applied to gangs who broke into factories and smashed machines. The image has become so deeply embedded in popular views of the Industrial Revolution that modern dictionaries define the term 'Luddism' as applying to any wrongheaded protest against the advance or progress of science and technology. Yet the story of the Luddites can be interpreted differently. They may be seen as people who opposed the social and economic changes brought about by the factory system and smashed machines not for what they represented technologically, but because they were the property of owners and part of the hated factories. If so, then, in one respect at least, the Luddites were correct – the factory did constitute a threat to their traditional way of life (based on cottage production), which it eventually replaced with a new form of production.

None of this should be taken to imply that technology was irrelevant to the rise of the factory. But it does raise strong doubts about whether technical change, in itself, is enough to explain the origins of factory production. Once factories were established there were indeed many significant technological innovations which took place within them. Certainly some later developments (e.g. the creation of moving assembly lines) would have been inconceivable without the factory form. Here, it would be as plausible to suggest that factories caused changes in technology as to argue that technical change caused the factory. The general form of the explanation advanced by those who see technological innovation as the cause of social and economic change is known as *technological determinism* (where technology is seen as the determining factor) and we will meet it frequently in our exploration of debates about the modern enterprise. Apart from detailed criticisms

11

of its application to particular cases, there are some standard theoretical objections to its mode of explanation (outlined in Box 1.2). Overall, the problems with technological determinism relate to the way in which human beings are seen as shaped by, rather than actively shaping, the technology which surrounds them. As isolated individuals, we may see our physical world as bounded by the opportunities and constraints built into our technology. Equally, we may recognize that, collectively, it is human beings who have created that technology, since its artefacts are not those found in nature without our intervention. By concentrating on the influence of technology on society we may produce a one-sided explanation which pays insufficient attention to social influences on technology – its purposes and uses.

Box 1.2

Technological determinism

Technological determinism refers to any theory which assumes that technology is the factor which determines or causes the nature of other factors – such as the organization of work, the nature of jobs, or the levels of skills. There are a number of standard criticisms of this view:

Alternative organization of technology. Any one technology may be used in a number of different ways. For example, an assembly line may be used with individual work stations, with workers repeating a single task, or it may be used with groups of workers moving along through the stages of assembly. There is social (probably managerial) choice in how the technology is to be used.

Alternative technologies. In many cases, if not all, there are a number of technologies available. For example, data can be entered into modern machine tools either via a computer program or directly by the operator. Again there is a social choice about which technology is to be adopted.

Social construction of technology. The alternative forms of technology which currently exist are produced within our society and reflect not only the body of technical knowledge but also the interests of those who create and adopt technology, and the investment of resources in their development. For example, non-technical decisions (primarily by politicians) sponsored the development of space technology whilst there has been relative underdevelopment of deep-sea technology. Thus any existing technology is the product of previous social choices.

Taken together, these points indicate that technology cannot be seen simply as determining people's experience – it is also the outcome of decisions which people have made.

Efficiency

Another common explanation of the rise of the factory depends not on the technological inevitability of this form of production, but on its evolution as the most economically efficient way of bringing workers and machines together. Here the argument is that, for a time, factories and cottages may co-exist, but the competitive advantages of factory production must force the cottages out of business. The classic statement of this view appeared early in the Industrial Revolution with the publication of Smith's *The Wealth of Nations* in 1776.

Smith argued that the competitive advantage of factories could be traced to the division of labour which could be found within them. In his famous pinmaking example he described how the process of pin production was divided into several minutely detailed operations each allocated to a different worker. This had three important consequences. First, each worker became more familiar with their own particular task, leading to an increase in dexterity and thus higher output. Second, since each worker performed only one operation, time was saved because there was no need to move from one machine or work station to another. Third, the close attention given to particular operations would stimulate the inventiveness of producers and encourage the development of labour-saving machines. These factors implied that the factory system was more economically efficient than its cottage competitors – it could produce more goods at less cost – and the 'laws' of the market meant that it would triumph over other forms.

Smith's argument has been attacked both for its identification of the advantages of the division of labour and for his overall claim that factories were more efficient. In relation to the division of labour, the third advantage – the stimulation of invention – was not well established and Smith himself later noted that workers carrying out minute tasks are unlikely to do much inventing of machines. Instead the development of the factory system led to an increasing distancing of those who invented machines from those who operated them. This is illustrated in the case of two textile machines. Hargreaves's spinning jenny of 1764 was invented for his own or his family's use; Roberts's self-acting mule of 1830 was intended to be used by other people. The key distinction between the two machines was that 'what Roberts set out to do was not, like Hargreaves . . . to make skill more productive. Rather he set out to eliminate skill so that the spinner was no longer needed except to supervise a set of machines' (Rosenbrock, 1985: 166). Roberts was then able to employ children where there had previously been skilled spinners. Whilst the factory division of labour may have changed the nature of invention, it is not clear that it necessarily increased its level.

Smith's second claim – that movement between operations was saved – suffers from a conceptual difficulty. There are two kinds of division of labour being examined at once. One divides a whole process into a series of detailed tasks; the other divides the work force into a number of detailed, specialized operators. The two steps are not only logically separate, they are also different in practice. Braverman, drawing on his own work experience, demonstrated how a tinsmith

13

would break down the task of making funnels into a number of separate tasks, and would make up batches of spouts, bowls, and rims before assembling them into several finished products. This would produce all the time-saving which Smith identified. 'The worker may break the process down, but he never voluntarily converts himself into a lifelong detail worker . . . the first step breaks up only the process, while the second dismembers the worker as well' (Braverman, 1974: 78). Thus, although the structuring of work operations is important, it does not explain the detailed subdivision of workers.

This leaves Smith's first claim – that the division of labour maximizes efficiency through increased dexterity. Here the case appears rather more substantial, although there are some difficulties in assessing the productive advantages of dexterity, as opposed to skill, which has been a major concern of those studying modern work forms. If we accept, for the moment, that there may have been some efficiency increases stemming from this source, we may find that there are other, stronger reasons, for the division of labourers. Charles Babbage in 1832 reconsidered the case of pinmaking, and stressed the importance of wage rates in the economic logic of dividing workers (Braverman, 1974). Where, in a group of workers, each one performs all the tasks in making pins, and some of these tasks require skills, then all must be paid the going rate for skilled workers. However, if it is possible to strip away some of the unskilled elements of the process, these can then be allocated to unskilled workers who earn a very much lower wage. The point here is that, even if the same number of workers produce the same number of pins (i.e. there is no increase in productive efficiency per person), the employer still achieves a lower cost of production. In the wage system of the 1830s the differences in pay were very marked and the corresponding effect on the cost of production was substantial (see Box 1.3).

These criticisms of Smith centre on the way in which he conducted his analysis. Other doubts have been directed at the assumption upon which the analysis was based – that the factories were actually more efficient. Marglin highlighted some difficulties in this view. He began by defining 'efficiency' in terms of the relationship between inputs and outputs, so that an increase in efficiency can be demonstrated when more output is achieved from the same input, or the same output from less input. Much of the success of the early factories came from a redistribution of output (so that the employer gained more of it) and from an increase in input (from the workers). Neither of these represented an increase in efficiency, and Marglin proposed an analysis which emphasized the social organization of production as the key feature leading to the rise of factories.

Control

In some respects the putting-out system offered many of the advantages later claimed for the factory. It offered the opportunity to develop a division of labour in which each cottage specialized in one part of the production process. It enabled

Box 1.3

Wages in nineteenth-century pinmaking

Task	Worker	Daily pay*	Index**
Drawing wire	Man	3s 3d	54
Straightening wire	Woman	1s 0d	17
	Girl	0s 6d	8
Pointing, twisting and cutting heads	Man	5s 3d	88
	Boy	0s 4d	6
	Man	5s 4d	89
Heading	Woman	1s 2d	19
Tinning or whitening	Man	6s 0d	100
	Woman	3s 0d	50
Papering	Woman	1s 0d	17

* Wages are shown in the now obsolete UK currency of shillings (s) and pence (d). One shilling was a twentieth of a pound sterling, and consisted of twelve pence.
** The relative wage levels are shown as a percentage of the highest rate for a skilled man.

Source: Babbage, 1832 (quoted in Braverman, 1974)

the putting-out master to control the product and meant that the cottagers were dependent on his organization of the overall process. It had a further advantage which proved difficult to establish in factories – the attachment of costs to products through the piece-rate system. However, the system had one important limitation.

> The minute specialization that was the hallmark of the putting-out system only wiped out one of two aspects of workers' control of production: control over the product. Control of the work process, when and how much the worker would exert himself, remained with the worker – until the coming of the factory.
>
> (Marglin, 1974: 237)

The putting-out master had difficulties in achieving the disciplining and super-vision of workers within their own cottages. This showed itself in two main ways. First, it was difficult to increase production by raising the effort levels of workers. The masters tried to control this through Acts of Parliament so that, in the woollen industry, work had to be returned within twenty-one days (1749 Act) and later within eight days (1777 Act). However, the use of legislation to increase pro-duction was clearly cumbersome. Second, the privacy of the cottage allowed the workers to manipulate production in their own interests. For example, they 'might exchange poor wool for good, or conceal imperfections in spinning, or wet the wool to make it seem heavier' (Marglin, 1974: 247). Again, this was addressed in the 1777 Act which allowed agents of the putting-out master to enter and search workers' cottages on suspicion of embezzlement. This law appears not to have been particularly effective, since an 1824 edition of the *Blackburn Mail* published an estimate that one-sixth of domestic cotton production was being embezzled within the cottages.

What the factory offered to the master was a building where workers could be supervised so that the length of time and the intensity of their work could be controlled, and their opportunities for fraud and embezzlement could be mini-mized. In short, the attraction (for the capitalist) of factory production was that it enabled the control of production as well as control of the product. With in-creased labour input (through longer, harder hours of work), and a greater share of output being gained by the employer (with goods being guarded by factory overseers), the factory could outperform the cottage, and the profits of the owner would rise. Marglin concluded that the decisive reason for its rise was that the 'factory effectively put an end both to "dishonesty and laziness"' (1974: 248).

Managing the early factories

This conclusion is somewhat premature. The early factory owners faced a long and difficult struggle actually to achieve the control of production which was potentially available in the factory form of production. Pollard (1965) charted the ways in which the problems of factory production were identified and solutions attempted.

Early managerial problems

The first problem facing the factory owner was that of *recruitment*. Workers were reluctant to enter the factories if any other choice was available, and this was particularly important for skilled men. In varying degrees the early employers relied on forced labour – criminals and wanted men, or women and children sent to the factory by male heads of households. As alternative cottage production declined, more and more men were impelled to move to factory employment, but shortages of skilled workers continued to be a problem well into the nineteenth century. From the complaints of many of the established capitalists of the period, it appears that 'poaching' of workers from other firms was a frequent response to these shortages, which they saw as a malpractice.

The second problem to be faced was that of *training*. For as long as the factories continued to use the familiar technology of the cottages, workers might be relied upon to bring their traditional skills with them, and to pass them on to younger workers through apprenticeship systems. Although production might take place upon the employer's premises, the actual working practices continued to be set by the workers themselves. As factory technology developed, and new technologies (such as those in the chemical industry) emerged, the need for new skills became increasingly important. Some of the leading employers of the period set up more or less formal training schemes (but often lost their workers through poaching) and combined this with a division of labour which narrowed the range of skills required.

Beyond technical skill there was concern with adapting workers to industrial routines. Thompson (1967) argued that, in the pre-industrial world, work rhythm had been dictated by nature or the cycle of tasks. The division of labour within factories put a greater emphasis on synchronizing and regularizing the time of workers and machines. The day was now not to be measured as the space between dawn and dusk, but carefully metered by the hour and the minute. Work was now subject to the 'tyranny of the clock' and time was perceived in different ways, producing a language with which we are familiar in the twentieth century – where workers 'clock on', 'time is money', and we 'spend time'. This new way of perceiving time and its relationship to work was a considerable break with traditional perceptions and values, and provoked resistance from workers. As the managerial systems of factories developed, other broad-ranging changes were sought by employers. The increasing use of paper for written descriptions, drawings, calculated dimensions, and printed instructions created a demand for a more literate and numerate work force. Thus, as the factories developed, there was an increasing emphasis on creating a new kind of worker to be employed within them.

This need showed itself strongly in the third major problem faced by owners – that of *discipline*. Workers, in the early years, were not willing to fit into the rhythms of the factory and there were high levels of absenteeism and labour turnover. In addition to wishing to observe traditional feast or holy days, workers would also celebrate 'Saint Monday' (and sometimes Tuesday) and try to make up for lost time by working day and night when they returned. After pay day there might be a spending spree and the workers would not return until the money was gone. Timekeeping was often irregular and employers tried to enforce stiff punishments for this. When workers were actually present there were problems with their application to the steady effort which employers wanted from them, and factories laid down bans on drinking, smoking, gambling, and leaving machines.

Overall, the early factories had many problems in the recruitment, training, and working practices of their employees. Descriptions of these places, and the complaints of their owners, hardly portray the efficiency which Smith cited as the reason for their rise, nor the control which Marglin thought they achieved. As one early owner, Edward Cave, observed of his workers, 'I have no great fascination in the prospect I have put myself into the power of such people' (quoted by Pollard, 1965: 181). The struggle to deal with these problems evolved over many years.

Early managerial solutions

The attempts by early entrepreneurs to create a new work discipline were categorized by Pollard as 'the proverbial stick, the proverbial carrot, and, thirdly, the attempt to create a new ethos of work order and obedience' (p. 186). At the start of the factory system deterrence was the main managerial tool, with poor work being sanctioned by fines and dismissals. Indeed, with the extensive employment of children, the stick was often literal, and there were widespread complaints about corporal punishment. Where workers attempted to organize in the early trade (labour) unions, or 'combinations', they were met with bans and blacklists.

On the more positive side of incentives to good work there was relatively little use of these as far as child labour was concerned (see Box 1.4). However, for adults there was an important development of pay systems. In the second half of the eighteenth century there was a widespread belief that workers sought only sufficient wages for their subsistence and that if pay awards for higher than target production were paid then they would absent themselves from the factory for longer periods. Thus higher pay would be followed by less work – a disincentive system. However, some entrepreneurs began to change their views on this and gradually pay incentive schemes were introduced. In the beginning these were based on prizes of cash, or in kind, to the best workers. Later they were tied to satisfactory working over a set period of weeks or months. In some cases pay was conditional on achieving a set level of production and bonuses were added if this was exceeded. Here we see the beginning of payment-by-results systems, which

Box 1.4

Managing child labour			
Number of firms using different means to enforce obedience among factory children, 1833			
Negative		*Positive*	
Dismissal	353	Kindness	2
Threat of dismissal	48	Promotion/higher wages	9
Fines, deductions	101	Reward or premium	23
Corporal punishment	55		
Complaint to parents	13		
Confined to mill	2		
Degrading dress, badge	3		
Totals	**575**		**34**

Source: Pollard (1965: 222)

were to become influential in the early twentieth century. But they were not used extensively in the early factories. Instead much of the attention of entrepreneurs was directed at the morals of the work force.

In attempts to establish a new work discipline the issue of drunkenness was often seen as central. Workers found to be drunk would be dismissed and, where the entrepreneur had sufficient local political power, public houses (or beershops) were banned. There were also campaigns to discourage idleness (or leisure) on Sundays, and children were required to attend church and Sunday schools. Additionally, employers were keen to eradicate swearing and other forms of indecency. Although these concerns clearly have an ethical or religious aspect (and were particularly important in social reformist and Quaker companies) they also had more practical business relevance. Many of the entrepreneurs believed that only if the 'character' of the worker could be transformed from indolence, improvidence and self-indulgence to industriousness, frugality, and sobriety could a new approach to employment be successful. In general, 'with some honourable exceptions, the drive to raise the level of respectability and morality among the working classes was not undertaken for their own sakes, but primarily, or even exclusively, as an aspect of building up a new factory discipline' (p. 231).

Thus in the early years of factory development we see a strong emphasis on the problems of existing workers and a number of hesitant first steps in creating managerial solutions to them. Equally important, we see an attempt to create a new kind of worker who would be more easily managed. Thus the social organization of production in the factory system also involved the social construction of the factory worker.

The development of the factory

As factories became more widely established and began to grow there were a number of developments which affected their social organization of production.

Entrepreneurs

Production under the putting-out system in the UK was generally controlled by merchants. Increasingly after the 1780s these merchants invested their surplus profits in manufacturing operations, often owning the land on which the factories were built. Factory owners also raised capital from their own and their families' fortunes, or from local banks. In some cases the merchants themselves became manufacturers. Generally manufacturers relied upon local merchants for the distribution of their products. Hence there were close ties between entrepreneurial owners and merchants in the early years of the nineteenth century. These ties existed as networks of kinship and friendship contacts and produced clusters of enterprises grouped together around the interests of business families. These were especially important where there were also strong religious bonds, such as among the Quaker families (the 'cousinhood') where banking, brewing, iron, and other enterprises were linked. As firms expanded, and the requirements for capital increased, these networks began to extend beyond the immediate social circle and finance was raised from a wider group of merchants and bankers, bringing in lawyers (who supervised clients' monies), goldsmiths, brokers, and later stock exchanges in London and the provinces.

This increased demand for capital, stretching the private resources of entrepreneurs and their immediate circle, led to a change in the legal arrangements for financing business. Provision was introduced (or rather re-introduced) for *joint stock companies*. Legislation in 1844–45 made it easier to set up companies where 'shares' of the capital were divided between a number of partners – initially restricted to twenty. This had been difficult since the 'Bubble Act' of 1720 which had been passed following a wild rush of share speculation. Repeal of the Act in 1824 opened the way for developing new forms of corporate ownership. The crucial feature of the legislation was the establishment of *limited liability* – a concept which, at the time, was controversial and seen by some as morally dubious. As the number of owners of companies increased, many were not in day-to-day touch with the uses to which their capital was put. They might well have shares in many companies. For as long as all their personal fortune could be called upon to settle any debts of their company, then they faced considerable risk to their wealth, and this acted as a deterrent to such investment. As remote owners they had much to fear from the incompetence or dishonesty of those who directed the affairs of the enterprise.

What limited liability offered was the protection that only the sum invested was at risk, not the personal fortune of the investor. Some opposed this change on the grounds that since owners were content to take all the profits they should be prepared to suffer all the losses as well. However, joint stock legislation was extended by further Acts in 1856 and 1862. This legal change was accompanied by a number of safeguards and provisions for the operation of enterprises. Directors were appointed to govern the business of companies, shareholders nominated one of their number as an auditor who could inspect company records, and rules for the winding-up of companies were enacted. These changes led to the spread of the joint stock form of enterprise, and fuelled the expansion of enterprises in the second half of the nineteenth century. One of the outcomes was that the entrepreneurs, who were already split 'into two personalities – the owner of capital, and the employer of capital' (Marx, 1894: 375), became socially divided into financial capitalists responsible for the provision of funds, and industrial capitalists who put these funds to work. Nevertheless, there were still many owner-managers who performed both economic functions, and whose involvement in production was much closer than that of the merchants.

Agents, contractors, foremen and workers

With the growth of enterprises, such entrepreneurial owner-managers employed others to manage their businesses. In the early factories the 'large-scale entrepreneur of the day began with very limited managerial, clerical or managerial staff: he wrote his own letters, visited his own customers, and belaboured his men with his own walking stick' (Pollard, 1965: 232). As these enterprises grew non-owners were involved in the tasks of administration and supervision.

Some of these non-owners may be described as *agents* – performing the more routine functions for which the entrepreneur had little time or inclination, and reporting to him. In the early days such agents were recruited from the kin of entrepreneurs, but increasingly they became separated from ownership and began to develop as a distinctive occupational group. At the beginning of the nineteenth century these people could be distinguished from other workers by their literacy and numeracy alone, but they increasingly took on a more professional image; initially as 'attorneys' – whom the entrepreneur might regard as 'my man of business' – and later as 'accountants' or 'company secretaries' (Reader, 1966). At a rather lower level, but still with quite widespread responsibilities, they were described as 'bookkeepers'. Such individuals were employees of the company, and were paid a regular wage or salary, but there were relatively few of them. Much of the organization of production was carried out by those with a different economic relationship to the enterprise.

In many factories work was organized not directly by the entrepreneurs or their agents but by *contractors*. Littler (1982) distinguished between external sub-contract systems where materials were bought in from 'outworkers', and various forms of internal sub-contracting. Internal contracting involved a deal between the entrepreneur (or agent) and an intermediary who would deliver production. Three common forms of this system were: family groups (where one member organized a small work force of kin and friends); craft groups (where a leading skilled worker organized a team of other journeymen and apprentices); and work gangs (a more assorted collection of workers controlled by a gang boss). What the different forms had in common was that the leading worker/boss recruited labour, allocated and organized tasks, directed work practices, instructed workers, distributed payment, and was responsible for discipline (including fines and dismissals). Littler claimed that such arrangements were widespread in the UK until the 1880s, and there were similar practices in US enterprises, where:

> The firm provided materials, tools, power, and a factory building. The employees – 'contractors' – in turn agreed to manufacture a particular object or component in a given quantity at a designated cost and by a specific date. Otherwise they retained virtually complete control over the production process. The contractor was thus an employee working for a day wage and an independent businessman working for an anticipated profit.
>
> (Nelson, 1975: 36)

At a rather lower level within the enterprise there were the *foremen* whose powers were less than those of contractors but far more wide-ranging than today's first-line supervisors. They were responsible for the hiring and firing of workers, specifying how work was to be done, and monitoring its quality and quantity.

21

Thus many workers were not directly employed by the owner of the factory, but were hired and fired and paid by intermediaries. The factories in which they worked were small (by today's standards), and we might think of them more as 'workshops'. In both the UK and the US firms employing over 200 people were rare up to the 1870s. Many working practices were traditional, passed down from one generation to the next, or were imposed by leading workers. Thus although workers were under the general direction of the owner, which Marx referred to as the *formal subordination of labour*, these owners were not yet in a position to dictate the precise nature of production – the *real subordination of labour*.

The transformation of society

Changes in business enterprises both reflected and influenced changes in broader society. In explaining the broader changes two main theoretical strands may be identified.

The first is termed *idealism*, where the power of ideas to transform the social world is emphasized. This view has entered into everyday consciousness in the words of the nineteenth century poet Bulwer Lytton, 'the pen is mightier than the sword'. In this perspective we are concerned with the rise of concepts and theories, values and beliefs, and how they change society. One such approach is that of Weber (1922), who saw the distinctive feature of change as the rise of rationality. The nineteenth century in Europe was seen as an 'age of reason' in which secular thinking replaced religious belief, and traditional or emotional (affective) action was increasingly being displaced by action based on the calculation of means and ends. For Weber, the capitalist enterprise was the social institution which most clearly demonstrated this rationality.

The second strand is *materialism*. Here the emphasis is upon the way that the physical world in which we live shapes the ways in which we think about our lives – our consciousness. The classic statement of this view came from Marx (1868), who argued that ideas were the product of society and depended, most crucially, on the ways in which people produced their goods and services. In production human beings enter into particular relationships with each other which constitute the social world. It is from these social structures that ideas (sometimes referred to as ideology) emerge – society's culture, law, politics, and so on. Here the forms of production and the social relationships of the capitalist enterprise are central to the creation of a new kind of society.

Although distinct enough in the abstract, these two fundamental forms of explanation tend to become less clearly different when particular analyses are addressed. Weber, for example, located his account of the rise of the rational enterprise in a discussion of the particular social institutions which supported it, including free markets, free labour, and a monetary economy. Similarly, Marx was clearly aware of the power of new ideas, such as in science and technology, to transform relationships between workers, and between employees and employers within production. Nevertheless, the different emphases of the two approaches produce rather different explanations of change in nineteenth century societies such as the UK and the US.

Broadly developing from the idealist perspective, the changes of the nineteenth century have been characterized as *modernization*. This approach emphasizes the role of political, legal, and educational institutions in creating a value system conducive to economic development. The culture of 'traditional' society was seen as a hindrance to the development of industry, which depended on: literacy and numeracy; economic and political freedom; the breakdown of barriers to social mobility based on ties of family, kin, status and religion; scientific thinking and technological innovation; and rewards for individual initiative.

In a materialist vein, others drew on Durkheim's (1893) discussion of the division of labour and focused on the way changes in production, especially in its technology, changed society. In one of the more extreme statements of this position, the transformation of *industrialism* was seen as having its own logic (Kerr *et al.*, 1960). Whatever the existing social order, and whatever the route that initial industrialization took, there was a process of convergence so that outcomes would be essentially similar patterns of social relations and ideas systems in all industrial societies.

Both the modernization and the industrialization views tended to see change in terms of evolution or progress along essentially similar paths. Marx's analysis emphasized specific social relations, embedded in the mode of production, which were the characteristic features of the development of *capitalism*. The central social relationship of capitalist enterprises (that between employer and employee) also produced the historically powerful relationship of capitalist society, between the industrial owning–ruling class (the bourgeoisie) and the industrial working class (the proletariat). More than any other social force, it was the struggle between these two great classes which shaped the transformations of the nineteenth century (and would, he thought, later lead to the overthrow of capitalism itself).

Thus, following different theoretical approaches, societies have been labelled *modern*, or *industrial*, or *capitalist*. Although the terms are overlapping, and any might be applied, they represent different kinds of explanation of societal transformation and its relationship to the enterprise. As competing perspectives they continue to influence debate on contemporary developments.

The enterprise at the end of the nineteenth century

The last quarter of the nineteenth century was a time of transformation for business enterprises in the UK and the US. The economic depression of 1873 to 1896 was exacerbated by increasing international competition as continental European countries, most notably Germany, began to industrialize. In the UK, profits as a proportion of industrial income fell from 47.7 per cent in 1870–4 to 37.8 per cent in 1890–4 (Littler, 1982: 72). Bankruptcies were widespread, and many of the small regional banks went down with the industrial enterprises in which they had invested. The banks reacted by withdrawing from long term investment in UK enterprises, and those firms which survived increasingly turned to the stock exchange as a source of capital (Armstrong, 1987a). In place of the family entrepreneur and closely associated local banks, shareholders became increas- ingly important in financing firms.

Within the enterprise the internal contract system was coming under increasing pressure both from above and from below. With profits being squeezed, the wealth of some of the largest contractors attracted the attention of factory owners, especially when, as Nelson (1975) noted of the US, they cut a fine figure at work with silk hats and fashionable coats. As entrepreneurs attempted to preserve their profits by cost-cutting on contracts, the relationship between contractors and their workers deteriorated. Whereas many had seen the system as beneficial to both sides, increasingly workers viewed it as a method of 'sweating' (Littler, 1982). In the UK unionism spread from craft workers (many of whom were themselves contractors) to semi-skilled and unskilled labourers, and the increasing resentment of the system found a means of expression. Gradually the system of internal contract, and 'the foreman's empire', began to crumble, and new forms of organization emerged based on the direct employment of workers by the enterprise, and the formation of a cadre of salaried managers to direct their activities.

Thus the end of the nineteenth century saw major shifts in the business enterprise which increasingly took the form with which we are familiar today (see Box 1.5). These changes brought with them new problems and there were a number of difficulties in generating solutions, just as there had been in the early factories. What was to be the relationship between the large number of remote shareholders and the entrepreneurs? How were the rising ranks of managers to be organized and controlled? How were the employees to be directed and production

Box 1.5

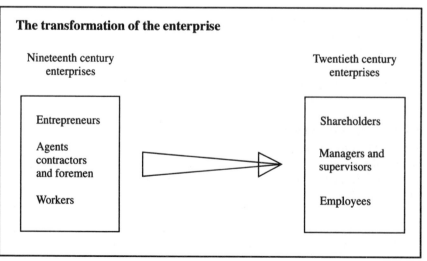

The transformation of the enterprise

Nineteenth century enterprises

Twentieth century enterprises

Entrepreneurs

Agents contractors and foremen

Workers

Shareholders

Managers and supervisors

Employees

organized? It was struggles over these questions which shaped the development of the modern enterprise and in which accounting was an integral part. The next section explores the relationship of accounting and enterprises during the period of the Industrial Revolution up to the 1880s. In doing so it deals with relationships between ideas and the material world in the creation of modern industrial capitalism.

THE RISE OF MODERN ACCOUNTING

Like the enterprise, forms of activity which may be described as 'accounting' have a long history which will not be detailed here. Instead the concern is to examine the ways in which accounting interrelated with the rise of the modern enterprise. Although modern accounting can be said to originate in the exposition of double-entry bookkeeping by Pacioli around the beginning of the sixteenth century, the 'evolution of the accountancy profession in Britain is inextricably linked with the history of the Industrial Revolution' (Jones, 1981: 19).

Accounting and management

At the end of the eighteenth century there were a number of men who described themselves as accountants, but generally they also performed other duties as writing masters, notaries, and agents. Often accounting was carried out by entrepreneurs for themselves and, 'undertaking simple (if detailed) bookkeeping in the counting house, they were capable of performing virtually all the calculations required for the practical operation of their businesses' (Jones, 1981: 25).

The accounting which they developed for their own purposes was adapted from three strands which existed prior to the factories (Pollard, 1965). Accounting had been used on the landed estates as a *stewardship system*, mainly as a check on embezzlement. As the landowners developed industrial interests – in mines, ironworks, canals, and factories – they continued to use this accounting but it provided little useful information on the efficiency of different parts of the activities or the overall profitability of the estate. Accounting had also been widely used in the *mercantile system*, where problems of complex transactions and large scale organization had been addressed. The system was far from ideal from an entrepreneur's point of view, since it was not directly concerned with production and did not deal with fixed assets, and although there was some rudimentary cost accounting it usually ignored overheads. The third source of accounting was the *putting-out system*, which preceded the factory. Here, although the accounting dealt with the production of goods, there was little need to deal with fixed capital, since the premises and machines were supplied by cottagers rather than masters.

Thus although accounting systems existed prior to the formation of factories, and were known by entrepreneurs (or their agents), they were not directly matched to the new circumstances. From the beginning, entrepreneurs had to develop their own procedures for factory accounts. These involved the creation of regular, periodic returns forcing 'the natural rhythm of work into a straitjacket of comparable sections of time' (Pollard, 1965: 215). Here, accounting both reflected the new imposition of time discipline (Thompson, 1967) and may be supposed to have provided one of the means of enforcing it – through the periodic measurement of performance. The same was true of the use of accounting to detect errors and fraud in production systems. It both shaped and was shaped by the concerns of the early factory owners.

Another potentially valuable contribution to be made by accounting developed more sporadically. In many enterprises it was difficult for entrepreneurs to discover the costs of particular products, and to relate these to the revenues received, so that they could not tell (with any certainty) which products contributed most to profit. Pollard ascribed this to three factors – incompetence, ignorance, or lack of staff. The last of these is striking. Arkwright's company, which must have been one of the largest, in 1801–4 employed 1,063 workers but only three clerks. There is considerable disagreement among historical researchers about the subsequent development of cost accounting in the nineteenth century. Armstrong (1987a) suggested that where costing was carried out in UK firms it was frequently developed by engineers and that cost 'accounting' was relatively uninfluential even at the end of the century. Hoskin and Macve (1988) identified the US armoury at Springfield as a crucial pioneer of new accounting in the 1830s and 1840s, but Tyson (1990, 1993) argued that this was not a significant advance on earlier cost accounting practices and major developments did not take place until the turn of the twentieth century. McKendrick (1970) found cost accounting systems in operation in Wedgwood's eighteenth century UK factory but argued that these were not developed in the next century – indeed they may have been forgotten.

Our knowledge of early costing practices is still narrow and uncertain, and as Ezzamel et al. (1990) warn, new cases are continually appearing which shift our understanding of the period. With some caution, we might describe the first half of the century as a period of patchy (and perhaps short-lived) developments in cost accounting within particular enterprises, which were only slowly diffused to other companies – although this appears to have been rather more extensive in the US than in the UK. Given a widespread use of contract systems where the cost of the product (to the entrepreneur) was agreed in advance of production, then calculations could be made without the need (for the entrepreneur) to be concerned about actual production costs. Indeed many commentators have seen the contract system as a substitute for cost accounting (e.g. Nelson, 1975; Littler, 1982). Where gang bosses and others were responsible for paying workers (within the agreed price) labour costs were not the direct concern of the entrepreneur. Such costs were, of course, relevant to the contractors, but it seems likely that the contractors were less concerned with the detailed measurement of labour costs, than with exacting the maximum effort from workers by driving supervision. Where the foreman system applied, the key issue for entrepreneurs was to

26

ensure that their subordinates would strive to achieve production targets, and thus accounting was important in providing controls and incentives for supervisors. In the Boston (US) mills of 1840, for example, there was 'a premium bonus system whereby the overseer whose workers produced at least unit cost received a cash payment which could amount to as much as $100, compared to an annual salary of $600' (Hopper and Armstrong, 1991: 414). Where piece-rates were used the paymaster would report monthly figures for the output, days worked and earnings of each operative. The figures were used to alter the rates so that earnings remained steady even where speed-up (of machines) and stretch-out (working more machines) meant that production was increasing. 'As a result of these measures, the workload of spinners and weavers [in Boston mills] more than doubled between 1840 and 1854 whilst wages remained substantially the same' (p. 414).

Similarly capital accounting was little developed in the early factories. Entrepreneurs, and their accountants, seem to have had difficulty in integrating the concept of fixed capital into their corporate accounts. In the early factories capital and revenue were often confused, and depreciation was seldom used. Again, underdevelopment (relative to modern practice) may have been of little importance. With Britain as 'the workshop of the world' and the US in its relatively isolated location, the returns on capital could be high and speedy. The capital cost of sinking a pit might be recovered in the first three months of operation, and the introduction of a new machine into a factory could produce great competitive advantages, if not the ability to manufacture an entirely new product. Where businesses were successful, partners tended to plough back most of the surplus, so the cost and availability of capital was not of crucial importance. Johnson and Kaplan (1987) argued that enterprises were usually based on a single product and there was little need to measure the relative profitability of different uses of capital since entrepreneurs were not faced with decisions about alternative investments.

In many mid-nineteenth century enterprises, accounting did not supply the kind of management information which it does today, but to describe this as a failure of accounting is to apply criteria which are coloured by retrospective vision since the circumstances then were very different. Pollard noted that 'accounting was used only minimally to guide businessmen in their business decisions and where it was used the guidance was often unreliable' (1965: 245). For Walsh and Stewart (1993) this misses the point. The move from early manufactories to the factory system entailed the creation of a new kind of bookkeeping based on people, actions, and abstract spaces. As the factories developed 'bookkeeping' (the recording of transactions) became 'accounting' – an analysis of production and a discipline aimed at continual improvement. Accounting had become an integral part of production, and it was this which was important rather than its contribution to particular decisions. In any case neither the lack of information nor the unreliability of that which was available seems to have been a crucial handicap to the early enterprises. For firms in quasi-monopoly positions in their local markets, the easy profit margins available 'explain not only the cavalier attitude to exact costing and pricing, but also the rapid growth of firms out of ploughed-back capital' (Pollard, 1965: 245).

After 1870 this began to change. Externally, enterprises faced economic depression and increasing national and international competition. Internally, the contract system was coming under pressure. Entrepreneurs responded by merging with other firms to form much larger and more complex units of production, and by dismantling the contract system to replace it with direct employment of both workers and managers. Thus the context of accounting underwent a transformation.

In the UK the response from accounting seems to have been rather slow, with accountants seen as scorekeepers rather than providers of managerial tools. 'The practice of using accounts as direct aids to management was not one of the achievements of the British industrial revolution; in a sense it does not even belong to the later nineteenth century but to the twentieth' (Pollard, 1965: 248). There was a more dynamic response in US enterprises. Developments which had already begun in some of the pioneering firms, most notably in the metalworking industries, spread quickly to other companies. Where workers were shifted from sub-contract to direct employment status, there was a demand from entrepreneurs for the creation of records of work done and wages paid. These provided the entrepreneur with cost information which was used to negotiate terms with contractors and to squeeze their profit margins (Clawson, 1980). Thus accounting responded to changes in work organization and also provided the means by which such changes could be achieved. Eventually the contractors were displaced, and a managerial system emerged in which accounting was increasingly important. Later, many of the US developments were imported across the Atlantic into Britain and shaped the development of its twentieth century accounting.

Accounting and ownership

In contrast with the development of (management) accounting within enterprises, the growth of external (financial) accounting seems to have been widespread. Changes in enterprises associated with limited liability and the rise of joint stock companies had an earlier and much more widespread impact both on accounting and on the development of the accountancy profession. In the UK the 1844 Joint Stock Companies Act required the production of a balance sheet which should be 'full and fair'. There was no clear indication of what this phrase meant and no requirement for a profit and loss account, but the Act began the modern system of financial reporting. Auditors were initially selected from among the shareholders, but the latter often drew on the services of public accountants. As auditing became an occupation conducted by accountants, enterprises increasingly employed their own (salaried) accountants to regulate their finances internally. A number of accountancy practices were founded in the 1840s – Deloitte's, Price Waterhouse, Young's – and the number of accountants listed in the London trade directories rose from 107 in 1840 to 264 in 1850 (Jones, 1981). When the Act was revised in 1856 it was recommended, but not required by law, that 'true accounts should be kept, a just balance of profit or loss should be ascertained and the auditors should check the correctness of the balance sheet' (Walton, 1991: 6). Double-entry bookkeeping was also recommended. The terms 'full and fair' disappeared and were replaced with 'true and correct'. Further legislation in 1862 required that both a profit statement and a balance sheet be presented at an annual general meeting of the shareholders, and provided a model balance sheet for guidance. This Act meant it was now virtually impossible to run a joint stock company without the services of an accountant. For this reason the Act has been nicknamed 'the accountants' friend' (Reader, 1966).

These legal changes were central to the development of the accountancy profession. At the beginning of the century, accounting was only one of the activities of those who called themselves 'accountants', or was 'practised as a sideline to some more lucrative occupation such as auctioneering, rent collecting, and stockbroking' (Reader, 1966: 158). By the middle of the century it had become a full-time occupation in its own right, although it did not enjoy the prestige of the established professions and its members 'tended to be of middle-class parents of modest means' (Jones, 1981: 35). The public image of these accountants was not always good and, since they had an increasing role in handling the financial affairs of businesses, there was concern about their competence and honesty. Worthington, in 1895, described accountants as 'mixed up in money lending, bogus company promoting, book-making, and other shady practices' (quoted in Jones, 1981: 70).

This mistrust of accountants was also fuelled by dislike of their activities. The 1848 Winding-up Act made the appointment of public accountants a virtual necessity and liquidation became an important part of their work. For example, between 1848 and 1880 some 70–90 per cent of the earnings of the accounting firm Whinney, Smith and Whinney came from insolvency work, and

> it appears that accountants did particularly well in times of financial disaster and depression, when bankruptcies brought extra and highly lucrative work. They were the rich undertakers of the economic world and gained disapprobation in consequence of profiting from the misfortunes of others.
>
> (Jones, 1981: 45)

Judge Quain complained, in 1875, that 'the whole affair of bankruptcy had been handed over to an ignorant set of men called accountants' (quoted in Jones, 1981: 70).

Accountancy is not the only occupation which we now regard as a pro-fession to have enjoyed low public esteem at the end of the nineteenth century. In the legal field the term 'attorney' was held in such public contempt in the UK that members of the occupation changed their name to 'solicitors' by Act of Parliament in 1874 (Reader, 1966). Accountants responded to the situation by creating new 'professional' institutes. The first of these were established in Scotland in the

1850s and then in England – in Liverpool (1870), Manchester (1871), London (1873), Sheffield (1877). In 1880 the English and Welsh societies were merged into the Institute of Chartered Accountants (ICAEW), which self-consciously set about the task of improving the image of accountants through setting up qualifying examinations and ethical standards for the conduct of its members.

Increasingly members of the ICAEW moved from a prime concern with insolvency to the preparation of financial reports and auditing. This shift was reinforced by changes in British banking (Armstrong, 1987a). As a response to the banking failures of the mid-Victorian period, banks in the UK generally decided to restrict industrial loans to the short term and to remain remote from the operation of individual companies. Lacking detailed knowledge of the products, production methods, and markets of companies, such banks relied on financial information from audits. The knock-on effect of this was that, since banks no longer supplied long term capital, enterprises looked to the stock markets through the public flotation of shares. Again audit, to confirm the basis of a company prospectus, became important.

ICAEW accountants concerned with this work were joined in 1885 by those of another association – the Society of Accountants, later renamed the Society of Incorporated Accountants. They both increased their membership, with the ICAEW growing from 578 members in 1880 to 2,702 in 1900 (Roslender, 1992). Other bodies, such as the Chartered Association of Certified Accountants, were formed around the turn of the century. Many of these accountants were grouped into partnerships, firstly on a local or regional basis and then at national level. By the end of the nineteenth century the names we are familiar with in accounting today – such as Coopers, Peat, Mitchell, Price Waterhouse, Whinney, Deloitte – had become important accounting houses. In the 1890s they began to spread their influence abroad, opening up offices in the colonies of the British Empire and in the US. Later, US firms such as Marwick, Arthur Young, Ernst, and Lybrand made the reverse trip across the Atlantic, some joining up with UK practices.

Changes in corporate structure – from the owner-manager entrepreneur to the joint stock partnership to the shareholding system – involved accountants in a number of difficult issues. How should the financial return to capital (interest) and to entrepreneurship (profit) be categorized and allocated? How should the early financial stake of the founding partners be related to the later investments of new shareholders? How was capital to be depreciated? All these were important to the central issue of the distribution of funds from the enterprise to its disparate collection of owners. Alongside these difficulties, there was ambiguity about what the accounts were thought to represent. The 1844 Act had talked of 'full and fair' accounts. In 1856 this became 'true and correct'. The Companies Act of 1879 reintroduced the term 'full and fair' but it disappeared again (from the statute books, at least) in 1900. From then until 1947 the term 'true and correct' reigned until it was replaced by the contemporary pledge of 'true and fair'. Whether these changes in terminology reflect either changing practice or changing perceptions of company accounts is not clear (Walton, 1991). But the concern with appropriate wording may be seen as a reflection of accountants' claims that accounting information was an essential element of owners' relationships with enterprises, whilst it was simultaneously asserted that there could be no standardized, guaranteed way of providing such information. The tension between the importance of accounting information and its uncertainty was increasingly seen (by accountants) as a matter to be resolved by professional judgement – that is, by accountants themselves. It was this view which the big accountancy firms and the professional institutes exported to the British Empire and the US.

The development of accounting knowledge

Until recently accounting history (as an academic discipline) has not been centrally concerned with the social analysis of the relationship between enterprises and accounting. Accounting historians were largely concerned with documenting the accumulation of accounting techniques and charting their development into modern practice. In recent reactions against this conventional approach, accounting history has been accused of falsely portraying accounting as a factual and objective form of knowledge (Loft, 1986); of being fixated on the question of 'who did what first?' (Hopper and Armstrong, 1991: 412); and of 'viewing the history of accounting as a natural evolution of administrative technologies' (Miller *et al.*, 1991: 396). To the extent that conventional accounting history rests upon some implicit notion of social change it would appear to assume a generalized evolution or progress in the development of ideas and thus to have links with modernization theory. In explaining why such progress took place in the nineteenth century, it has been widely assumed that accounting responded to the needs of businesses to improve their efficiency – paralleling the assumptions of industrialization theories. In the last decade or so, this conventional approach to accounting history has been challenged by a wave of research based upon social analysis. As Miller *et al.* noted, the 'broadening of accounting history is at an early stage and it is only just becoming possible to discern the contours of the emerging landscape' (1991: 397). However, with some oversimplification, two important strands can be detected.

One has involved attempts to locate accounting practice more firmly in its social context and has drawn widely on Marxian approaches. As we have seen, changes in accounting practice have been related to the internal conditions of the enterprise – for example, the demise of contract systems. There have also been analyses of the influence of change external to the enterprise – for example, the withdrawal of UK banks from long term investment in companies. Of particular importance in such studies is the identification of differences between countries at both enterprise and societal level. This has highlighted variations in accounting practices, so that they are no longer viewed as the inevitable outcomes of the evolution of accounting theory. Instead they are seen as embedded in specific social formations.

Another strand has been concerned with the location of accounting modes of thought in broader intellectual developments. For Weber accounting was the purest expression of the rationality of the capitalist enterprise, and hence an exemplar of modern ways of thinking. Weber's work has had little impact on the new accounting history, but there has been much interest in the way accounting as a discipline/practice relates to broader developments in knowledge. Much of this work draws on that of the French social theorist Foucault, who examined the construction of knowledge as 'discourse' – the theories, concepts, and practices of the 'human sciences'. Those who have used this approach have linked developments in accounting discourse with the wider codification, regimentation, and examination of human beings in nineteenth century prisons, armies, schools, and hospitals, as well as factories (Hoskin and Macve, 1986, 1988: Loft, 1986; Miller and O'Leary, 1987; Walsh and Stewart, 1993).

These two strands may be seen as representing the different perspectives of the materialist and idealist positions, and there has been some hostility between the two camps (see Neimark, 1990). However, as noted above, the distinctions can be exaggerated, and there is much overlap in the work of the new accounting historians. In particular, both approaches have been concerned with the role of the accountancy profession in creating, organizing, and applying accounting knowledge. Rather than treating the development of accounting as simply a response to the needs of enterprises, the process has been analysed in terms of the ways accountants have been involved in the identification of 'problems' and the construction of 'solutions'. Here, what the enterprise *is* (and hence what constitutes its needs) is inextricably linked with how it is *seen* (what constitutes problems and solutions). Accounting, towards the end of the nineteenth century, was becoming increasingly important as a way of seeing – and, as such, was both influenced by the nature of enterprises and shaped the way those enterprises developed.

REVIEW

Short questions

What are the distinctive features of the cottage, putting-out and factory systems of production? What three types of explanation have been offered for the rise of the factory? Why does Marglin say that he is not convinced that factories were the inevitable result of new machinery and new forms of power? What three features of the factory division of labour did Adam Smith identify as leading to efficiency? What criticisms have been made of Smith's argument, and what is the significance of Babbage's study of wage rates? What is meant by 'technological determinism' and why has it been criticized? What two key control problems does Marglin identify, and what evidence does he have for this? What three managerial problems does Pollard identify in early factories and how did managements deal with them? What is 'limited liability' and why was it important in the development of enterprises? What is meant by 'internal contract systems' and what forms did they take? How did nineteenth century foremen differ from today's first-line supervisors? What are the distinctive features of 'idealism' and 'materialism' as forms of explanation? What particular views of the Industrial Revolution are implied by the terms 'industrialism', 'modernization', and 'capitalism'? What key changes were influencing the enterprise at the end of the nineteenth century?

Which three forms of accounting does Pollard identify prior to the rise of factories? What competing descriptions are there of the incidence of cost accounting in the nineteenth century? Why is it argued that capital accounting was not crucial in the management of enterprises? How did late nineteenth century changes affect accounting within enterprises? What strands of a 'new accounting history' can be identified, and what are their central concerns?

Discussion points

How were technological, economic, political, and social factors related to the rise of enterprises? What was the role of accounting in this?

Part I

CAPITAL

Debates on ownership and control

2

CONTROL OF THE ENTERPRISE

In the late nineteenth and early twentieth centuries UK and US enterprises began to grow rapidly and develop forms of ownership based on dispersed holdings of stocks or shares. In place of the single entrepreneur or small joint stock partnership, as the controlling head of the firm, the modern corporation was owned by hundreds, then thousands, then hundreds of thousands of individual investors.

The rise of big business provoked a long-lasting debate on whether this development constituted a fundamental change in the nature of the capitalist enterprise, and in the nature of wider capitalist society. This debate is concerned with identifying changing patterns of ownership, interpreting the consequences of such changes for the control of enterprises, and their impact on the goals which are pursued. For some, the changes amounted to a revolution in which managers replaced owners as the central force within business and which led to a decline in the importance of profit as the defining enterprise objective – and to the development of 'post-capitalist' forms of society. In opposition to this, others interpreted the changes as a restructuring of capitalist ownership and continued to emphasize the pursuit of capital accumulation – within forms of society termed 'finance capitalism' or 'impersonal capitalism'. This chapter reviews this debate and identifies some key issues in the construction of theories of the enterprise at the end of the twentieth century.

MANAGERIALISM

Managerialism is the term generally given to a collection of theories which state, in essence, that owners have lost control over large enterprises, that managers have gained power, and that this has led to the rise of corporate goals other than profit. Two broad strands of this argument can be identified. One emphasizes the surrender of ownership control and the rise of social responsibility as the prime corporate goal. The other identifies the growth of management power as leading to a range of managerial goals for the enterprise.

Community interests and social responsibility

The most influential contribution to the first strand of managerialism is the work
of Berle and Means (1932). They argued that individual owners were becoming
increasingly unable to control the business activities of the firms in which they
invested. The twin factors which gave rise to this development were the *dispersal*
of ownership among a large number of small investors, and the *disorganization*
of these individuals so that they could not combine to form an effective voting
block in order to safeguard their interests.

The evidence for such a change came from their 1929 study of the 'Top 200'
(i.e. largest) US non-financial corporations. Assuming that only a relatively small
group of investors could organize themselves effectively, they attempted to
discover what voting power such a group could muster. Where this was
sufficiently large the corporation was deemed to be under owner control. Such
firms were categorized into three broad bands – private, majority and minority
control (see Box 2.1). Owner control, they argued, could exist even with only a
20 per cent holding in the company, provided that the other shares were so widely
dispersed that victory in any voting battle, although not guaranteed, was probable
for the group which held the 20 per cent block of shares. Below this 20 per cent
level, owner control was significantly weaker, and if the largest voting block was
less than 5 per cent then owner control could not be exercised. Where such a
power vacuum existed, effective control was in the hands of management. In
1929, they concluded, such *management control* had already emerged in 44 per
cent of the largest US companies, and a further 21 per cent rested on the brink of
this situation.

This separation of ownership and control meant that owners could no longer
impose their interests on many giant US corporations. Freed from the dominance
of owners, how would managers now operate these enterprises? In their original

Box 2.1

Control of the top 200 non-financials, US, 1929		
Proportion of shares in largest block (%)	*Type of control*	*Proportion of companies (%)*
80 and over	Private	6
50–79	Majority	5
20–49	Minority	23
5–19	Joint/Legal device	21
Under 5	Management	44

Source: adapted from Berle & Means (1932)

work Berle and Means considered three possibilities. First, that the new controllers (i.e. the managers) might act as trustees of the owners' funds and continue to operate the businesses for the sole benefit of the owners; second, that managers might use enterprise resources to pursue their own interests; and third, that the rights of 'the community' might dominate the management of corporations. The first and second of the potential outcomes, however, were suggested only as logical possibilities and were quickly dismissed. Owners, 'by surrendering control and responsibility over the active property, have surrendered the right that the corporation should be operated in their sole interest'. Similarly, managers had never laid:

> a basis for the alternative claim that the new powers should be used in the interests of controlling groups [i.e. managers]. The latter have not presented in acts or words any acceptable defence of the proposition that powers should be so used. No tradition supports that proposition.

Thus, using a language of 'claims', 'rights', and 'tradition', they focused on the third possibility.

> Neither the claims of ownership nor those of control can stand against the paramount interest of the community . . . It remains only for the claims of the community to be put forward with clarity and force . . . It is conceivable – indeed it seems almost essential if the corporate system is to survive – that the 'control' of the great corporation should develop into a purely neutral technocracy, balancing a variety of claims by various groups in the community and assigning to each a portion of the income stream on the basis of public policy rather than private cupidity.
>
> (1932: 312)

This prediction of the replacement of *private greed* with *public need* as the prime goal of the largest US corporations was elaborated in Berle's later work. He argued that, in balancing the interests of all parties in the community, managers were guided by 'corporate conscience' (moral rules adopted within enterprises) and 'public consensus' (attitudes in society). Thus 'soulful corporations' had emerged within a 'People's Capitalism' where US businesses were collectively owned by citizens and served the needs of the American people (Berle, 1960). Further, since these developments were inextricably linked with the increasing size of enterprises, this 'corporate revolution' was a general historical process which would transform capitalist economies around the world. Changes in corporate ownership patterns would deliver control to managers who would run socially responsible enterprises.

Apart from their own research, US evidence to support the starting point of Berle and Means's thesis – the spread of ownership among a large number of small investors – came from a number of sources (Goldsmith and Parmalee, 1940; Gordon, 1945). Larner, in a study of the 'Top 200' US non-financials in 1963, classified 84 per cent as 'management controlled', and concluded that 'it would appear that Berle and Means in 1929 were observing a "managerial revolution" in process. Now, thirty years later, that revolution seems close to complete' (1966: 786). In Britain, apart from the work of Florence (1947, 1953, 1961), there were no similar studies until the 1970s. Florence discovered a trend towards greater share dispersal in the UK 'Top 100' non-financials between 1936 and 1951, though dispersal was far less widespread than in the US. For some, this was enough to indicate that Britain had already begun to experience the 'managerial revolution' first begun in the US. Dahrendorf (1959), drawing heavily on Berle and Means's work, portrayed Britain as a 'post-capitalist society' in which enterprises were effectively under the control of propertyless managers. Their position was based not on capital, but on authority – their professional expertise and its legitimate exercise and 'Never has the imputation of a profit motive been further from the real motives of men than it is for modern bureaucratic managers' (Dahrendorf, 1959: 46).

Although the evidence for Britain was hardly extensive, it seemed to many to confirm Berle and Means's thesis of managerialism. Means was confident enough to introduce the fourth edition of their book by stating, 'The fact of the corporate revolution is now so widely accepted that statistical evidence is no longer needed to establish its occurrence' (Berle and Means, 1968: xxix). This view was echoed by Dahl, who asserted, 'Every literate person now rightly takes for granted what Berle and Means established four decades ago in their famous study' (1970: 125). Managerialism, in the form constructed by Berle and Means, seemed to have become established not only as social science orthodoxy, but also as the common-sense view of those informed about business.

Management interests and corporate goals

Whilst the foundation of Berle and Means's view – that control had passed from owners to managers – was widely accepted, not all accepted their view that this resulted in the replacement of *profit* with *social responsibility* as the prime objective of large enterprises. Instead a number of alternative goals were proposed which reflected the interests of managers rather than those of the community.

Galbraith was happy to agree that control had shifted, and that 'decisive power in modern industrial society is exercised not by capital but by organisation, not by the industrial capitalist but by the industrial bureaucrat' (1967: 17). His explanation of this change stressed, not the dispersal of share ownership, but the complexity of decision-making in the modern enterprise. It is this which limits the power of owners to intervene. Decision-making is conducted by teams, or networks, of managers from the level of executive director to first-line supervisor. This collectivity of decision-makers – the 'technostructure' – determines the goals of 'the mature corporation', with which managers identify. However, such goals can be described as socially responsible only to the extent that 'What is deemed to be sound social purpose is a reflection of the goals of the corporation and the members of the technostructure' (p. 174).

For Galbraith, the first technostructure goal is the survival of the organization itself, which depends upon achieving and maintaining corporate autonomy. This involves freeing the enterprise from control by markets. Management can loosen the constraints of capital markets by providing the minimum level of dividend acceptable to shareholders and then ploughing back the rest of the profits internally. It can abolish markets for raw materials and semi-finished goods, and wholesale and retail markets by vertical integration – buying-out its suppliers and distributors. It can weaken the hold of product markets by horizontal integration – take-overs, mergers, or collaborative agreements with competitor firms. The remaining power of consumers to choose can be manipulated by 'demand engineering' so that consumer taste is shaped by advertising and marketing which designs the customer.

Through these strategies management attempts to gain independence – from owners, from suppliers and distributors, from competitors, from consumers – and shape its own destiny. When this has been achieved,

> there is then a measure of choice as to goals . . . there is little doubt how, overwhelmingly, this choice is exercised: it is to achieve the greatest possible rate of corporate *growth* as measured in sales. [Such growth serves the interests of technostructure members since it] is wholly consistent with the personal and pecuniary interest of those who participate in decisions and direct the enterprise.
>
> (Galbraith, 1967: 179)

Closely associated with corporate growth are goals of technological virtuosity and innovation. Only after the satisfaction of these goals does the technostructure attend to lesser objectives which may be termed 'socially responsible'. Here giant enterprises attempt to create the very values and attitudes to which they claim to respond. Enterprises serve social need only to the extent that they define what that need is.

Like Berle and Means, Galbraith saw these changes as a general historical process. In his case, since it is decision-making, rather than dispersal of ownership, which is the motor of change, not only capitalist but also 'socialist' economies will experience it. The state is no more able to intervene in the affairs of the technostructure than is the small shareholder. This strand of managerialism followed the second line of possibility that Berle and Means had so quickly dismissed – that managers would seize the enterprise they controlled and use its resources in their own interests. Galbraith's general emphasis on growth finds support in managerial economics. Baumol (1959) cited maximization of sales revenues (subject to a profit constraint) as the prime business objective; Williamson (1966) stressed growth maximization (constrained by fear of take-over); and Marris (1964, 1972) identified the need for security as a constraint on the central goal of growth. For these writers it was growth, rather than profit, which had become the defining feature of the large enterprise. Growth contributes to salaries, fringe benefits, career prospects, and prestige, and hence serves managerial, rather than capitalist, purposes.

Occupying a position somewhere between Berle and Means and Galbraith is the view advanced by behavioural economists such as Simon, Cyert and March. Simon (1945) argued that uncertainty about the environment of enterprises means that decision-makers are never in a position to maximize any single goal – whether it be profit or growth. Instead, managers attempt to create outcomes which are 'good enough' or 'satisfactory'. The enterprise is seen as a coalition of managers, owners, customers, workers, and creditors, each of whom makes a contribution and must be satisfied with the returns they receive (Cyert and March, 1965). In this way corporate managers are portrayed as *satisficing* – balancing the interests of all those who are connected with the enterprise. To the extent that managers concentrate on satisfying the needs of others this might be termed socially responsible; but to the extent that managers serve their own interests companies pursue managerial goals.

This strand again drew close links between the increasing size of firms, the decline of owner power, the rise of management power, and changes in organizational goals. Although the two strands differ in their view of whether managers run enterprises in their own interests or in the interests of the community, the central emphasis in both is that the interests of owners no longer dominate, and that profit maximization is no longer the prime goal. The wider implication is that, if capitalists do not even rule enterprises, they can hardly be seen to dominate society – hence capitalist society has been transformed in the twentieth century.

CRITIQUE OF MANAGERIALISM

Despite the confidence that the theory of 'corporate revolution' had, by the 1960s, become fully established as the orthodox theory of the enterprise, there were counter-voices. In the US, Lundberg's (1937) studies of the holdings of wealthy families and, in Europe, Hilferding's (1910) analysis of finance capital had presented quite different views of developments. In the 1970s managerialism came under increasing attack from sociologists and economists, who reassessed and reconstructed all aspects of the thesis.

Attacks on managerialism

Corporate goals

Some critics accepted the first claim of managerialism – that owners have lost power and no longer control the firm – but argued that this does not make a great difference to the goals pursued by the enterprise. In the US, Larner concluded, 'the effects on the profit orientations of firms, and on stockholders' welfare have been minor' (1970: 66). In the UK, Nyman and Silberston (1978) could find no clear pattern emerging that indicated management-controlled firms were less profit-oriented and more concerned with growth.

The view that managers, once they are in control, will change the goals of the firm rests upon the assumption that they are, in some significant ways, different from owners. Nichols (1969), in a study of six firms in the North of England, suggested that such differences may be exaggerated. He found that the background and values of managers were similar to those of owners. Three-quarters of the sixty-five directors and senior managers he interviewed were drawn from the 'upper middle class' (i.e. had fathers who were directors, small business owners, managers, or professionals) and many (63 per cent of directors, 44 per cent of senior managers) had attended Britain's elite public schools. Both in their families and in their schools, managers had experienced a common pattern of socialization which was unlikely to be hostile to shareholders. Indeed as Florence (1961) pointed out, they were likely themselves to be shareholders. Although their holdings might be small in relation to the total ownership of the enterprise, these holdings might well have a high significance for their personal finances and attitudes. Nichols also discovered considerable difficulty in separating such goals as 'profit', 'social responsibility', and 'growth' in the views of managers. Whereas for some academics these might appear to be distinct categories, for managers these concepts merge in their discussion of business goals. Some managers see a reputation for social responsibility as an aid in maintaining the long term profitability of the firm and which will permit growth; others see profit as a measure of how well the firm is satisfying the needs of customers and regard failure to maximize the benefit to owners (in the short or long run) as socially irresponsible.

This raises uncertainty about the meaning of the labels attached to corporate goals. In explaining their actions, managers may draw on a 'vocabulary of motives' (Mills, 1940) thought acceptable to the audience. Organizations may have a 'front' and a 'back' (Cicourel, 1968). Managers may believe that some motives are socially acceptable and can be publicly expressed, whereas other motives might be seen by outsiders as illegitimate and are to remain unspoken. The relationship between such vocabularies of motive and the goals of firms is problematic. Williams (1959: 184) claimed that the separation of ownership and control shows that 'the "profit motive" is not a motive at all . . . it is not a psychological state but a social condition'. This view has been echoed by de Vroey (1975a), who rejected the idea that corporate goals are merely dependent on the 'motivations' of managers, and Zeitlin (1974), who argued that profit is 'an objective requirement'.

All these criticisms suggest that we have much to disentangle in order to test the proposition that corporate goals have shifted from 'profit' either to 'social responsibility' or to 'growth' or to some other managerial goals. It is not clear how managers perceive these objectives, whether they see them as alternatives, or how far they are able to choose between them. This uncertainty is connected with what is meant by 'management control'.

Management control

Critics have found a number of shortcomings in the managerialist concept of management control. The term *management* is often applied in a very general fashion by managerialist writers. Berle and Means (1932) referred to a 'neutral technocracy'; Galbraith (1967) to a 'technostructure'. Both terms suggest a broad collective of technical experts who are the new controllers. There are difficulties in applying these terms in many British companies either because managers lack technical qualifications – ironically labelled 'technocracy without technocrats' (Nichols, 1969) – or because where there are technical experts they do not see themselves as in control (Nichols and Beynon, 1977). A number of critics have also been concerned to differentiate between managers. Management may be vertically differentiated between top and middle in terms of *strategic* versus *operational* management (Pahl and Winkler, 1974; Scott, 1985). In addition there may be important dissimilarities horizontally between managers carrying out different *functions* or drawn from different *occupational specialisms* – for example, between engineers, accountants and personnel managers (Armstrong, 1985).

Thus, rather than being a cohesive force which gives a single direction to corporate affairs, management may be a loose coalition with internal fractures running vertically and horizontally. Goals, to the extent that they are determined within the enterprise, may be the outcome of unstable patterns of competition and co-operation in decision processes involving different managerial perceptions, values and interests. In this view enterprises do not have a single organizing intelligence, nor a 'visible hand' of management (Chandler, 1977). There may be 'no "essential function" of the firm which subordinates all others . . . [but] a set of more or less ambiguous objectives towards which an institution, firm or enterprise might be working' (Thompson, 1982: 234). These criticisms raise problems about which managers are supposed to be in control of enterprises: directors, executives, middle managers? Accountants, engineers, sales and marketing, or general managers? They also question whether management in general, or some section of management, is capable of imposing any single goal.

This leads us to the issue of what is meant by 'control'. Berle and Means saw control as resting upon the voting power of shares in selecting members of the board of directors. Others have extended this to cover all means of determining corporate policy (Goldsmith and Parmalee, 1940). Instead of two concepts – 'ownership' and 'control' – some have preferred to use three (Renner, 1904; Hilferding, 1910). *Legal ownership* refers to shareholders' legal right to benefit from the application of their funds by enterprises. *Economic ownership* is concerned with a social relationship in which some individuals or groups direct the use of capital. When only some of the shareholders exercise control, or when non-owners (such as banks with outstanding loans) intervene, then the category of economic owners overlaps but is not identical with that of legal ownership. Economic owners are those who have effective *possession* of the enterprise

(Poulantzas, 1974; de Vroey, 1975a; Scott, 1985). Scott associated this with 'strategic control', which:

> involves deciding on the source and level of investment funds, the allocation of these funds to alternative uses, calculation of the rates of profit to be earned in different parts of the enterprise, the recruitment of top executives, and the resolution of such constitutional issues as mergers, take-overs, and liquidation [as distinct from 'operational control', which is] the implementation of corporate strategy and thus the immediate day-to-day administration of corporate operations at plant level.
>
> (1985: 44)

Although managers may have operational control in administering the enterprise this does not necessarily mean that they are able to direct strategy or set corporate goals. To determine control over the enterprise, rather than control within it, we have to discover who has ultimate power to direct the use of capital.

This raises a second major problem with control. If it is defined as ultimate power, then this may be exercised infrequently and thus may be difficult to detect. Nichols argued that owners seldom intervene, but this is because 'in the generality of cases, such shareholders are satisfied that their interests are reasonably well served' (1969: 104). What we are concerned with is the potential to intervene in corporate strategy, rather than regular interventions. Zeitlin's (1974) discussion of the US Anaconda company demonstrated how difficult it may be to detect the potential for intervention. Anaconda was one of the companies deemed to be under management control in Berle and Means's 1929 survey and Larner's 1963 survey. In 1971 Anaconda found its copper mining operations in Chile nationalized, without compensation, at heavy loss to the firm. Within two months owner intervention produced a new chief executive (who was a vice-chairman of Chase Manhattan Bank), the chairman took early retirement, and 50 per cent of corporate (head office) staff were fired. For over forty years it had been thought Anaconda was management-controlled, but when a crisis occurred capital was able to dispose of the management. A similar story is told by Nyman and Silberston (1978) of two UK firms – Vickers and Debenhams. Both experienced low and falling profitability in the 1960s. At the end of the period both experienced major shake-ups following interventions from owners – a grouping of banks, insurance companies and investment trusts. Vickers found it had a new managing director and financial director and many senior executives were replaced. Several business interests were sold off, there was a 15 per cent reduction in staff, and the company's profitability rose. In Debenhams' case almost the entire board was changed, including the chief executive and chairman, and there was a 30 per cent reduction in personnel.

These case studies suggest two possibilities. Either owners had the potential for intervention over many years but had chosen not to exercise it: or, when faced with corporate operations which failed to satisfy them, the owners were able to organize themselves effectively to generate such power. Whichever is the case, the studies demonstrate the danger of assuming that day-to-day control implies ultimate control of enterprises.

Ownership

Such indications of potential owner power provoked a re-examination of the basic plank of the managerialist platform – that ownership was highly dispersed and disorganized. A number of researchers re-evaluated the original Berle and Means 1929 study and found it defective in a number of respects. For many of the firms Berle and Means studied, they admitted there was little evidence, and they 'presumed' management control in the case of forty-four corporations (Zeitlin, 1974). The existence of 'nominees' (individuals or companies who hold shares for others) means it is difficult to detect the ultimate owners. This problem is exacerbated when company records are an unreliable guide to share ownership. Burch (1972) contrasted the US Securities Exchange Commission's official records with the information gained from reports in *Fortune, Time, Business Week, Forbes*, and the *New York Times*, and found very considerable disparity. These issues, together with other technical problems in the methods of Berle and Means and later managerialist researchers, have led to strong doubts about the statistical validity of the findings. Researchers in both Britain and America stressed the continuing importance of family control of firms, and the rising role of financial institutions in both countries. These findings have led to sharply downward revisions of the number of corporations which might be classified as management-controlled – however we define that term.

The end of managerialism?

Although managerialism seemed to be firmly established as social science orthodoxy at the end of the 1960s, the 1970s saw a ferocious assault on all aspects of the thesis. Weaknesses were found in its empirical foundations; in its concepts of 'ownership', 'management', and 'control'; and in its conclusions that there had been a fundamental change in corporate goals with a declining importance of profit. Zeitlin (1974) branded managerialism a 'pseudofact', and Scott (1984) a 'myth'. These attacks considerably damaged the managerialist thesis, perhaps beyond repair. However, even pseudo-facts and myths may be highly influential, and managerialism has permeated thinking in many areas of social science and business. Thus it would be premature to suggest that managerialism is dead.

One of the reasons for the success of managerialism was that it offered a broad, organizing framework for understanding changes in the modern corporation. In the 1970s much of the critical attack on managerialism was concerned with chipping away at its monolithic structure rather than creating an alternative thesis. However, the critics of managerialism were not arguing that there had been no significant change in the capitalist enterprise. From the wreckage of managerialism some very different views of the development of capitalism emerged.

DEVELOPMENTS IN CAPITALISM

Two strong themes developed in the critique of managerialism. First, a stress on the continuing importance of *personal* ownership and control through individuals and families. Second, the identification of an increasingly important trend for ownership to pass from persons to *institutions* – especially financial institutions such as banks, insurance companies, investment trusts, and pension funds.

The first theme is the argument that wealthy individuals and families have been able to maintain control over vastly grown commercial empires by drawing on the funds of many small investors. Since these small investors did not at any stage in the development of corporations hold control over corporate policies, it cannot be claimed that they have lost or surrendered such power. Instead the dispersal of share ownership consolidated the position of founding families by enabling them to become the 'economic owners' of huge business units which far exceeded their own personal wealth. Thus there has been a concentration of power in the economy with the development of oligopolistic and monopolistic enterprises. Instead of *people's capitalism*, this has been labelled *monopoly capitalism* (Lenin, 1917; Aaronovitch, 1955; Baran and Sweezy, 1966).

The second theme is the argument that in those cases where individuals and families have lost personal control of enterprises, power has shifted, not to the managements of enterprises, but to financial institutions. Not only has the financial stake of such institutions in enterprises increased considerably, but they can no longer be regarded as 'sleeping partners' remote from business decisions, since they now actively intervene in the direction of business policy (de Vroey, 1975b; Nyman and Silberston, 1978). This results from a mobilization of finance where the small contributions of savers, insured persons, and pre-pensioners are aggregated into concentrated units of capital by large institutions. Banks are seen as especially important in this process whereby the *industrial capitalism* of the nineteenth century was replaced by *finance capitalism* in the twentieth (Hilferding, 1910; Schumpeter, 1919; Sweezy, 1956). Where relationships between and within the large units of industrial and banking capital are regulated or mediated by governments, and where these governments take on extensive economic functions, this is seen as producing *state monopoly capitalism* (Aaronovitch, 1961).

Individual, family and institutional ownership

In the US, Lundberg's (1937) early work on the holdings of America's sixty wealthiest families pointed to considerable concentration of ownership. Burch (1972), from a study of 300 large US corporations, concluded that 45 per cent were 'probably', and a further 15 per cent 'possibly', under family control. The families of Ford, Rockefeller, Du Pont, Mellon, and others continue to figure strongly in corporate control (Scott, 1986). In the UK, Nyman and Silberston's (1978) study of the 'Top 250' discovered that founding families continued to be strongly represented through ownership and/or the occupation of top corporate positions such as chairman or managing director. Influential families include Guinness, Whitbread, Cadbury, Lever and McAlpine. Scott concluded that 'family control remains important in both countries and is especially important in the "smaller" of the large enterprises' (1985: 83).

Also significant is the rise of institutional forms of ownership. In the US, over a third of corporate stock was in the hands of financial institutions by the late 1970s (Kotz, 1978; Herman, 1981). Pension funds are the biggest investors, most of whose investments are managed by banks. In addition, the banks invest directly in enterprises. There is interlocking ownership of companies and banks through individual and family holdings. Banks own shares in other banks, and also hold their own shares (Chevalier, 1969). The issue of *bank control* is complicated by these intricate ownership patterns (Zeitlin, 1974).

In Britain, financial institutions have also grown in importance. In 1963 they held 30 per cent of equity shares; by 1975 the figure had risen to 48 per cent, and it reached 58 per cent in 1981. Pension funds and insurance company investments are the most significant. Whilst banks are relatively unimportant as direct investors in industry, they do provide significant amounts of capital through loans (Diamond Report, 1975) and this may give considerable indirect influence. Despite the extensive privatization of nationalized industries and public utilities in the 1980s, with the number of share owners in the UK now 11 million (London Stock Exchange, 1991), the proportion of shares held by persons has continued to fall – from 54 per cent in 1963 to 21 per cent in 1989 (see Box 2.2). Again the situation is complicated by the various connections and overlaps between families, companies, and financial institutions.

Box 2.2

Ownership of UK equity shares (%)		
Sector	*1981*	*1989*
Personal	28.3	21.3
Financial	57.6	57.9
Pension funds	26.7	30.4
Insurance companies	20.5	18.4
Unit trusts	3.6	5.9
Other financial	6.8	3.2
Overseas holders	3.6	12.4
Others*	10.5	8.4

* Including charities, companies, central and local government.

Source: London Stock Exchange (1991)

In these complex patterns of ownership, control can no longer be traced to any single source – an individual, family, company, or institution – but is to be located in the network itself. Here control is characteristically through a *constellation of interests*. This applies to situations where the largest shareholders do not form a stable cohesive group but have the potential to form alliances and to intervene when corporate policy threatens their interests:

> No coalition [of owners] can achieve a stable position of control, but the board cannot disregard the interests of those in effective possession. The major shareholders have effective possession, yet this constellation of interests has no unity and little possibility of concerted action. The major shareholders may be able to co-operate in order to determine the composition of the board, this composition depending on the balance of power among them, but co-operation beyond this is unlikely.
>
> (Scott, 1985: 50)

Owners do not set corporate strategy on a permanent basis, but they cannot be ignored by those who do. This implies that control over the enterprise is dependent on the interplay of interests at the level of the board of directors, which is the locus of connections between enterprise management and ownership networks.

Control and the board of directors

Scott analysed boards in terms of three kinds of actors – entrepreneurial, financial, and internal capitalists. The *entrepreneur* has a high degree of personal ownership of particular enterprises either as tycoon or as representative of the founding family. The *financier* represents those with diverse interests in many companies through a portfolio of shares. The *executive* (internal capitalist) is a salaried manager who is also likely to hold shares (or share options) in the enterprise. Together these three actors are the constituent elements of the 'dominant coalition' which determines the strategy of the business enterprise (Child, 1972). Each of the individuals may represent a different interest, and hence the board is an 'arena' within which there is a 'struggle for control' (Scott, 1985). However, since this struggle is carried on under the general surveillance of a constellation of ownership interests which has the potential to intervene, the differences between the three kinds of individual actors are constrained within a field of possible strategies.

Of particular importance are financiers on boards of directors, and financial institutions in ownership constellations. There are connections between corporations through individuals who sit on several boards of directors. This creates an 'interlocking directorate'. By counting the number of connections between enterprises we can measure the strength of the 'inter-corporate network' in the US and UK (see Box 2.3). Both countries display strong connections at board level.

Firms which at first appear to be isolated enterprises are linked through spiders' webs of interlocking directorships. At the hub of these webs there are

Box 2.3

The distribution of interlocks in the top 250 enterprises

United States		United Kingdom	
No. of interlocks per enterprise	No. of enterprises	No. of interlocks per enterprise	No. of enterprises
0	16	0	61
1–4	61	1–5	112
5–9	75	6–10	54
10–14	56	11 or more	23
15 or more	42		

Source: Scott (1985)

major banks who, through the management of institutional funds and the provision of credit, create spheres of influence which connect enterprises (Scott, 1985). They are 'nerve centres of the communication network' between enterprises (Mokken and Stokman, 1974). This gives a very different picture of enterprise control from that developed from an emphasis on the individual enterprise. So too do studies which change the focus from individual owners to an owning class.

Class, corporate ownership and control

If the owners of firms are seen as isolated individuals, their power may appear low, but if we view them as members of an owning class, then a basis for general control of enterprises may be revealed. The concept of class, however, is open to a number of definitions, and various authors have stressed different aspects of class formation.

Studies of the distribution of wealth, in both the US and the UK, have shown that it remains highly concentrated (Lundberg, 1969; Atkinson, 1972; Westergaard and Resler, 1975). The 'top 1 per cent' and 'top 5 per cent' categories continue to hold a very large proportion of all those shares which are in private hands. Rather than the dispersal of share ownership leading to a widespread property-owning democracy, it is probably better characterized as producing a pattern of portfolio holding in which wealthy individuals have diversified their investments.

Such a *wealth class* may be merely a statistical category of unconnected individuals. However, there is also evidence that there are a number of links between wealthy individuals so that they can be seen to constitute a *social class*. Social cohesion is created through similarities and connections in family background, education, marriage, and social or leisure activities (Lupton and Wilson, 1959; Scott, 1982) which create social networks where 'the families of officers, directors and principal shareholders are bound by interwoven kinship ties' (Zeitlin, 1974: 1,109). Evidence for a relatively small wealth class, whose members are linked as a social class, is not sufficient to demonstrate a basis for control of enterprises. For this to be established, two further elements are needed.

First, the existence of common interests among members of the wealth class, so that they constitute an *economic class*. De Vroey (1975a) argued that, in the nineteenth century, the twin functions of providing capital and putting capital to work were united in the person of the entrepreneur. In the twentieth century these two functions separated into fractions of *finance capitalists* and *industrial capitalists*. Whether the specific form of financial return is 'interest payments' (a financial return on the provision of capital) or 'profit' (a financial return on the entrepreneurial use of capital), both forms are aspects of the overall pursuit of *capital accumulation* – the increase of owners' wealth – which constitutes the 'logic of capitalism'. Child (1985a) has similarly suggested that there is a unifying goal of 'profitable growth' – the term preferred by company directors. This view dissolves the supposed conflict between profit and growth as competing enterprise goals. Instead, the interests of the wealth class are unified around the pursuit of capital accumulation.

Second, members of the wealth class must be able to mobilize and express their interests as a *business class*. Scott (1982) argued that, although not all its members are economically active, the business class constitutes a pool from which business leaders are drawn. Through the networks of interlocking directorates business leaders, especially financiers, direct individual enterprises and influence overall movements in the economy. In doing this the (small) active element of the business class has access not only to the large holdings of capital of the wealthy, but also to the aggregated investment finance of numerous small contributors. Thus a vast supply of capital is channelled between enterprises, and directed within enterprises, by a tiny proportion of the population – a few hundred controllers. Although 'legal ownership' may have been more widely distributed, 'real economic ownership' has become more concentrated.

The rise of impersonal capitalism?

This form of economy may be termed *impersonal capitalism*. Here the providers of capital are remote from the destination of their funds, which are spread between many enterprises. Most have no direct attachment to particular enterprises, nor any specific control over them. Their funds are professionally managed for them by finance experts. In the nineteenth century it may have been possible for entrepreneurs to impose their own personal goals on enterprises – perhaps selecting security or reputation above profitability at some stages in corporate life. They could dispose of their own capital in any (legal) way they saw fit. Large enterprises are no longer open to such personal choices but instead are governed by a more abstract need to provide financial returns to the generalized owner. Since capital is dedicated not to any particular enterprise but to enterprises in general, failure to meet market expectations of financial returns may be penalized by switches in investment to more lucrative opportunities. In both Britain and the US this has led to the view that enterprises have become focused on short term financial results to the detriment of more strategic long term aims.

The shift of emphasis from individual ownership of individual enterprises to impersonal ownership of enterprises in general also directs attention to the role of the state in managing the collective affairs of enterprises. The state influences the operation of the modern business system through the legal framework of regulation; the construction of an infrastructure of education, welfare, transport, and communication; the encouraging and discouraging effects of taxation and subsidy; and the general management of the economy. It may also intervene more directly through its own economic activities such as production for military purposes or in nationalized industries. Although different political parties, when in government, have adopted different stances on the proper role of the state, there may be a general move from the state being concerned with the construction and maintenance of the conditions for enterprise activity to a concern with more directive policies. The 'move from facilitative to interventionist mediation appears to be an irreversible feature of the development of modern capitalism' (Scott, 1985: 225).

The rejection of the managerialist view that power has shifted from owners to managers led to new theories which focus attention elsewhere. The role of finance professionals in directing capital, and the role of the state (both in creating the framework for this and in making specific interventions) have been highlighted – capitalism may have developed from an 'entrepreneurial' to a 'modern' form based on impersonal ownership, financial control, and state mediation. Such patterns may not be universal and international comparisons suggest there are significant variations between capitalist societies.

INTERNATIONAL COMPARISONS

The conclusions about modern enterprises produced by managerialism, in both of its forms, were seen as indicating a key trend in capitalist society. The newer theories are more sensitive to international variations. The notion of management control has been difficult to sustain on its home territory, in the US and UK, but it has been even harder to defend elsewhere. Distinctive national patterns have been identified which suggest there is no single path which capitalism follows. For example, in Australia the concern has been with foreign ownership of firms (Wheelwright and Miskelly, 1967). In Sweden, one family – the Wallenburgs – has extensive ownership of industry (Scott, 1985). In Belgium, one financial institution – the Société Générale de Belgique – is dominant (de Vroey, 1975b). These variations suggest that patterns of ownership and control of enterprises are dependent on broader historical and social differences between countries rather than on the outcome of some inevitable trend in the development of enterprises and capitalism. Such societal differences are demonstrated in the cases of Germany and Japan.

Enterprises in Germany

The German pattern of enterprise ownership and control is strongly influenced by the country's banking system. This pattern emerged from restructuring after the slump of the 1870s. *Mobilier* banks, which channel the funds of small depositors to industry, were established in the 1850s. When the 1870s slump caused widespread industrial (and consequently banking) failures, German bankers responded by combining into large *universal* banks, and reorganizing industrial production through mergers (Scott, 1985). In Britain the banks' response to the same slump was to adopt a 'borrow long, lend short' policy – an attempt to create security by encouraging depositors to leave funds with banks for long periods, whilst giving short term loans to a diverse range of companies (Armstrong, 1985). This led German banks to close, long term connections with groups of enterprises with which they enjoyed a special relationship. In Britain, by contrast, banks developed a more distant, hands-off relationship with enterprises. These banking policies meant that the pattern of share ownership characteristic of the UK and the US was not so dominant in the German economy. Instead, the big three German banks – the Deutsche, Commerz-, and Dresdner – became highly important providers of capital. By 1975 their direct investments, and the funds for which they were trustees accounted for 35 per cent of the holdings in the seventy-four largest German enterprises. The holdings of other banks and investment companies made up a further 28 per cent (Smith, 1983). Around each of the major banks is a relatively stable grouping of industrial enterprises. Although these are independent companies, they can be described as a loosely knit corporate family (Benjamin, 1991).

A second significant feature of the German pattern developed from industrial restructuring following World War II. Under pressure from the Allies, and with the encouragement of the Catholic Church, the German government introduced a system of co-determination in which company executives are responsible to a supervisory board which balances owner and employee interests. Again banks dominate the owner interests – in 1980 about one-fifth of the seats on supervisory boards of the top seventy-four companies, and half of the chairman positions, were occupied by bankers (Smith, 1983). Overall, bank power appears to be much stronger in Germany than in either the UK or the US.

Enterprises in Japan

Patterns of ownership and control of Japanese enterprises are also influenced by developments which go back to the last century. The Meiji government, established in 1868, encouraged industrialization and fostered the development of *zaibatsu* – business groupings created by the wealthiest Japanese families. These combines were dominated by family-owned holding companies under which were banks, insurance companies, and manufacturing industries. These in turn had their own subsidiary enterprises.

This system was restructured after World War II, when the US government required wealthy families to sell their shares. These shares were eventually acquired by companies within the combines, and the *keiretsu* system emerged. Here there is a closely knit family of companies with interlocking shareholdings. The biggest of these are the industrially centred Mitsui, Mitsubishi, and Sumitomo combines, and the financially centred Sanwa, Fuyo, and Daiichi Kangyo. These combines are now the largest business groupings in the world. Each constituent company of these combines is likely to have directors from other companies within the combine. Strategic direction is through the 'Presidents' Club' of chief executives of each company (Scott, 1985). In addition to these combines there are also large 'autonomous' companies, such as Hitachi, Nissan, Toyota, and Sony, which form extensive industrial groupings through long term connections with contracted suppliers. In both forms capital is provided within organizational structures. It has been claimed that 'the Keiretsu and industrial groupings are in fact the most dynamic and efficient system of raising industrial finance yet devised' (Benjamin, 1991).

Through this system of contracted suppliers these large enterprises extend their control over a large number of smaller firms in the Japanese economy. This system has been described as 'organization-oriented' rather than 'market-oriented' (Dore, 1989) and suggests a high degree of business planning and management of relationships between units, in contrast with the competitive regimes of the UK and US.

The development of combines and industrial groups has been strongly influenced by the Japanese state. Since World War II the Ministry of International Trade and Industry and the Japan Development Bank have strongly influenced economic development (Benston and Lloyd, 1983). The government has identified key product markets for exploitation, and selected technologies for importation and development. Responsibility for these products, markets and technologies has been allocated to particular combines or industrial grouping in a planned state approach to industrial expansion (Fransman, 1988).

Contrasts with the UK and US

The German and Japanese patterns of enterprise ownership and control display a very different development from that in the UK and US. The role of small individual shareholders has never been as important in Germany or Japan, hence the theory that dispersal of share holdings leads to the rise of management control has had little relevance. Scott (1985) has described the German pattern as 'oligarchic bank hegemony' – a situation in which strong influence, but not absolute power, rests in the hands of a few big banks. In Japan the situation might be described as 'group hegemony', with small and medium-sized enterprises drawn into the industrial/financial networks of the giants.

Although the four countries display different patterns there may be some broad similarities in the forms which have been created. None of them fits the model of entrepreneurial capitalism where there are strong connections between personal capital and enterprises. Instead the 'variant forms of intercorporate shareholdings which exist in capitalist economies point to a transition from a system of personal possession to one of impersonal possession' (Scott, 1986: 26). Power no longer rests with individual owners, but with the intercorporate networks at the centre of which lie financial institutions (UK and US), or banks (Germany), or combines (Japan).

THE DEBATE ON OWNERSHIP AND CONTROL

Research over recent years has moved the debate from rather simplistic analysis in terms of a shift of power from owners to managers towards a view of power as generated within intercorporate networks of control. Here power is an ultimate, though unstable, ability to determine corporate strategy in pursuit of the general interests of owners. This power is not stable, since it depends upon temporary alliances forming dominant coalitions. It is not specific, since it is constructed from a constellation of interests rather than any single owner interest. It is activated when, or if, managerial decisions or actions stray too far from owner interests. Thus control does not show itself in the operational management of enterprises, but in the constraints within which managers exercise their delegated powers. The arena where strategic control and operational management meet is the board of directors.

Here, in both the UK and the US, financial intermediaries are seen as especially important. They stand between the investor and the enterprise. It is their assessment of company performance which is crucial in determining whether or not owner intervention is required. Unsurprisingly, many authors see these assessments as based on accounting reports of financial performance. Thus Zeitlin argued that,

> whether or not managers are actuated by a 'profit motive', as a subjective value commitment, 'profit maximization' is an objective requirement, since profit constitutes both the only unambiguous criterion of successful managerial performance and an irreducible necessity for corporate survival.
>
> (1974: 1,097)

In a similar vein Scott concluded,

> Operational managers experienced the constraints of de-personalized capital through the strategic control exercised by the finance capitalists and internal capitalists who filled the boardrooms of the large enterprises. As a

result, the 'profit motive', far from declining in importance, has become institutionalized in the control systems of the modern enterprise.

(1985: 262)

The debate leaves a number of issues unresolved. If we accept that the notion of 'management control' should be abandoned and replaced with a concept of 'delegated authority' there remains the possibility of considerable variation in the operational management of different enterprises in different societies. Although we have seen that, in extreme cases, owners can intervene when their interests are disregarded or unfulfilled, managers may still exercise considerable discretion in the short term. Although we have evidence that owners, through financial intermediaries, can attempt to ensure the pursuit of their general interests, we cannot be certain that they are always (or even usually) successful in this. The role of accounting is stressed but not examined. We will turn to this last issue in the next chapter.

Most particularly, for our purposes, we need to question the validity of the view that financiers can use financial measures of performance as an effective check on managerial action. Scott introduced a word of warning on this:

> although the size and rate of 'profit' earned by an enterprise are dependent on its accounting practices and may not, therefore, provide strictly comparable yardsticks, many investigations have attempted to relate strategic control to measures of profit.

(1985: 187)

Within accountancy there have been claims that financial measures not only fail to provide Zeitlin's 'unambiguous criterion' but may be thoroughly suspect even as Scott's 'yardstick'. If 'impersonal capitalism' is driven by financial control, then accounting is placed at centre stage of the debate as the key link between operational managers and strategic controllers. The debate on ownership and control has largely assumed, rather than investigated, this link, which has now become a crucial aspect of our understanding of the modern corporation. In the next chapter we will explore the relationship between accounting and the control of enterprises.

REVIEW

Short questions

What two factors did Berle and Means identify as leading to loss of owner control? What evidence did they have for this? What three possibilities did they consider as the goals of 'the modern corporation', and which did they decide was the most likely? How does Galbraith's approach to managerialism differ from that of Berle and Means, and what is meant by the 'technostructure'? What are the goals of the technostructure? What do Simon, Cyert and March mean by 'satisficing' and how does it relate to the other approaches to managerialism? Why does Nichols think that managers are unlikely to have goals which are hostile to owners? What is meant by 'strategic control' and 'operational control'? Why does the view of power as a 'potential for intervention' cause difficulties for the study of control? Why is it difficult to be certain about who owns modern enterprises? What two forms of ownership are stressed by critics of managerialism and how have these been changing? What does Scott mean by a 'constellation of interests', and who are the key actors at the level of the board of directors? What different concepts of class are used, and what does a class analysis suggest about ownership and control? What is meant by 'impersonal capitalism' and what does this suggest about the goals of enterprises? Why has financial control become more important in UK enterprises? How do patterns of ownership and control in Germany and Japan differ from those in the United States and the United Kingdom?

Discussion points

Is 'managerialism' dead, and should we see modern societies in terms of 'impersonal capitalism'? What unresolved issues are there in the debate on ownership and control, and how might we address them in building new theories of the relationship between capital and management?

3

ACCOUNTING FOR THE ENTERPRISE

This chapter is concerned with three overlapping issues – the influence of social science theories on accounting thought; the interrelationship of the nature of the enterprise and accounting practices; and how the study of these practices may modify existing social science theories of the enterprise.

CORPORATE REPORTING

From the middle of the nineteenth century accounting became increasingly important in reporting the activities of UK and US enterprises to outsiders as a means of monitoring their internal management. What is reported, and how this is done, has a considerable impact on the way enterprises are perceived. With the growth of large numbers of remote owners, who had little detailed knowledge of the enterprise, accounting information became a means of judging performance, and a basis for future decisions to intervene in corporate affairs or transfer capital elsewhere. For most of this century accountants have widely assumed that owners are the key users of corporate reports, and that content must therefore be determined by their interests. This was concisely stated in a report to the Institute of Chartered Accountants of England and Wales in 1952: 'the primary purpose of the annual accounts of a business is to present information to the proprietors, showing how their funds have been utilised and the profits derived from such use' (ASSC, 1975: 32). Over the last twenty years or so there have been challenges to this view. Some have come from accounting academics and commentators who shared some of the assumptions of managerialism. They have questioned the definitions of both the users and the purposes of annual reports.

Corporate social accounting

In the 1970s, in both Britain and the US, there was a rise of interest in broadening corporate reports to place less stress on owners and their economic interests, and more on the general influence of enterprises on society. Definition of *users* of reports was widened to include all 'stakeholders' in the enterprise, which *The*

Corporate Report (ASSC, 1975) listed as equity investors, loan creditors, employees, analyst–advisers, business contacts, and the government. Others widened this list to include consumers and the community or neighbourhood (e.g. Ramanathan, 1976). At its broadest, the concern of supporters of corporate social accounting (CSA) was that reports should be relevant to society in general. Alongside this was a reconsideration of the *content* of reports to reflect broader, and more varied interests. For external reporting, Ramanathan (1976) argued that the accounts should portray the 'social contribution' of the firm. This aspect – social responsibility accounting (SRA) – might involve statements dealing with: client satisfaction with goods and services; the effects of corporate policies on local education; crime prevention; pollution; conservation; urban renewal; traffic; the hiring and firing of female employees and those from racial minorities; sponsorship of recreation, the arts, and culture; medical care; contributions to charity; and energy saving (Council for Economic Development, 1971; Estes, 1976; Ramanathan, 1976).

In the US much of the early interest in SRA was aimed at producing internal information for management on the social impact of their organization, including employment reports. In addition, in both the US and the UK there was concern to provide information to lower level enterprise members through employee accounting (EA). *The Corporate Report* suggested that such reports might include:

> numbers employed (analysed in various ways); location of employment; age distribution of workforce; hours worked during year (analysed); employee costs; pension information; education and training (including costs); recognised trade unions; additional information on race relations, health and safety statistics, etc; and employment relations.
>
> (Maunders, 1981: 181)

Both SRA and EA represented a considerable shift from the traditional concerns of corporate reporting and were seen by some as amounting to a 'revolution' in accounting (Glautier and Underdown, 1974; Flint, 1980). What brought accounting academics to recommend such fundamental changes?

Roots of corporate social accounting

In identifying the need for change, supporters of CSA adopted three rather different positions. Firstly, some saw change in terms of a *moral imperative*. They regarded those in charge of enterprises as insufficiently aware of the social consequences of their business activities and/or as unwilling to be held accountable for their social responsibilities (Dierkes and Bauer, 1973). They advocated that the accounting profession should forsake its usual conservatism and take a lead in changing those attitudes. 'Is it asking too much for accountants, just for once, to take an initiative?' (Owen, 1982: 6). Accountants, they thought, should create CSA techniques and use the power of corporate law to impose them on enterprises. Such pressure was required, since 'without a strong motivational incentive system on the part of management to publish accurate and realistic social accounting information, there is little reason to expect that social accounting will ever be more than a mirage' (Monsen, 1973: 112).

A second position was based on the assumption that sufficient *external pressure* on enterprises to demonstrate their social responsibility already existed. As managements increasingly recognized this, there would be a need for accounting to respond. Some saw this external pressure diffused throughout society.

> Any social institution – and business is no exception – operates in society via a social contract, expressed or implied, whereby its survival and growth are based on: (i) the delivery of some socially desirable ends to society in general, and (ii) the distribution of economic, social, or political benefits to groups from which it derives its power.
>
> (Shocker and Sethi, 1974: 67)

Ramanathan adopted this view in his definition that 'the purpose of social accounting is to help evaluate how well a firm is fulfilling its social contract' (1976: 519). Other advocates of CSA identified pressure in more specific locations, such as central and local government, public pressure groups, and large institutional investors – Churches, foundations, universities, and so on (Parker, 1986). Both the managements of enterprises and the accountancy profession would (sooner or later) have to respond to changing perceptions and expectations in wider society, since the demand for social accounting appeared to be substantial and growing (Estes, 1976).

The third approach to CSA took the view that enterprises had already been transformed by *internal change* which created the need for a new form of accounting. The view adopted in *The Corporate Report* was that the ICAEW's stress in 1952 on proprietors and profit

> was no doubt correct at its time of issue, but with the passage of time it has become increasingly clear that it is incomplete and unsympathetic to modern needs . . . distributive profit can no longer be regarded as the sole or premier indicator of performance.
>
> (ASSC, 1975: 38)

A similar assumption introduced the Flint Report to the Scottish ICA:

> the primacy of the position of the owners or shareholders has gone and the current philosophy is to recognize as stakeholders all those with an interest in business performance or conduct . . . responsibility to and accountability to the stakeholders is . . . a fact.
>
> (Flint, 1980: 4)

Although the accounting academics who advocated CSA rarely dwelt on the social theories which underpinned their position the identification of internal change as lessening the power of owners and the importance of profit, the citing of external pressure from a 'public consensus', and the moral imperative towards a 'corporate conscience' are indicative of the influence of managerialism on accounting thought. That this is not explicitly recognized in CSA writing may be a symptom of the way that social science theories become embedded in everyday thinking – and may show that the Berle and Means thesis had, by the 1970s, become what 'every literate person now rightly takes for granted' (Dahl, 1970: 125).

Responses to corporate social accounting

Even if notions of the social responsibilities of enterprises were widespread in the 1970s, the recommendations of CSA were not universally accepted by accounting academics. Many warned of the technical difficulties that accountancy would face in attempting to construct appropriate techniques, since:

> Very few matters of social concern lend themselves readily to objective and verifiable quantification. . . . Accountants simply do not have the knowledge, qualifications or expertise to be able to measure levels of pollution or to assess the sociological or economic impact of a factory on a community.
> (Perks and Gray, 1979: 22, 23)

The uncertainty of any information which CSA was likely to produce implied that 'the social responsibility of accountants can be expressed best by their forbearing from social responsibility accounting' (Benston, 1982: 102). Scepticism about the ability of accounting to respond to change was accompanied by questioning of the need for it to do so. Perks and Gray (1979) warned that the moral desirability of CSA was not as clear-cut as was assumed by its advocates. Accountants attempting to construct new techniques might find themselves the pawns of interested parties concerned to generate partial or politically oriented information. 'Anti-capitalists' might seek to use CSA to attack enterprises, whilst 'corporate defenders' would wish to polish their public image. Even if accountants resisted these pressures, they themselves might be accused of having a vested interest in using CSA to boost their own fees, and anyway accountants might not be the best people to act as guardians of public morality (Puxty, 1986). Given its technical difficulty, its reliance on subjective judgements, and its dubious desirability, Perks and Gray (1979) were concerned that CSA, if adopted, would bring traditional accounting into disrepute and warned accountants, 'Beware of social accounting.'

Outside the academic world CSA had a mixed reception. In the UK legislation on employment and charity donations led to the production of some limited forms of CSA, but Roslender (1992) argued that the US has been in the forefront of voluntary social reporting, even though it was not incorporated into legislation. This reflected a long tradition of community involvement by enterprises, supported by Internal Revenue Service practices and encouraged by public campaigns on consumer rights and equal opportunities for employees. In the UK there was more general hostility to some of the broader claims for CSA. The recommendations made by the committee which produced *The Corporate Report* seem to have been a considerable surprise to those who had set it up and 'it was received with horror by large sections of the accountancy profession, business and the Conservative Party' (Roslender, 1992: 100). Within enterprises the response was patchy and selective. Although a number of companies made statements of commitment to social responsibility in principle (Melrose-Woodman and Kverndal, 1976), the annual ICAEW survey of 1979 found only thirteen out of 300 firms publishing any form of social accounts (Perks and Gray, 1981). After 1983 questions on social accounting were dropped from the survey (Herte and Owen, 1992). A study of fifty-seven accountants in six large enterprises in 1979–80 found that, after a decade of academic interest, CSA was still virtually unknown to practitioners in industry. Although there might be some generalized support for the notion of socially responsible business at the highest levels, this had not been translated into actual accounting practice, and for most accountants 'profitability was seen as the central managerial purpose' (Jones, 1990: 280).

If there was little active support for SRA, the same was not true of EA. All six of the companies studied in 1979–80 (Jones, 1990) had introduced some kind of EA and it received the support of many accountants, particularly at senior levels. This was not based on some generalized sense of social responsibility but was seen as a means of achieving profitable production. Its attraction was that it offered managers an opportunity of influencing employees' attitudes to managerial decisions and legitimizing the profit-oriented goals of enterprises. Typically enterprises used the same initial data as those used for the annual accounts, but presented them in the form of Value Added Statements. These identified the 'Wealth Created' and showed how it had been distributed. The glossy graphics which were generally used in Employee Reports carried the strong message that the vast bulk of value added was returned to employees in the form of wages, or paid on their behalf as tax contributions. Few companies went beyond this form of accounting to report on the non-traditional items discussed in *The Corporate Report*. Although companies did adopt some form of EA, it hardly constituted the radical break with established reporting practices which the advocates of CSA hoped for.

The failure of corporate social accounting?

By the mid-1980s many supporters of CSA were concerned that their fears that it would be dismissed as 'an indulgent fad of an affluent society' (Gambling, 1978: vii) had come true: it was being written off as 'a child of the 1970s' (Puxty, 1986: 107). Enterprises had, in general, not embraced the philosophy and practices of CSA and the revolution in accounting had not happened. CSA was seen as an 'opportunity . . . which the [accountancy] profession has not seen fit to grasp' (Owen, 1992: 26).

Some of the reasons for this may be ascribed to particular features of the CSA movement, and to the conservatism of the accountancy profession. The more grandiose of the CSA schemes, aspiring to report the whole impact of enterprises on society, were so ambitious that they could readily be dismissed as impractical. Narrower proposals for change, responding to public concern expressed through pressure groups, did meet with some success by forcing companies to disclose more information or to change their policies – for example, British Nuclear Fuels after the Chernobyl disaster, and Barclays Bank in relation to its South African investments. These, however, were isolated developments and there was no unifying theme around which pressure groups were able to organize a more general and sustained impetus towards greater social responsibility and account-ability on the part of enterprises. Indeed the very diversity of CSA proposals – concerned with issues of gender, race, pollution, energy, arts, recreation, em-ployee rights, and more – may have made it difficult to create a clear focus of support for CSA. Neither did those groups which were attempting to build pressure on enterprises gain much sympathy or support from the UK and US governments of the 1980s, which, under Thatcher and Reagan, were more con-cerned with the economic performance of their countries and building a competitive 'enterprise culture'.

The problems faced by CSA may have been much deeper than these particular issues. Each of the different positions adopted by CSA supporters assumed a weakening in the power of owners and a corresponding decrease in the im-portance of profit. These changes were presented either as an established fact (internal change), or as something increasingly being imposed upon firms by 'the public' (external pressure), or as an imminent change to be brought about through initiatives (moral imperatives) from the accountancy profession. Whereas there might have been a plausible theoretical basis for these assumptions in the early 1970s, when managerialism was still widely accepted, the later studies of social scientists showed them to be both theoretically and empirically dubious. Some of the early support for CSA can be seen as over-optimistic, or perhaps naive, in assuming the displacement of profit by social responsibility as the goal of enterprises. Some accounting academics responded by concentrating on more specific and less ambitious objectives for CSA which recognized the continuing importance of profitability for enterprises. For example, Gray *et al.* (1987) called for 'compliance with standard' reporting in which companies would report their performance against requirements already enacted in national legislation. This, they felt, would be practical and acceptable to industry. Even this more restricted form of CSA gained little support and by the end of the 1980s CSA appeared to be becoming a relatively minor academic backwater. At the same time, though, new developments were emerging which were to revitalize some of the issues in CSA and refuel the debate on corporate accountability.

Green accounting

This new impetus was heralded by Gray (1990b) as creating a new role – 'the accountant's task as a friend to the Earth'. Again, the concern was that accountants should report on more than the use of funds and profitability of enterprises, but the focus was upon responsibility for the natural environment rather than to society. Green accounting (GA) proposals were directed at both internal and external reporting of corporate performance as part of the 'greening' of enterprises. For internal uses, the functions of accounting should include 'developing information systems capable of capturing the cost effect of adopting environmentally friendly practices [and] the design of, recognition of, assessment of and control of information systems in an organization' (Owen, 1992: 7). Assuming that managers would wish to improve the Green performance of their enterprises, advocates of GA proposed specific initiatives such as environmental audits, environmental budgets, environmental hurdle rates for new investment, and environmental asset maintenance (stewardship of natural capital). For external reporting, there were calls for enterprises to disclose 'environmental policy; capitalization of environmental spending; environmental contingent liabilities; spending on environmental protection; anticipated spending in excess of contingent liabilities; [and] environmental activity and performance' (Crowe, 1992: 132).

The roots of Green accounting

Interest in GA emerged from what appeared to be a widespread rise in awareness of environmental issues in which public consciousness and concern were stimulated by reports of holes in the ozone layer, global warming, greenhouse effects, acid rain, threatened extinction of flora and fauna, and specific environmental disasters such as those involving Bhopal, Chernobyl and the *Exxon Valdez*. More broadly there was the identification of a need for 'sustainability' in enterprises' use of resources. Although increasing concern over the natural environment had been evident since the 1960s, until the mid-1980s it was limited largely to natural scientists and small environmental pressure groups. The rise of more general public awareness of environmental issues in the 1980s appeared surprisingly rapid. To one observer of the UK scene it seemed that:

> suddenly everyone *was* 'Green' – there were Green votes to be had; Green consumers popped out of the closet; products were Green; advertising went Green; ethical investment trusts got a Green dimension; Britain got a Green Minister of State for the Environment, a Green Bill, the possibility of Green taxes; and Mrs Margaret Thatcher, the UK Prime Minister, gave a speech to the Royal Society in September 1989 in which she became Green too.
>
> (Gray, 1990a: 7)

Although, as Gray noted, much of this may have been 'hype', the sudden greening of public awareness influenced the accountancy profession. Gray's own work had been funded by the Chartered Association of Certified Account- ants (ACCA) and he was able to cite twenty Green accounting articles in the UK accounting press during the previous year. Two years later a compilation of articles on GA (Owen, 1992) drew on contributors from three UK professional bodies (ACCA, ICAEW and CIMA) as well as accounting academics. It seemed that both professional and academic accountants were willing to accept the connection claimed in the title of the compilation – *Green Reporting: Accountancy and the Challenge of the Nineties.*

As with CSA, support for GA demonstrated a strong moral dimension. For example, if accounting could assist in decision-making which offered even the slightest possibility of minimizing, or repairing environmental damage, 'then I suggest that accountants convert this possibility into a personal duty, a duty which should override any environmentally detrimental activities of their employers' (Adams, 1992: 85). This time, however, the moral imperative seemed to be more certainly supported by a groundswell of public opinion. This was reflected in the growth of pressure groups such as Friends of the Earth and Greenpeace, of Green parties in Europe, and in publications such as *The New Consumer* and *Green Magazine*. National governments appeared willing to consider legislation which would require enterprises to be more environmentally responsible. In addition, supra-national organizations, such as the European Commission and the United Nations, produced guidelines and recommendations.

There was also some indication that enterprises might be changing: partly owing to recognition of the potential funds available from 'ethical investment' sources, but also because of re-evaluations reflecting more traditional concerns. For enterprises primarily concerned with the pursuit of profit, the cost-saving potential of programmes of energy efficiency, better means of waste disposal or recycling, and reduction of excessive packaging were immediately attractive. So too was the marketing potential of 'environment-friendly' claims in appeals to Green consumers. Here the issue would be 'How do the costs associated with environmental issues affect the bottom line?' (Filsner and Cooper, 1992: 121). This central concern of enterprises was thus linked with the generation of accounting information, and GA was given public support by representatives of the Confederation of British Industry (Blaza, 1992), the Institute of Directors (Buck, 1992), and the British Institute of Management (Lester, 1992).

Prospects for Green accounting

In comparison with the fate of CSA, the prospects for GA appear brighter. The moral and practical case for environmental reporting, and its urgency, seem much clearer than for the disparate elements of SRA. Its potential is being recognized by professional accounting bodies as well as by academics. There seems to be an extensive and well organized network of external groups putting pressure on enterprises, and some support has been voiced by governments. Questions of sustainability may have changed the business agenda. All this could indicate a coalition of interests in support of GA.

However, the very diversity of support for GA creates some problems. Some GA supporters adopt positions identical to those of CSA twenty years ago.

The traditional view is that a company is accountable to its shareholders but these, by any measure, are a tiny, unrepresentative group. By contrast, the 'stakeholder' concept of corporate responsibility is increasingly being recognized as valid by major companies. This argues that several groups of people have a right to information about operations and policy – the shareholders, employees, consumers of the goods or services provided, the social community, and the community world-wide, particularly with respect to environmental issues.

(Wicks, 1992: 110)

If one of the reasons for the failure of CSA was the over-optimism or naivety of its supporters in the face of the power of owners and the importance of profit, then this may weaken the cause of GA. Other supporters of GA were more aware of the potential friction between enterprise interests and environmental concern. Comparing GA to the 'social audit' element of CSA, Geddes argued that both 'are linked to a critical politics, and unite in their opposition to the economics and politics of "the market"' (1992: 237). Here proposals for a new accountability are seen as implying either 'a fundamental challenge to the private ownership and control of the economy' or a confrontation with 'certain capital decisions to replace the unacceptable face of capitalism with a human face' (p. 237). Whereas Wicks presented GA as a development of existing accounting practices, Geddes would require a transformation of them, since 'Conventional accounting attempts to reduce the social to the economic, and the economic to the cash nexus' (p. 237) in ways which leave little room for reporting on, and being accountable for, social and environmental responsibilities. This divergence of positions reflects the broader rifts in environmental politics – between 'light Green' reformers and 'dark Green' radicals. The central issue is whether the development of new forms of accountability can be affected by amending business practices within their current enterprise framework, or whether a fundamental transformation of the economy and its governance is required in order to secure change. If the latter view is followed then perhaps accountants as 'the technicians of money' (Geddes, 1992) must be stripped of their current influence in economic, political and social decisions as a prelude to the emergence of environmentally responsible production.

This issue confirms the similarity between CSA and GA. Both propose forms of accountability which displace profit as the sole or prime criterion for the measurement of the performance of enterprises. As was the case with CSA, UK companies have (as yet) shown little indication of giving a high priority to reporting on social/environmental issues and fears have been expressed that any information which is provided is highly selective and driven by public relations (Harte and Owen, 1992). Claims by business spokespersons that industry is enthusiastic about environmental issues may (again) represent the 'public face' of enterprises rather than any considered and detailed intention to change management practices. Like CSA, GA may be seen as the child of relatively affluent economies. The world economic downturn of the early 1990s has caused some to raise the question 'Can the environment survive the recession?' (Lynn, 1991). If GA is to be constructed and implemented its supporters will need to address the issue of the relationship between environment and profit in the control and goals of enterprises.

There are broader questions about the ways in which environmental and social issues are incorporated in GA proposals. Many of the supporters of GA had previously been associated with CSA, and they have tended to bring with them its diverse elements. For example, an early CSA advocate, Owen (1981, 1982), and Gray – first a critic (Perks and Gray, 1979, 1981) and then a convert (Gray *et al.*, 1987) – have both been leading advocates of the greening of accountancy, and their social concerns have influenced their view of the desirable course of new developments. In some respects making a close connection between ecological and social issues is justified – because any society must exist within a natural environment and because concern with environmental issues has exerted social pressure on enterprises. However, the social and natural aspects of enterprise environments interrelate in various ways. Sometimes issues are compatible – for example, programmes to reduce toxins in products are likely to gain the support of ecologists and employees alike. But there may also be tensions – for example, the identification of coal as a 'dirty fuel' has not been greeted enthusiastically by mining communities in the UK, or the activities of the International Whaling Commission by whaling communities in Norway and Japan, where people feel their livelihoods and life-styles are threatened by outside interests. Such tensions are most potent in the 'Third World', where those in 'underdeveloped' countries are differently placed in relation to policies for satisfying needs, rather than gratifying wants, from those in the 'advanced' world of Europe and America who propose such policies.

The response from supporters of GA to this tension between social and ecological rationales has generally been that the threat to the survival of the planet is so dire and imminent that petty differences of interest between individuals and groups must be set aside in order to act effectively and quickly. Exploring ways of doing this will involve the generation of new ways of thinking about society. Since the Industrial Revolution social theorists have generally assumed the dominance of society over nature – that the natural world has become (largely) tamed, organized, and controlled by human beings. The concerns of social science, from nineteenth century writers Marx and Weber to 'postmodernists' of the 1970s and 1980s, focused on the study of interrelationships between people in their social milieux. Now, at the end of the twentieth century, concern is returning to the relationship between people and their natural environment. Social theorists are only slowly formulating ways of rethinking this relationship. The conceptual and practical difficulties faced by accountants in creating GA are part of this rethinking.

If GA is to make a positive contribution to protecting and repairing our natural environment by creating new forms of reporting through which enterprises are held accountable, its supporters will need to grapple with issues concerning the nature of enterprises (about which social science has a lot to say) and the relationship between the social and natural worlds (where social theorists are struggling to create new approaches). The immediate starting point for this is a reflection on the fate of CSA. As one leading advocate of GA, attempting to learn from past mistakes, put it:

> The social responsibility debates of the early 1970s looked dramatic and appeared to signal a substantive reappraisal of organisational life but, leaving only a small legacy, the energy passed away quite rapidly . . . it would be well to learn from the 1970s and remember that all the rhetoric in the world, all the promises of legislation, are insufficient to actually achieve anything in the way of change . . . The same opportunity offers itself again. It would be foolish to let such an opportunity slip by a second time and, one rather suspects, the business world and the accounting profession are unlikely to get away with it so easily this time.
>
> (Gray, 1990a: 17, 19)

Perhaps this time there is more genuine support for changing reporting practices among decision-makers in enterprises and the accounting profession. Perhaps this time there are more accounting academics who are aware of the difficulties they face and the nature of the enterprises they seek to influence. If so, the (necessary) optimism of those who wish to change corporate reporting will be better justified, and their impact greater. There will be many who hope this is the case. It certainly promises to be a lively debate.

ANNUAL ACCOUNTS AND AUDITING

It is perhaps ironic that, while some academics were proposing wide-ranging new forms of accountability for enterprises, others were becoming increasingly critical of the way accountants were performing the traditional role of reporting to owners on the use of their funds. These concerns covered both general issues of the nature of the information provided in the annual accounts of enterprises and specific questions about the accounting practices through which such information is generated.

Accounting information and corporate control

The development of forms of enterprise in the UK and US, depending heavily on bank lending and stock exchange transactions in the provision of capital, was associated with the rise of financial accounting as a key source of information. Investors and potential investors sought to monitor the performance of established enterprises through their annual reports, and to assess the viability of new ventures through their prospectuses. In both, accounting information played a major role. The relatively remote, or 'hands-off', relationship between finance capital and industrial capital meant that providers of capital had a less detailed knowledge of R&D and manufacturing strategies, product lines, and potential markets than their counterparts in Germany and Japan. In place of this knowledge, financial reports were used as a proxy for such information, and hence accounting came to occupy a pivotal position between owners and managers – thought to represent 'the bottom line'.

Short-termism

Given the significance of accounting to the owner/manager relationship, the particular ways in which it represents enterprises take on central significance. Annual accounts focus on profit, or the maximization of shareholder wealth. This has been identified as generating short-termism in the goals of enterprises. One standard UK textbook remarked:

> Conventional financial reporting information may be criticised . . . [because] profit is highlighted as the 'keynote' figure. This may lead users of statements to believe that maximization of short term profit is the sole aim of modern business enterprises when this is not so. This may also cause management to concentrate on short term results.
>
> (Gee, 1985: 111)

This is a highly complex statement and raises a number of difficult issues. It claims that accounting information is capable of shaping the beliefs of users. That in the case of short term profit these beliefs are not valid. Finally, that managers may respond to these (erroneous) beliefs and begin to pursue short term profit (presumably making it the actual aim of the enterprise). For Gee the nature of accounting practices can determine the direction of enterprises. Against this view it can be argued that accounting does not determine corporate goals but merely reflects the interests of owners – and that these are frequently short term. In economies with volatile stock exchange trading, where executives are either fearful of take-overs and mergers, or are aggressive corporate predators, then the perspective of decision-makers is likely to be within a close horizon. This can generate a 'casino economy' in which there is 'an obsession with reported "profits", earnings per share, the short-term and growth by acquisition at the expense of investment, research, development, and long term competitive strength' (Mitchell *et al.*, 1991: 4). Such short-termism appears particularly pronounced in the UK, where banks and stock exchanges together have not given enterprises access to the amounts of long term, external finance available in other economies such as Germany, Japan and the US (Williams *et al.*, 1983). Pollard (1984) claimed that this situation was worsened by UK government economic policy (dominated by the Treasury) which persistently identified investment as an item to be sacrificed in response to short term economic difficulties.

The policies of UK financial institutions and governments have been cited as a key factor affecting enterprise management. Williams *et al.* argued that there 'can be no doubt that the lending practices of the banks and the new issue market powerfully conditioned the calculations of manufacturing enterprise' (1983: 83). Pollard concluded that, faced with government decisions resulting in 'sudden lurches in policy, sudden increases in the cost of capital and the sudden wrecking of markets . . . [businesses] acted sensibly, logically and naturally in the conditions' (1984: 106) by holding back on long term investment. He detected a tendency for US governments to adopt similar policies and predicted similar economic consequences. If accounting is inclined towards a short term view then this may be not an inherent feature of its theory and/or practice but a reflection of its social context – the way it responds to enterprise managements' accommodations to pressures from outsiders – owners and governments.

Historical orientation

Another general criticism of financial reporting is that it is essentially past-oriented, and therefore not appropriate to the future decisions of users of annual accounts. Some have argued that companies should publish their forecasts, plans, and budgets, because these are the guidelines for managerial decisions and actions and are hence relevant to investors' assessments of likely company performance. Similarly, there have been calls for cash flow data 'since cash is the lifeblood of all businesses. Yet published accounts continue to give prominence to profits rather than cash flow' (Mitchell *et al.*, 1991: 20). Opponents of such changes have reaffirmed the advantages of historical cost accounting on the grounds that its data and calculations are open to objective verification, whereas future-oriented information is more subjective and speculative. However, 'subjective opinions and estimates play an important part in historical cost accounting' (Gee, 1985: 116). Critics of conventional practices have thus dismissed claims that future-oriented information would lead accountants into newly subjective territory, since the information provided is (inevitably) partial.

Monetary measurement

A third general issue goes to the heart of financial accounting by questioning its assumptions about monetary measurement. The information conventionally provided by accountants rests upon two fundamental assumptions – that all business assets, liabilities, and transactions can be quantified in monetary terms; and that the monetary unit of measurement is a stable standard. We have already seen doubts raised about the first assumption in relation to social and environmental reporting. But the issue goes deeper, since the central concept of accounting – the notion of 'value' – is not an objective measure, and even if 'price' is taken as a proxy for value this cannot always be established. When enterprises are treated as 'going concerns', the value of an asset must be estimated rather than taken as the price agreed through market exchanges. The second assumption has also caused difficulties, since it depends upon units of money having fixed values. This assumption is untenable in modern economies where money is permanently in

70

flux. Inflation within one currency regime (so that £1 in 1994 does not equal £1 in 1995) and variations between currency regimes (so that the 1994 £ : $ exchange rate is not the same as the 1995 £ : $ rate) mean that accounting's basic unit of measurement – money – is constantly changing. Either this variation is ignored (as in historical cost accounting) or various adjustments are made (as in a number of inflation accounting practices, and in different treatments of currency exchange fluctuations). Whatever method is adopted, it inevitably results in a particular portrayal of situations or events – against which there could be other portrayals. In this sense any 'bottom line' of a cash figure can never be an absolute measure.

Accounting entity

The way in which accountants proceed in gathering data and applying calculations is (loosely) guided by various basic 'concepts', 'assumptions', and 'principles'. These provide a framework within which distinctive accounting portraits of enterprises are produced. The enterprise 'for accounting measurement purposes . . . is regarded as an entity quite apart from its owners or proprietors. The business owns it own assets and owns the claims (liabilities) against those assets' (Gee, 1985: 115). This formulation, codified in company law, presents a 'legal fiction' in which an enterprise is treated as though it were a person. Whilst for many purposes this 'entity' concept may be convenient, it is certainly not a natural or commonsense view – it is a very particular theoretical construction. So too are other basic components of conventional accounting concerning how the entity is to be reported, such as the 'objectivity principle' (which urges impartiality embedded in objective facts) and the 'prudence concept' (which prescribes systematic bias towards conservatism).

The accounting view

These ingredients (together with many others) imply that accounting does not simply 'tell it the way it is' in reporting on enterprises. Accounting contains distinct views about how the enterprise is to be regarded, what data are to be taken as relevant, and what ideas should guide the processing and presentation of these data. This results in a particular way of seeing enterprises. In this sense accounting information provides a view of enterprises which is different from that which derives from other forms of information – manufacturing, marketing, personnel, research and development – which could also be relevant to determining future action. To the extent that accounting is accepted as an authoritative view and owners and managers decide and act on this view, then it shapes not only how enterprises are seen, but also what they do.

However, accounting does not provide a single view of enterprises. Such is the general and vague nature of the guidelines, and so numerous and different are the ways of applying them, that there is no single account of the firm – even within the distinct accountancy perspective. Within accounting frameworks a multitude of different accounts can be generated. Individual accountants are involved in selecting which of these accounts is to be presented and this has been the root of more particular concerns over recent years.

Creative accounting

In the previous section we saw two arguments about the role of accounting information. First, that accounting – by its very nature – may influence the judgements and actions of owners and managers (for example, by leading to an emphasis on the short term). Second, that accounting should be seen as responding to the external pressure from users of annual accounts (so that short term reporting was a response to owners' inclinations). In this section a third argument is introduced – that managers of companies (together with their accountants) construct annual accounts in order to influence owners. Here the notion of 'users' of accounts is reinterpreted. Is the 'user' the person who reads the accounts (as conventionally assumed) or is it the person who constructs them (as a tool for their own purposes)? Concern with 'creative accounting' has led to an emphasis on the ways in which managements manipulate corporate information.

Griffiths defined creative accounting as 'an above-the-board means of achieving underhand ends', and claimed, 'Every company in the country [UK] is fiddling its profits. Any accountant worth his salt will confirm this is no wild assertion' (1986: 1). In his view, major financial decision-making power resides with a small number of financial advisers in the commercial heart of London ('the City') which 'is rapidly becoming a handful of key analysts and institutions who between them have enormous power, and whose influence can make or break a company' (p. 4). Companies target these analysts and institutions as the most important recipients of annual reports and tailor accounts to their expectations and aspirations.

The central concern of this tailoring is to portray the company as achieving steady growth in earnings and profits. Suppose over a four-year period a company achieved £15 million profit. This might be presented chronologically as: Year I, profit £4 million; Year II, loss £1 million; Year III, profit £15 million; Year IV, loss £3 million. If the company were to use 'profit-smoothing' techniques then the same four-year period could be presented as Year I, profit £1 million; Year II, profit £2 million; Year III, profit £4 million; Year IV, profit £8 million, thus producing the desired impression of steady improvement rather than haphazard performance, and reducing the perceived risk.

The bulk of Griffiths's book then set out, with worked examples, methods by which accountants manipulate data in order to achieve the desired effect (see Box 3.1). A skilful accountant can, within some limits, determine when income is to be recognized, defer or capitalize expenses, direct money from pension funds into profits, and then attempt to defer tax on the enhanced profits through careful interpretation of company plans and forecasts. For the careless or unskilled reader of accounts, profit figures which have been constructed from selective treatment of shifts in exchange rates or revaluation of fixed assets may appear to indicate success in the production and trading of goods and services. Prospective bad news for future years may be hidden through postponed depreciation of assets, or by not declaring pending lawsuits as potential liabilities (on the grounds that they have no genuine legal substance), or by valuing stock by the most favourable of the many allowable methods.

Over the short or medium term it is possible for companies to produce the kinds of accounts which analysts want to see – a progressive improvement in performance. If, in any one year, the company exceeds expectations, the finance director may save some of the surplus in the 'bottom drawer', thus 'putting a bit aside for a rainy day'. However, Griffiths argued that creative accounting cannot in the long run save a company which is economically unsound and that the company will eventually collapse. Between these two extremes of over-profitability and unprofitability will be many companies which have enhanced their profit figures by drawing upon all the ingenuity of their accountants and find it increasingly difficult to sustain the illusion through creative accounting. At this stage, and especially if financial analysts are already becoming suspicious, companies are likely to take the sudden step of announcing losses (known as taking the 'big bath'). These (until recently) could be declared on an 'extraordinary' basis and, given sufficient reserves, need not affect dividend payment for the year. When this happens the guiding principle appears to be 'get rid of all the bad news in one go', and financial directors can not only clear their desks of a backlog of embarrassing items but also anticipate future problems. This will prepare the way for the production of positive results over subsequent years. Since the declaration of loss is clearly a sensitive issue, companies need to be careful in deciding when it is to be done. One senior accountant told me a preferred time is the year following the departure of one chief executive and the appointment of a replacement. Here loss can be attributed to the old regime and promises made that a revitalized

Box 3.1

Techniques of creative accounting

How to:

- increase income
- pilfer the pension fund
- tamper with taxation
- get around goodwill
- cultivate current assets and liabilities
- brush up borrowings and cash

- expand expenditure
- pamper presentation
- fiddle foreign currency translation
- flatter fixed assets
- smarten stock
- sharpen share capital
- operate off-balance sheet financing

Source: Griffiths (1986) chapter titles

---

management under new leadership will improve performance speedily. Creative accounting can then be used to demonstrate that these promises have been met.

The people most at risk from the rise of creative accounting may be the small shareholders, and for them the 'myth that the financial statements are an irrefutable and accurate reflection of the company's trading performance for the year must be exploded once and for all' (Griffiths, 1986: 190). On the other hand, independent analysts and those working for the large financial institutions may be sufficiently aware of creative accounting practices, and more broadly informed on corporate performance, not to be deceived. This view is known as the theory of the 'sophisticated investor', who is presumed to be able to ascertain the 'real' value of a share behind the actual market price generated by creative accounting. However, through his study of a number of business scandals in the US, Tinker (1985) discovered that many of the smartest business people in the country were drawn into bogus investments. After the collapse of the National Student Marketing corporation, in the early 1970s, investors lost $100 million and they included Citibank, Morgan Guaranty Trust, and the Harvard University Endowment Fund. Despite the scrutiny of the Securities and Exchange Commission, large and small investors alike had been deceived by the company accounts. In this example, creative accounting was deemed to have crossed the boundary between the enhancement of results and fraud – two Certified Public Accountants were jailed for their part in the scandal. The case is not unique. Tinker also examined an oil drilling company which didn't drill any oil, and a coal mining firm which never mined coal, both of which were, nevertheless, able to produce fine prospectuses and later published glowing reports which appeared to be supported by the accounts.

So-called 'sophisticated investors' could be seen as victims of their own professional expertise. In the 1970s Wall Street thinking was dominated by the formula of 'earnings per share' as the prime means of valuing a company. This formula 'took on an almost mystical quality . . . it provided a rationale for actions and decisions in situations in which decision-makers would otherwise be impotent' (Tinker, 1985: 59). This rationale encouraged some managers to pay dividends out of capital rather than profit, thus enhancing share price. Whilst the contents of the accounts presented a misleading picture of companies, the calculations by which the figures were arrived at were declared to be in accordance with 'generally accepted accounting principles'. Thus investors' perceptions of companies rested upon two related beliefs – the validity of the earnings-per-share measure, and the reliability of the accounting figures. Accountants had become the 'paper prophets' of business in a modern world where accounting was accepted as 'the word' on corporate performance.

Auditing

The activities of creative accountants within enterprises may be restrained through audit of annual accounts. From the middle of the nineteenth century onwards auditors have been appointed to monitor the financial information supplied by directors to shareholders and other outsiders. Gradually this activity was monopolized by members of the accountancy profession and became a central feature of the work of accountancy firms.

By the 1980s the accounting names of the late nineteenth century – such as Price Waterhouse, Cooper, Marwick, Mitchell, Andersen, Ernst and Young – had amalgamated into a number of giant partnerships. In the US they were known (for a while) as the 'Big Nine' and each of them was large enough to have appeared on *Fortune*'s list of the Top 500 US companies had they been industrials. In 1981 these giants audited 493 of the *Fortune* 500, employed 170,000 people in over a hundred countries, and included almost a third of all the members of the American Institute of Certified Public Accountants (Tinker, 1985). These huge practices are unique among the professions. Although there are some quite large international legal firms, they do not approach the size of the accounting houses. The accounting giants in 1981 each earned ten times as much as the largest law firm, and employed as many lawyers.

In the 1980s these giants continued to grow and merge, and expanded their non-audit activities, particularly in management consultancy. They have gained enormous influence in the accountancy profession in both the UK and the US, supplying a large proportion of the senior members responsible for creating the principles, and monitoring the practice, of public accounting. They occupy a central position in the debate over auditing.

Boundaries of acceptability

In recent years there has been growing criticism of audit's role in relation to creative accounting on both sides of the blurred boundary between (legally) enhancing performance figures and (illegal) fraud. Some of the fiercest of these critics in the UK have been the team of Mitchell, Sikka, Puxty, and Willmott. This group is an interesting phenomenon in its own right, being composed of (respectively) a Labour Party Member of Parliament and three academics – two accountants and a sociologist. They have persistently harried the accountancy profession through academic papers and newspaper articles, on political platforms and in Parliament. Their concern focuses on the role of accounting and auditing as 'the police force of capitalism' where they claim current activities are in disrepute. They have pointed to the collapse of numerous companies whose annual accounts had not indicated impending failure to their shareholders but were, nevertheless, audited as 'true and fair' statements (see Box 3.2).

They listed four major creative accounting techniques which were increasingly being used by major companies. In *foreign currency fun* assets held overseas appear to go up or down in value in line with exchange rates. The changes are not related to the yearly trading performance of the companies but may be taken into the profit and loss account (or may be left out). In some cases where such changes produce 'gains' they are included, but when there is a 'loss' they are

Box 3.2

True and fair?

Question. What do the following companies have in common?

Polly Peck	British & Commonwealth	Sock Shop
Coloroll	Rush & Tomkins	Parkfield
Johnson Matthey	Sound Diffusion	Eagle Trust
Corton Beach	British Island Airways	Leavitt Group

Answer. 'Company accounts showing strong asset positions and healthy profits . . . accepted as "true and fair" by auditors, but followed, in weeks, by the collapse of the companies.'

Source: Mitchell *et al.* (1991: 3, 8)

---

excluded. As an *interesting event*, some companies take interest payments (which should reduce profit) and capitalize them 'to flatter income statements and balance sheets, a process which makes assets and profits look better' (Mitchell *et al.*, 1991: 6). Accountants have also become willing to move away from traditional practice to value brand (trade) *names as assets.* Not all companies do this, and there are many methods used by those that do, hence comparability between firms is weakened. These practices and others are intended to make the economic performance of enterprises look better than they otherwise would, but 'all of this is lawful and permitted by current UK accounting rules' (Mitchell *et al.*, 1991: 7).

At the head of their list of dubious accounting practices was the *exceptional/ extraordinary game.* Here corporate accountants used the flexibility of accounting guidelines to define unusual events either as 'exceptional' (which would affect the declaration of earnings per share for that year) or as 'extraordinary' (which would not). In whatever ways these two terms might be defined in dictionaries, or contemplated in philosophical discussion, many accountants were merely concerned with the consequences of selection – if the event helped profits then it was treated as 'exceptional'; if it hurt them it was 'extraordinary'.

On this item of the Mitchell *et al.* hit-list there has been some general agreement and in autumn 1992 the UK accountancy profession changed its guidelines so that the extraordinary/exceptional distinction was modified. It is not suggested here that criticism of the practice by Mitchell *et al.*, or by other academics, (Humphrey *et al.*, 1991, 1992) was directly responsible for changing the accounting guidelines. Certainly there were many practitioners who found the situation unsatisfactory, and there may well have been pressures from other quarters. However, the outcome does suggest that, while creative accounting may (from the corporate accountant's viewpoint) be marvellously manipulative, it is not infinitely so. Some practices, though technically feasible and perhaps having some justification in logic and theory, may become socially unacceptable. The boundary between acceptable and unacceptable accounting is not only blurred, it is also a shifting terrain.

Monitoring the boundary

The patrollers of this indistinct and shifting frontier are auditors, who have been assigned the task of ensuring that guidelines are followed. The way they have been doing this, and their reluctance to 'blow the whistle' on companies which stray too far into the grey area between acceptable and unacceptable practices, have attracted much recent criticism. Mitchell *et al.* asserted that auditors 'supposed to be the watchdogs, should safeguard investors . . . They don't' (1991: 7). In principle auditors are independent of companies and act as representatives of owner interests. In practice they are nominated by directors and through 'secrecy, influence, apathy and lack of time/interest, the shareholders are asked to rubber-stamp the directors' choices' (Mitchell *et al.*, 1993: 5). Once appointed, according to a recent UK court ruling (*Capara Industries plc* v. *Dickman et al.*, 1990), auditors do not owe a duty of care to individual shareholders. The large accounting houses now derive a considerable proportion of their income from management consultancy services which are often sold to the same companies which they audit. Indeed, the big firms seem to regard audit as a loss-leader which gains them the opportunity to market their more lucrative consultancy services. This builds up close links between auditors and enterprises and calls into doubt claims of independence. As part of their efforts to gain the initial auditing work, the large firms may stress their own competence in creative accounting – as Price Waterhouse did in one tender which announced their 'acknowledged track record in constructive accounting solutions' (Mitchell *et al.*, 1991: 8). Rather than restraining creative accounting practices, auditors are accused of supplying them and, given the looseness of accounting guidelines, all this can be done quite legally.

As well as criticisms of the way auditors may assist managers in presenting information in ways which suit them, there has been concern over the failure of auditing to reveal corporate fraud. Following spectacular collapses of major companies (see Box 3.2), investors who lost their money turned back to the annual accounts and found no indication of impending doom, with enterprises being treated as 'going concerns'. Where later investigations revealed fraud on the part of corporate executives, investors tended to blame 'audit failure'.

The accountancy profession has responded by citing an 'expectations gap' (Humphrey *et al.*, 1992). The claim is that the public misunderstand the role of auditors, who do not have a statutory duty to detect and report fraud. Auditors have a narrower duty in relation to accounting procedures – attesting that accounting figures have been produced, collated, and presented in accordance with professional practice. The solution to the problem (a mismatch between public expectations and audit practice) preferred by the profession is that public attitudes

77

must be changed. Alternative suggestions that audit practice should be changed have been strongly resisted on the grounds that this would increase costs and impair the trust between auditors and enterprises even if it were practical. The values of 'privacy' and 'property rights' are stressed in claiming that too much disclosure of information and too restrictive regulation can reduce competitiveness. In short, the profession (backed by the law) claims that auditors should be watchdogs, not bloodhounds; critics complain that they have become lapdogs.

Monitoring the monitors

Major corporate collapses are usually followed by some kind of investigation. In the UK these are conducted by the Department of Trade and Industry (DTI), which typically handles over a hundred cases each year (Sikka and Willmott, 1991). In most cases the DTI has appointed two inspectors for the inquiry – one a lawyer, the other an accountant. Usually accountants are recommended by the ICAEW and are often partners in one of the giant accounting practices. Frequently the reports of these inquiries are treated as confidential, with the ICAEW being the only external body to receive them. In those reports which are published there are sometimes strong criticisms of the auditors who, because of the size of the enterprises involved, are often drawn from the giant firms (see Box 3.3).

This has not prevented accountants from these same firms being accepted by the DTI as future inspectors, and in at least one case the accountant appointed was

Box 3.3

Inspecting the auditors

The Department of Trade and Industry (UK) has authorized over 2,000 investigations since 1971: fewer than 100 of the reports have been published. Here are extracts from some of those that have been published:

'Price Waterhouse's conduct as regards the non-executive directors and incoming auditors is indefensible.'

(Ramor Investments report)

'Thompson McLintock failed to exercise reasonable skill and care.'

(Roadships report)

'Arthur Young's errors were serious: overall this was a very poor auditing performance.'

(Milbury report)

Thornton Baker 'failed to exercise proper professional judgement'.

(Gilgate Holdings Report)

Source: Sikka and Willmott (1991)

---

himself at the same time the subject of a continuing previous inquiry (Sikka and Willmott, 1991). The DTI has not acted against any of the audit firms criticized in its reports. It prefers to leave discipline to the professional bodies. This hardly seems to have been rigorous, since the ICAEW has never investigated the overall standards of any auditing firm, nor has it taken action against any individual auditors debarring them from conducting audits (Mitchell *et al.*, 1993).

'True and fair'

These issues of the role of auditors in scrutinizing annual accounts revolve around the notion of 'true and fair'. It is something of an in-joke among auditors and financial accountants that this focal point of their activities is incapable of precise definition – indeed that it is so vague that auditors are effectively operating in a vacuum (Griffiths, 1986). However, the vagueness of the term does not imply that it has no meaning. As we saw earlier (Chapter 1) the terms used have changed over the years from 'full and fair' (1844 Act) to 'true and correct' (1900 Act). The modern usage stems from the 1947 Act, when the UK government was persuaded by the ICAEW that the term 'correct' was too strong, since there could be no standard of absolute truth which would imply that only one set of accounts was appropriate and that all others should be rejected as incorrect (Walker, 1984). Instead the signing of annual reports was seen as dependent upon the professional judgement of auditors. The social significance of this is that guidelines are to be created by the profession rather than imposed by the state.

The importance which the accountancy profession attaches to maintaining this position can be seen in the development of the European Community's Fourth Company Law Directive (Walton, 1991). The process of drafting this directive began in 1966, when the UK was not a member of the EC, and seems to have been strongly influenced by German accounting traditions. The first draft referred to 'principles of regular and proper accounting' and called for accounts to be as accurate as possible. When British accounting influence entered the process these phrases were removed and replaced in the second draft (1974) with 'true and fair'. Following some dissent from other EC members, the final draft was amended (perhaps slightly changing the meaning of the phrase) but the outcome was that the Anglo-American emphasis on 'true and fair' was exported to Europe. The debate over the directive had involved two different accounting traditions – one (in Germany and France) of state prescription of proper methods, and the other (from the UK and US) of professional judgement and self-regulation.

Reforming annual accounts and auditing

Griffiths (1986) concluded his discussion of creative accounting by tentatively suggesting that it should be tempered with realism and that changes in company law – especially in relation to disclosure of accounting policies – might encourage this. He was not particularly optimistic about the prospects and warned that if shareholders were being misled by accounts they should not expect third parties to come to their rescue. Instead they were urged to be more vigilant and cynical. Other critics were prepared to go further and made a series of detailed and wide-ranging demands for reform in accounting and auditing practice. Mitchell *et al.* (1991, 1993) recommended that annual reports should be systematic, future-oriented, registered within ninety days of year end, and should contain information on the market values of fixed assets, cash flow data, and analysis of current assets and liabilities. In addition, they urged the profession to outlaw, or rigorously standardize and control, the major creative accounting practices which they had identified.

If these demands for change caused some disquiet among those in prominent positions in the profession, their broader recommendations for change were even more uncomfortable. Mitchell *et al.* were concerned not merely with eliminating some specific 'fiddles' but with transforming the social organizations and processes which, in their view, systematically created and maintained an accounting/ auditing regime in which creative accounting was endemic. Here their recommendations aimed at establishing greater independence for auditors. Auditors should be barred from selling management consultancy services to the enterprises they audit; they should be regularly rotated so that they do not build up a cosy relationship with executives; and they should themselves be publicly accountable and subject to disciplinary action. Such reforms would not merely change particular accounting methods but would redefine the position of audit firms in relation to enterprises and professional bodies. Since this might well constitute a challenge to the profitability of the giant accounting partnerships Mitchell *et al.* anticipated heated resistance to their proposals but warned, 'There are already calls for the abolition of external audit . . . If auditing is to have any social value then far reaching reforms must be instituted' (1993: 26).

How were such sweeping changes to be achieved? The present form of annual accounts and auditing has developed in the context of a self-regulating profession which (to a very great extent) constructs its own accounting rules, applies them, identifies dubious applications, investigates them, decides whether rules have been transgressed, and – if they have – determines and carries out disciplinary action (if any). In short, in present circumstances members of the accountancy profession are not only the defendants, investigators, prosecutors, juries and judges, but also the legislators as well. Given the social organization of the profession, the key figures in many of these roles are drawn from the ranks of partners in a handful of giant accounting houses. This has led to the allegation that a central feature of the governance of enterprises – the reporting of financial information to owners – is dominated by a small elite who are not publicly accountable.

The solution proposed is the dismantling of the self-regulatory institutions of the profession and greater involvement of the state in the creation and monitoring of accounting. Many have pointed to the US as providing a more suitable model for the regulation of accounting through legal requirements, the Financial

Accounting Standards Board, and the Securities and Exchange Commission. Despite these institutions, many US observers have been equally concerned with current practices, and public unease with accounting has been rising.

> Bank failures, overcharging by major defense contractors, profit man-ipulation by managers on a widespread scale, the proliferation of debt defeasance and other off-balance sheet financing techniques, and failure to resolve ongoing controversies over accounting for pensions, taxes, and inflation are all blamed – in varying degrees – on accountants.
>
> (Tinker, 1985: 204)

In the US, as in Britain, the accountancy profession is coming under increasing public criticism and facing doubts about its ability and willingness to reform its own practices. The profession remains hopeful that it will be able to re-educate the public to accept that it can be trusted to continue to organize the flow of information from managers to owners – preferably with the minimum of change to current practices.

ACCOUNTING AND THE DEBATE ON CONTROL

Debates in accounting over the purpose and nature of corporate reporting have much in common with the social science theories discussed in Chapter 2. The earlier discussion of corporate social accounting reflected many of the assump-tions and concerns of the managerialist tradition and later discussions began to address issues which had been reinstated in the debate through attacks on this approach. The argument about annual accounts and auditing paralleled the in-creasing emphasis placed on financial control by Scott (in the UK) and Zeitlin (in the US). Scott's analysis of the importance of financiers in creating social networks through which flows corporate information was matched by the identi-fication of a handful of financial analysts as the key recipients of accounting information, through their role as interpreters, adjudicators, and advisers in the City (Griffiths) or on Wall Street (Tinker). Alongside banks, pension funds, insurance companies, and investment trusts, as increasingly dominant owner institutions, we find the giant accounting partnerships as the creators, monitors, and arbiters of corporate information.

There is, however, one very clear difference between the discussion in ac-counting and the wider social science debate. Zeitlin had argued that 'profit maximization' is 'an objective requirement, since profit constitutes the only unambiguous criterion of successful managerial performance and an irreducible necessity for corporate survival' (1974: 1097). What the debate in accounting has shown is that profit cannot be taken as an unambiguous criterion. Whether we take the view of Griffiths that all companies are fiddling their profits, or the official view of the profession that there can be no 'correct' account, accountants do not believe that they provide the benchmark which Zeitlin assumed. Indeed the profession's successful espousal of the 'true and fair' position has ensured that this is not the case in Britain and America. Scott's approach was rather more guarded than that of Zeitlin, recognizing that 'the size and rate of "profit" earned by an enterprise are dependent on its accounting practices and may not, therefore, provide strictly comparable yardsticks' (1985: 187). Nevertheless, he concluded that 'the "profit motive" . . . has become institutionalised in the control systems of the modern enterprise' (p. 262). The debate in accounting has thrown doubt even on this more modest version of the 'financial control' theory. Over the short term, and perhaps for many years, managers appear to be able to manipulate accounts in presenting corporate performance in ways which meet the aspirations and expectations of owners and analysts. This does not, in itself, assure that profitable growth (capital accumulation) is the central purpose of managerial actions under the control of owners. The study of corporate reporting suggests that financial controls are neither as certain, nor as restrictive, as is assumed in current social science theories of the enterprise.

This should not be taken to imply that accounting is so flexible that it offers no means of control over managers, nor that capital accumulation is no longer relevant. Although there is considerable (perhaps vast) scope for managerial discretion hidden behind creative accounting it is not limitless. First, although technically feasible, some devices become socially unacceptable, so they are withdrawn by the profession (as was the case with under-the-line extraordinary items) or fall so far into disrepute that their use in constructing annual accounts would cause raised eyebrows among analysts. Second, annual accounts are not the only source of accounting information about enterprises (especially for those financiers who sit on boards of directors), nor is accounting the only form of information which is relevant (e.g. news of research breakthroughs may quickly affect share prices). Third, creative accounting may suffice in the short or medium term, but it cannot prevent companies from going bankrupt – as the many 'scandals' show. Although some slick financial operators and dodgy executives may benefit in the short term, companies which trade unprofitably, or fail to meet the expectations of owners do not survive unchanged in the long term. The threat of liquidation, take-over, or merger is an ultimate discipline on the actions of management as a whole even if the fortunate few can escape detrimental consequences.

This analysis of the role of accounting in mediating the relationship between the owners and managers of enterprises suggests re-examination of some of the fundamental questions posed by social scientists. Rather than asking, 'Who controls the enterprise?' and 'What are its goals?' it may be more useful to view control as a struggle between different people occupying different positions and pursuing different interests. The power of (various) owners and other outsiders, and the power of executives and managers, is likely to fluctuate. The goals actively pursued by enterprises will reflect this shifting balance of control and interests. Accounting is a resource used in such struggles for control and a means of expressing the achievement of goals. It both influences, and is influenced by, these social processes.

In the UK and US specific forms of development of enterprises and society have led to accounting gaining a pivotal position between owners and managers. As the dominant medium of corporate information, what it reports (and does not) has crucial importance. In both societies corporate reporting activities are dominated by the accounting profession – especially by the partners of the giant accounting houses. In Germany and Japan accounting has not had this dominant role. The different, closer connections between financial and industrial capital in those countries have produced flows of information and forms of corporate control which are not so strongly centred on accounting and auditing. However, there are signs that this may be changing. A combination of factors – internal problems with their national economies, attempts at the global harmonization of financial accounting, the spread of multinational corporations using Anglo-American accounting practices, and the ambitions of the giant accounting partnerships to become business advisers to the world – may be shifting patterns of corporate governance closer to those of the UK and US. If so, accounting will again have played an important role not only in reporting on enterprises, but also in shaping those enterprises on which it reports. Or, as Hines put it, 'in communicating reality, we construct reality' (1988).

REVIEW

Short questions

What changes were proposed by advocates of corporate social accounting? Why did they think these were important? How did the accountancy profession and businesses respond? How can we explain the rise of interest in Green accounting? What different views of the role of accounting do its supporters adopt? What general concerns with annual accounts have been identified? How does Griffiths define 'creative accounting'? What four elements of creative accounting are highlighted by Mitchell *et al.*? Why have auditing practices been criticized and what reforms are proposed? How has the profession responded? What is the significance of self-regulation in the monitoring of auditing?

Discussion points

Are the prospects of Green accounting in the 1990s any better than those of corporate social accounting in the 1970s? Do annual reporting and auditing need to be reformed and, if so, how? Does accounting supply owners with information which enables them to control enterprises, or are managers able to manipulate accounts to free themselves from the demands of capital?

Part II

MANAGEMENT

Debates on organization

4

ORGANIZATION OF THE
ENTERPRISE

At the end of the nineteenth century the growth of corporations produced uncertainty among business owners about the prospects for managing large-scale enterprises. Under contract systems the organization of production had been undertaken by internal contractors who had a profit stake in the performance of their work gangs. With the growth in the size of enterprises, new forms of organization began to emerge. Littler (1982) described the period 1880–1914 as one of 'experiments and hesitancies' with a number of employment forms being tried out. These included profit-sharing schemes, and co-partnerships of owners and managers. Many owners were wary about the direct employment of managers rewarded through salary. They feared that managers would divert corporate resources to their own pockets or schemes, and that supervisors would be open to bribery and favouritism in their hiring and firing practices. As owners became more remote from production and operational management was devolved to non-propertied personnel within the enterprise, a central concern was that, without the profit motive, salaried officials could not be relied upon to pursue the interests of the owners.

Managerialist writers thought these fears well founded and concluded that the rise of salaried, professional managers did indeed mean that owners no longer dominated the enterprise and that profit was no longer the prime goal. Critics of this view generally held that no such managerial revolution had taken place but that a more complex struggle for control among different ownership interests had emerged at the level of the board of directors. The competing sides of the debate on ownership and control portrayed managers either as a 'neutral technocracy' (Berle and Means, 1932) or as technical specialists 'constrained to pursue long-term profitability' (Scott, 1985: 185). This chapter is concerned with theories of the nature of this management and its organization of corporate activity.

ORGANIZATION AND BUREAUCRACY

In analysing the structures and processes of the management of modern enterprises, three broad approaches can be identified. First, the view which dominates economics and functional organization theory, that organizations are shaped by functional requirements in their pursuit of *efficiency* in their responses to environments. This view tends to assume an essential similarity between all forms of large-scale administration – in factories, schools, prisons, hospitals, and so on – and detects some general characteristics of efficient social organization. Second, views such as those of cultural organization theory, that organizational forms are a reflection of the *values* of members and broader society. These emphasize distinctive organizational cultures, which may relate to different national characteristics. Third, views drawn from sociology, especially but not exclusively Marxian analyses, which stress the need for *control* as the major factor shaping management. Here the focus is upon the social relations of capitalist enterprises.

Although these three strands generate very different explanations of organization they each draw upon the work of Max Weber, who, at the beginning of this century, developed a highly influential model of a specific form of organization which he labelled *bureaucracy*. In his view this was the most rational form of administration. Much of the debate about the organization of enterprises has been shaped by differing interpretations of what is meant by rationality in the context of business structures and processes.

The rise of bureaucratic organization

Weber's (1922) account of the rise of modern organization placed it in the context of changing modes of thinking. He argued that before the nineteenth century authority was usually based on tradition (for example, in monarchies) or on charisma – the supernatural/superhuman qualities attributed to certain individuals (for example, in religious movements). In the nineteenth century such forms were increasingly being replaced with rational modes of thought based on calculation. This form of calculative thinking was most clearly identifiable in the capitalist enterprise, particularly in its accounting regimes, which produced 'rational administration'. In its purest form this is expressed as bureaucratic organization.

Weber's construction and use of the concept of bureaucracy has caused some difficulties in the debate on organization in the twentieth century. His discussion centred upon an 'ideal type' – a model which attempts to extract the essence of the notion of bureaucracy from the trends he observed. The concept itself is not a description of any particular organization, nor a prescription for the best way to manage; instead it is a tool for the analysis of long term developments in society. This ideal type is constructed of two elements – the characteristics of bureaucratic administration, and the role of individuals within such an organization (see Box 4.1). The brief meaning of bureaucracy is 'rule of office', and Weber's two elements delineate the nature of offices and of the officials who carry out their functions. At the centre of his discussion was the stress on rules – both legal (such as precedent) and technical (such as engineering principles) – in creating a framework within which officials acted. These rules constitute a legitimate basis for administration when they are accepted as rational by members of the organization. The official acts not on the basis of tradition (custom, or habit), nor emotion, nor following the personal inspiration of corporate leaders: instead the bureaucrat impersonally calculates means and ends in applying the abstract body of rules to particular cases.

The organizational form of this rational action is one where tasks are divided and allocated as duties attached to closely defined offices (or positions). These

Box 4.1

A model of bureaucracy

Characteristics of bureaucratic organization

Fixed jurisdictional areas where there are detailed official duties, whose conduct is limited by rules and which are methodically provided for each organizational activity.

A *firmly ordered hierarchy* of superior and subordinate offices.

Offices are both a centre of *written documentation* of activities, and a post (or position) whose *public resources* are clearly separated from the *personal funds* of the office-holder.

A prescribed course of *expert training* (through formal education and/or experience) which prepares the individual to hold office.

The holding of office is the *primary activity* of the office-holder, who is rewarded by salary.

The conduct of each office, and relations between them are covered by *general rules* (which may also state how rules are to be changed).

The position of the official

Office-holding constitutes a *vocation*, which the individual undergoes *prescribed training* for and carries out as a matter of *duty*, having an *impersonal loyalty* to the organization. Proper carrying out of rules provides officials with an 'ideological halo' which protects them from criticism or sanction whatever the outcome of their activities.

The personal position of the official offers *social esteem* (based on level in the hierarchy), and is based on *appointment* according to rules of educational qualification, experience, and seniority. The appointment is permanent and gives *life tenure* (unless the rules are broken). It is rewarded by *salary*, and by promotion to higher bureaucratic levels, and thus constitutes a *career*.

Source: adapted from Weber (1922)

---

offices are arranged hierarchically into superior and subordinate posts, with clear lines of command and communication. In return for salary, status, and career prospects, experts (appointed on the basis of their educational qualifications and administrative experience) carry out the routine of decision-making as their primary, long term, and secure employment (unless they depart from the rules and hence fail in their duty). Weber predicted that administrations which more or less fitted this form would become the dominant form of organization in the twentieth century. Not only the civil service (of which the term bureaucracy is often used pejoratively), but also armies, political parties, trade unions, hospitals, schools, among others, would increasingly take on bureaucratic form. However, the purest form of the development of this rational administration in capitalist societies was the business enterprise. In socialist (or soviet) type societies, the replacement of markets by state planning, and the overall regulation of social life would lead to an even greater spread of bureaucracy. Thus the development of rationality as the dominant mode of thought in modern society would lead to a bureaucratization of social organization.

Weber's concern was with the analysis of contemporary trends, but at the same time there were others who were more concerned with prescription – with recommending certain organizational forms to business. In the US, Taylor (1911) advanced his 'Principles of Scientific Management'. In France, Fayol (1914) and, in the UK, Urwick (1928) attempted to produce templates for efficient organization. Although these management consultants offered plans which differed from each other in detail they, together with other writers such as Follett (1924), Gulick and Urwick (1937) and Barnard (1938), produced what is now termed 'classical management theory', which shared many characteristics with Weber's analysis of bureaucracy. In particular they advocated functionally separate departments to replace the generalized responsibilities of early managers, to create clearly demarcated spheres of responsibility. Through their work these consultants created a view of management as an expert activity in its own right, resting on certain universal principles of organization from which specific enterprises could derive their structures and procedures.

Organization and efficiency

The work of early management consultants stressed the efficiency gains which would result from the adoption of particular management forms. Similarly, but in more general terms, many economists have tried to explain the growth of *managerial hierarchies* as creating greater efficiency than could be achieved in *markets*. Chandler (1962, 1977), Williamson (1975) and Ouchi (1980) developed transaction cost theory which focused on the flow of raw materials, semi-finished goods, and final products. Where there are many small firms this flow passes through markets between enterprises. The growth of enterprises through vertical integration led to multi-function firms involved in all aspects of production – from the extraction of raw materials to the retailing of final products. Thus external markets were replaced by internal transfers, Smith's (1776) 'invisible hand' of the market being replaced by the 'visible hand' of management (Chandler, 1977).

This internalization of the flow of goods led to changes in organization structure. Firms which had been single-function units operating either independently or as loosely associated subsidiaries of parent holding companies became divisions of larger multi-functional corporations. For transaction cost theorists, the development of multi-divisional organizational structures is to be explained as an outcome of the pursuit of efficiency – the costs of allocating resources are lower when transactions take place within the enlarged enterprise.

This emphasis on efficiency also appears in economists' discussion of processes within management – for example, in decision-making. Here the *rational* model of decision-making is dominant. It can be summarized as a number of steps, portraying decision-making as the most efficient utilization of resources in maximizing the achievement of objectives:

1. Faced with a given problem,
2. a rational man first clarifies his goals, values or objectives and then ranks them or otherwise organizes them in his mind;
3. he then lists all important possible ways of – policies for – achieving his goals
4. and investigates all the important consequences that would follow from each of the alternative policies,
5. at which point he is in a position to compare consequences of each policy with goals
6. and so choose the policy with consequences most closely matching his goals.

Some people define a rational choice as one which meets these conditions. Others have merely claimed that these are the steps that any rational problem-solver should take. Either way, these steps constitute a classical model of rational decision.

(Lindblom, 1968: 12)

Such accounts of organizational structures and processes equate 'rationality' with 'efficiency' and claim that these reach their highest level in highly structured, rule-based enterprises. As Weber put it,

the decisive reason for the advance of bureaucratic organization has always been its purely technical superiority over any other form of organization. Precision, speed, unambiguity, knowledge of the files, continuity, discretion, unity, strict subordination, reduction of friction and of personal costs – these are raised to the optimum level in the strictly bureaucratic administration.

(1922: 973)

The efficiency approach to organization has come under attack both for its description of enterprise structures and processes, and for the explanations that are advanced for their development. In particular, bureaucratic organization has been challenged as ineffective – either universally, or in specific circumstances. At the most general level some writers have seen bureaucracy as the epitome of inefficiency, corresponding to its everyday, commonsense stereotype. Muir (1910) complained that it generated 'Red Tape, Mystery Mongering, Jack-in-Office, Gentlemanly Malingering'. This hostility was also apparent in the work of psychologists, who saw a fundamental disparity between the conception of managerial behaviour as impersonal calculation, and the motivation of real managers. The Human Relations movement, led by Mayo (1933, 1945), stressed that managers needed to exercise social skills, rather than objective calculation, in their organization of production. Equally important, managers themselves could not conform to the robotic stereotype of impersonal calculation, and attempts to make them do so would lead not to efficiency but to alienation, stifling managers' initiative, enterprise, and imagination. (For critical reviews of such approaches see Perrow, 1972, and Salaman, 1981.) Thus each organizational 'advantage' of bureaucracy can be reinterpreted as a 'disadvantage' from the human relations perspective (see Box 4.2)

Apart from these general attacks on bureaucracy, there were more specific challenges to the claimed effectiveness and efficiency of this form of organization. One of the earliest critics was Woodward (1958), who tested classical management theory against a sample of firms in south-east England. She found no overall correlation between organizational form and performance. Instead, successful organizations appeared to be clustered around three different forms, dependent on the production technology of their different industries – unit and small-batch, large-batch and mass, and process production. Each seemed to generate its own distinct pattern of organization in terms of the number of levels

Box 4.2

'Advantages' and 'disadvantages' of bureaucracy			
Advantages from a Scientific Management perspective			
Conformity	Equality	Consistency	Routine
Stability	Standardization	Clarity	Co-ordination
Responsibility	Predictability	Specialization	Guidance
Disadvantages from a Human Relations perspective			
Over-supervision	Impersonality	Inflexibility	Rigidity
Ritualism	Insensitivity	Poor communication	Centralization
Buck-passing	Frustration	Narrowness	Restriction

in the hierarchy and span of control (i.e. the number of subordinates to each superior). The large-batch and mass-production industries were the only ones which appeared to fit the case advanced by classical management writers. Instead of one superior blueprint, the relationship between type of production technology and organizational form was important.

At around the same time, Burns and Stalker (1961) found that organizations which closely matched the bureaucratic model (which they termed *mechanistic*) developed into alternative forms when faced with technological and market change. Scottish firms entering the new electronics markets of the 1950s moved to *organic* forms where organization charts are torn up, jobs are broadly concerned with problem-solving, horizontal communication is stressed, authority is delegated, flexibility is encouraged, and change is normal. These two forms are seen to fit, respectively, stable and unstable conditions – the 'beginning of administrative wisdom is the awareness that there is no one optimum type of management system' (1961: 125).

In the US, Dalton's (1959) study of four manufacturing companies also called into question the economic performance of bureaucratic administration. The formal presentation of organizations, in charts and job profiles, gave little or poor indication of what actually happened in enterprises. Instead of a manager's authority being impersonally determined by organizational position, power was created and used through cliques, deals and alliances, with the personal characteristics of the officer (e.g. Protestant or Catholic; membership of elite social clubs; bullying or friendly behaviour) being crucial to the practice of managing. Aside from the formal presentation of the enterprise, *informal organization* was extremely important in the conduct of the enterprise.

These interesting field studies of enterprises were quickly assimilated into the fashionable theoretical framework of the 1960s – 'open systems theory'. The view adopted here was that enterprises responded to their *environments* and thus displayed a range of organizational forms. No one form could be seen as most efficient; instead each enterprise sought a fit between organization and environment. The environment might be outside the firm in markets (capital, product, labour, raw materials) or outside management in enterprise size and production technology. The most elaborate of such approaches in the UK produced 'contingency theory' (Pugh and Hickson, 1976; Pugh and Hinings, 1976) which aimed to generate a taxonomy (complete classification) of organizational structures linked with the environmental variables which had determined them. In the US Lawrence and Lorsch (1967) followed a similar line in linking sub-systems within enterprises to sub-environments outside.

Perrow (1970a) provided an overview of this relationship, suggesting that bureaucratic organization is associated with routine conditions (with uniform raw materials and well understood processes applied to them) whereas non-bureaucratic forms emerged when non-routine conditions were faced. He soon amended this position (Perrow, 1972) and argued that there is an underlying tendency to 'routinization' in business which means that non-bureaucratic forms are essentially unstable and that formal, rule-based bureaucratic forms will re-emerge. For this reason he concluded that:

> bureaucracy is a form of organization superior to all others we know or can hope to afford in the near and middle future; the chances of doing away with it or changing it are, probably, non-existent in the West in this century.
>
> (1972: 7)

Open systems approaches were based on the assumption that enterprises could be studied as though they were natural, biological phenomena, and that organizations could be seen as adapting to their environments. A major problem with this approach is that it fails to explore the mechanisms through which such adaptation is supposed to take place. The field studies of Burns and Stalker, and Dalton stressed the importance of individuals and groups of managers in shaping organizational structures and processes. Burns and Stalker insisted that structures are 'explicitly and deliberately created and maintained to exploit the human resources of a concern' (1961: 119) and noted the resistance from middle management which chief executives had to overcome in making changes. Dalton showed how social relations between managers shaped the creation, amendment, and abandonment of particular systems. The notion of 'efficiency', as measured and reported through accounting systems, was the result and not the cause of social structures and processes (see Chapter 5).

Viewing enterprises from a natural science perspective tends to obscure the personal and social influences on organization. By focusing on the organization as an entity in its own right, systems approaches generated a concept of efficiency which assumed that the enterprise pursues its own goals and adapts itself so that these may be achieved economically. For critics of this approach, it is people rather than organizations who have goals and these may be multiple, changing, vague, and often conflicting (Salaman, 1979, 1981; Pfeffer, 1981). Similarly, environments do not operate on firms simply as the objective reality beyond their boundaries. They are identified and interpreted by individuals and groups, who then relate the external changes they perceive to the internal changes which they plan. Their perceptions and plans may vary considerably. To move beyond the mechanistic view of managers as impersonal calculators embedded in a bureaucratic machine, we need to study the ways in which managers (individually and collectively) actively construct the organizational forms of enterprises. We need to understand how they think about managing.

Organization and values

Some of the writers involved in linking the organization to the modes of thinking of enterprise members have drawn on a different interpretation of Weber's work from that adopted in the efficiency approach. This involves a reconsideration of rationality. Weber's discussion of rational administration was located in a wider exploration of different forms of authority. Authority is defined as a form of legitimate power, and Weber began his account of bureaucracy with the assumption that a legal norm may be established, by agreement or by imposition, on grounds of expediency, rational values, or both, with a claim to obedience on the part of members. Bureaucracy was developing as the dominant form of organization because rationality (rather than tradition or charisma) was increasingly becoming the most acceptable basis for a claim to obedience. Thus the rise of bureaucracy was inextricably linked with changing values in modern society.

Perrow (1972) developed this view in relation to large US enterprises. Despite often expressed complaints about the evils of bureaucracy, he argued that it reflects the values of US and other Western societies. The principles embedded in bureaucratic organization include: equal treatment of all under the law or rules; the separation of public resources from personal finances; individual ability rather than favouritism as the basis of office; regulation rather than arbitrary decisions; and clear assignment of responsibility. All these are represented in the wider value-systems of modern society. It is when enterprises do not conform to the values of bureaucracy that they are seen as illegitimate and unacceptable. Disquiet is experienced by organization members when promotion is seen as depending on who you know rather than on what you know; when decisions are made on a whim rather than through proper procedures; when managers use the resources of their office for their personal advantage; when rules are waived for favourite people or projects; when managers dodge responsibility by passing the buck. Those who feel they have lost out when these things happen complain about others 'feathering the nest', demand that 'there ought to be a rule', and ask, 'Who's in charge round here?' (1972, chapter 1 sub-headings). Although the substance of particular rules may not be accepted by everyone, there is general acceptance that administration ought to take a rule-based form.

For Gouldner (1954) the form and substance of rules could not be so easily separated as components of a value-system. From his field research in a US gypsum mine and its alabaster plant, he concluded that the content of rules was vital to their acceptance. Criticizing Weber for failing to explore the way in which rules gain legitimacy, he identified three types of bureaucratic rules. *Representative bureaucracy* most closely fits the Weberian model where those who make the rules and those who are subject to them share the rational values exemplified by the rule (e.g. a ban on smoking underground where mine gases made it dangerous). But Gouldner also found *mock bureaucracy* where rule-breaking was common among enterprise members and senior managers contrived to avoid noticing the frequent infringements (e.g. smoking in the factory, or late arrival at work). He ascribed it to an 'indulgency pattern' where managers and workers who had grown up together within the local community forged a loose, informal contract on acceptable behaviour. Here rules-on-paper were not translated into rules-in-practice. When a new general manager was appointed from head office this cosy world was disrupted. Insisting that rules were followed, the new manager created a *punishment-centred bureaucracy*. Infringements were penalized by suspensions and sackings. Whilst in abstract discussions the proper carrying through of rules might be equated with efficiency, in this particular case it resulted in an unofficial (wildcat) strike at the plant. This study showed the varying forms that rules may take in the enterprise, and the way these are influenced by social relations between those who create rules and those who are subject to them. Some rules were mutually accepted and implemented; others were barely tolerated or ignored; others were imposed and resisted. This underlines the connection between rules and values.

In the 1980s management writers began to explore how this connection related to wider values in society – *culture*. Hofstede (1980), from an international study of IBM, argued that the US and the UK share a value-system which stresses individualism and is ambition-oriented, especially towards quantity of things owned rather than quality of life. Handy linked social values with particular organizational forms, where within

> organizations there are deep-set beliefs about the way work should be rewarded, people controlled. What are the degrees of formalization required? How much planning and how far ahead? What combination of obedience and initiative is looked for in subordinates? . . . These are all parts of the organization.
>
> (1985: 186)

Drawing on the work of Harrison (1972), he identified not only a 'role culture' (bureaucracy), but also a 'power culture' (e.g. in nineteenth century enterprises), a 'task culture' (e.g. in project teams and matrix organizations) and a 'person culture' (e.g. in professional partnerships). These organizational cultures may be linked with societal cultures which differ between countries and over time.

In such approaches the link between society, organization and culture is frequently unclear. For example, Handy preferred the term 'culture' to Harrison's original use of 'ideologies' because 'it conveys more of the feeling of a pervasive way of life, or set of norms' (p. 186). This, coupled with his views that beliefs are deep-seated in people, might lead us to conclude that enterprise structures are generated from long term, society-wide values. However, he also argued that cultures were influenced by a number of factors specific to the enterprise – its history and ownership, its size, its technology, its goals and objectives, its environment, and its people. Here organizational cultures would appear to be the outcome of existing enterprise structures and processes. Hence it is not clear whether organizational culture is to be seen as something which is the cause or the effect of the ways enterprises are managed.

A further complication is that it is also claimed that organizational culture can be chosen for an organization. If so, then managers can identify successful cultures in other companies and adopt them for themselves, or even design new cultures. The most prominent exponents of this approach in the popular management literature are Peters and Waterman (1982), who advocated an eight-point corporate culture to managers 'in search of excellence'. One of the problems with such approaches is that any checklist of successful cultures (even supposing we could clearly define success) might merely be the particular characteristics of specific enterprises in a strictly limited time and place. Another issue is whether such cultures should be viewed as ideological – as a set of ideas serving to legitimate corporate practices, aimed at securing their acceptance by organization members and the wider society. At one extreme, 'culture' may be seen as internal propaganda and external public relations, which disguises rather than constructs enterprise practices. As we saw earlier (Chapter 3) this was one of the fears of those advocating social responsibility accounting and Green accounting – that the values which underlie them are being exploited rather than implemented.

Overall the exploration of ways in which rules are created and maintained and how this relates to the values of organization members and society is an important ingredient in our understanding of the management of enterprises. However, there are a number of unresolved difficulties here. As Handy admitted, many management writers have been content to accept that 'culture cannot be precisely defined, for it is something that is perceived, something felt' (1985: 197). This vague entity is also variously treated as cause, effect, choice or ideology. As Morgan concluded, although a study of culture may offer some valuable insights into enterprises, 'it is unlikely that these insights will provide the easy recipe for solving managerial problems that many writers hope for' (1986: 139).

The idea that organizational forms are affected by the values of individuals and reflect differing beliefs also led to a re-examination of the rational model of decision-making. Simon attacked it as a mechanistic and unrealistic portrayal of actual decision-making. He labelled it 'preposterous', and described it as 'having great intellectual and aesthetic appeal but little discernible relation to the actual or possible behaviour of flesh-and-blood human beings' (1976: xxvii). Goals are seldom clear, or given, and instead must be searched for (Scott, 1967; Lindblom, 1968). Since organizations have limited resources – of time, finance, and expertise – any hope of identifiying and investigating all important alternatives is unrealistic. Given ambiguity and/or disagreement about the goals of decisions, there cannot be clear, agreed criteria for making the best (most efficient) decision. Thus 'It is impossible for the behaviour of any single, isolated individual to reach any high degree of rationality' (Simon, 1976: 79) if rationality is defined in the manner of the classical model. The reason is 'the inability of the human mind to bring to bear upon a single decision all the aspects of value, knowledge and behaviour which would be relevant' (p. 108).

In place of this abstract, efficiency approach to decision processes Simon offered an *administrative* model. Here the rationality of managers is expressed in decisions which aim to 'satisfice' rather than maximize the outcomes of managerial action (see Chapter 2). The decision-maker 'recognises that the world he perceives is a drastically simplified model of the buzzing, blooming confusion that constitutes the real world' (p. xxix). This perspective was based upon the social psychology of decision-makers and the organizational contexts of the decisions. First, the individual decision-maker is seen as limited in skill, values and knowledge potentially relevant to the decision. Since individuals are seen as varying widely in these respects – having different skills, values, and types of knowledge – the calculations they make will also vary. Second, the specific organizational contexts of decisions create 'givens' – the taken-for-granted assumptions which specify the 'problem'. These become the 'premises that are accepted by the subject for his choice' (p. xxix). Although the decision-maker may be 'intendedly rational', business decisions have a 'bounded rationality' – bounded by personal subjectivity and organizational rules and norms. In these circumstances not all alternatives are explored, and decision-makers begin a sequential search from the *status quo* (the here and now) shaped by conventional treatments of uncertain areas, until a course of action that is satisfactory or 'good enough' is discovered. Rationality is seen not as the process of producing solutions which maximize efficiency, but as action which is practical and realistic within personal limitations and organizational constraints.

In later work some of Simon's colleagues produced accounts of decision-making which challenged the rational model even further. Cohen *et al.* (1972) proposed a *garbage can* model of decision-making, originally intended as an analysis of US universities, which they described as 'organized anarchies', but later writers found little difficulty in applying their ideas to business decisions. Decision processes involve 'problematic preferences' (we aren't certain where we want to go), 'unclear technology' (we aren't certain how to get there), and 'fluid participation' (we – the decision-makers – keep changing as each decision stage involves a different membership). In this chaotic world there is no logical connection between given problems and optimal solutions. Instead, participants in decisions arrive with varying definitions of what the problems are, carrying ready-made solutions, looking for acceptance whenever a 'choice opportunity' is identified. These loosely connected elements – problems, solutions, participants, choice opportunities – swirl round in the space where decisions are made (the garbage can). Out of all this emanates not one decision but streams of decisions which become the backcloth for future decisions. After the event, people may be able to look back and provide some reasoned explanation for what happened (*post hoc* rationalization), but any observer of the process as it happened would see randomness of procedure unshaped by any clear managerial intention. In management writing this approach is probably the furthest extreme, which takes us to, and beyond, the boundary between rationality and irrationality. The portrayal of individuals having sharply different perceptions and values which make it difficult to construct collective action brings into doubt the very concept of 'organization' and whether it can be applied to enterprises.

Approaches to organization structures and processes which examine the perceptions and values of individuals and groups provide an important antidote to the mechanistic portrayal of enterprises as vast calculating machines unerringly pursuing efficiency. They remind us that environments do not directly impinge on organizational forms – they are perceived and interpreted by managers. Goals and problems are not given – they derive from the values of organization members. What we may lose sight of in such approaches are wider social structures and processes. Individuals may vary not only in their perceptions and values, but also in their power to impose their views on others. In part, this power rests upon the position they occupy in the enterprise structure. This can also generate differing interests which they pursue. The claim that managers have taken over the enterprise and are now free to do with its resources what they wish has been strongly rejected by many authors. Economic owners are seen as retaining control over the enterprise and merely delegating authority to managers for day-to-day operations. Where there are conflicts between the interests of owners and of managers, organization may be concerned with resolving them. This is the central concern of the third major approach to organization, which places control at the centre of the analysis.

Organization and control

Critics of the efficiency and values approaches to organization in general refocused attention on specifically capitalist features of enterprises and their management. The central concern was with organization as a form of *control*. Structures and processes within enterprises are outcomes of attempts to harness lower-level members to the interests of those in more powerful positions, ultimate power resting with capital. This approach often begins with rejection of the efficiency model, which involves another reassessment of Weber's discussion of rationality. Albrow (1970) argued that no clear connection between rationality and efficiency was intended in Weber's work, nor is it possible to construct one. Since then most sociologists have broadly accepted this interpretation (see Lee and Newby, 1983).

Weber distinguished two forms of rationality which underlie rational action. *Formal rationality* refers to 'the extent of quantitative calculation or accounting which is technically possible and which is actually applied' (1922: 85). It is concerned with the form of thinking which takes place, with procedures and rules, with the means through which people pursue their ends. *Substantive rationality* (as it applies in business) is 'the degree to which the provisioning of given groups of persons . . . with goods is shaped by economically oriented social action under some criterion . . . of ultimate values . . . [which are] bases from which to judge the outcome of economic action' (pp. 85–6). It is concerned with the substance or content of thinking, with the ends that are pursued as well as the means of achieving them. Both forms are rational but they can produce different outcomes. By following the letter of the law (formal rationality) decisions may be made which go against the spirit of the law (substantive rationality); a slavish application of bureaucratic rules may result in managers losing sight of the purpose of those rules. There are underlying processes of 'routinization' which lead to the increasing dominance of form over substance, of procedures over outcomes, of

99

means over ends. Here it is difficult to see how the two forms of rationality can be combined into a single force which could be labelled 'efficiency'.

Sociologists in the 1970s and 1980s began to construct theories which emphasized the ends which enterprises served, and re-emphasized the politics of management. Salaman (1979, 1981) argued that Weber's work had more in common with that of Marx than it did with that of the later organization theory writers, stressing Weber's comments that bureaucracy became an 'iron cage' where individuals were no more than cogs in a giant social machine and that bureaucracy suppressed democracy. Bureaucracy is not a social mechanism producing efficiency, but a political device to control the actions of enterprise members. Goldman and Van Houten studied the development of bureaucracy in US business between the 1890s and World War I, and concluded that in 'addition to the rhetoric of business efficiency which accompanied this development there was a stress on the need for social control over the growing ranks of managers'. What bureaucracy provided was a 'fixed chain of command [which] allowed early entrepreneurs to expand their businesses while leaving day-to-day operations at dispersed sites to trained and usually highly paid subordinates' (1980: 121). Thus the constraining features of bureaucracy, identified by Human Relations writers, may not be an unfortunate side effect but its central purpose. In response to the issue which had troubled owners at the turn of the century – how were non-profit-taking managers to be trusted to pursue profit – a powerful form of social organization was developed which provided a system of hierarchical control through a framework of rules, and the monitoring of performance.

This approach adopts a Marxian perspective and locates the rise of managerial bureaucracies specifically in the framework of the capitalist enterprise. This draws on Marx's distinction between two functions of management. Given any kind of division of labour – the separation of tasks and their allocation to different individuals or groups – some form of organization is required to relate the discrete activities to the overall purpose of the collective organization. This would apply in any kind of society; to any kind of production. Marx referred to it as *co-ordination and unity*. However, where individuals pursue different interests there are issues not only about how activities are to be organized, but also about what these activities should be. Marx saw the difference between the interests of capital and those of labour as crucial in capitalist society and its systems of production. Hence, in capitalist enterprises organization must also be concerned with *control and surveillance* to deal with struggles about how resources are to be used, and for whose ends. These twin functions of management mean that the organization of capitalist enterprises must always be related to both co-ordination and control. Bureaucracy was constructed in enterprises as the outcome of two related political processes. First, the rise of salaried managers as the co-ordinators and controllers of labour replacing the internal contractors. Second, the practices of top executives (as agents of capital) in co-ordinating and controlling the growing ranks of middle and junior (supervisory) management.

The twin functions of co-ordination and control may be in tension with each other. The construction of 'low discretion jobs' which constrain middle-level managers to act in standardized, rule-bound ways may be seen by senior executives as a necessary strategy where there are 'low trust relations' (Fox, 1974). Middle managers subject to such constraints may react with attempts to circumvent official rules, with acts of resistance to the demands place upon them, and with an overall low level of commitment to the enterprise. In such circumstances the benefits of bureaucratic control (in terms of detailing the use of enterprise resources) may be outweighed by its costs (in requiring even more monitoring of activities). Here organization is seen as a (potentially) fragile, and (usually) shifting balance between the needs to draw upon the abilities of managers and to channel these abilities towards the interests of owners. Any particular organizational form will depend on historically, and socially, specific features of the relationship between superior (owner) actions and subordinate (manager) reactions. Organizational structures and processes are constructed in an arena of political conflicts and compromises between individuals and groups within management in the course of struggles for co-ordination and control (Salaman, 1979, 1981). Individual managers occupy different positions within the enterprise, vertically segregated into senior, middle and junior ranks, and horizontally segregated by department and occupational specialism. These different positions generate differing interests – objectives which derive from the location of individuals in social structures rather than from their personal values. These positions also generate differing levels of power – the ability to advance or protect interests.

From these ingredients – positions, interests, and power – a third view of decision processes has been constructed based on *political* models (Pfeffer, 1981). Although there could be as many political models of organization at the level of the enterprise as there are at the level of the state, one model has dominated management writing – *pluralism*. This portrays decisions as the outcome of processes of bargaining and compromise between many individuals and groups who have different preferences. These groups may be based on factors outside or within the organization. Goals are seen not as organizational objectives nor as premises, but as the outcome of competition between the preferences of such groups. Decisions are shaped by shifting interests, strategies, and alliances. Here 'managing' may be seen as an activity of a pseudo-governmental form, balancing the demands of all of the interest (or pressure) groups. Alternatively, management itself may be seen as the most powerful of such groups.

In *Marxist* models of managerial decision-making it is capital which is seen as the dominant interest. The enterprise is a site of endemic conflict of interest between capital and labour. Managers stand in an ambiguous position between these interests, since they are simultaneously controllers – of labour – and controlled – by capital (Carchedi, 1977; Wright, 1978). Decisions are not simply the outcome of the preferences of participants, but are structured by wider social forces. This approach shares much with the pluralist view, but the language is less of 'bargaining and compromise' than of 'struggle and resistance' (Salaman, 1979). Such struggle includes competition between different occupational specialisms or departments to specify and enact strategies which both serve the interests of owners and promote their own position within the enterprise (Armstrong, 1985).

The control approach to organization and political models of decision-making make an important contribution to our understanding of management by relating structures and processes to the purposes of enterprises rather than to some abstract notion of efficiency, or vaguely specified values. However, issues of efficiency and value cannot be ignored. In managerial struggles claims to be able to contribute to efficient operation are important power resources for competing groups. Managements which are thought inefficient are likely to come under pressure through owner intervention. Equally, positions do not determine the interests of those who occupy them. Without understanding what it is that people value, we cannot identify what it is in their interests to achieve. Such issues may be under-examined in the control approach. This in turn may be a product of an overemphasis on control and an underemphasis on co-ordination as sociologists criticize those who uncritically accepted organization as solely concerned with co-ordination. As Burawoy (1979) pointed out, everyday life in enterprises is characterized much more by consent than by conflict.

PROFESSIONALISM

The approaches outlined in the previous section take the enterprise as the focus for a study of managers. The hidden assumption here is that managers' main identification is with the organization of which they are members. However, managers' collective identity may vary. Gouldner (1957) distinguished two kinds of manager. One, the 'local', is a long term member of the organization within which he or she builds a career. The other, the 'cosmopolitan', moves freely between companies as he or she seeks and gains promotion. For cosmopolitans it is not the organization which constitutes their primary membership, but their occupation – they see themselves not as employees of a particular company, but as engineers, sales people, personnel managers, or accountants. Freidson (1971) characterized two main forms of organization in modern society. One centres on the 'administrative principle' and is most clearly demonstrated in bureaucracy; the other revolves around 'the occupational principle' and is most clearly demonstrated in professionalism. These two principles are fundamentally opposed to each other, and he argued that the second principle was gaining ground at the end of the twentieth century – that the great juggernaut of bureaucracy was being turned back by the rise of professionalism. Others argued that professional occupations are themselves increasingly subject to bureaucratic control and the status of professionals is being reduced (Oppenheimer, 1973). This section explores this debate on professionalism.

The nature of professions

A recurring feature of the debate about professions is their identification as special occupations. They have been seen as having a special importance in industrial society and to its citizens. They have been identified as having a special sense of independence which is linked to their special *knowledge* and special *morality*. Thompson set the scene for much of the discussion when he claimed in 1857, 'The importance of the professions and the professional classes can hardly be overrated; they form the head of the great English middle class, maintain its tone of independence, keep up to the mark its standard of morality, and direct its intelligence' (Reader, 1966: 1). A similar view was expressed some seventy years later by Carr-Saunders, who went on to argue that 'professional men collectively possess the ability to perform all those skilled services upon which the continuing functioning of modern society depends' (1928: 3).

Knowledge and morality

Much of the subsequent discussion of the professions has been concerned with matters of definition – just what is meant by the term, to whom does it apply, is there any particular process of becoming professional? In everyday usage the term *professional* has a number of meanings, including receiving payment (as opposed to an amateur), being competent (as opposed to being unprofessional), as well as signifying high social status, position, and career (as opposed to workers, who merely have jobs). Sociologists have attempted to refine, or strip away, these meanings in their delineation of certain occupations as professions. Greenwood, in a widely quoted model of this kind, claimed,

> After a careful canvass of the sociological literature this writer has been able to distill five elements, upon which there appears to be consensus among the students of the subject, as constituting the distinguishing attributes of a profession.
>
> (1957: 10)

Such models (see Box 4.3) are labelled either as *trait* (attributes of individual professionals) or as *functional* (services to society provided by the profession) theories of professionalism. They identify the key characteristics of an occupation that is properly to be called a profession and then assess particular claims – is this occupation a 'profession', a 'semi-profession', a 'quasi-profession', or merely an occupation attempting to gain professional status? Stress is placed on the theoretical nature of professional knowledge: the way an abstract set of principles is applied to concrete practical tasks. Professionals have 'esoteric knowledge' (Leggatt, 1970: 156) which is concerned with 'the ability to manipulate ideas and symbols rather than things and physical objects' (Pavalko, 1971: 20). The identification of a special kind of professional morality, directed towards social values rather than money, was also echoed by other writers in terms such as 'service orientation' (Goode, 1961), 'service ideal' (Wilensky, 1964) and 'commitment to a calling' (Moore, 1970). Perhaps the most extreme statement of this approach to professionalism is that supplied by Legatt, who declared that professionals 'are the elect, in a true sense of the most knowledgeable and morally superior of men whose dealings are with other men in the conduct of practical affairs' (1970: 159).

Box 4.3

Attributes of a profession

Systematic body of theory
> 'The skills that characterize a profession flow from and are supported by a fund of knowledge that has been organized into an internally consistent system, called a body of theory.'

Professional authority
> 'Extensive education in the systematic theory of his discipline imparts to the professional a type of knowledge that highlights the layman's comparative ignorance. This fact is the basis for the professional's authority . . . The authoritative air of the professional is a principal source of the client's faith that the relationship he is about to enter into contains the potential for meeting his needs.'

Sanction of the community
> 'Every profession strives to persuade the community to sanction its authority within certain spheres by conferring on the profession a series of powers and privileges . . . [which] constitute a monopoly granted by the community to the professional group. Therefore, when an occupation strives towards professional status, one of its prime objectives is to acquire this monopoly.'

Regulative code of ethics
> 'A monopoly can be abused; powers and privileges can be used to protect vested interests against the public weal [welfare] . . . Were such abuses to become conspicuous, widespread, and permanent, the community would, of course, revoke the profession's monopoly. This extreme measure is normally unnecessary, because every profession has a built-in regulative code which compels ethical behaviour on the part of its members.'

Professional culture
> 'If one were to single out the attribute that most effectively differentiates the professions from other occupations [it is a culture where] . . . A career is essentially a calling, a life devoted to "good works" . . . The professional performs his services primarily for the psychic satisfactions and secondarily for the monetary compensations.'

Source: Greenwood (1957: 11–17)

Unsurprisingly, this kind of eulogistic treatment of the professions has exasperated some critics. The special knowledge–morality approach has been seen as little more than a celebration of the pious claims put forward by some occupations; its authors attacked as public relations propagandists for professional associations rather than careful social analysts. Roth argued that the approach was 'contaminated with the ideology and hopes of professional groups rather than an independent assessment of what they achieve' (1974: 17) and Daniels recommended that 'what professions say about themselves in justification of their privileged status might better be studied as political ideology rather than as an indication of intrinsic differences between professions and other types of occupation' (1971: 56). The knowledge–morality approach has thus been accused of reinforcing a 'myth of professionalism' (Esland, 1976).

Ideology and power

In opposition to the trait or functional approach to professions, critics have investigated the nature of professional *ideology* – the set of beliefs which professionals have about themselves and/or present to the public. Roth (1974) treated the five elements listed by Greenwood as typical of the claims put forward by occupations hoping to achieve, or maintain, professional status. These claims give only a partial view of occupational activities. A lengthy period of training may be sought in order to legitimate the claim that a body of systematic theory exists, even when its connection with practice is tenuous or dubious. The client may not accept the authority of the professional but demand particular services, or shop around for the 'best buy' (a practice which is discouraged in those professions which do not advertise). Community sanctions may be based on the view that only insiders (fellow members of the profession) are in a position to judge the performance of professionals, but this perception may have been constructed by the deliberate creation of a jargon and mystique which exclude non-professionals. The code of ethics may 'have almost no protective value for the clientele or the public. Indeed, the existence of such codes is used as a device to turn aside public criticism and interference' (Roth, 1974: 10). Finally, on professional culture and the service ideal, professions may not be more altruistic than other occupations, merely more sanctimonious. Every occupational group claims to be providing a valuable service to society – 'including prostitution' (p. 11), often referred to as the oldest profession.

The questions raised by this attack on the knowledge–morality approach are not about whether this or that occupation can properly be deemed 'a profession', but about the kinds of claims which are advanced, and the conditions under which they gain (or fail to gain) public acceptance. Jamous and Peloille's study of the French university-hospital system was concerned with the ways in which certain groups attempted to claim a professional knowledge base for their activities. They divided knowledge-based activities into two categories around the concepts of 'technicality' and 'indetermination'. When looking at the outcome of professional activity – its product – they defined *technicality* as 'the part played in the production process by "means" that can be mastered and communicated in the form of rules' (1970: 112). *Indetermination* refers to 'the means that escape rules and, at any given historical moment, are attributed to the virtualities [= personal experiences, knowledges, and skills] of the producers' (p. 112). An occupation whose knowledge base is mainly technical – standardized procedures applied to a well known body of facts – is likely to be seen as technician-level. An occupation whose knowledge base is solely indeterminate – based entirely on personal opinion – is unlikely to be valued. Only those occupations which strike a successful balance between objective, factual, codified technique and a high level of personal, individualized judgement are likely to be accepted as professions.

The issue here is how such a balance between two forms of knowledge is to be established – how does it become accepted by other people? Jamous and Peloille's answer was that this involves a 'twofold dynamic'. First, an internal creation of knowledge which generates demand for the professional product. Second, an external recognition of the truthfulness and importance of this knowledge. Here the acceptance of new knowledge as being both true and important depends upon the credibility of those who advance and support the claim. If the public accept those who already hold authoritative positions as the arbiters of new knowledge, then the acceptance of an occupation as a profession, either reinforcing existing claims or supporting new ones, is crucially dependent on the *power* of the advocates and supporters of an occupation/profession – it is a 'self-perpetuating system'.

These approaches raise questions about professionalism revolving around concepts of knowledge, morality, ideology and power. Other writers have tried to apply these concepts in examining how particular occupations have become established as 'professions' (medicine, law, the Church, architecture, accounting), as semi-professions (social work, teaching, nursing), or as latent professions (potentially, systems analysis) and to contrast them with those which have failed to impress (estate agents/realtors, or personnel/human resource specialists). Here the emphasis is not upon whether these occupations have or do not have the appropriate attributes (which verdict is likely to depend on whether or not the decider is a member or supporter of one of these occupations) but rather upon the historical, social processes through which claims either gain social acceptance or are rejected.

The rise of professions

Reader pointed out that our modern conception of professions emerged, over a long period, from occupations which were very different from those of today. In the eighteenth century in Britain the liberal, or learned, professions – the Church, the law and medicine – were seen as occupations fit for gentlemen equipped with a liberal education in Greek, Latin, and mathematics. Then:

nobody thought it necessary to make a strict inquiry into a young man's knowledge of divinity, physic or law before he took up the practice of these professions . . . until well into the nineteenth century the ancient liberal professions had found no use for written examinations of any sort.

(1966: 11, 42)

The development of education in and examination of the body of knowledge which today seems such a vital element came not from the 'established' professions, but from the lower branches of the occupation. In medicine the process was begun not by the elite physicians, but by the lowly surgeons and apothecaries. In law, it was not the higher barristers, but the despised attorneys who reconstructed their occupation. Attorneys were frequently employed as 'my man of business', as advisers to entrepreneurs, and were sometimes directly employed as agents (or managers) in industry itself. Despite their low public standing attorneys became the first of the 'professional managers' of business, and 'inside the eighteenth century attorney half a dozen later professional men – the accountant, the land agent, the company secretary, and others – were struggling to get out' (p. 27).

In examining the rise of such professions, Johnson (1977) utilized concepts of technicality and indetermination but changed the focus from the power of academic supporters to the ability of an occupation to serve the needs, and hence gain the support, of capital. Drawing on Marxist approaches, especially the work of Carchedi (1977), he divided managerial functions into two general areas. First, those which consist of the *global functions of capital* – and are concerned with control and surveillance. Second, those which are part of the *functions of collective labour* – concerned with the co-ordination and unity of production. Those occupations which perform essentially the global functions of capital have their indetermination/technicality claims accepted and become professions. Those which carry out the functions of collective labour will remain technicians. Thus the rise of professions is dependent on external power and in order to gain status occupations must demonstrate that they are 'servants of power' (Baritz, 1960).

Other approaches have focused on the internal strategies of occupations as they attempt to gain power for themselves. Parkin (1979), drawing on Weberian sociology, emphasized the importance of *social closure*. To achieve a privileged position in labour markets, occupations must sharply delineate themselves from other occupations (potential competitors) and limit the number of insiders who are deemed to have the special knowledge. Such social circles may be constructed in a number of ways. The most obvious form of closure in the history of professions has been the exclusion of women. The reader may have noticed how frequent the use of 'he' and 'his' has been in the debate on professionals. For the 'established' professions in eighteenth century England recruitment was limited to 'gentlemen' – from families of high social status and with a liberal education at Oxford or Cambridge University. In the twentieth century such exclusionary practices have been challenged, but there remain considerable inequalities in professional recruitment. Often closure is achieved through *credentialism*. Here only those who hold the necessary certificates of competence, usually based on examination and (sometimes) practical experience, are admitted into the profession. Here the social function of a long and rigorous training period, and high failure and drop-out rates, is not primarily to ensure that all members have acquired a high level of command over the complex and necessary body of theory. Instead its significance is that it enables the profession to control entry by granting or withholding credentials. In this way occupations may manipulate labour markets by determining the supply of professional skills.

The other side of this coin is the manipulation of demand. Professionals' organizations (their institutes and associations) attempt to ensure both that their services are highly valued and that they cannot be obtained from elsewhere – from some competing occupation. The strongest assurance of this comes from government legislation which licenses only those with approved credentials to engage in professional practice. At a lower level, general acceptance among employers or clients that only a properly qualified person may undertake certain duties is also advantageous, and professional organizations attempt to create such perceptions. The extension of training periods and the increasingly esoteric nature of theory are not the inevitable result of increasing technical complexity and difficulty in professional practice. They are a result of strategies pursued by professional organizations to improve the market situation of the occupation by manipulating supply and demand, and 'if there is no systematic body of theory, it is created for the purpose of being able to say there is' (Freidson, 1970: 80). For the individual, education becomes the basis of attempts to enter privileged occupations rather than providing the essential knowledge for their practice. As Weber put it,

> The development of the diploma from universities, and business and engineering colleges, and the universal clamour for the creation of educational certificates in all fields make for the formation of a privileged stratum in bureaus and offices . . . When we hear from all sides the demand for an introduction of regular curricula and special examinations, the reason behind it is, of course, not a suddenly awakened 'thirst for education' but the desire for restricting the supply for these positions and their monopolization by the owners of educational certificates.
>
> (1922: 241)

In this debunking of professional ideology, those business professions which are likely to extol the virtues of 'the free market' are themselves seen as constructed through manipulation of the market to create monopolies. Although individuals are not formally excluded on grounds of gender or race, to the extent that inequalities exist within education systems these will continue to be reflected in entry to the professions.

The two approaches to the rise of professions dealt with above emphasize, respectively, the external power of capital and the internal power of occupations. These elements have been combined by Larson (1977) in her discussion of *collective mobility projects*. Occupations adopt strategies of manipulating supply and demand in labour markets within the wider constraints of capitalist society. Armstrong (1985) applied this framework to the analysis of managerial occupations. He portrayed management as composed of competing specialisms (for example, accountancy, engineering, and personnel) which rival each other in bidding to be accepted as the key agents for owners. Managers do not simply serve the needs of capital; instead groups within management strive to define what these needs are and promote their servicing contribution. They seek to define the key problems, to which they then claim to have the most important solutions. There is little doubt that, in the UK and US, accountancy has been one of the most successful of these competing managerial groups, but this is not an inevitable feature of business, rather it is the result of specific historical circumstances and strategies.

Overall, in rejecting models of professions which see knowledge and morality as intrinsic qualities of certain occupations, historical approaches to the rise of professionalism have emphasized the strategies, constraints and struggles through which occupations have attempted to create and maintain an ideology of specialness. Those which have succeeded are recognized as professions. This may have important consequences not just for professionals' position in labour markets, but also for the way they are employed within the enterprise.

Professionals in enterprises

Many early professionals traded as independent practitioners or in small group practices where they supplied fixed services to specific clients and were remunerated through fees for the work carried out. Today large numbers of professionals are employees of large scale organizations, where they have permanent employment, work under superiors, and are rewarded by salary. Despite the fact that some professions were always engaged within organizations (e.g. management accountancy) many sociologists have seen the move from independent practice to organizational employment as a key trend which has influenced the professions in this century. For some this has produced important tensions between bureaucracy and professionalism. These tensions relate to the employment relationship, the design of managerial jobs, and forms of supervision and control.

Scott argued that:

First, professionals participate in two systems – the profession and the organization – and their dual membership places important restrictions on the organization's attempts to deploy them in a rational manner with respect to its own goals. Second, the profession and the bureaucracy rest on fundamentally different principles of organization, and these divergent principles generate conflicts between professionals and their employers in certain specific areas.

(Scott, 1966: 268)

Professionals resist bureaucratic rules, standards, and supervision, and have only conditional loyalty to the organization. They wish to follow rules laid down by their own associations and to be judged against professional standards. They look for considerable autonomy at work, but where supervision or leadership is necessary would prefer it came from peers – fellow professionals. Since their skills give them many career opportunities they do not feel tied to any enterprise in particular and thus are not fully committed to one. Although the potential for such conflict exists, Scott suggested that there are forms of accommodation to them which lower the tension. The bureaucracy allows more freedom to those professions which have very high prestige and centrally important skills than to other managers. Professions which are weaker in this respect find their members taking on a 'bureaucratic orientation' – they are deprofessionalized.

Freidson concentrated on the first of these processes and argued that for professional employees 'management can control the resources connected with work, but cannot control most of what the workers do and how they do it' (1971: 22). This is because the professional 'has managed to persuade others that he and only he is competent to do so' (p. 24). For Freidson, this 'limits seriously the traditional authority of management' (1973: 51). To the extent that, in modern society, professional knowledge and skills are becoming increasingly important, bureaucratic control will become less applicable. In direct opposition to this view, Oppenheimer predicted the victory of bureaucracy, leading to the downfall of professionalism. He argued that, in bureaucracies, professionals would increasingly experience conditions which were more like those of factory workers than those of their colleagues practising independently. Increasingly, they would be rule-bound, given routine tasks to perform which would fall short of the high expectations they had acquired as students, would find their income level stagnant or declining, and men would find their job security attacked by an influx of female alternatives. The outcome of these factors would be the proletarianization of professionals – the reduction of their elite status to the conditions of working class employment.

Johnson (1977), in reviewing the Freidson and Oppenheimer approaches, argued that each identified trends which might affect different occupations in different ways. Drawing again on the work of Jamous and Peloille, he argued that occupations high in 'technicality' (reducible to technical rules) might well be rationalized, restructured, and degraded in bureaucracies. However, those high in 'indetermination' (characterized by subjective judgement) would be immune from such processes. Since for Johnson claims to professionalism could be successful only 'where the ideological and political processes sustaining indetermination coincide with requirements of capital' (1977: 106), only those

110

occupations which primarily carry out the functions of capital could resist rationalizing tendencies which would degrade their employment. The implication for the work of professionals in enterprises is that some business professions, those which can claim that they make a major contribution to the needs of capital, will experience jobs significantly different from those of other organization members. Since their tasks are essentially indeterminate – they cannot be structured by bureaucratic rules, but depend upon broad, business judgements based on experience – their work cannot be codified, routinized, and fragmented. Whilst others may experience low-discretion jobs, they will be able to retain high-discretion roles which give them space to use their personal expertise to determine, as experts, not only how they will perform their duties, but also (for the elite) what those duties should be. In short, bureaucratic control is not appropriate for such agents of capital.

Here we return to the issues of knowledge, ideology, and power. Why must management allow special consideration for certain kinds of professional employees? Is it because there are essential, intrinsic qualities in certain professions which make their work impossible to standardize? Is it because they have successfully built an image of their occupation which inclines people to accept this view? Or is it because they have generated sufficient social power to resist managerial attempts to impose external authority upon them? At the turn of the century there were many workers who claimed special status in organizations, generally justified on the grounds of craft knowledge and skill. Yet these workers found their tasks restructured by managerial initiatives. Why are the elite professions not subject to the same fate?

One answer to this question was supplied by Salaman (1981). It returns us to the issue raised at the beginning of this chapter – how can owners trust their employees to pursue the interests of ownership rather than their own interests? As we have seen, one possible answer is the development of bureaucracy – a system of organizational rules which constrains managers to act in regulated, directed ways. A second possibility is to recruit and socialize managers who have internalized rules consistent with the interests of owners, and then to monitor not their activities, but the outcomes of these activities. In employing 'business professionals' enterprises are hiring people who have been steeped in business principles, ideology, and ethics for a long period, both in education (for example, in business schools) and in their professional training. Great care is taken in the selection of the right people. Once they enter enterprises they may be further socialized by colleagues, and more formally in training schools, to develop the appropriate attitudes. Their careers, even if they choose to leave the particular enterprise, are influenced by their 'track record' – their past ability to deliver what was required. The non-organization rules which they bring with them have been created by professions which wish to impress business with the usefulness of their specialist services.

Overall such employees may be trusted by employers to pursue the interests of the enterprise, without needing expensive systems for detailing individual tasks

(Armstrong, 1987b). Since these professionals are likely to occupy sensitive decision-making positions within the enterprise, the need for commitment and consent may be more important than the detailed control of particular activities (Littler and Salaman, 1984). Once owners have employed expert managers to act as their agents, to coordinate and control lower-level employees, they may not be able to intervene operationally. Instead they may concentrate on strategic intervention, determining who their agents shall be, what targets are set, and monitoring performance.

Here accountancy may have a particularly important place among business professions. Not only may its members be most deeply socialized by the 'business ethic' but their professional services include the means of monitoring the performance of other managers. For accountants, at least, the notion of some deep-seated conflict between bureaucracy and professionalism seems implausible.

INTERNATIONAL COMPARISONS

Much of the above discussion of managers as officials and/or professionals reflects UK and US perceptions and practices. As Lane (1989) pointed out, even the term 'manager' is distinctively a product of Anglo-American culture, and its use in other societies is more restricted, or more recent. In France the word *cadres* is typically used for management and, more informally, *patron* for individual managers. In Germany *Unternehmer* (entrepreneur) is applied to senior executives, and *Leitende Angestellte* (leading employees) to middle managers. Similarly, Larson (1977) claimed that the concept of a 'profession' is particularly strongly developed in the UK and US but of less significance in continental European societies. Here strong central governments with highly developed bureaucracies did not generate the growth of a large number of self-regulating occupations.

Not only may we find differences in the concepts of 'management' and 'professionals' in other societies, but their organization may reflect other social values. Hofstede (1980), from a survey of IBM in forty countries, analysed four dimensions of national culture which influenced organization. In comparison with the UK and US, some societies (e.g. France and Belgium) prefer a much higher concentration of power among 'bosses'. Countries such as Austria and Italy were found to be more concerned with 'uncertainty avoidance' and controlling future events. Individualism was most strongly valued in the UK and US, and collectivism most strongly demonstrated by Venezuela and Pakistan. In Scandinavian countries the quality of life, and inter-personal relations were stressed more strongly than material ambitions. There are clearly dangers in attempting to sum up an entire population as sharing some key personal characteristics. Nevertheless, to the extent that nations have distinctive histories, traditions and cultures these may become embedded in the taken-for-granted world-views of members of enterprises. This field of difference may be narrowed by the spread of multinational corporations, the movement of managers between countries, and the export of (especially US) management practices. Such differences and similarities can be explored in relation to German and Japanese management.

Enterprises in Germany

As it is Weber's birthplace, we might expect Germany to correspond most closely to his bureaucratic model. Indeed German management is often characterized as highly authoritarian and rule-bound. Lane argued that this portrayal is now outdated, especially in relation to large-scale enterprises. The post-war development of co-determination, and government legislation on employment and industrial relations issues have curtailed some employer prerogatives and encouraged the development of more co-operative management styles.

> In Germany the production department is central, and the other departments are considered to be at its service. Boundaries between departments are fluid and the relation with maintenance and technical services is one of mutual interaction and support and of close cooperation.
>
> (1989: 48)

The number of levels of management also appears to be smaller than is typical of UK and US companies. Maurice *et al.* (1980) concluded that German management may be more personal than bureaucratic.

German managers may also differ in terms of their occupational training and identity. In Britain and the US there is a concept of 'general management' which emphasizes all-rounder skills which may be demonstrated by MBA (Master of Business Administration) graduates of business schools. In Germany, although the notion of profession (as a self-regulating occupation) is less applicable, managers typically see themselves as technical specialists. Certainly, the peculiarly British notion of managers as 'gifted amateurs' has no place in German firms (Lane, 1989). In the production-oriented German enterprises, engineering is particularly valued and there is a high proportion of specialists at senior levels in the firm. In contrast, of the limited numbers of vocationally trained managers in UK firms, accountants are the most widely represented specialism at senior levels. Overall, German managers have been characterized as pursuing technology-led strategies in their organization of enterprise activities (Lane, 1988; Sorge and Maurice, 1990).

Enterprises in Japan

The organization of large Japanese enterprises is usually characterized as 'team management'. Top management has been described as 'multi-disciplinary with a strong engineering voice' (Currie, 1992). This top management is responsible for constructing the Long Range Strategic Plan, which is 'an all-embracing assessment of where the business is in relation to production and markets, an integrated technology/market approach' (Jones *et al.*, 1993) which, typically, covers a five-year period. At the next level, 'directors' convert this into a three-year Long Range Operational Plan which sets the framework for 'managers' to construct their Annual Operating Plan. At each hierarchical level decisions are taken by teams drawn from a number of managerial specialisms in a process which is often labelled 'management by consent' (Hodgson, 1987; Oliver and Wilkinson, 1987). Although, to many Western observers, this may appear to generate a great deal of time-consuming discussion, it can be argued that it facilitates the implementation of strategy since all relevant managerial parties become committed to particular decisions.

This collective approach to management is facilitated by the nature of occupational specialisms in Japan. New recruits to managerial ranks, who in the large companies are generally graduates, attend company technical colleges or schools, where they learn about corporate objectives and strategies, not merely about the particular function to which they have been assigned. These colleges also provide later post-experience training, which is also broadly based – for example, Advanced Manufacturing Technology courses cover both engineering and accounting aspects (Currie, 1992). Once through initial training, recruits are moved through a variety of functions during their career in the enterprise. Movement between enterprises is discouraged, and Japanese managers are highly critical of the 'job hopping' which they observe in the UK and US (Hodgson, 1987). As one put it, 'a person loses something each time he leaves a company'. The gender-specific nature of this comment is important here as the above comments refer only to men – women are expected to leave the firm on marriage. Management in Japan is a male occupation which is neither 'generalist' in the UK and US sense, nor 'specialist' in the German sense. Instead, technical experts have a broader knowledge base, are closely attached to the enterprise, and are engaged in collective organization.

Contrasts with the UK and US

Although in broad terms German and Japanese enterprises may correspond to the bureaucratic model of organization – with rule-oriented, hierarchical structures and processes – there are more detailed differences which may be important. There are less strictly defined demarcations of functional departments with clear-cut duties. In Germany this situation is represented by fluid relations between specialists; in Japan by team management. The construction of business professions as self-regulating occupations which are the guardians of special knowledge does not follow the UK/US pattern. To the extent that specialist occupations exist, enterprises are led by different groups. The US enterprise has been described as sales-led (Perrow, 1970b) and the UK enterprise as finance-led, or accounting-dominated (Armstrong, 1985, 1987a). In contrast, in both Germany and Japan engineering seems to be the most influential function within management. Thus, although overall similarities exist, management 'styles' may differ widely.

THE DEBATE ON ORGANIZATION

In this chapter three broad approaches to bureaucratic organization have been discussed which emphasize, respectively: efficiency; values; and control. In order to present them clearly these have been sharply distinguished. In the works of particular authors, however, such distinctions are less clear-cut. Perrow (1972), for example, argued that bureaucracy both reflected modern values and was the most efficient form of administering routine activities. Goldman and Van Houten (1978) explained the rise of bureaucracy in terms of the need of capital for both efficiency and control. Although the various authors may have been keen to promote their own approach as superior to others' (e.g. Salaman, 1979, 1981; Pfeffer, 1981) we may be able to combine elements of each approach in analysing enterprises.

One common strand is the continuing influence of Weber's ideas in the debate. Most authors have wished to enrol his views as support for their arguments. Here there are considerable difficulties. Lee and Newby may be correct in stating that 'to conflate "rationality" and "efficiency" would be to offend against Weber's view that science cannot arbitrate on questions of values and should not make value judgements about outcomes' (1983: 193). But it may also be true that Weber himself offends against this view. At one moment Weber seems to distinguish strictly between rationality and efficiency, but at the next to fear that the efficiency of rational administration makes it inescapable. This suggests that a re-examination of the concept of rationality would be helpful in further exploration of managerial activity. (This will be attempted in Chapter 8.)

A second common strand, for the UK and US at least, is the continuing emphasis on bureaucracy as the dominant organizational form. There have been attempts to modify Weber's original model or to suggest alternative models. There are occasional suggestions that some widespread cultural shift in values will destroy bureaucracy and replace it with more open, flexible, or democratic forms (Bennis, 1966; Abell, 1982) which Perrow dismissed as 'the science-fiction wing of organizational theory' (1972: 175). Such cases may be treated as exceptional, and even some of those arguing that we should attempt to create more democratic forms accept that these will remain in a bureaucratic framework (Clegg and Higgins, 1990). Most attempts to pinpoint non-bureaucratic enterprises involve a rather tedious use of Weber's characteristics as a checklist against which to assess particular firms to see whether they have or do not have these features. It is probably more useful to use Weber's model in the way he originally intended – as a tool for the social analysis of developing processes. Thus we should be concerned not with questions about whether any particular enterprise 'is' or 'is not' bureaucratic but with how and why managers seek to create rules, or implement them more rigorously, or change them, or allow them to be ignored. We also need to consider the content of such rules and the ways in which they gain acceptance or are rejected. Similarly, much of the sociology of professions has been concerned to label particular occupations as full, semi-, or quasi-professions (and some as failed professions). Whilst this debate has produced some interesting insights into various features of professional organization, perhaps the emphasis needs to be placed more on the processes by which occupations attempt to promote their interests, how they construct their knowledge base, and the consequences both for professionals and for their employment and for the non-professionals who are affected by these processes. The next chapter will discuss the role of accounting in the organization of enterprises and the relationship of the accountancy profession to management.

REVIEW

Short questions

What key problems of employing managers were identified at the end of the nineteenth century? What three broad approaches to studying organization are discussed in the chapter? What key characteristics did Weber identify in his model of bureaucratic organization? What is the position of the official in a bureaucracy? What is meant by functional organization (as recommended by early management consultants)? What does Chandler mean by 'the invisible hand' and 'the visible hand'? What are the key features of the 'rational' model of decision-making and what are its limitations? What attacks have been made on the claim that bureaucracy is the most efficient form of organization? What is the open systems approach and what are its limitations? What modern values does Perrow identify in bureaucracy? What is meant by 'organizational culture' and how is it used to explore management? What are the key features of the 'administrative' model of decision-making and what are its limitations? What is Weber's distinction between 'substantive rationality' and 'formal rationality'? What is Marx's distinction between 'co-ordination and unity' and 'control and surveillance'? What are the key features of the pluralist and Marxist 'political' models of decision-making and what are their limitations?

What is distinctive about 'trait' and 'functional' approaches to professionalism? What five attributes does Greenwood identify? How can this list be seen as 'ideology'? What do Jamous and Peloille mean by 'technicality' and 'indetermination', and what is their importance in establishing an occupation as a profession? How does Johnson relate this to the power of capital? How does Parkin use 'social closure' and 'credentialism' to explain the rise of professions? How does Armstrong combine these approaches in his discussion of 'collective mobility projects'? What opposite views of the future of professionals are adopted by Freidson and Oppenheimer? How does Johnson combine these? What differences in management and professions can be identified in German and Japanese enterprises?

Discussion points

How can we explain the organizational forms taken by enterprises? How are occupations established as professions, and what is the significance of this status for the employment of professionals? What is the relationship between professionals and managers, and between professionalism and management in enterprises?

5

ACCOUNTING AND MANAGEMENT

In UK and US enterprises accounting has achieved an important (some would say dominant) position in management. This chapter is concerned with three related issues – the relationship of accounting information to management decisions; accounting systems as regimes of management control; and the position of accountants as managers and/or professionals.

ACCOUNTING AND MANAGEMENT DECISIONS

Accounting is frequently seen as centrally concerned with the provision of information for decision-making. This was the basis of the American Accounting Association's definition that accounting is 'the process of identifying, measuring and communicating economic information to permit informed judgements and decision by users of the information' (quoted in Drury, 1992: 3).

Perspectives on decision-making

The models of decision-making discussed in the previous chapter generate very different views of the nature of facts, information, and decisions. They provide distinctive perspectives on the roles of accounting in enterprises.

Accounting and the rational model

The dominant view of decisions in management accounting textbooks draws upon the rational model – indeed Emmanuel and Otley (1985) claimed this was the sole theoretical base in conventional discussions. Facts are seen as objective truths about enterprises and are carefully gathered so that they are comprehensive, valid, and reliable. They are selected on the basis of their relevance to particular decisions, are processed through the application of universally established accounting techniques, and presented to decision-makers as the necessary information from which decisions will flow. Accounting information should provide definitive answers to questions of finance so that decision-makers can reach the best solution. Accounting is a technical activity and accountants are placed outside the decision-making process itself, which is the responsibility of managers. Accounting is rational because it deals with facts rather than opinions, prejudices or guesses, and because it operates with standardized, formal procedures (validated against profession criteria) rather than hunches, feelings, or other idiosyncratic methods. Here the term 'rationality' is closely linked with 'logic'.

Hopper *et al.* (1987) labelled this approach to management accounting *conventional* and explored its role in mainstream textbooks and research. Management is portrayed as a neutral group impartially organizing the enterprise and 'management accounting is presented as a politically neutral instrument' (p. 441). A committee set up by the (then) Social Science Research Council (in the UK) to investigate potential developments in accounting research brought together a range of criticism of this approach. They rejected the narrowly technical view of accounting and insisted that it should be seen as a social and political activity (Hopwood, 1985a). In their discussions 'technical' was variously linked with the terms 'calculative', 'neutral', 'professional', and 'uncritical', and to a belief in 'progress' and 'efficiency'. Their characterization of conventional accounting was shared by others in the UK (Tricker, 1975; Loft, 1986) and, in the US, Tinker complained that accounting students 'are trained to become greyhounds in bookkeeping and ignoramuses in social analysis' (1985: xxi). Conventional accountants, in the eyes of their critics, wrongly saw accounting as merely a technical activity producing objective, factual and neutral information in the pursuit of efficient business decisions.

Accounting and the administrative model

Some early attempts to construct a different view of accounting drew on the administrative model. The purpose of accounting is not to supply all relevant information, but merely to assist decision-makers to move sequentially through their explorations of a limited range of possible decisions until a satisfactory outcome is agreed. Information is shaped by the particularities of individuals and their organizations. Accountants identify and select facts on the basis of their subjective perspectives and values which are influenced by particular experiences (in education, training, and employment) and personal status (in terms of age, gender, race, and other factors). The way individuals do this is constrained by organizational factors such as decision rules (formal and informal), lines of communication, corporate strategies, and professional practices. Rationality refers to the practicality with which accountants (aware of their own limitations and organizational practices) provide information which is appropriate and sufficient to produce a satisfactory decision. Since a range of different decisions may be deemed satisfactory, variations between individual accountants and the information they provide is not a crucial issue.

This perspective on accounting has been labelled *naturalism* (Tomkins and

Groves, 1983). It breaks with the view that accounting knowledge is the product of a kind of scientific method resting firmly on objective facts. Instead account- ants are portrayed as social actors who create meaning through interaction with others. They generate and communicate particular kinds of information about the enterprise. 'Far from providing a secure or accurate depiction of reality, ac- counting is seen to represent a language system furnishing a partial and particular type of (socially created) perspective on everyday life' (Hopper *et al.*, 1987: 142). In concentrating on individual and group processes, and being concerned with perception, rules, culture, and language, naturalism has been accused of failing to deal with broader questions relating to social structure and forces within which individual interaction takes place. These are more centrally the concern of the third approach to decision-making.

Accounting and political models

Political perspectives on accounting information begin with the view that there is no single, agreed goal (or set of goals) towards which decisions are oriented. Individuals and groups occupy particular positions within enterprises which generate interests. Accounting is implicated in the ways in which individuals pursue these interests through struggles and compromises with others. Facts are closely related to power. On the one hand, if statements are accepted as facts they become powerful – and so do those who provide them. On the other hand, being successful in persuading others to accept a statement as a fact can be a reflection of the power of those who make the claim. When accounting information is accepted as factual this is simultaneously a cause of power (aiding some to gain advantage) and an effect of power (being accepted by others as authoritative statements). In this way the creation and use of accounting information are seen as a political activity. For some, this approach would appear to deny that accounting is a rational activity – it is certainly a long way from the objective, factual, neutral view. However, there is still some notion of rationality here. Accountants and decision-makers are involved in calculating their own interests, seeking alliances, constructing information to suit their purposes, and predicting the outcomes of decisions and actions. This pursuit of self-interest may (to a greater or lesser extent) be rational in relation to their positions in the enterprise.

Naturalism adopts a pluralist approach to the politics of decision-making. Competition and conflict are located in relationships between individuals or groups within the enterprise as a result of varying perceptions and values which are incompatible (Covaleski and Dirsmith, 1983). This approach is relatively unconcerned with these people's location in social structures and with issues of control over and within enterprises. Such issues have been addressed in *critical* perspectives which draw on Marxist models. Here accounting is seen as centrally concerned with the allocation of resources and distribution of rewards, and with the management of conflict over these – 'accounting practice is a means for resolving social conflict, a device for appraising the terms of exchange between constituencies, and an institutional mechanism for arbitrating, evaluating and adjudicating social choices' (Tinker, 1985: 81). Although, in the abstract, accounting is not necessarily politically partisan, its existence within social contexts means that sides are taken. Information is not impartially provided; it is provided for particular users, and for some purposes and not for others. Thus when textbooks claim 'accounting is concerned with providing information that will help decision-makers to make good decisions' (Drury, 1992: 3) this prompts the question 'Good for whom?' Attempts to avoid this issue on the grounds that it is irrelevant to accounting, or that there is no real conflict, means that the partisan nature of accounting is reinforced because it is unquestioned (Hopper *et al.*, 1987).

The creation and use of accounting information

These different perspectives on accounting contain very different views on the nature of the information provided and its relationship with decisions (see Box 5.1). 'Facts' are variously portrayed as objects which exist in the external world, subjective perceptions of that world, or deliberately constructed claims to truth. The information which is generated through accounting procedures – collection, collation, categorization, comparison, evaluation, presentation – is seen as an objective presentation of enterprise reality, as a selective representation of this reality, or as self-serving manipulation. The purpose of all this may be to maximize the achievement of a given goal or set of goals, to reach some satisfactory resolution, or to advance particular interests.

This is further complicated when accounting is viewed as having a number of roles in decision-making. Burchell *et al.* (1980) argued that accounting has many possible uses. They analysed these in terms of 'uncertainty of objectives' (do we

Box 5.1

Accounting and decision perspectives			
	Rational	*Administrative*	*Political*
Facts	Objective	Subjective Rule-based	Subjective Interest-based
Information	Relevant Representational	Selective Partial	Selective Purposeful
Purpose	Maximization/ Optimization	Satisficing	Sectional
Key concepts	Technique	Perception Values	Interests Power

know where we want to go?) and 'uncertainty of cause and effect' (do we know how to get there?). Much discussion about accounting assumes that goals are known and agreed, and that the relationship between action and consequence is unproblematic. Using a 'machine' analogy, they located accounting in contexts where these assumptions were relevant and then explored those where they were not (see Box 5.2). Where objectives (ends) and cause and effect (means) are relatively certain, accounting has the role of answer machine – computation can solve problems and decisions are programmable. When ends are clear, but means less so, then techniques such as 'what if' models and sensitivity analysis can be a way of exploring uncertainty, with accounting acting as a learning machine.

Accounting can act as an ammunition machine when organization members do not know, or cannot agree, appropriate goals but where the outcomes of particular decisions are predictable. Accounting information may then be used to make some short term consequences look attractive whatever the long term goal might be. Although it is unlikely that anyone could ever fully capture accounting for their own purposes – even accountants are constrained by their own rules – it can be mobilized by particular individuals or groups to promote their own interests. It is influential in setting the agenda for decisions since it creates 'mechanisms around which interests are negotiated, counter-claims articulated, and political processes explicated' (Burchell *et al.*, 1980: 17). The final category is perhaps the most difficult to define and identify, but it is likely to be very familiar to accountants in enterprises. This is where neither ends nor means are clear but decisions still have to be made. In such circumstances, 'decisions, once made, need to be justified, legitimated, and rationalized . . . a need for retrospective understanding of the emergence of action' (1980: 18). Here accounting information offers *post hoc* rationalization – it is brought in after decisions have been

Box 5.2

Uncertainty, decision-making and the roles of accounting			
		Ends	
		Certain	Uncertain
Means	Certain	Answer machines	Ammunition machines
	Uncertain	Learning machines	Rationalization machines

Source: adapted from Burchell *et al.* (1980)

made in order to make them appear sensible and convincing. Thus it does not 'inform' decision-makers; it gives them a way of justifying decisions.

This discussion of the uses of accounting suggests different roles for accountants. Accountants can be viewed as *scorekeepers* who keep track of events and report them. They may be seen as *gatekeepers* (letting through some, but excluding other, information) or as *guardians* of the bureaucratic rules of enterprises and the guidelines of the accounting profession. In doing this they may be seen as *servants of power*, supplying dominant managerial interests with the ammunition and rationalizations they demand, whilst also being *political actors* in their own right – pursuing their own interests whilst appearing to serve those of others.

ACCOUNTING AND MANAGEMENT CONTROL

Apart from supplying information for decision-making, accountants are involved in constructing and operating systems of management control. Although accounting is not the only aspect of management control, it has gained considerable importance in UK and US enterprises. The concept of management control has been seen as having two dimensions:

> Firstly, there is the idea of control as domination; the person 'in control' is the one who has the power to enforce his will on others. Secondly there is the idea of control as regulation; here the controller detects the difference between 'what is' and 'what ought to be' . . . and this difference acts as a stimulus to action.
>
> (Emmanuel and Otley, 1985: 6)

The split of 'domination' and 'regulation' has much in common with the dual view of management as 'control and surveillance' and as 'co-ordination and unity' (discussed in the previous chapter) and demonstrates the same tensions. As noted in a standard US textbook, 'Accountants often face a dilemma because they are supposed to fulfil two conflicting roles simultaneously. Firstly, they are seen as watchdogs for top management. Secondly, they are seen as helpers for all managers' (Horngren, 1977: 11). This tension, once noted, is often swept aside in accounting texts. Horngren called upon managers to accept accounting systems 'as positive vehicles for company improvement, departmental improvement and individual improvement' (p. 155). Similarly, in his UK text, Drury, after noting managerial suspicions about accounting, claimed that problems resulted from the 'incorrect managerial use of accounting information rather than the system itself' and that there was an 'educational role' for accountants, who should persuade managers to 'see the accounting system as there to assist them, rather than judge them' (1992: 599). These responses pretend either that there is no tension, or that it can be blamed on managers rather than accountants, or that managers can be persuaded to ignore it. As Hopper *et al.* (1987) argued, this hardly deals with the issue which these texts themselves raise and then dismiss. It is a central issue in debates on management control.

Accounting and formal control

Accounting provides a battery of techniques for management control which can be found in all the standard texts. Apart from the overall appraisal of corporate performance through measures such as profit, earnings per share, return on investment, and volume of sales, there are more detailed techniques applied to divisions and departments, and their managers. One key technique is budgeting, which has many different functions – authorization, forecasting and planning, communication and co-ordination, motivation, performance evaluation and control, and decision-making (Emmanuel and Otley, 1985). Enterprises vary in their use of budgets. Hopwood (1972) identified a 'budget-constrained style' in which managers' performance is tightly monitored against their short term budgets. This was forcefully expressed to me in one company:

> Each manager's performance is monitored and levelled as against a budget. If he beats his budget then he's a good bloke. If he doesn't beat his budget then he's not such a good chap – unless outside influences affect him. You've got to stand back and say, 'Well is this guy doing his job properly? Is this department a profitable investment or not?'
>
> (Finance manager, quoted in Jones, 1990: 281)

But Hopwood also found a 'profit-conscious style' where budget information was used in a less direct and more flexible manner, alongside other information, as part of a more general evaluation of managerial performance.

Both of these approaches generate mechanisms by which the financial expression of overall corporate performance is brought down to successive divisional and departmental layers of managers. In accounting debates there has been increasing emphasis on treating enterprise sub-units as though they were mini-businesses – treating them as cost, profit, or investment centres 'buying' and 'selling' materials and goods in contracts with other sub-units. In such regimes there appears to be an attempt to construct managers as mini-entrepreneurs who respond to pseudo-markets within the enterprise. However, managers are not entrepreneurs in the usual sense – since they do not provide capital and take profits – and hence companies attempt to create a simulation of these conditions. Here systems of managerial reward become a crucial issue.

Vancil's (1979) survey of US companies found that nearly all profit centre managers received annual bonuses based on performance measures which they thought were derived solely or partially from a strict financial measurement formula (65 per cent), or by the use of less clearly defined accounting information (31 per cent). Only a tiny minority (4 per cent) thought that accounting was unimportant to their rewards. These bonuses typically amounted to about a quarter of the annual salary of the managers. In the UK such (financial) performance-related rewards have been less common but Ezzamel and Hilton (1980a, b) found that, in over half the companies they surveyed, profit measures were seen as a major factor in the promotion of managers.

The use of accounting to align the action of managers with the interests of owners has been the subject of much recent accounting debate. In *agency theory* there is a basic assumption that remote owners (principals) have delegated decisions to managers (agents) whose interests are different, who must therefore be controlled, which results in agency costs (Jensen and Meckling, 1976). Owners are unable to specify exactly what managers should do, since they lack either the time or the expertise – this is why they have appointed them as agents (Shapiro, 1987). Rather than detailing specific actions, principals contract with their agents in terms of outcomes and rewards. The aim is to minimize managers' inclination to be lazy or to divert effort towards non-owner goals. However, managers are in a position to shape the information which they provide to owners and so there must be a means of monitoring this. All of this adds costs. For advocates of agency theory in accountancy (Jensen and Meckling, 1976; Fama, 1980; Watts and Zimmerman, 1986) what accounting offers to principals is a potential for regulating their relationships with agents at minimum cost. They have attempted to calculate ways in which to optimize the benefits of control against its costs. However, what this ignores is that monitors are also agents and so monitoring the activities of monitors produces another tier of complexity and cost. The logical outcome of agency theory is an endless chain of regulatory relationships – of agents monitoring other agents monitoring yet other agents (Armstrong, 1991).

Agency theory addressed an issue which has been central to the organization of the enterprise since the late nineteenth century – under what conditions can owners entrust their capital to managers? One answer to this followed the route of bureaucracy in attempting to specify the duties and responsibilities that each manager must carry out. Agency theorists proposed instead a system of contracts covering the outcomes of action and a reward system which would give managers incentives to fulfil these contracts. Their fundamental assumption was that the sole motive of human action is individual utility maximization – the calculation and pursuit of specific interests. Enterprises were viewed as sets of contracts between individuals where owners 'sell' their capital and managers sell their services. In this way agency theory stressed market forces, rather than bureaucratic rules, as the regulatory system of enterprises.

Problems with this approach relate to the role of information. We saw earlier how enterprises use creative accounting to construct the information provided to owners. Within the enterprise, managers faced with financial performance indicators 'might also be tempted to indulge in a little creative accounting of their own' (Griffiths, 1986: 135) and divert their efforts into constructing acceptable information rather than concentrating on productive activities. Alternatively, accounting may lead managers to focus their attention only on those items which are highlighted in their regular reports at the expense of other factors which may be crucial to long term success (Hopwood, 1974). In either case, the existence of the monitoring system will affect the information which is supplied. One financial controller I interviewed recently expressed this as a fundamental feature of organizational life: 'The minute you say that "that" is what you are measuring, if you haven't a balance and a check within the system, "it" will get better!' Providing such balances and checks further complicates the system and increases costs. In this respect, attempts to create ever more sophisticated accounting control systems can exacerbate problems as a proliferation of 'controls' leads to greater difficulty in obtaining overall 'control' (Drucker, 1964).

Accounting, informal control and trust

There are limits to the extent to which managers can be controlled through the formal application of accounting techniques. Managers resist attempts to control them, and manipulate information to show desired results. Extensive systems of monitoring can become prohibitively expensive. The very reason why principals appoint agents – because they have neither the time nor the expertise to run businesses on a day-to-day basis – means that detailed and comprehensive control is impossible. Thus managerial jobs may be described as 'high-discretion roles' (Fox, 1974) and 'if some crucial organisational roes are essentially complex, containing discretionary elements, and requiring skill and judgement, then the commitment and "trustworthiness" of these members is most important' (Salaman, 1979: 98). This is inescapable and the issue is 'deciding who – not whether – to trust' (Armstrong, 1991: 13).

From an agency theory viewpoint the necessity to trust managers, rather than relying on systems of control, may seem an insurmountable and possibly fatal problem for the enterprise. From a social perspective the difficulties are less perplexing. Salaman (1979) argued that there are a number of features of the employment of managers which facilitate reliance on their unsupervised discretion. First, managers often come from backgrounds with strong business connections and are unlikely to be actively hostile to enterprise goals (see also Nichols, 1969). Second, many will have been educated in university courses aimed at producing potential managers and steeped in business ideology – even if this is the 'hidden curriculum' rather than the overt syllabus. Third, considerable care is taken in the recruitment and selection of managerial personnel and the shaping of their subsequent careers. For example, Ford recruiters stressed 'the importance of the candidate's knowledge of, and sympathy with, the values and beliefs current within the organisation' (Salaman, 1979: 193). Fourth, once within enterprises, managers experience further ideological shaping through graduate-entry training courses, briefing sessions, and mission statements. Those with non-business educational backgrounds may be sent on MBA courses. At the same time, managers are actively involved in articulating business ideology when they explain and justify their decisions and actions – both to superiors and subordinates. Fifth, managers are rewarded not only for performance against some technical standards or targets, but for their overall commitment to 'appropriate' ways of thinking and acting:

First there is the work itself. This tends to be intrinsically satisfying and challenging, less controlled and supervised, more demanding and interesting. Then there are the conditions of work security, work surroundings and support facilities, status and prestige, fringe benefits, pensions, career prospects, levels of pay, etc., etc. Although it might be too cynical to suggest that the normative commitment of senior and expert organisational members is *bought* by granting them high levels of remunerative rewards, it is undoubtedly important to note that this commitment is associated with privileged organisational positions.

(Salaman, 1979: 119)

Rather than treating rewards simply as an incentive to achieve particular targets (as in agency theory) this analysis suggests that the occupancy of managerial positions itself creates a moral obligation of duty to the enterprise.

In addition to technical expertise, enterprises look for trustworthiness in their managers. This is related to two key factors. One is their *socialization* into general business values and particular organizational cultures. This encourages the internalization of rules so that they become part of managers' self-control. The other is a generalized development of *commitment* to these values and cultures which they themselves articulate as part of their job and which legitimates their privileges in enjoying life-chances and life-styles which set them apart from other employees. Not only is the adoption of an appropriate managerial perspective an ingredient in individuals becoming managers, but this perspective itself serves to justify managers' authority and rewards on the grounds that they are serving the interests of the enterprise.

In the UK and US, accounting has gained central importance in both these aspects of managerial perspectives. It is a core element in educational courses directed at the production of managerial recruits, training within firms, and MBA courses. Non-accounting managers explain and justify their decisions to executives using accounting calculations, terminology, and logic. The ability and willingness of potential managers to view the enterprise through accounting perspectives not only influence the way their seniors judge particular decisions and actions, but are also a distinctive characteristic which marks them out for promotion to higher levels – to become part of the management team (Dugdale and Jones, 1993). Here the importance of accounting lies not so much in its specific measures and criteria as in the regime of accountability it creates, in which managers use accounting as a language which explains decisions and actions to others – and also to themselves (Jones and Dugdale, forthcoming).

Formal *versus* informal control?

There is likely to be a tension between formal and informal aspects of control. Attempts to monitor the detailed activities and results of managers imply a lack of trust which they may resent, resist, or evade, which (in turn) means they are less trustworthy and hence require more control. On the other hand, enterprises which give free rein to managers may find that senior executives become more remote from management and hence more dependent upon managers' discretionary actions. From this it might be supposed that organizations face a choice between 'control' or 'trust' strategies.

In practice, it is unlikely that any enterprise can rely solely on one or the other approach. The complexity of modern enterprises means that no control system can cover all decisions and activities – there must be some discretion and, hence, some trust. On the other hand, to assume that managers have sufficiently internalized business ideology not to need monitoring would be to adopt an 'over-socialized conception' (Wrong, 1961) which replaces the agency theory view of people as economic calculating machines (utility maximizers) with an equally inadequate model of them as social robots (programmed by society). Enterprises are likely to display a balance of social control and socialization elements in which accounting is influential. The dual aspect of management – 'control and surveillance' and 'co-ordination and unity' – implies that any balance is likely to be unstable because of tensions within enterprises. Armstrong identified this as a basic contradiction 'because employers and managers are faced with the inescapable problem of achieving co-operative activity by antagonistic means' (1991: 6). Even if accountants were able to persuade managers to view accounting only in its coordinating role (as suggested by Horngren and Drury) this could only be a partial and temporary resolution of conflicts of interest within management or between managers and owners.

One further point needs to be made. Although accounting has been identified as an important element in management control, it is by no means the only one. Apart from the two management styles already discussed, Hopwood (1972) discovered a 'Non-Accounting Style' where financial information was not seen as a crucial measure of managerial performance, or as a basis for reward. Even where accounting is emphasized, it co-exists with other forms of information and is influenced by decisions and actions which are not based on an accounting rationale. Thus, not only are there contradictions within management accounting, there are also tensions between accounting and other information and managerial activities. These are explored in the next section.

ACCOUNTING IN ACTION

Management accounting textbooks tend to draw a clear distinction between accounting-for-decisions and accounting-for-control. In practice the distinction is less clear-cut. This section presents three classic studies which link decisions and control. They concern different enterprises in different countries at different times. What they have in common is that they confront the clutter of everyday life in enterprises rather than simplifying it into neat categories, models, or stereotypes. They provide rich pictures of accounting in practice.

Capital justification

This discussion is drawn from Wilkinson's (1983) study of a US-owned machine tool manufacturer operating in the UK. In the late 1970s the company began to introduce computer numerical control machine tools (CNCs) for its own production use. Formal investment decisions were made at policy meetings of key manufacturing managers. This group collected brochures and other kinds of information on the available technologies and decided which machine was most suitable. Then a production engineer was given the task of drawing up a capital justification (a written explanation supported by accounting information) for submission to the company's directors. He explained, 'With justifications we look at machines against the type of work anticipated, then justify them solely on the grounds of cost – payback periods and so on.'

Although the justification was expressed in accounting terms, Wilkinson argued that this was an 'economic rationale' or 'gloss' on the decision, which had involved much broader social and political considerations. Various sections within management had different aspirations for the new technology. Senior managers appeared to prefer machines which would enable office staff to be responsible for all programming, including the final editing when programmes were tested. However, they had only recently taken over, following the acquisition of the company, and were reluctant to intervene yet in operational decisions. Manufacturing supervisors, on the other hand, were generally suspicious of office workers and favoured machines which encouraged editing on the shopfloor. In particular they stressed machinists' craft skills, which could be extended through training in programming. These two different views of CNC were shared, respectively, by the programmers (who wanted office editing) and machinists (who wanted craft editing). Middle management identified this as the crucial social choice which they had to make. As one put it, 'The firm has to go one of two ways. We can retain skills on the shopfloor and have manual data input, or transfer skills into here [the office] with more tape control.' Arguments were put forward for each route but in the end the committee decided to recommend the adoption of a technology where the control box could be locked and accessed only by office staff.

This commitment now made, the capital justification was written. Thus accounting information was sought only after the crucial social choice had been made. The justification did not dwell on the debate over control, and its resolution in favour of the office was represented as cost reduction in the employment of skilled machinists. Since the firm was moving into unfamiliar territory by adopting CNCs, the costs and benefits could not be established with any certainty. Nevertheless, the use of accounting information gave the impression that the decision was based upon the cost–benefit balance conceived in narrowly economic terms and established through technical calculations.

The study tells us a number of interesting things about the relationship between accounting and decisions. It demonstrates how accounting can be used as a language which communicates decisions to senior levels of the enterprise. It shows accounting being brought late into the decision-making process to legitimate choices selected without accounting criteria. Managers played down the social and political factors, including disagreements within management, so the decision appeared to be the outcome of careful calculations of economic efficiency. Accounting served to legitimize managerial actions – so much so that a casual observer might assume that the decision was made in conformity with the rational model.

There was a sting in the tail of this study. Once purchased, the machines were not used in the way anticipated. Instead the keys to the control boxes remained on the shopfloor, and four years later machinists had established new programming skills. Thus neither the social and political reasons for the decision, nor its accounting justification (savings on skilled labour), represented the actual implementation of the technology.

Information and control systems

The second study deals with performance measures of managers and the way they were influenced by accounting information and control systems. It is drawn from Dalton's (1959) discussion of 'Milo', a large US engineering company in the 1950s. At Milo there was considerable concern with efficiency – seen in terms of reduction of operating costs. The performance of middle managers was assessed at monthly meetings of top management and 'efficiency ratings' were generated and published. Reports applauded efficient managers (whom Dalton labelled 'Team A') and shamed the inefficient ones ('Team B'). The ratings were constructed from accounting information on managers' performance against their budgets. Dalton explored one element of these budgets – maintenance costs – and showed how these were generated through a complex and changing system of social relationships.

At the outset of the study there was an old accounting system which had been in operation for ten years. The Maintenance Department recorded labour time and material for each of the jobs it carried out in the production areas, and sent the information to Auditing, who calculated costs and charged them to each Operations Department. Each production manager applied direct to Maintenance for repair work. This caused some inter-departmental friction. Maintenance staff complained that production managers put in unreasonable requests for immediate repairs; Operations managers claimed production was being hampered by a backlog of uncompleted jobs on their machines. When the issue eventually came to the attention of top management, it investigated and discovered that some managers had hundreds of outstanding requests whilst others had none. The backlog belonged to Team B managers. They merely put in requests and waited for them to be fulfilled. Team A managers used friendships, bullying, bribery, favours and threats to get their jobs moved to the top of the queue. They spent less money on regular maintenance but when their machines broke down they were repaired immediately by pulling maintenance workers off other jobs. Hence they minimized their maintenance costs but still managed to ensure that production targets were met. This was one of the reasons why accounting information showed them to be efficient managers. Top management was concerned about the overall level of backlog, and the amount of production which was being lost, and decided to install a new system.

A Field Work Department (FWD) was set up which would act as a buffer between Maintenance and Operations Departments. The new unit would log in each request, give it an account number and priority status, estimate the costs, and send instructions to Maintenance. When the new system went into operation some surprising anomalies appeared. In some cases the 'actual' costs of repair jobs were two to three times higher than estimated costs; in other cases repairs appeared to be completed with no costs being incurred. In addition, the monthly efficiency ratings began to alter significantly. Operations managers no longer had direct access to Maintenance, but had to go through the FWD. All their bullying, cajoling, and wheeler-dealing tactics were no longer effective in getting priority on repair work. This immediately led to Team A managers finding their efficiency ratings slipping. Worse, from their point of view, some maintenance staff who had long resented the tactics of these managers decided to get their own back. They used their new-found freedom to do favours for Team B managers by recording some of the costs of their repairs against Team A account numbers – a few minutes here, a few components there. This produced the disparity between estimated and actual costs, and led to Team B managers rising in the efficiency ratings. The new system was now producing some very bad news for Team A managers. The accounting information reviewed in monthly meetings showed that managers once thought efficient (and seen as whiz-kid go-getters) were recording lower production and increased costs. At the same time, other managers (once dismissed as dozy no-hopers) were improving rapidly. Team A managers attacked the new FWD system. The FWD was abolished in an atmosphere of antagonism with each group blaming the other for its failure.

The story of Milo's information and control systems shows how closely accounting is interrelated with the events it reports. The data it uses are socially constructed through the activities of many people in changing social relationships. The information it produces shapes not only perceptions of 'costs' and 'problems' in production, but also the 'efficiency' of departments – leading to personality characterizations of good and bad managers. Accounting is itself influenced by the social relations of the enterprise. In this case the new accounting information was seen as unacceptable and the control system which produced it was scrapped. For the politically powerful Team A managers, accounting information was regarded as valid only when it served their interests.

Performance measurement and profitability

The third study is drawn from Hopper *et al.* (1986) and Berry *et al.* (1985a, b).

This team of academic accountants were investigating the use of accounting information in a major UK nationalized industry – the (then) National Coal Board (NCB) – in the early 1980s when their research was overtaken by the events of a long and bitter industrial dispute.

The NCB was set up in 1947 and adopted a highly centralized structure organized around a national board accountable to the government through the Department of Energy. Below this there were divisional boards with area and colliery management teams. Those in charge of operations were usually mining engineers whilst industrial relations, manpower and welfare, marketing and finance managers were treated as staff advisers. In the 1970s colliery and area-level accountants produced information on standard costs but this was regarded by mining engineers as an unreliable and inappropriate measure of performance, and they preferred to use physical measures – such as metres of coal cut, machine working time, and output per miner/shift. The power of these managers ('the mining mafia') was such that financial information was not an important element in colliery decisions.

After the election of the Conservative government in 1979, the Department of Energy (and the Treasury) took a more active role in regulating the industry and in 1982 instituted monthly meetings with the NCB. These relied heavily on financial information, and by 1984 this was influencing area and colliery management through new information systems and performance indicators. Although resented by some mining engineers, accounting became a key factor in the government's drive to remould the NCB in line with its views on 'rationality', 'efficiency', and 'market fitness'. In 1984 the NCB announced a pit closure plan and the National Union of Mineworkers (NUM) responded with a national strike that lasted a year. The public controversy over these actions was significantly shaped by the financial information constructed by NCB accountants. The head of the NCB, Ian McGregor, stressed the 'facts of life' which meant that 'uneconomic' pits had to be closed. This was based on figures in the F23 – the colliery-level profit and loss account. It was used to target twenty pits for closure. In public the NCB presented the F23 as an objective statement demonstrating that there was no choice but to shut these pits. The NUM did not challenge the information directly, but argued that broader social considerations, the economic welfare of mining communities, and the nation's energy requirements should lead to pits being kept open. The NUM seemed content to leave accounting to NCB management and to argue on other grounds.

There was, however, a challenge to the NCB accounts from the team of academics who were studying the industry. Berry et al. (1985a) argued that the F23 was a 'fundamentally flawed' tool for decisions on closure. It was constructed on an absorption basis (which meant it was difficult to appraise the relative contribution of individual pits); not all costs were included; an inappropriate method of depreciation was used; and, as an historical account, the F23 was an unreliable means of predicting future profits. Taking one colliery which the NCB cited as the clearest case of an uneconomic pit – Cortonwood – they demonstrated how the NCB's identification of over £6 per tonne 'loss' could, given different assumptions, be portrayed as a positive 'contribution' (see Box 5.3). They described the NCB accounts as 'a mine of misinformation'.

Since the NCB had used F23 information to convince the public of the necessity of closure (implying that taxpayers lost over £6 every time a tonne of coal reached the surface) the academic challenge to their 'unchangeable facts' was greeted with some hostility. Apart from an immediate response (Harrison, 1985), the NCB commissioned an 'independent' team of accountants to review

Box 5.3

Short run contribution analysis of Cortonwood Colliery (£)				
		Assumptions		
	1981/82	1	2	3
Per tonne	F23	1983/84 basis	1981/82 basis	1981/82 basis
Net proceeds	44.30	44.30	44.30	44.30
(operating costs)	(50.50)	(50.50)	(50.50)	(50.50)
Profit/(loss)	(6.20)	(6.20)	(6.20)	(6.20)
Less				
Unavoidable costs:				
Surface damage		2.73	2.44	nil
VERS[*]		1.14	0.83	0.36
Depreciation		3.99	2.78	2.78
Overheads/services		3.79	3.94	3.94
Total		11.65	9.99	7.08
Contribution		**+5.45**	**+3.79**	**+0.88**

Assumptions

All three assumptions are based on published statistics in which the average costs are unclear.

1. Based on average costs for 1983/4. Assumes depreciation of 7.9% of average costs, and overheads/services at 7.5% of unit costs.

2. Based on average costs for 1981/2. Assumes depreciation of 5.5% and overheads/services at 7.8%.

3. As 2 but assumes surface damage costs can be avoided and government subsidy has been deducted from VERS.

* VERS = Voluntary Early Retirement Scheme.

Source: Berry *et al.* (1985a)

the issue. Within the broader industrial conflict there was a mini-dispute over the role of accounting in presenting the case for closure and targeting collieries. By the time the independent experts produced their report, the NUM strike had been broken, the miners were back at work, and the closure plan moved ahead. The dispute over accounting no longer occupied the public spotlight. The report did not resolve the accounting controversy since both the NCB and the hostile academics claimed it supported their original views.

This study gives important insights into the political roles which accounting can have. In the 1970s accounting information was relatively unimportant in local management, being rejected by the powerful mining engineers. It gained importance in the 1980s when it was adopted by the government as a means of securing tighter regulation of the industry. Here it played a crucial part in converting uncertainty into a kind of certainty. Since much coal was transferred to other nationalized industries, rather than sold on an 'open market', it was difficult to establish an economic revenue figure for NCB production. However, accounting information reinforced the government's view that national coal production was too high. Decisions to cut back production and/or close pits could have been made on geological information (on the life expectancy of seams) or technological information (on the suitability of pits for mechanized production under the MINOS computer system). The NUM's own mining experts might then have argued about the validity of such information. Instead accounting was used to provide a simple and hard 'bottom line' figure about the unprofitability of certain pits.

In this way uncertainties about the prevailing conditions, and the merits of closure decisions, were absorbed into accounting and a conclusion emerged. It is not clear whether accounting was the cause of the closures. Some saw the government's actions as essentially political rather than narrowly economic – retribution for the NUM strike of 1974 (when the previous Conservative government had called an election and lost it) and/or a symbolic warning to other union members that their power was to be broken. The NCB claimed that it had not actually used the F23 to make closure decisions (but did not disclose what information had been involved). What is clear is that accounting was central in the presentation of decisions both within the NCB and in public debate. The NCB presented accounting as the neutral and factual basis of rational economic decisions, but this was challenged by academics more sympathetic to the NUM, and the independent report did not resolve the differences. The way in which the two sides produced different accounts demonstrates how accounting can be manipulated and mobilized in support of particular political positions.

ACCOUNTANTS AS MANAGEMENT PROFESSIONALS

Accounting textbooks tend to draw a clear distinction between accountants (who provide information) and managers (who make decisions). This enables the claim to be made that 'a major reason for some of the dysfunctional effects of accounting control systems appears to be incorrect managerial use of accounting information rather than the defects of the system itself' (Drury, 1992: 599). Even in textbooks, this distinction quickly breaks down when claims are made that management information and management control are quintessentially the domain of accounting. It is blurred where a high proportion of senior managers are recruited from the ranks of accountancy, and when a move to general management is a realistic career aspiration for many accountants. Are accountants to be seen as professionals who advise managers, or as managers in their own right?

Accountancy and professionalism

In order to address this question we need to examine the construction of accountancy as a profession. In the debate on professionalism the conventional view was that it centred upon certain special attributes of occupations such as those listed by Greenwood (see Box 4.3). Matching these against accountancy, some appear to fit fairly well. From their beginnings in the 1880s the national bodies instituted examinations, made claims to ethical conduct, and have been increasingly successful in persuading governments to sanction self-regulating powers and the monopolization of certain business activities. Against this it can be argued that accountants' theory is not their own property but imported from elsewhere (notably economics) and business clients and employers are not financially ignorant lay people who must rely unquestioningly on their expertise. Most of all, the underlying assumption that professionals have a 'calling' to good works, and are oriented to service rather than money, hardly seems applicable to accountants.

Social closure in accountancy

Recent approaches to professionalism have stressed the importance of social closure in regulating the supply of expertise. Accountancy bodies operate as qualifying associations examining candidates on technical competence, which in the UK demands long periods of study, often in low-paid and uninteresting employment. This 'sacrifice' may be enough to deter some, and high failure rates exclude others. Accountancy does not appear to have the same degree of direct inheritance as some other occupations (e.g. medicine, where a high proportion of doctors are the children of doctors). However, entry to the public profession is now virtually restricted to graduates, and hence is likely to share the social class profile of higher education institutions, which recruit disproportionately from upper and middle class families. Like other elite occupations, accountancy (particularly as represented by the ICAEW) has been concerned with the social status and life-style of its recruits (Harper, 1988a).

More striking is the gender composition of accountancy. Attempts to gain access for women were resisted in the UK before the First World War on the grounds that women in general were more suited to the 'professions' of matrimony and motherhood; and because upper class 'ladies' would not apply, lower class women entrants would lower the social status of the profession (Lehman, 1992). It was not until 1921 that the first woman was admitted to the ICAEW, although some US states had accepted women a few years earlier. In the UK, female membership of the institutes ranges from 7 per cent (CIMA) to 12 per cent (ACCA), which is low even by general standards of professions (Roslender, 1992). In the US a 1986 Census Bureau report found that 45 per cent of all those classified as 'accountants and auditors' were women, but their average earnings of less than three-quarters the rate for men indicates that they were still disproportionately concentrated at lower levels (Lehman, 1992).

There are few studies of the racial composition of accountancy. One exception is Hammond's (1991) US history of African-American accountants. She found that obstacles to their enrolment as Certified Public Accountants (CPAs) came from state accountancy societies (e.g. the Texas society did not accept black entrants until 1952) and from the requirement for practical experience when the existing (white) CPAs would not accept black trainees. Although in the early years of the century a few states did allow qualification without the practice element, by the mid-1930s there were still fewer than ten African-American CPAs in the US. Between the First World War and the 1960s virtually the only route into the profession was to work for one of the very few African-American CPA firms already established (e.g. from 1942 to 1967 there was only one such firm in the state of Michigan) and today African-Americans still represent less than one per cent of US CPAs. Hammond concluded that the main reason for this has been the exclusionary practices of the American profession.

Although recruitment practices in the UK and US have changed over the last couple of decades, accountancy still reflects the legacy of social closure – in terms of social class, gender and race – of its formative years. These exclusionary practices can be seen as part of the occupation's efforts to construct itself as a profession whose social organization provides both a source of identity and a career, and a means of social control which go well beyond the boundaries of particular enterprises.

Judgement, independence and employment

Apart from regulating its personnel, the profession also attempts to influence the way services are provided. It claims not only a technical body of expertise in which its members are competent, but also that this must be exercised through the application of professional judgement. Sound accounting depends upon the subjective judgements of accountants – trained, guided and regulated by the profession. The implication of this view is that accountants should be independent pratitioners, self-disciplined by the rules they have internalized from their professional culture.

However, most accountants are not independent in terms of their employment relationship, since the majority of financial accountants, and nearly all management accountants, work as employees in non-accounting organizations. Some have argued that such employment situations generate a tension between the principles of professionalism and the organization. Roslender argued that those strictly defined as accountants (rather than managers of other accountants) were increasingly experiencing routine, formalized tasks, deteriorating work situations, decreasing opportunities for promotion to management, and were in danger of further erosion of their occupation through the implementation of information technology. All this implies that, despite efforts to create an elite occupation, many professionally qualified accountants should now be seen as 'the managed working class' (1992: 86). Only those who manage accountants can be seen as part of management.

This view perhaps puts too much emphasis on managing as the direction of labour, ignoring other functions where managers act as the agents of capital – such as determining the allocation of resources and the distribution of rewards. Rather than seeing accountants in conflict with the bureaucracy, it may be more appropriate to view them as the creators, monitors, and guardians of bureaucratic rules. The depiction of this as a routine activity disregards the level of indetermination involved in such tasks and the implied need for commitment from those who exercise managerial–professional judgement. Even if the prospects for accountants are currently declining, what is remarkable is the extent to which the profession has been successful over this century in establishing itself as a central business function, and the way in which its members have achieved senior positions in UK and US enterprises.

The rise of accountants in management

The rise of accounting (and accountants) in enterprises might be seen as the logical outcome of the need for financial information and the usefulness of accounting. Indeed much conventional accounting history presents it as an inevitable march of progress (Loft, 1986). In a series of papers Armstrong (1985, 1987a, 1987b, 1993) traced accounting in UK management from the late nineteenth century to the present day and found its development far more complex than this view would imply. By the early years of this century, the dispersal of share ownership and active capital markets had produced a strong audit base from which the profession extended its intervention in the life of enterprises. This extension was enhanced by the actions of the UK government during the First World War in attempting to preserve a 'business as usual' policy under wartime conditions whilst restraining profiteering in war-oriented industries. The solution adopted was contracting with firms for war goods where prices were based on production costs plus allowed profits. To enable this, leading accountants from accounting practices were co-opted into the war ministries to construct cost accounting systems. At the same time clerks within enterprises extended their own costing skills.

Following the war there was considerable controversy within the profession about whether to regard costing as a proper element of accounting or to treat it as a lower-level, technical activity suitable only for clerks (Loft, 1986). The ICAEW, perhaps reluctantly, included cost accounting in its examinations, but in 1919 a new body, the Institute of Cost and Works Accountants, was set up, aimed specifically at a membership within enterprises. Thus by the early 1920s the established financial reporting and auditing roles of accounting were being supplemented by a more managerially oriented concern with costing. In the economic slumps of the 1920s and 1930s, the position of accountancy was reinforced when financial accountants became the key providers of diagnoses of companies' economic ills, and prescribers of remedies for them. Crises were interpreted in financial terms as problems of profitability and liquidity, and tighter financial controls recommended. Accountants typically advocated a *holding company* corporate structure where the 'parent' group would regulate subsidiary units through regimes which paralleled existing external reporting patterns. Financial control within enterprises became more important as budgetary and costing systems developed and, simultaneously, career opportunities were opened up for accountants both within management and on boards of directors.

There was a similar pattern of government stimulation during the Second World Word, followed by post-war reconstruction. Growing concern with Britain's poor economic performance prompted UK enterprises to despatch productivity teams to the US in the late 1940s and early 1950s to study modern production methods and organization. The accountancy members of these teams returned with a new concept – 'management accounting' – and an admiration of American budgetary control and standard costing techniques. These had been developed in US *multi-divisional* forms of corporate structure rather than in the holding company pattern typical in the UK. Divisions were governed by a more deliberate rationalization of business activities, allocation of resources, and performance-related reward systems. Rescinding the advice of an earlier generation of UK accountants, these newly conceived 'management accountants' recommended the abandonment of holding company forms and their replacement with multidivisional structures, to be facilitated through merger and take-over. Again, accountants were key players in the identification of problems and recommendation of solutions, and a new breed of Financial Controllers emerged in the UK.

Much of this activity was dominated by financial accountants but the US notion of management accounting fuelled the ambitions of 'humble' UK cost accountants. Claiming new-found importance, they cast their role in strategic and executive terms. This new ambition expressed itself in changes to syllabuses and examinations (where there was a new emphasis on 'corporate strategy') and was symbolized by the changing titles of journals (*The Cost Accountant* changed to *Management Accounting* in 1965) and of the professional body (from Institute of Cost and Works Accountants to the Institute of Cost and Management Accountants in 1972, and then the Chartered Institute of Management Accountants in 1986). The junior costing wing of the profession sought, with some success, to establish itself as a managerial profession in competition not only with its non-accounting rivals (e.g. engineering, marketing, and personnel occupations) but also with the more elite, longer-established financial accountants.

Armstrong's analysis of accounting as a managerial profession located its rise in particular historical and societal conditions. It showed how accountants had played an important part in promoting their own specialism. While textbooks identify a clear distinction between 'accounting' and 'managing', the professional bodies have been seeking to weld the two together – and their success may be measured by the large numbers of senior managers, executives and directors from accounting backgrounds.

The fall of management accounting?

The importance of accounting in UK management owes much to ideas and techniques imported from the US. Ironically there has been a major debate over whether accounting was becoming irrelevant to US enterprises during the same period. In one of the most influential books of the last decade, Johnson and Kaplan argued that 'today's management accounting information . . . is too late, too aggregated, and too distorted to be relevant for managers' planning and control decisions' (1987: 1). In their view, conventional accounting is of little help in attempting to reduce costs and improve productivity, fails to give accurate product costs, and causes managers' time-horizons to contract to the short term cycle of monthly profit and loss statements. These failings lead to managers wasting their time justifying irrelevant variances, and making misguided decisions on pricing and product mix. They also discourage long term investment – especially in new technology. This was becoming increasingly damaging in the US in the 1980s, since enterprises needed to make significant improvements in their competitiveness in the face of increased international pressure, especially from Japan.

Much of Johnson and Kaplan's book was an historical examination of the way management accounting had come to lose its relevance for management. In nineteenth century enterprises accounting provided information relevant not only to decisions, but also to the motivation and evaluation of managers. In the early years of the twentieth century it responded to the development of larger, more diversified enterprises engaged in both manufacturing and marketing – led by pioneers such as DuPont and General Motors. 'By 1925 virtually all management accounting practices used today had been developed: cost accounts for labour, material and overhead; budgets for cash, income and capital; flexible budgets, sales forecasts, standard costs, variance analysis, transfer prices, and divisional performance measures' (p. 12). But at this point management accounting innovation appeared to stop. Although companies continued to grow in size, diversity, and complexity, accounting stagnated in its increasingly irrelevant 1920s form. The two key causes of this were over-emphasis on financial reporting and the pursuits of academic accountants. The requirements of audited reporting led to a concern with verifiable figures, and costing became a simplistic tool for valuing inventories, based on historical cost. This information was adequate for financial reporting purposes, and the auditors who advocated it did so for good reasons, but it became less useful for managers. Cost management deteriorated into mere cost accounting. This might have been noted and rectified by academics, but they were led astray by simple economic models of the firm based on outdated one-product/ one-process assumptions. They failed to test their academic theories against modern enterprises, where a variety of raw materials might be converted through many processes into a vast range of products sold in different markets. These two influences combined disastrously when academics (using their too simple models) advocated the use of financial accounting information (designed for other purposes) as the key means of running enterprises – creating 'managing by the numbers'. Before the 1920s managers had an intimate knowledge of the products and processes to which accounting figures related. The next sixty years saw the evolution of an elite, business school-trained cadre of executives, remote from production, who used highly abstract financial indicators which they could not see were becoming increasingly irrelevant.

This sweeping attack on conventional management accounting has been criticized on a number of grounds. Johnson and Kaplan claimed their approach was based on transaction cost theory, which assumes that enterprises' growth in size and complexity was due to internal costs being lower than market costs – the giant corporations were more economically efficient. However, their analysis was concerned with the systematic development of an irrelevant accounting which hindered economic efficiency. Thus the *theoretical base* of this work has been found inadequate or inappropriate. The *empirical* base of their history of enterprises has also been attacked. Ezzamel *et al.* (1990) argued that long before the 'watershed' of the 1920s, attempts to discover the 'real' costs of production, and to manage companies on such knowledge, were problematic. Management accounting – from early developments in the US Springfield Armory in the 1830s – was part of a broader emergence of disciplinary practices in which 'individuals' (in education, the military, and industry) become 'subjects' to be examined, marked, graded and rewarded. Hopper and Armstrong (1991) questioned the interpretation of events after the 1920s. Enterprises did not merely become more complex; managers were faced with the growing strength of organized labour which meant that it was increasingly difficult to translate information on costs into practices of cost reduction. The giant enterprises were forced to come to terms with their work forces and were able to pass on increased costs to their customers (in quasi-monopoly US markets) and to smaller firms which had to bear the brunt of economic fluctuations (and passed this on to their own less protected workers). Thus management accounting had not mysteriously become irrelevant, but had to contend with the new relevance of organized labour. Whatever explanations are offered, it is clear that the rise of accounting in management cannot be regarded as an obvious, commonsense, inevitable outcome of the progressive development of modern enterprises.

ACCOUNTING AND THE DEBATE ON MANAGEMENT

This chapter began with a view of accounting as a rational activity at the heart of business affairs which enables managers to make decisions and control the operation of enterprises. The discussion has shown the theoretical and practical complexity of these processes and how they are enmeshed in their social context. This has implications not only for our understanding of accounting, but also for broader social science theories of the enterprise.

In identifying rationality with efficiency, some have portrayed accounting as promoting successful business performance, but research has shown how notions of 'efficiency' are socially constructed and that accounting information cannot be separated from the social relations it reports. For those who emphasize the role of values in organizations, accounting may be seen not only as a means of their expression – measuring and reporting important items – but also as shaping the values of managers by highlighting some issues whilst neglecting others. Indeed accounting itself may be regarded as a modern corporate value – a preference for quantitative rather than qualitative approaches to management. For control approaches to enterprises, there are important issues about the way accounting – both formally and informally – constructs 'accountability' within the enterprise, and the tensions this entails.

Each of these approaches draws upon various interpretations of Weber's classic discussion of rationality. Weber identified accounting as central to the *formal rationality* of enterprises – stressing its measurements and calculative techniques – expressed in its bureaucratic organization. This chapter has shown the way subjective perceptions and values permeate accounting, and how it is strongly influenced by its social context whilst simultaneously shaping that context. The analysis of accounting as informal control, implicated in the construction of trust relations, is an important counterpart to the more usual emphasis on formal control. This implies a need for social scientists to reassess not only their view of accounting, but also their analysis of organization. The rise of accounting as a central business function is often seen as representing a routinization in which formal rationality comes to dominate. It may be more appropriate to see accounting as absorbing, obscuring and recreating values – reflecting the interests of particular sections within and outside the enterprise, providing an economic rationale for decisions and control, and generating its own perspectives on the means and ends to be preferred. In this way accounting is concerned with *substantive rationality* – with criteria of ultimate value – even though it may present a technical face to the world. The image of objective calculation disguises controversies and conflicts below the surface.

The discussion has also shown that accounting has not gained importance merely as a result of the increased rationalization of enterprises. Accountants themselves – individually and through their professional associations – have been instrumental in managing the supply of expertise, and increasing the demand for their services. Theories of professionalism, built on the model of the 'established professions' of Church, law, and medicine, do not fit accountancy well. And yet accountancy may be seen as one of the most successful managerial professions. This reinforces criticism of conventional approaches which identify professions as distinctive occupations in terms of their traits or functions, and supports alternative emphases on social closure and collective mobility projects. It also suggests that the assumption of a fundamental conflict between the principles of professionalism and bureaucracy is inappropriate to the analysis of enterprises. Different occupational specialisms compete with each other in creating bureaucratic rules and gaining bureaucratic positions.

In the UK and US accountancy has been remarkably successful in this competition and is now routinely regarded as a central business function. The same does not apply in enterprises in some other economies. In Germany, the accountancy profession has not developed the same self-regulatory powers and many activities which would be carried out by accountants in the UK and US are the responsibility of technical managers – especially engineers – who have been educated in 'business economics' alongside their technical studies (Strange, 1991; Currie, 1992). In Japan, distinctions between occupational specialisms are not so clear-cut, and accounting is not accorded a special role in managerial decisions and control (Jones et al., 1993). The rise of accounting in enterprises is thus a particular phenomenon of certain times and places rather than an inevitable outcome of business development. This has led some to argue that many of the problems of competitiveness in UK and US companies stem from over-reliance on accounting, which should now be given much less importance (Johnson, 1992a). This is unlikely to be easy, since 'there are certain structures and ways of intervening which, once invented, have proved so powerful and compelling that they cannot be denied', but such is the current concern with changing UK and US enterprises that a 'convincing solution to the problem of "managing by the numbers" will be irresistible' (Ezzamel et al., 1990: 157, 165).

REVIEW

Short questions

What different perspectives on accounting information are generated by the three decision models? What roles of accounting are identified by Burchell et al.? What dual roles of accounting in management control are identified in accounting textbooks? What three management control styles does Hopwood identify? What is agency theory and what problem does Armstrong find with it? What five factors does Salaman list as conducive to management trust? Why does Wilkinson suggest that capital justifications are 'economic rationales' rather than determinants of decisions? How did accounting information influence perceptions of efficiency in Dalton's study? Why do Hopper et al. see NCB accounting as political?

What features of social closure can be identified in accounting? What is the social significance of a stress on professional judgement? How did 'costing' become 'cost accounting' and then 'management accounting' in the UK and what are the implications for the employment of accountants? Why do Johnson and Kaplan argue that management accounting lost its relevance in US enterprises? What alternative explanations have been offered?

Discussion points

Is accounting only concerned with the 'formal rationality' of calculation, or does it also embody a 'substantive rationality' of goals and values? Are accountants professionals who stand outside management and advise decision-makers, or are they managers themselves actively involved in making decisions?

Part III

LABOUR
Debates on Production

6

PRODUCTION IN THE ENTERPRISE

At the end of the nineteenth century managers of enterprises were increasingly taking direct control of production. Under earlier systems those who organized production had dictated the length of the working day, the place of work, and to whom the work would be allocated. But much of how work was actually done – the productive operations themselves – was still determined by workers following the traditions of their craft, or informal patterns developed within work groups: the 'capitalist had little choice but to take labour power – skills and the organization of work – as he found it on the market' (Thompson, 1989: 41). When the UK was 'the workshop of the world' its competitive advantage was such that these traditional or informal patterns of working were not a hindrance to the profitability of UK enterprises. But as new industrial competition appeared – in the US, Germany, France, Belgium, and elsewhere – the pressure for productivity increased. This pressure was reinforced by the profit squeeze during the Great Depression of 1873 to 1896 (Littler, 1982). Thus the decline of earlier systems of work organization was accompanied by greater urgency in reforming production to regain competitive advantage.

WORK, WORKERS AND PRODUCTION

In the twentieth century a central concern of writers on the business enterprise has been to advance either prescriptive approaches to increasing the productivity of labour, or analytical approaches to the practices adopted by managements. These prescriptions and analyses have generated a debate on the nature of workers and how they are, or should be, managed. These theories of work and workers are the concern of this chapter. Four strands of the debate may be identified which (respectively) emphasize *technology* or *efficiency* or *motivation* or *control* as driving forces shaping the nature of work.

Technology and the division of labour

Many discussions of modern production begin with the concept of the *division of*

147

labour. The term is used in two main senses. At one level, the *social* division of labour refers to the separation of activities into different, specialist, occupations. Here the development of modern industry is seen as creating thousands, even hundreds of thousands, of new occupations and generating major changes in existing occupations. This is widely ascribed to two processes. First, the increase in specialized knowledge which becomes the basis of particular expertise. Second, the rise of new production technologies which create needs for different mechanical skills. At another level, the *detailed* division of labour refers to the breaking down of an occupation into a number of discrete tasks which are then allocated to particular employees. Here the concern is with the way production is specified within the enterprise – with job design and work organization. Again, technology is often seen as a crucial determining factor in these detailed arrangements.

The view that there is a strong and direct relationship between production technology and the division of labour was central to the work of Blauner. He sought to link technology with the nature of tasks performed; with the 'bundle of work tasks constituting a "job"' (1964: 9); and to whether workers experienced in this work 'a sense of meaningful purpose rather than futility, a sense of social connection rather than isolation, and a sense of spontaneous involvement and self-expression rather than detachment and discontent' (p. vii). Technology shapes tasks, and occupations, and workers' reactions to these. Blauner defined technology quite broadly as 'the complex of physical objects and technical operations (both manual and machine) regularly employed in turning out the goods and services produced by an industry' (p. 6). This technology differed considerably between industries, being determined by three main factors: the existing scientific-technical knowledge; the economic and engineering resources available; and the nature of the product. There were two key phases of twentieth century technological development – *mechanization* (the increasing use of tools, instruments, and machines as elements in production) and *automation* (the linking of such elements by transfer machines, and their monitoring and control by mechanical or electronic devices). Industries move firstly through mechanization, and then automation, in a process of increasing technological sophistication.

In order to investigate the impact of this technological progress on work and workers, Blauner selected four US industries at different stages – the early stage of mechanization (printing), its mid-development (textiles), to its highest point (car assembly), and automation (chemical processing). In the print industry craft jobs depended on high skill, passed from one generation to the next through systems of apprenticeship. In the textile industry workers had lower skill levels and were machine-tenders. At the extreme point of mechanization jobs entailed unskilled machine-minding activities completely dominated by the technology. Hence mechanization is a technological development which results in the 'de-skillization' of workers. However, in the chemical industry automation had reversed this trend and 'responsible technicians' worked in teams with mixed skills and had a strong sense of control and responsibility over the technology.

The progress of technology influenced workers' experience of work as either 'alienation' or 'freedom'. Alienation was measured in four dimensions: *powerlessness* – where workers feel controlled by the technology; *meaninglessness* – where workers see only individual tasks and do not identify with the overall process or its end-products; *social isolation* – where workers do not feel members of a work group or industrial community; and *self-estrangement* – where work is not seen as drawing on workers' intelligence, knowledge, skill, or initiative (the properties of their inner selves). Bringing together these ingredients – technological progress, industries, jobs, and experience – Blauner produced his now notorious 'inverted U-curve graph' (see Box 6.1).

This view of work is essentially optimistic. In the longer-term future the wider spread of automation will repair the harm done to the work experience of employees by reversing the deskilling tendencies of mechanization. Even in the short term prospects were brighter, since 'Automation is eliminating unskilled factory jobs at a faster rate than they are being created through the further deskillization of craft work' (p. 169). Although in some industries craft jobs are still being degraded into unskilled labouring tasks, 'with automated industry there is a counter-trend, one that we can fortunately expect to become even more important in the future' (p. 182), which will produce a new kind of technician employee with 'the social personality . . . of the new middle class' (p. 181).

Blauner has come under strong attack for this depiction of the development of work in the twentieth century. His empirical account of the nature of work in

Box 6.1

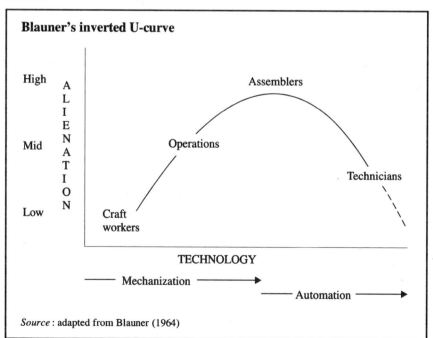

Blauner's inverted U-curve

ALIENATION

High

Mid

Low

Craft workers — Operations — Assemblers — Technicians

TECHNOLOGY

Mechanization ———→

Automation ———→

Source: adapted from Blauner (1964)

149

different industries, particularly chemicals, has been challenged by other studies (e.g. Nichols and Beynon, 1977; Gallie, 1978). His theoretical framework has been attacked as a form of 'technological determinism' (see Box 1.2). UK writers following a socio-technical systems approach argued that there are a number of forms of work organization which are compatible with any particular technology and hence there is a degree of choice (Trist and Bamforth, 1951; Rice, 1958; Trist *et al.*, 1963). This focuses attention on management's role and intentions in selecting particular patterns of work organization. Similarly, it has been argued that worker reactions are not immediately caused by the technological environment – they are shaped by each worker's motivation or orientation. Nevertheless, Blauner's work remains widely cited in writings on organization and it represents a particularly clear statement of a general approach to production which views technology as the driving force behind change and sees current developments as leading to a 'golden future of automation' (Thompson, 1989: 108). It suggests a one-dimensional source of change leading to a single (or convergent) outcome in enterprises. Managers would appear to have little control over the process of change – or its outcomes.

Efficiency and job design

Taylorism

A similar single-track view of the development of production can be found in the work of those who place emphasis not on technology *per se*, but on a more general notion of efficiency. The beginning of this century saw the rise of the Efficiency Movement in the US. The leading figure was Taylor, who inspired an approach to production termed either 'Taylorism' or 'Scientific Management'. His early experiences in industry (which included being an engineering apprentice and a gang boss) convinced him that massive increases in productivity could be achieved through the restructuring of work practices. He set out to achieve this through the application of science to the organization of production.

For Taylor, the key problem of US industry at the end of the nineteenth century was that work was still being carried out by 'rule of thumb' methods adopted by workers. Managers, being relatively ignorant of production operations, could not determine how work was to be conducted, and hence could not specify the level of output to be achieved. They depended on general exhortations and the arbitrary use of power to increase effort. In place of this, Taylor proposed an elaborate system of work study, selection and training, pay incentives, and close supervision. It is difficult to give a concise account of these, since they differed in various applications and because Taylor appears to have been an unreliable witness to his own activities (Nelson, 1975; Littler, 1978; Kelly, 1982). In general, his approach was to make a detailed study of work either by observing workers as they performed their tasks (as he claimed in the notorious pig-iron study of the worker Schmidt) or by undertaking the tasks himself (as in the case of high-speed metal cutting). Once this was done he specified the 'one best way' of performing operations, with detailed timings of each part of the activity, and (sometimes) its fragmentation so that different workers performed separate elements of the task. He then selected the 'first class man' most suitable for the activity, and trained him in the required operations. If the worker proved capable of producing the output level that measurement had shown to be possible, he would be rewarded with a relatively high wage – 'a fair day's pay for a fair day's work'. In order to facilitate the implementation of this work regime, the Taylor system also included proposals for factory layout, machine maintenance, restructuring supervisory positions, and developing departmental management structures.

The outcome was the setting up of standardized systems of production in which management would detail both the precise ways in which tasks were to be performed and the time allowed for this. This led to the creation of standard times for each product and hence standard costs for direct labour. The system was dependent upon the creation of detailed work instructions and records for every aspect of production:

> The work of every workman is fully planned out by the management at least one day in advance, as each man receives in most cases complete written instructions, describing in detail the task which he is to accomplish, as well as the means to be used in the work.
>
> (Taylor, 1911: 39)

This, in turn, necessitated the creation of large numbers of clerical office jobs (a growing element of indirect labour) which would also be scientifically studied to determine the most efficient way of organizing them.

Although Taylor did produce some technological innovations, most notably his high-speed steel for metal cutting tools, he did not regard technology as the determining factor in work organization. Instead he emphasized management determination of how work was to be performed. Workers would respond favourably to this managerial initiative provided that payment was 'fair', since 'what the workmen want from their employment beyond all else is high wages' (1903: 22). The key to efficient production was that management must scientifically study and redesign individual tasks so that work was no longer under the command of workers. Instead, thinking must be removed to the managerial offices and workers must follow detailed instructions.

Fordism

At around the same time Ford was developing production systems at his Highland Park plant in Detroit. These showed many of the characteristics of Taylorism, and became almost synonymous with mass production in the twentieth century under the banner of Fordism. In Fordism the relationship between technology, efficiency, and production is rather more complex. When Ford began producing cars in 1903 he used a gang of skilled assemblers who finished, and pieced together, parts bought in from other car firms. Then, with the development of more accurate machine tools, Ford was able to produce his own components which could be assembled without the requirement for final machining. This technological change was one of the factors which triggered a series of developments which eventually led, in 1914, to the establishment of the Fordist assembly line system of production (Russell, 1978; Gartman, 1979). Since today there is much discussion of the emergence of new forms of production, labelled 'post-Fordism', it is worth looking in some detail at the way Fordism originally developed.

Beginning in 1908, Ford first changed the factory geography so that functional layout (similar machines grouped together, as advocated by Taylor) was replaced by progressive layout (where machines were located close to the place where their components would be assembled). Then unskilled workers were employed to carry components from these machines to the workhorses where Model T cars were assembled by stationary work gangs of skilled assemblers. The next stage was the fragmentation of tasks so that each gang would assemble one set of components and move on to the next vehicle to repeat the same task. This enabled Ford to employ unskilled labour and, with very limited training, set them to assembly. In 1913 this system was changed so that, originally, workers would push the Model T chassis from one work station to the next, and then managers attached a rope to the chassis and pulled it through the shop using a ship's windlass. In January 1914 this moving system was operationalized in full production, using two electric chain-driven assembly lines.

These two lines demonstrated the key features of Fordist production. The vehicles were now in constant movement through the shop whilst unskilled workers, at individual work stations, each fitted only one (or a very few) components to the car in tasks which lasted the minimum possible time (a few seconds to a minute or so). Some indication of the detail of the task specification is given by one worker who described his job as 'I screwed on nut No. 58' (ex-Ford worker, quoted by Gartman, 1979: 203). The amount of labour time taken to assemble the Model T fell from 12 hours 28 minutes in stationary assembly in 1913 to 1 hour 30 minutes in moving assembly by April 1914.

Fordism in 1914 was not merely about detailed job design and the moving line. The early development of the line in 1913 was associated with extremely high labour turnover rates, with many workers quitting their jobs. In 1913, 52,000 men were recruited to fill only 14,000 jobs at Highland Park, and even with minimal training requirements the cost of this amounted to $2 million – compared with the capital cost of the plant of $6 million (Russell, 1978). Ford responded in a number of ways. He offered a new 'profit-sharing plan' under which workers could earn $5 a day, twice the usual labouring rate in Detroit. This was introduced in January 1914, two days before the electric-powered assembly lines were switched on. In order to earn such money workers needed a positive report from their production supervisors that they were capable of keeping up with the line. In addition, they needed the approval of Ford's Sociology Department, which made home visits to ensure that workers met the company requirements for 'thrift, honesty, sobriety, better housing, and better living generally' (Meyer, 1980: 70). Workers who failed this test were given six months to reach Ford standards or be sacked. Further, Ford set up an English School to prepare immigrant workers for employment, to instil proper attitudes and habits. This school provided courses in: industry and efficiency; thrift and economy; domestic relations; community relations; and industrial relations. In adapting workers to the new production systems, as one of the Ford educators put it,

> This is the human product we seek to turn out, and as we adapt the machinery in the shop to turning out the kind of automobile we have in mind, so we have constructed our educational system with a view to producing the human product in mind.
>
> (Marquis, 1916, Quoted in Meyer, 1980: 74)

Thus, originally, Fordism was about more than flowline technology and job fragmentation. It involved not only a restructuring of work, but also attempts to mould the kind of worker who would do it. Although technology is implicated in this process, the assembly line was the outcome of Ford's drive to achieve high-volume, low-cost production, not the cause of it. The creation of unskilled, fragmented tasks was one of the intentions of Ford's mechanization of production, not an unfortunate side effect of progress. In the early years the strategy was highly successful; from Ford being a very minor car producer in 1903, by the early 1920s one car in every five on the planet was a black Model T Ford.

Production and efficiency

From these early beginnings Taylorism and Fordism became bywords for efficient production. From the US these ideas spread to the UK in the 1920s and 1930s – although in different contexts and circumstances – and had a considerable impact (Littler, 1978; Lewchuk, 1983). Taylor's practices were exported by management consultants and became established under labels such as 'Work Study', 'Time and Motion Study', or 'Industrial Engineering', in small and medium-sized batch engineering companies. Taylorism was diffused through the work of Gilbreth, Emerson, Leffingwell, Gantt, Bedeaux, and others in the US, UK, France and Germany. They reached into Russia through Lenin's advocacy of Scientific Management after the 1917 Revolution as one of the vital ingredients of an economically successful socialist society. Many of Ford's production techniques were also widely copied (but not the Sociology Department or the English School) and became incorporated in production systems for a vast range of mass-production, mass-consumption products.

Although there are significant differences in the detailed practices of Taylor and Ford (see Box 6.2), there are broad similarities in their approaches to job design and work organization. Both stressed the need for management to determine the nature of work through a detailed division of labour into brief fragments of activity, carefully measured and monitored, requiring little skill. Both emphasized

Box 6.2

Production under Taylorism and Fordism		
Aspect	Taylorism	Fordism
Job design	Empirical/analytical Fragmentation (variable) Deskilling	Analytical Fragmentation (high) Deskilling
Work organization	Functional layout Detail division of labour (individual)	Progressive layout Detail division of labour (group to individual) Flow line technology
Management control	Coercive: direct Economic: fixed 'fair' rate	Coercive: technical/direct Economic: $5 day Political: Sociology Department Ideological: English School
Employment relationship	Minimal	Attached
Management structure	Functional Planning Department	Personnel and Production Departments

high pay (relative to other unskilled workers) as a means of securing cooperation, although Ford's difficulties with labour turnover and absenteeism led him to concern about attitudes as well. For those who followed Taylor and Ford, and implemented their ideas, the nature of work – tasks, jobs, and occupations – was not something dictated by technology. Instead it was management's responsibility to design all these so that they would maximize the economic efficiency of enterprises. It would be wrong to see Taylor and Ford as theorists producing some kind of social analysis of work. Nevertheless, they have probably had a greater impact on management thinking about production in the twentieth century than all the academics and popularizers of management theory put together.

Motivation and the nature of workers

The practices of Taylor and Ford have been subject to much critical scrutiny from academics. Taylor is often treated as a theory-producing social scientist – although, interestingly, Ford has not suffered the same fate. The early attacks originated in industrial psychology, where Taylor's prescriptions were first challenged from the viewpoint of human physiology, and the optimum performance of the human body. Here he was criticized for selecting only the best subjects rather than a 'scientific' sample; for attempting to combine the fastest elements in the work of different subjects despite their physical differences; and for failing to recognize that an overall rhythm of work might be important in maintaining optimum performance (see Rose, 1975, for a review of such criticisms). The major attack from industrial psychology was, however, to come from a different source. It concerned Taylor's conception of the nature of workers, and how this related to the managerial task of achieving, and maintaining, high levels of performance in production.

Human relations

The leading figure in this attack was Mayo, who drew upon studies at the Western Electric company's plant in the suburb of Hawthorne, Chicago. This much celebrated research, involving a series of experiments and counselling sessions mostly carried out between 1926 and 1933, has now become so embedded in the mythology of management theory that it is difficult to disentangle fact from fiction. The lasting outcome of the Hawthorne story is Mayo's interpretation of it, which has been described as 'the twentieth century's most seductive managerial ideology' (Rose, 1975: 124). Part of its success may be ascribed to the view that it derives from the first rigorous social analysis of workers, although it is not clear how much connection Mayo himself had with the original field research (Rose, 1975) and despite some fierce attacks on the adequacy of this research (Carey, 1967).

Mayo (1933) dismissed Taylor's view of workers (as primarily, if not solely, concerned with money, and working best as individuals) as a 'rabble hypothesis' based on a narrow rational–economic view of human motivation. Workers should be seen as essentially social actors, who seek social relationships with others in groups, and who wish to work in an industrial community. Work groups create norms of performance to which group members conform, whilst those who produce significantly more than the norm ('rate-busters') or less ('chisellers') find themselves socially excluded. Thus what determines the output of workers are not the factors identified by Taylor – scientific measurement, individual ability, payment systems – but the nature of the work group. Managers and supervisors can influence work groups through a 'friendly' approach, making workers feel part of the family of the workplace, using group bonus payment systems and other devices which lock the worker, through the work group, into the enterprise. The overall message to managers was that 'the happy worker was a more productive worker' (Salaman, 1981: 77). High productivity was to be achieved not through the application of the methods of natural science by managers armed with stopwatches and calculators, but through the insights of social science applied by managers with inter-personal skills.

By the time the Hawthorne studies were actually published (Whitehead, 1938; Roethlisberger and Dickson, 1939), Mayo's views were already receiving widespread attention in the US, and may well have been used retrospectively in interpreting the findings (Rose, 1975). In analysing the central experiments, which involved groups of six women, the researchers ascribed increases in productivity to the satisfaction of the workers' social needs. However, as Carey

(1967) pointed out, the increased output – to the extent that it was ever properly identified in the studies – could just as well have been explained as deriving from driving supervision and new payment systems. This would hardly have surprised Taylor. Nor would another Hawthorne finding – that in the group of male workers output was restricted to a norm well below the level of the highest producers. This observation had been the main reason for Taylor's insistence that work groups should be broken up and employees treated as individuals, which was central to his treatment of yard labour at the Bethlehem Steel Works. Thus there are alternative explanations of the Hawthorne studies.

However, it was Mayo's 'social' explanation that was seized upon and a vast body of research was generated which was concerned with 'group dynamics', 'leadership style', and 'job satisfaction'. Perrow (1972), in his review of this research, found it characterized by strong value judgements but weak empirical evidence. Despite the apparently sound common sense of the view that satisfied workers will work harder, or that there are some special attributes which attach to good leaders, research results have failed to lend any consistent support to these propositions. Nevertheless, the model of successful managers as socially skilled leaders who can simultaneously maximize productivity whilst creating a happy, psychologically satisfied work force has proved highly attractive to many people. Human relations were taken up by management consultants and educational institutions which offered to provide managers with the necessary social skills (Perrow, 1972). The values espoused in this approach to work – of participation, democratic leadership, harmony, cooperation, and openness – may be consonant with the values of US society, or at least may be part of the favoured self-image of its managers.

One issue that the Human Relations movement did not address was the design of work itself. In the Hawthorne studies, whilst the 'friendly' approach of supervisors may have been novel, the tasks which the workers carried out seem to have remained close to the 'principles' of Taylorism. The central concern of the Human Relations writers was with the social environment of work, not work itself. This focus was changed by a later generation of industrial psychologists in their construction of what became known as Neo-Human Relations. There were two main strands of this later development. One, largely US in origin, emphasized job design in relation to individual motivation. The other, beginning in the UK but more widely developed in Scandinavia, focused on work organization and collective worker participation.

Neo-Human Relations I: job enrichment

The first strand drew its view of motivation from the study of the maturing of individuals. Maslow (1958) presented motivation as a 'hierarchy of needs' (see Box 6.3). As the more basic needs at the foot of the pyramid were met, they became weaker drivers of individuals, and the higher needs became more important. At the top of this hierarchy were the needs of the fully mature

Box 6.3

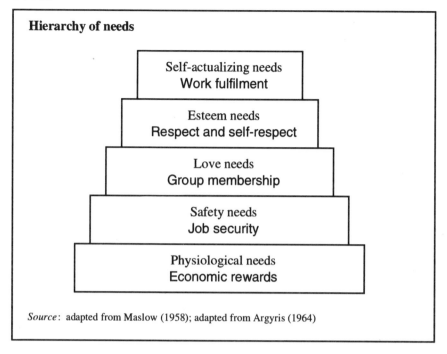

Hierarchy of needs

Self-actualizing needs
Work fulfilment

Esteem needs
Respect and self-respect

Love needs
Group membership

Safety needs
Job security

Physiological needs
Economic rewards

Source: adapted from Maslow (1958); adapted from Argyris (1964)

personality where the inner self, and all its potential, was the driving force in 'self-actualization'. Argyris (1964) took this notion of self-actualization (derived from studies of children) and applied it to workers. He argued that although workers' lower needs could be satisfied by pay, and then by working in groups, the more powerful motivating forces at the top of the pyramid could not be released in many existing jobs. Taylorism had produced fragmented, unskilled, unsatisfying tasks: now jobs should be redesigned in order to draw upon powerful drives deep within workers – this would raise motivation and result in better performance, greater productivity.

Pursuing this theme, Herzberg (1968) identified 'hygiene factors' which produced dissatisfaction (which workers try to avoid) and 'motivators' which create satisfaction (which workers actively seek to gain). Insisting that dissatisfaction is not the opposite of satisfaction, he located hygiene factors in the 'job environment', whilst motivators were about 'job content' (see Box 6.4). In order to achieve a highly motivated work force, jobs needed to be redesigned on principles other than those of Taylor. Herzberg dismissed two forms of redesign – 'job rotation' (switching tasks periodically) and 'job enlargement' (adding similar tasks together) – as irrelevant to motivation, and advocated 'job enrichment' – the building-in of higher-level activities as a principle of job redesign. Workers should be self-supervised (but still accountable); they should receive feedback on their progress, be able to learn more about their work, and conduct their own quality control.

Box 6.4

Motivators and hygiene factors

Motivators producing satisfaction	*Hygiene factors* producing dissatisfaction
Achievement	Supervision
Recognition	Working conditions
Work itself	Salary
Responsibility	Colleagues
Advancement	Status
Growth	Security

Source: adapted from Herzberg (1968)

In the 1970s, Herzberg's theories were widely influential in academic circles and his popularization of these ideas was welcomely received in enterprises. In the US (e.g. AT&T) and the UK (e.g. ICI) many leading companies claimed to be following his job enrichment approach with impressive productivity results (Cotgrove *et al.*, 1971; Bosquet, 1972) and there were signs that 'managements are now beginning to put together again the jobs they earlier disassociated following the dictates of Taylorism' (Nichols, 1975: 249). Phrases such as 'the humanization of work' and 'the quality of working life' were bandied about as symbols of some large scale, wide-ranging transformation of management thinking in enterprises – the 'de-Taylorization' of work.

Some caution is needed here. Herzberg himself did not (in his written work, at any rate) advocate such a sweeping transformation, although his disciples may have done so. He placed careful limits on the utility of his job design principles, which should be adopted only when '(a) the investment in industrial engineering does not make changes too costly, (b) attitudes are poor, (c) hygiene is becoming very costly, and (d) motivation will make a difference in performance' (1968: 61). Thus not all jobs can be enriched, nor do all jobs need to be enriched. The original study which led him to these views was based on 200 engineers and accountants. Many later applications concern managerial, professional, technical, supervisory, administrative, and clerical employees. However, many saw job enrichment as a universal solution and claimed it could be applied to production workers. Some of these claims appear rather thin. Changes at ICI (Gloucester) reported by Cotgrove *et al.* (1971) seem to be more along the lines of the (dismissed) job enlargement approach than to represent an application of job enrichment; many of the changes at ICI (Avonmouth), to the extent that there were any real changes, look more like job rotation. Managers were explaining their actions in a language which drew upon the then popular jargon of enrichment (Nichols, 1975). Although there certainly were a number of new initiatives in the organization of work in the 1970s and 1980s, it is not clear that they were the result of the adoption of a new psychology of workers.

Neo-Human Relations II: participation

Herzberg insisted on treating workers as individuals and allocated responsibility for job design to managers alone – this much at any rate he shared with Taylor. He advised managers to 'Avoid direct participation by the employees whose jobs are to be enriched' (1968: 61). A quite different approach was adopted in the second strand. Emery prescribed 'autonomous work groups' as the superior form of organization, and, finding little support in the UK, moved to Scandinavia and developed this approach in collaboration with Thorsrud (Emery and Thorsrud, 1969, 1976). The foundation of their work was the belief that those who know most about production are the producers themselves. Hence the starting point of job redesign ought to be the participation of workers in reconsidering and restructuring their working practices. The way this was done emphasized groups within the work force. Work organization is concerned with the delineation of the tasks to be done, and the identification of workers with the skills to carry them out. Once these workers, as a group, are allocated tasks they should themselves decide their working practices. Again impressive productivity achievements were cited to support this form of job design and work organization (see Jenkins, 1974).

Again there are signs of the de-Taylorization of production. The design of work is taken away from 'scientific managers' and given back to workers. Although both strands may represent a rejection of Taylor's ideas, the pre-scriptions offered were quite different. Emery's broader project of developing 'industrial democracy' was in fundamental opposition to Herzberg's managerial concerns. This brings into question whether any set of specific consequences can be attributed to such a diverse body of theory. Although there have undoubtedly been changes in working practices over the last two decades, it is not clear that these have stemmed from the development of improved theories of motivation which have swept aside the outdated principles of Scientific Management (Kelly, 1982). Certainly, the notion that managements' job redesign and organizational restructuring are driven by their eager adoption of the latest academic ideas hardly seems plausible, despite frequent textbook models of work being shaped by successive waves of theory – Scientific Management to Human Relations to Neo-Human Relations and beyond.

This is not to say that academic theories have no impact on work and workers. To the extent that managers are exposed to such theories – for example, through undergraduate and MBA courses in business schools – we may expect new vocabularies to enter managerial language. Similarly, we may find the books of Herzberg and popularizations of modern management thinking on managers' shelves (Nichols and Beynon, 1977). However, these works maybe provide merely a new means of describing long-established practices, or explanations of changes which emerged for quite different reasons.

MANAGEMENT CONTROL AND THE LABOUR PROCESS

The debate on the nature of work underwent major shift in the 1970s. This followed Braverman's highly influential analysis of labour in the US, which he linked with general developments in capitalist economics (and also Soviet societies). Braverman dismissed explanations based on technological determinism (such as Blauner's), arguing that technology is chosen by managers in their pursuit of the interests of capital. He claimed that, far from leading to a utopian future of automation, 'The "progress" of capitalism seems only to deepen the gulf between worker and machine and to subordinate the worker ever more decisively to the yoke of the machine' (1974: 231). Similarly, he dismissed the view that industrial psychologists had displaced Scientific Management:

> Work itself is organized according to Taylorian principles, while personnel departments and academics have busied themselves with the selection, training, manipulation, pacification and adjustment of 'manpower' to suit the work process so organized . . . Taylorism dominates the work of production; the practitioners of 'human relations' and 'industrial psychology' are the maintenance crew for the human machinery.
>
> (p. 87)

Labour process theory

Braverman's analysis of production centred on the concept of the *labour process*. Whilst many writers use this term in a very general way to refer to work, or production, Braverman remained close to Marx's original use of the term, which refers to the way human labour acts upon raw materials, transforming them into products, within specific social relations of production. In capitalist production the products are commodities to be exchanged in markets in a process of capital accumulation. In the labour process there is a crucial distinction between labour and labour power. *Labour power* is a worker's total physical and mental ability to work – it is a potential to produce. *Labour* is the amount of work which is actually done – that which is realized in production. The central task of management, acting as an agent of capital, is to ensure that the maximum amount of labour is extracted from the labour power bought by enterprises, and at the least cost. Although labour power may be bought (like any other commodity) the difficulty is that it cannot be separated from the workers who supply it. In order to control production, managers must control labour, which means they must control the workers who supply it. This is the central role of management, and the process which shapes production.

The key managerial control strategies of the twentieth century involved the detailed specification of work practices (Scientific Management) and the development of new production technologies. Taylorism was part of a general development of management methods aimed at extracting the highest level of labour from labour power. Taylor's contribution, through his work study methods, was to capture workers' knowledge of production, to transfer this knowledge to the office, and then to dictate to workers precisely how tasks are to be performed and at what speed. The essence of the process was the 'separation of conception from execution' (p. 114) – thinking became a managerial responsibility; doing was the worker's role. Since the unity of mental and manual aspects of production (thinking and doing) was the basis of skill, separating them meant deskilling. This not only increased managers' control over labour, but simultaneously re- duced the cost of labour power.

Similarly, technology should not be seen as a neutral or external force in the relations between managers and workers. The separation of conception from execution led to science becoming a commodity monopolized by management and used to create technologies which reduced the thinking input of workers. Technical control, especially through computers, was built into the machinery itself. Superficially this may look like machines determining the nature of work, but it is the intentions of management (lying behind the creation, adoption, and use of technology) which are the real cause. The purpose is control, and the result (again) is the deskilling of workers. The development of production produced 'the degradation of work in the twentieth century' (the subtitle of Braverman, 1974) through both management practices and technology (see Box 6.5).

The labour process debate

Braverman's stark portrayal of management and production, with its theme of the deskilling of work and workers, prompted a vigorous debate. This challenged almost every aspect of his argument and produced a great deal of interesting empirical evidence and many important analyses. We can explore this 'labour process debate' by examining the basic concepts laid out in Box 6.5.

Skill

To begin with, the concept of *skill* has been dismantled. Researchers have questioned whether productive skills are based on some clear body of knowledge which managers are capable of capturing. Shaiken (1979) claimed that metal cutting, which was one of Taylor's key studies, remained more of an art than a science, and others argued that skill can be based on 'tacit knowledge': workers are not formally conscious of the origins of their skill, which may appear as knack, gut-feeling, or merely habitual practices. Thus managers have found it difficult to codify such knowledge and to eliminate the need for skilled workers in many areas of production. Although the introduction of computer-controlled machines may eliminate some skills, workers may later re-establish them ('claw-back') or develop new skills (Wilkinson, 1983). The issue is further complicated by the question of whether skill refers to productive operations (skilled work) or to those who carry them out (skilled workers). Skilled workers

161

Box 6.5

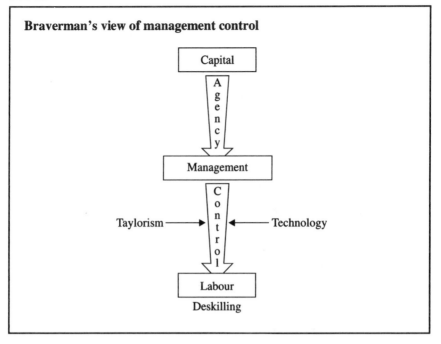

may well perform a number of unskilled tasks, and the definition of who is, or is not skilled depends on more than strictly technical factors. The label 'skilled' may indicate a relative scarcity of particular personnel in labour markets or may be the outcome of bargaining between managers and unions. Cockburn (1983) showed how the label is more readily gained by male workers, which suggests a prejudice that 'if women can do the job, it can't really be skilled, can it?' Skill can be seen as a social construction – both of what tasks are to be defined, and of which workers are to be recognized, as skilled.

Control and consent

Braverman's identification of *control* as the central function of management has also been challenged. Edwards (1979) disputed the dominance of Taylorism and took the view that US industry had generally moved through three control phases in the twentieth century. The early stage of 'simple control', where supervisors directly observed and exhorted workers to greater effort, was widely replaced by 'technical control' (e.g. through Fordist assembly lines). This in turn was replaced by 'bureaucratic control' based on regulatory systems of rules and procedures similar to those employed in the administrative offices of enterprises but now extended to production itself. Here, long term employees would be promoted up a series of grades constituting an internal labour market, gaining pay and privileges

162

in return for adherence to corporate rules (see also Burawoy, 1979). Edwards argued that the move from one stage to the next was initiated in core firms (those central to the US economy) in response to the activities of organized labour. In smaller companies and workshops on the periphery of the economy the earlier control types could still be found. In the UK, Friedman (1977) identified two broad types of control: *direct control* (e.g. Taylorism) and *responsible autonomy*, where workers have more scope to determine how tasks are to be carried out in order to meet targets set by management. Those workers whose tasks are seen as central to the enterprise's operation, or whose market and/or industrial relations strength means they can put pressure on management, are more likely to experience responsible autonomy in their employment.

These approaches criticized Braverman for his focus on only one kind of control – Taylorism. Other writers have gone further and questioned whether any focus on control, however broad, is enough to explain the development of production practices. Alongside, or instead of, control managers need *consent* – some minimal level of cooperation from workers – for production to take place at all. Managers may seek increases in productivity through encouraging greater willingness on the part of workers, rather than by ever more coercive means (Littler and Salaman, 1984; Thompson, 1989). In some approaches this appeared as a stark choice facing managers – either they followed the Taylor route of coercion or they took the alternative path of management by agreement. Thompson (1989) argued that these are not so much alternatives to choose between as aspects which are differently balanced in all forms of work organization in enterprises. Even Taylor insisted on a 'fair day's pay' to secure worker acceptance of his regime, and Ford intended the $5 day, Sociology Department, and English School to achieve a social construction of the cooperative worker. Control and consent are embedded in most, and possibly all, management practices. In examining how consent may be constructed in enterprises, Burawoy emphasized the 'games' that workers play. Within the rule systems created by management, workers develop their own informal responses which are directed at relieving boredom and fatigue, achieving production targets, and gaining their living. In 'making out', workers' participation in game-playing 'has the consequence of generating consent to the rules, which define both the conditions of choice and the limits of managerial discretion' (1979: 199). Whilst workers are controlled by the system created by management, through working the system they come to consent to it.

These criticisms suggest that there has been too great a concentration on management as control and surveillance and insufficient attention to coordination and unity. By focusing on the production of commodities to be sold for profit ('exchange value') we may neglect the fact that commodities are also of social worth ('use value'). Even where workers find little satisfaction in their actual tasks (in highly controlled, unskilled work) they may still take a pride in the production of some socially valued end-product. This may differ considerably between different kinds of product and production. As Beynon (1973) noted, the relationship between miners and coal is very different from that between assemblers and cars.

Subjectivity

This last point leads us to questions about the ways in which workers experience, and respond to the work they do – their 'consciousness' or 'subjectivity'. Goldthorpe *et al.* argued that workers' personal experience of work was shaped by their expectations and aspirations – which they termed *orientation* towards work. In their study, many relatively well paid manual workers came to work expecting it to be boringly routine and unskilled, but were prepared to carry out their tasks provided the wages were attractive enough. This form of instrumental orientation applied when 'Workers act as "economic man", seeking to minimize effort and maximise economic returns, but the latter concern is the dominant one' (1968a: 39). This 'instrumental worker' was prototypical in the UK (1968a: 175) and the rise of such affluent workers would have widespread impacts on the class structure and political life of the UK (1968b, 1969).

This image of the worker – making a wage–effort bargain with the employer, and emphasizing the wage side of the equation – seems closely in line with Taylor's view. But here it is not seen as natural (stemming from human biology or genetics), nor as psychological (stemming from universal human drives or motivations). It is the spread of Taylorist and Fordist production methods, mass consumer markets, and the break-up of occupational identities which are seen as the social origins of worker orientation. Braverman referred to this as the 'habituation' of workers – their accommodation to the limited choices available to them. Others have argued that people only regard themselves as 'producers' whilst at work; outside work they see themselves as 'consumers' (Dubin, 1956). The modern employee may be shaped more by the world of consumption than by that of production. This implies that broad, societal factors outside the enterprise may have considerable impact on its internal practices. Gallie (1978) showed how French and British workers in divisions of the same company, British Petroleum, responded quite differently to conditions of work. The pay of BP workers in France was very much higher than the going rate in local labour markets, whereas in the UK it was only marginally higher. Nevertheless, it was the British workers who were relatively satisfied with their wages, whilst the French workers were not. UK workers tended to compare their wages with those of other workers, whilst French employees related them to BP profits and the company's ability to pay. This was rooted in differing trade union ideologies and practices, and in the wider cultural context of employment.

This suggests there is no direct connection between work and workers' experience of it; instead the relationship is mediated by the 'subjectivity' of workers – their attitudes, expectations, aspirations, and values. These, though social in origin, may become deep-rooted in individuals. In some cultures certain jobs may be regarded as 'men's work' and labouring tasks may be valued as representing the rugged masculinity of hard work (Willis, 1977); and 'macho' world views may shape the relationship between workers and managers (Knights and Collinson, 1987). This subjectivity suggests that workers' responses may not simply reflect technology, or management practices, or some universal human psychology, but may be shaped by wider social processes.

Labour markets

Such differences may be reinforced when recruitment to work is itself socially structured. Those who have researched labour markets have identified connections between kinds of jobs and the kinds of people thought suitable to fill them based on social, rather than technical, evaluations. Nelson's (1975) study of early twentieth century management in the US disclosed a form of racial stereotyping where Poles and Hungarians were thought suitable for heavy work; Italians, Portuguese, and Jews for light repetitive work; and British and German workers for engineering. Other writers pointed to gender stereotyping of jobs as 'men's work' and 'women's work' (Pollert, 1981; Cockburn, 1983).

This produced the view that labour markets are segregated into different categories of worker. Edwards (1979) identified three labour markets in the US – the 'independent primary' (from which craft, technical, supervisory, administrative, and professional employees are drawn); the 'subordinate primary' (the source of employees in relatively secure but routine production and clerical jobs); and the 'secondary' labour market (which feeds into casual, low-paid jobs such as migrant agricultural labour; low-level jobs in catering, wholesaling, and retailing; and marginal labouring and clerical tasks). These three segments are characterized by different race and gender composition. In the first segment there is a high proportion of white males; in the third might be found many black or Hispanic workers, single-parent mothers, and elderly people, who constitute a high proportion of America's working poor. Edwards argued that the existence of these three labour market segments was an outcome of three forms of management control within the enterprise – simple, technical, and bureaucratic – and found strong links between forms of management control, the nature of jobs, the social segmentation of workers, and the class structure of US society (see Box 6.6)

Resistance

Edwards viewed the three forms of management control as historical phases in the development of enterprises, with shifts occurring when managers reorganized production in response to problems experienced under earlier forms of control. This draws attention to the question of worker resistance to management control. Managers are not omniscient (all-knowing) when devising control systems: nor omnipotent (all-powerful) when implementing them. If workers resist management control, and managers respond by changing their control systems, then production must be viewed as the outcome of changing social relationships

Box 6.6

Control, labour markets and class

Control type	Labour market	Fraction of the working class
Simple	**Secondary**	**Working poor**
Personal power of entrepreneur (or agent) over labour	Casual workers in lowest-level production, service, retail/wholesale, clerical, migrant agricultural jobs. Low levels of education and training, pay, and job security. Non-unionized	High proportion of workers black/Hispanic/elderly/ or female heads of household. Concentrated in rural areas and inner cities
Technical	**Subordinate primary**	**Traditional proletariat**
Technology directs and paces labour	Workers in jobs requiring skills specific to particular enterprises. Unionized, long-term, better paid employment with some promotion prospects	Long term wage labourers in working class communities or stable ethnic neighbourhoods
Bureaucratic	**Independent primary**	**Middle layers**
Impersonal control of labour through organizational rules	Workers with general marketable skills. More senior jobs in clerical, secretarial, sales, technical, and supervisory positions; craft workers; professionals. Well developed career ladders	People between lower-level administrative/production workers and executives/owners. Large proportion of white males

Source: adapted from Edwards (1979)

between managers and workers, rather than as the result of management intention alone. Resistance may show itself at an *individual* level by the withdrawal of labour (absenteeism, labour turnover), by reluctant compliance and restriction of output, or by undisciplined behaviour and sabotage (Beynon, 1973; Brown, 1977). Resistance may also appear in *collective* form, either through informal action in work groups, or through the more formal unionization of organized labour.

Some writers argued that in America and Western Europe there was a rising tide of resistance in the 1960s and 1970s which forced managers to abandon earlier forms of control. This was linked with broad educational and cultural changes in these societies which meant that previous control strategies became outdated. Bosquet (1972) identified rising levels of strikes, absenteeism, labour turnover, and recruitment problems as indicating a general crisis of management. Taylorism, aimed at achieving profitability through maximum efficiency, had now become self-defeating, since the costs of implementing it were rising drastically. Both the problem and the solution seemed clear enough – Taylorist production must be abandoned and the approaches of industrial psychologists implemented in order to maintain profitable production. This was not because managers had been won over by academics' theories of motivation, but because Taylorism had outlived its usefulness. There was a sting in the tail of this argument. The new solution – job enrichment – encouraged workers to emphasize the 'meaning' of work (its personal skills and satisfactions), but this would lead on to a re-examination of its 'purpose' (the social objective of production). This would lead workers to question the purposes which managers pursued and to seek a say in determining them – 'Job enrichment spells the end of despotic authority for bosses great and small' (Bosquet, 1972: 34). The 'paradox, whose truth managements have found it so difficult to accept, is that they can only regain control by sharing it' (Flanders, 1970: 172).

Such sweeping generalizations need to be treated with caution. In the first place it is not clear that the different elements of the evidence cited – strikes, job changing, sabotage, etc. – are indicative of a more militant work force, or a rejection of Taylorism. Even if such were the case, job enrichment schemes in the 1960s and 1970s were not generally introduced in those areas where managements faced the greatest resistance (Nichols, 1975). Instead they were applied to clerical, technical, supervisory, and professional personnel, or to manual employees who hardly fitted the model of militant worker. The changes may have been more apparent than real, and in some cases restricted the power of employees to intervene in local management decisions, despite much talk of participation (Nichols, 1975; Nichols and Beynon, 1977).

There was a broader concern, especially strong in the UK, that organized labour was increasingly posing a threat to managements' *right to manage*. It was felt that managers could not implement practices in the ways they wished, and that this was a severe check on productivity and profitability. Despite the claim by Goldthorpe *et al.* (1968a) that union members were becoming increasingly 'economistic' – concentrating on pay and security rather than posing a 'political' challenge to management – there was a widespread view that the power of organized labour had a significant impact on managements and governments (Nichols, 1986). Storey's (1980) survey of UK industrial relations practices in the 1970s gave little support to the idea of a national-level challenge to the authority of governments. It did, however, find significant changes within enterprises. Here, union representatives elected from the work force (shop stewards) had succeeded in opening up new areas of negotiation where there had previously been management-only decisions, and had strengthened their position in existing areas of negotiation. These changes were identified across a broad range of enterprises and industries, and interpreted as a shift in the *frontier of control*. On one side of the frontier were management-only decisions (e.g. investment, appointment of managers, promotions); on the other were worker-only decisions (e.g. job demarcation, overtime rostas). The frontier itself was marked by issues subject to negotiation (e.g. shift working, work force levels, discipline, speed of work). In Storey's view the 1970s saw an upward shift of this frontier which constituted a 'challenge to management control'.

Adopting this view of the 1970s, some have seen the 1980s as an era in which managements attempted to restore their old powers through an 'employers' offensive' where 'unilateral enforcement of what was once called "managerial prerogative" today seems necessary for capitalist production to remain viable, in order to restructure production without the need to buy out workers' resistance' (Hyman and Elger, 1981: 117). Restructuring involved detailed changes to existing work methods – seen by managers as 'restrictive practices' – and a general reassertion of 'directive control' by employers, aided by the Thatcher government, in the face of a weakening of unions in the periods of high unemployment of the early 1980s and early 1990s. By these means the frontier of control would be shifted downwards.

There is an alternative explanation of what was happening in the 1970s and of developments up to the 1990s. The expansion of negotiated issues in the 1970s may not have been solely an indication of union power. Storey concluded that managers faced a choice as to whether to take on workers and their unions in a battle for control, or whether to draw them into decisions in an attempt to manage by agreement. The attractions of the second approach were noted in the 'ChemCo' studies, where it was managers who were keen to develop (and thus shape) unionism within the enterprise (Nichols and Beynon, 1977). Similarly, Gallie (1978) found that British managers of BP appeared to prefer a 'semi-constitutional' form of industrial relations. The image of Britain in the 1980s as an arena of intense power struggle between employers and employees, which produced a new 'enterprise culture' for the 1990s, is a powerful one. Many politicians and newspapers portrayed it this way and highlighted leading employers such as Edwardes (British Leyland), Murdoch (Times Newspapers), Shah (Today Newspaper), and McGregor (British Steel/National Coal Board), winning out against recalcitrant workers and bloody-minded unionists. However, in other enterprises, in less publicized ways, other employers may have continued with a strategy of incorporating workers into the enterprise. It seems more than coincidence that one of the most outspoken industrial critics of the Thatcher government's confrontational approach was Harvey-Jones of ICI – an enterprise most closely associated with the job enrichment, participation, and management-by-consent thinking of the 1970s. Again, it would be unwise to assume that broad changes in the environment – in this case in the climate of industrial relations – will have any single consequence upon production in enterprises. Instead, this environment constitutes part of the context within which managers choose how they manage.

Managing the labour process

The labour process debate which followed Braverman's original statement challenged many of his ideas. Writers explored various aspects of skill and what constitutes deskilling. They questioned both Braverman's narrow view of control as dominated by Taylorism and the broader issue of whether control is solely, or always, the purpose of management. Instead, consent was advanced as an alternative concern. His conception of labour has been attacked as monolithic – failing to encompass individual subjectivity and labour market structuring – and as failing to address race and gender issues in the social construction of the working class. Further, by failing to explore worker resistance, Braverman ignored ways in which labour shapes production – both directly and by prompting managers to change existing practices. His view of management as a coherent, single-minded entity has been contradicted, and its role as agent of capital has been found to be much more problematic than his treatment of it. In all this subsequent work our knowledge of production – its operations, its organization, its environment – has been greatly enhanced. Rather than the simplistic (one-best-answer) approaches implicit in earlier discussions of technology, efficiency, motivation, and control, we now have a complex body of work which raises questions about all aspects of production (see Box 6.7).

Theories of work and workers

In introducing these theories of production I have made them appear distinctly different. Certainly there are fundamental differences in the approaches discussed. Blauner, despite his occasional protestations to the contrary, essentially saw production as driven by the technology available and actually used. He left little room for managerial manoeuvre within this technological domain. Neither, in another way, did Taylor leave much scope for managers, who must be guided by 'science' to the one best way of managing which produced maximum efficiency. Psychologists concerned with motivation often produced universal models of 'the worker' which paid little attention to variation in the social construction of workers through their differing race, gender, age, family, education and experience, or to differences in the social contexts within which they live and work. Whilst the control approach was centrally concerned with social relations of production, Braverman's statement of it was insensitive to individual, organizational, and societal differences. Hence, each of the approaches discussed here offers us insights into production which are driven by particular theoretical concerns.

However, once we look more closely at particular issues, these distinctions may become blurred. Braverman assumes that Taylorism is indeed the one best way – from capital's point of view. The concern of labour process theorists with 'consent' has connections with psychologists' discussion of 'motivation'. Although the view that technology determines production may be rejected, the constraints

Box 6.7

Concepts in the labour process debate

Questioning Braverman's view of the labour process (see Box 6.5)

Skill. Is skill an art or a science? Are skills permanently eliminated or is there scope for claw-back? Are skills technical features of the world of production or are they determined by market exchange? To what extent are they socially constructed? Are they based on tacit knowledge? Is skill the only factor which generates worker control?

Taylorism. How important is Taylorism? Are there different forms of management control? Has Taylorism been replaced by newer control forms?

Control. Is consent an alternative to control? Or do all control approaches require an element of consent? Are there contradictions between needs for control and surveillance versus coordination and unity?

Labour. What is the role of individual and collective worker resistance in shaping labour? How does worker subjectivity affect the experience of and reaction to work? Are workers divided by segmented labour markets? How do forms of control relate to labour markets? How important are differences in product markets for job design? Is there an increasing need for more versatile employees? How central is labour to managerial concerns?

Management. Does Braverman portray managers as omniscient and omnipotent, when perhaps they may be ignorant and incompetent? Should management be seen as a holistic block or is it fragmented into different sections? What is the importance of competing rationalities between different managerial specialisms? Is management united by organizational culture? Can we find any distinctive management strategies?

Agency. Do managers act as agents for owners or do they pursue their own interests? Does bureaucracy act to restrict the activities of managers? How important is managerial resistance and struggle in the shaping of production?[1]

Capital. Is capital a single block or is it fragmented into industrial and financial fractions? Do owners have any clear objectives in relation to management and labour? Does corporate strategy dictate management strategy? Do high levels of overseas investment and short term financial goals mean that capital is not invested in production technology which might offer management control over labour?[1]

Technology. Are there factors other than the need to control production that shape the nature of technology? Is technology designed to meet managerial needs? Does the use of technology match managerial intentions?[2]

[1] See earlier chapters. [2] See next section.

---

which particular technologies impose on managers may sometimes leave them little room to manoeuvre if their enterprises are to remain competitive. What emerges from theories of work and workers is a picture of a complex social arena in which many factors interact, and in a variety of changing ways.

Whilst this rich, complex picture may bring us closer to the real world of production, there is a danger that it will serve to confuse our views of enterprises rather than raise our understanding of them. We are moving towards a social analysis in which production is seen as the outcome of relationships between differing social actors in different social contexts – and almost impossible to generalize about. But we are also moving to the view that managers have to manage within this social world – they are required to decide and act – whatever its complexity. The next section addresses the issue of how they do this through an analysis of managerial initiatives and responses in recent changes in production.

MANAGING CHANGE

Much of the discussion in the previous section emphasized ways in which production is shaped by the relationship between managers and workers. There was a widespread feeling that patterns of work established in the early years of this century were beginning to break down by the 1970s. Such views gathered more support in the 1980s and led many to see the 1990s as an era in which new forms of production would come to dominate. These theories not only looked at internal relations between managers and workers, but also related these to external changes – most importantly to technologies and markets. Discussion moved from a focus on the de-Taylorization of work to a broader claim that enterprises now operate in a post-Fordist environment.

Technology and change

Technology on the shopfloor

Although there have been many changes in manufacturing technology over the last twenty years, few have had such a general widespread influence as the linking of computers to production machines. Here we will examine one example of this change and the ways in which it has been analysed. Machine tools remove metal from blocks (or partly finished items) by drilling, boring, turning, and grinding. They are important in the production of components used throughout manufacturing industry and have been around for a long time – indeed they were the objects investigated by Taylor in his high-speed cutting tests in the last century. Shortly after the Second World War, numerical control (NC) was added to such machines, whereby cutting operations would no longer be dictated by the operator but would be fed to the machine by instructions coded as holes in a paper tape. In the 1970s this system was developed so that a small computer could be bolted on to the machine with instructions stored as electronic programs – computer numerical control (CNC). The next phase of technical development involved a mainframe computer so that a group of machines could be networked to create flexible manufacturing systems (FMS). What shaped these developments?

One of the earliest discussions of NC came from Braverman (1974), who saw it as a microcosm of the general trends in control and deskilling. The knowledge of the machinist had first to be captured by management, then converted into programs, and thus would result in the removal of brainwork from the shopfloor and deskill machinists. Management would gain absolute control of machining processes, which was the intention behind technical change. However, studies of NC in use soon showed that the process of change was not as simple as this. In the US, Shaiken (1979) argued that the knowledge of machinists had proved difficult to capture. This meant that managers had to leave some discretion with workers in order for production to proceed. He found examples of workers using this discretionary space to resist managerial intentions of gaining control over machining. In the UK, Jones (1982) found great variety in the use of NC machines, with no clear-cut managerial intention apparent. He argued that factors such as existing organizational structures, trade (labour) union membership and practices, length of production runs, and many others, all influenced NC use.

One aspect of NC use which has been studied in some depth is editing. With CNC machines part-programmers prepare the initial set of commands which are then proved (i.e. tested) on machines. Inaccuracies or errors in the program are amended before full production begins. This may be done in two ways. Either the programs can be edited through the computer directly attached to the machines, or they can be removed to the office. In most circumstances in the UK this choice is also seen as one of whether the editing is to be done by the machinist (at the machine) or by the programmer (in the office). The technology itself does not determine how editing is to be done, and thus this choice, which is simultaneously technical (how editing is to be done) and social (who shall do it), is seen by many managers as a 'political hot potato' (Jones, 1988).

Wilkinson's (1983) study of UK companies showed a number of factors which influenced the way this choice is made. Often machinists wished to do the editing, and generally programmers attempted to keep it their own hands. In this struggle, machinists were often supported by shop management, whilst senior managers preferred editing to be an office responsibility. Each group mounted arguments in support of its claims and these became part of a negotiation of CNC use. Informal negotiation continued even after choices had been made, since statements about intended working practices made when the machines were adopted were often contradicted by actual applications which emerged during the implementation (or 'debugging') of the technology. The outcome, in some cases, was that machining became a routine, low-skill activity; in other cases, machinists developed new (and unexpected) skills in computer programming. Black's (1983) study of NC decisions in the UK subsidiary of a US company found machine shop super-intendents enthusiastic about the purchase of new machines, whereas in the assembly areas (which received components from the machine shops) superintendents opposed their introduction. Investment in NC was supported by quality control, planning, and plant engineering managers; but opposed by senior managers in manufacturing and accounting (because appraisals predicted a poor return on investment). It was from these departmental disagreements that the eventual decision to purchase NC emerged.

These studies demonstrate that there are a number of different managerial intentions behind the adoption of technology, and differences between intentions and actual implementation. Managerial differences reflect the different positions which managers occupy within the enterprise, both vertically (junior, middle, senior) and horizontally (line/staff, machining/assembly); and their differing backgrounds and occupational specialisms. Wilkinson (1983) noted that some engineering managers, who had themselves once been craft workers, put considerable emphasis on skill as a vital ingredient of effective production – particularly in relation to quality. Kelly (1982) found that personnel managers, who had encountered industrial psychology theories, supported changes leading to 'job enrichment', whereas industrial engineers adopted a more Taylorist approach involving unskilled work and monetary incentives. Technological change is seen as a process involving social (managerial) choice, with considerable variation in the way this choice is exercised and this reflects the different positions and attitudes of managers. The outcome is a view which stresses the malleability of computer-controlled technology – the ways in which its use is shaped by a broad range of factors, and the ways in which these are variously perceived, interpreted, and acted upon by managers.

Technology in the office

Computers have also been at the centre of considerable technological change in the provision of services, and in the administration of enterprises. Studies of office automation have been concerned with the introduction of various stand-alone devices (such as word-processors) and the development of large-scale, computer-based, information systems. As with shopfloor studies, much of the early work was heavily influenced by Braverman.

Wordprocessing (WP) was quickly identified as having a strong impact on the numbers of clerks and typists in employment (overwhelmingly women workers) and on the skills of those who remained. Downing quoted claims that WP operators could do between two and a half and five times as much work as typists and concluded, 'This is no empty sales talk' (1980: 276). She argued that this would eliminate a large number of clerical jobs, and those that remained would be deskilled in a number of ways. At the most immediate level, the knowledge required to produce good-quality documentation, laid out according to business conventions, had been transferred to standard settings in the WP program. The ability to produce work requiring the minimum of correction had become less important because of the ease of computerized editing. An office supervisor stated, 'A less experienced typist is able to produce the same quality of work as a really skilled girl and almost as quickly' (p. 284). A typist's job traditionally involved much more than sitting at a keyboard entering symbols; other tasks involved leaving the typewriter – to file or retrieve documents, collect stationery, and deliver urgently required letters. The WP incorporated functions which replicated or replaced these activities. Since WP systems are often introduced following some kind of time-and-motion study leading to office reorganization, 'the typist's job becomes further fragmented, so that she can work, in theory, continuously in front of her machine' (p. 284). The study produced an image of WP creating clerical jobs more akin to many on the shopfloor – deskilled machine operating in the office.

Change also affected the social relations of the office. In some cases typists were removed from offices in close proximity to managers, and relocated in WP centres. Here WP operators, continuously at their work stations, received material despatched to them from distant sources, prioritized by computer scheduling systems, and their performance was electronically monitored through their machines. Operators no longer had personal contact with the origins or destination of their work; local technical control replaced the traditional 'patriarchal' relations of the office – male boss and female subordinate – so that the 'social office' disappeared (Braverman, 1974). Opportunities to escape such jobs through climbing the secretarial career ladder were declining. With increasing managerial concern about indirect labour costs and white-collar overheads came pressure to reduce the number of secretarial employees, retaining only a few personal secretaries or personal assistants for the highest managerial levels – acting as 'office wife', dealing with the enterprise's most sensitive and confidential documents, and extending hospitality to important visitors. In this polarization of the office work force, the 'top' or 'private' secretary would be increasingly remote from the main mass of routine clerical employees, who would be increasingly experiencing factory-like conditions (Harman, 1979), and firmly located in the working class (Braverman, 1974).

The introduction of large-scale computer systems also transformed activities and occupations in administration and the provision of services. In areas such as banking and insurance, the mass production of financial services was seen as increasingly factory-like in terms of tasks, skills, management control, career structures, and working environments (Glenn and Feldberg, 1979). This was the result of standardization of procedures, which simultaneously enabled activities to be programmed and reduced the requirement for skill and discretion in the bulk of routinized office work. Crompton and Jones found a consistent impact in three organizations – a bank, an insurance company, and a local authority – and concluded that, 'as far as clerical work is concerned, computerisation "deskills" tasks, enhances the level of function specialization, and centralises control within the organization' (1984: 53). This deskilling of tasks was not necessarily per-ceived as the deskilling of clerical workers. The vast majority of those who carry out clerical tasks are women, and in general they are more likely to take career breaks from employment. The majority of workers had not been continuously employed before, during, and after the introduction of computer systems, and thus had not personally experienced the process of computerization. This process was an extension of the deskilling, standardizing, and centralizing tendencies which had long been apparent in large offices. Whatever the personal experience of individual clerical workers, and whatever the force behind change, the outcome was uniform:

> the vast majority of the clerical and administrative employees we interviewed were in jobs that required them to exercise little in the way of skill; work tasks were on the whole governed by explicit rules and few could exercise discretion or self-control in their work.

> (p. 64)

Early research into the impact of both stand-alone and systemic office automation induced a view that change was leading inexorably to a more factory-like form of employment and work organization in offices. This seems surprising, since at the same time shopfloor studies were suggesting that factory work itself was highly varied in its forms. The single-track view of office change – decline in skill, increase in technical control, erosion of career paths – may have been the result of important differences in shopfloor and office change. There is some reason to suppose that this could have been the case. The lower levels of office work tend to be occupied by women, who may not regard their current employment as their 'central life interest' (Dubin, 1956). Of the relatively small number of men who occupied such positions most fell into one of two categories: either young men at the start of their career or older ex-manual workers who had been moved to lighter work at the end of their careers (Stewart *et al.*, 1980). All these workers may have had less attachment to their current employment position, and its 'job rights', than those permanently located in manual work. If so, then there was likely to be less worker resistance, or greater difficulty in mobilizing and organizing such resistance, than in shopfloor change. This would imply that the implementation of office automation may have been closer to original management intentions. This might explain the apparent unilinearity of office change.

On the other hand, it may be that the early studies of office automation did not probe as deeply as those of the shopfloor. Certainly it is clear that there are choices for office managers about which technology is adopted and how it is to be implemented. WPs, in themselves, do not demand the setting up of WP centres, nor that wider work tasks are stripped away – indeed this may lower office productivity:

> instead of 'de-skilling' a clerk/typist in order to make her into a WP operator it might be far more appropriate and consistent with organizational needs for her to become an information assistant perhaps using a word-processor but also interrogating data bases, handling electronic mail and so on, on behalf of a manager or group of managers.

> (Damodaran, 1980: 5)

Later researchers discovered variation in office automation. Webster's study of WP use in eight UK companies 'showed a massive diversity in the technology already adopted and their organization of work around the new technology' (1986: 130). Similarly, Baran's (1988) overview of change in US insurance enterprises suggested different technological impacts at different levels. At the lowest levels, jobs disappeared; at middle levels there was a decline in promotion prospects; and at the higher levels there were relatively undemanding and uninteresting tasks for college-educated women in most of the managerial–professional positions occupied by them. However, to the extent that 'bottom' jobs were disappearing and the proportion of 'top' jobs was increasing, the overall skill levels of the female office work force might be rising.

Further research may show that the impact of new technology in the office is as varied and complex as that discovered on shopfloors. If so, issues of social choice and political negotiation are likely to be of central significance. If not, then another intriguing question will need to be addressed. Why, given the claimed flexibility of modern technology, do office managers consistently implement it in similar ways which decrease skill and increase management control?

Management strategy

The diverse nature of new technology and its uses, widely noted in shopfloor studies and rather less so in offices, suggests that change is neither predetermined by the technology itself, nor the outcome of a single managerial intention. Existing organizational and production arrangements influence the direction of change and, even in relatively similar contexts, managers have a degree of choice over which possibilities are realized. Here we meet the issue of *strategy*.

Child (1972) argued that 'strategic choice', constructed by the 'dominant coalition' at senior management level, was a crucial feature in the development of organizational structures and processes. Although each management may be pursuing 'profitable growth' the routes taken to achieve it may be quite different. Nevertheless, his studies of shopfloor and office automation led him to the view that 'four managerially initiated developments, facilitated by new technology' (1985a: 107) were of widespread significance. First, automation was frequently aimed at the *elimination* of direct labour from the production of goods and services. This might be achieved by abolishing the need for any workers, or by decreasing the need for regular employment of workers, thus moving them from primary to secondary labour markets. Second, a growth of *contracting*, so that staff who were once employees of the enterprise would become employed by other agencies, or self-employed workers supplying services on a fee-paid basis. The third strategy was *polyvalence*, which meant that 'workers perform, or at least are available to perform, a range of tasks which cut across or extend traditional skill and job boundaries' (1985a: 125). Fourth, *degradation* of work, in the way the term was used by Braverman – fragmentation, deskilling, direct control – was also widely found. Although not directly causing such outcomes, new technology facilitated managerial initiatives in these directions, and tended 'to be a vehicle for significant changes in the organization of work' (p. 107). Managers do not necessarily choose one direction or another, but apply each strategy selectively to suit particular circumstances. Overall managerial intention is to weaken the enterprise's dependence on its work force by removing the need for workers (elimination), moving workers outside the enterprise (contracting), and reducing requirements for particular kinds of skill (degradation). For those workers whom the enterprise cannot marginalize in these ways managers attempt to create employment practices which make the widest possible use of their skills (polyvalence). Thus there is a 'portfolio' of management strategies towards change.

Objections to such an approach have suggested that management decision-making may be less coherent than this implies. Rose and Jones (1985) found it difficult to detect technology strategy – defined as a coherent and coordinated set of policies formulated specifically with the labour process in mind and implemented throughout the organization. Instead technological change was piecemeal, uncoordinated, and pragmatically developed from existing circumstances. Child (1985a), in turn, complained that the definition of strategy used by Rose and Jones was so demanding that no form of human action could be so categorized, but this did not mean that managers did not have collections of intentions for change which shaped their introduction of technology, and which would have both direct and knock-on effects on labour. In part the disagreements between Child and Rose and Jones may have originated from studies of rather different technological changes. Much of Rose and Jones's work was based on the adoption and use of stand-alone shopfloor machines (Jones, 1982). Here we might expect departmental managers, within their own budgets, to pursue individualistic paths. In contrast, Child had studied more overall changes having broader impacts on business systems, especially in banking (1985b). Here we might expect a more coherent top-down approach which reflects managers' strategic considerations.

This dispute was narrowly focused on the relationship between new technology and the labour process. Beginning with questions about whether technological innovation is implemented with any particular management intentions towards labour, it raised more general issues. Instead of being a long term, coherent view, managers' approach to change may be a series of short term, fragmented responses to the many constraints, uncertainties, and changes they face. Ramsay, for example, raised a sceptical eyebrow at the notion of strategy:

> Almost every management text now has 'strategy' in its title. And no self-respecting manager would be caught dead admitting to anything but a 'strategic' approach to whatever function she or he performs . . . there must remain some considerable suspicion that much purportedly strategic behaviour is a mirage, more public relations thunder and post hoc rationalisation of decisions than genuine substance.

> (Ramsay, 1990: 8)

However, even if decisions are not seen as 'strategic' they may reflect broader, historical changes which managers face both within and outside the enterprise and hence have a general character. Some writers have identified such changes as a fundamental transformation at the end of the twentieth century – producing a 'new manufacturing environment'.

Flexible specialization and post-Fordism

Changes in production

An early approach to change in production systems was that of Emery, who identified the central characteristic of mass production as the 'fractionating' of operations into a series of separate tasks – the detailed division of labour. He argued that 'the logic of the car assembly line is a keystone, probably *the* keystone, to prevailing 20th century concepts of human management' (1977: 1, emphasis in original). Fordist assembly-line production addressed four key issues (see Box 6.8) but there were limits to such an approach and there were no more gains to be made by pursuing it further. The solutions which Ford had developed had now reached their technical limits. It was this, rather than the need for higher motivation, or the resistance of workers, which was the driver of change. The technical limitations of Fordist production were increasingly highlighted by changes in product markets which were putting new demands upon production. Coriat's (1980) account of the reorganization of production in Renault plants in France reads almost as though the history of Fordism was being replayed – but backwards. In the 1970s Renault began by breaking up its assembly lines (Ford 1913) to introduce benchwork (Ford 1908), and then brought in group working (Ford 1903). But, of course, history can never simply be replayed – in any direction – and the explanations offered for these changes needed to be located in a new era.

Kelly identified three broad categories of work restructuring in UK enterprises in the 1970s (see Box 6.9). The changes occurred in enterprises facing 'a diversified and fluctuating product market' (1982: 78). Here the principles of mass production, which had served Ford well, were increasingly inappropriate. Ford's system was designed to meet the requirements of long run, high volume, standardized products; in some new markets there was a demand for a wide range of short-lived products which put pressure on existing production systems and highlighted the technical limitations which already existed in flowline production.

Flexible specialization

This view was generalized into a theory of global change by Piore and Sabel. The economic difficulties experienced by enterprises and nations in the 1970s and 1980s were not simply part of a normal cycle of boom-and-trough experienced by economies, but signalled a major shift in the nature of economic life – 'the second

Box 6.8

Technical problems and solutions in assembly-line production

1 *Transfer costs* involved in moving products from one place to another and *waiting time* when goods are stockpiled reduced by the continuous flow of products
2 Assembly of large numbers of different components into finished products achieved through *standardization* of parts
3 Bottlenecks and idle areas eliminated through the *balancing* of production elements by means of 'scientific' work study
4 The *pacing* of work determined by external supervision through the speed of the line

Source: adapted from Emery (1977)

Box 6.9

Job redesign in UK enterprises

Reorganization of flow lines	where long chains of work roles are either broken up into several shorter chains or replaced by individual work stations
Flexible work groups	where a number of work roles are amalgamated and distributed to work groups within which labour is allocated between jobs as and when required
Vertical role integration	where a number of work roles are carried out by different workers or are amagamated into the job of one worker

Source: adapted from Kelly (1982)

---

industrial divide' (1984, title). The first industrial divide had appeared in the mid-nineteenth century when industrialists faced the choice of whether to continue with craft forms of working or move towards mass production. The US, more than any other country, chose the mass-production route and developed powerful industrial systems which used low-skilled labour to supply products to mass markets and competed on price. Taylorism and Fordism were some of the central ingredients in this development. The UK also followed this route, although less comprehensively (Smith, 1989). Other countries, most notably Germany and Italy, retained much of the craft form of work, and thus took the alternative path from the first divide. Choices made in the mid-nineteenth century shaped the economy of the US, and greatly influenced the nature of global competition for

179

the next hundred years. By the 1970s significant shifts in the nature of the global economy had begun to emerge. Consumer behaviour was becoming increasingly fragmented. This showed itself in two ways. First, consumers were becoming more *differentiated*, so that each customer, or small group of customers, wanted products tailor-made to their own tastes. Second, these tastes were becoming more subject to fashion changes, so that they might last only two or three years. This produced a crisis in mass markets, with a consequent effect on mass-production systems which had been created to serve these markets. This crisis constituted the second industrial divide, and the choice facing industrialists was whether to attempt to recreate stable mass markets on a global scale – 'multi-national Keynesianism' – or to develop new responses to fragmenting markets through 'flexible specialization'.

Although Piore and Sabel were careful to say that this was a genuine choice facing industrialists and that they could not predict its outcome, it was clear that what excited them were the possibilities for flexible specialization, and it was this that attracted later writers. *Flexible specialization* refers to production systems which handle a broad mix of products (goods or services), can move between them as market conditions dictate, and can change rapidly to new ones. In this way they can exploit opportunities when market 'niches' open up, change, and then close again. Flexible technologies are now available which suit these new requirements; in particular, computer-based systems which are capable of being rapidly reprogrammed offer the possibility of 'soft' automation to replace the 'hard' (i.e. dedicated, inflexible) automation of mass production. Flexible work organization would facilitate the workers' movement from one type of production to another, and draw upon their knowledge to aid change. Workers should have a broad range of skills as 'crafticians' (a cross between craft workers and technicians). Since competition is increasingly based on design and quality, rather than cost, the drive to cheapen labour through deskilling will be weakened. Organization structures must also be flexible to deal with the new environment and its demands. Decentralized decision-making in small enterprises, or in more autonomous units of larger enterprises, needs to be directed as much towards cooperation with other units and enterprises as towards competition with them, since each occupies a separate market niche. Piore and Sabel concluded that some countries, most notably Germany and Japan, were well placed to pursue this route. The US, on the other hand, might have become so committed to the former path that its enterprises were no longer able to change direction.

The flexible firm

The discussion of flexibility in the UK has been more narrowly focused, and has generally concentrated on new patterns of employment. Atkinson (1984) identified three forms of flexibility which were pursued by UK firms in the 1980s. *Functional flexibility* involves moving 'multi-skilled' workers between tasks (and even occupations) in response to production changes; *numerical flexibility* is aimed at increasing and reducing the organization's 'head count' (i.e. the number of people employed) rapidly in response to market demand; and *financial flexibility* promotes the altering of pay levels to react more quickly to changes in supply and demand in product and labour markets, and facilitates numerical and functional flexibility. The ways in which enterprises were implementing these three forms of flexibility resulted in a new employment model – 'the flexible firm' (1984: 29). This model consists of a core group of employees, surrounded by several other categories of workers who are becoming increasingly distant from the central activities of the firm and who constitute its periphery (see Box 6.10).

> Workers in the core group are full-time permanent career employees: say, managers, designers, technical sales staff, quality control staff, technicians and craftsmen. Their employment security is won at the cost of accepting functional flexibility both in the short term (involving cross-trade working, reduced demarcation, and multi-discipline project teams) as well as in the longer term (changing career and retraining) . . . the central characteristic of this group is that their skills cannot readily be bought-in. The firm is therefore seeking to separate them from a wider labour market'.
>
> (Atkinson, 1984: 29)

For those outside this group, who do not have 'firm-specific' skills (i.e. those particular to the enterprise's core activities) there are a number of different employment practices. Some are unskilled workers employed on short term, part time, or casual contracts. Others have general, marketable skills and are employed on a freelance, fee-paid basis. Where enterprises are seeking flexibility by sub-contracting some of their production, or are buying-in components (outsourcing) rather than manufacturing these themselves, we find workers moving outside the enterprise to employment with the agencies.

This view of the flexible firm had strong links with Child's (1985a) discussion of management strategy. Polyvalence might be applied to those employees at the core; the strategies of degradation and contracting would push more workers to the periphery; and elimination would remove them completely. There were also echoes of Edwards's (1979) discussion of segmented labour markets in the US, and if enterprises did pursue this route to flexibility we might expect it to deepen social divisions, including those of race and gender, between the relatively protected core and the more turbulent periphery.

Discussions of flexible specialization and the flexible firm suggest a diversity of practices in managing change which affect different kinds of work, and different kinds of worker, in differing ways. In place of emphasis on control as the central managerial issue, the buzz word of the 1980s and 1990s was 'flexibility' in a rapidly changing world. This was seen as a result of the decline of mass markets and the consequent pressure on mass production. As the bandwagon gained pace, and more people jumped aboard, the world of the end of the twentieth century was heralded as a new era of 'post-Fordism'.

Box 6.10

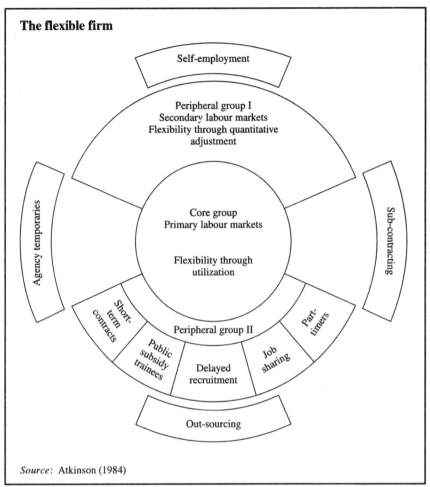

The flexible firm

Self-employment

Peripheral group I
Secondary labour markets
Flexibility through quantitative
adjustment

Core group
Primary labour markets

Flexibility through
utilization

Agency temporaries

Sub-contracting

Short-term contracts

Public subsidy trainees

Peripheral group II

Delayed recruitment

Job sharing

Part-timers

Out-sourcing

Source: Atkinson (1984)

The myth of flexibility?

As ever with such broad generalizations, some caution is needed with the theory of post-Fordism. Piore and Sabel had not argued that the development of flexible specialization was inevitable, nor that all enterprises, or all nations, would pursue it. In their various writings on the subject they tended to produce vague and shifting definitions of what the changes actually amounted to (Smith, 1989). We find modest claims for the emergence of 'neo-Fordism' and 'flexible assembly lines' (Sabel, 1982: 209, 211) alongside much more ambitious claims that there may be a shift from Fordist production to new 'high-technology cottage industry' (Sabel, 1982: 220) with echoes of organizational forms antedating the Industrial Revolution. The evidence for the more ambitious view was very sketchy and seemed to depend heavily upon particular organizational examples – such as firms in the Emilia-Romagna and Tuscany regions of Italy, and the New York City garment district (Smith, 1989). Certainly the concept of flexibility was very much part of the language of managing change, but its significance is much less clear. Sir Adrian Cadbury, of the Cadbury-Schweppes food group, told French industrialists in 1982 that he expected

> people to adopt a more individual life-style in the years ahead and to be less ready to accept the offerings of the mass market. The problem for us as manufacturers will be to meet these individual needs without losing the advantages of long production runs.

> (Quoted in Smith, 1989: 213)

This would appear to support the assumption of market fragmentation, but the company was actually abandoning low-volume products, and promoting core brands through global advertising:

> For all Sir Adrian Cadbury's worry, Cadburys has been warmly embracing Fordism, reducing the number of products by over half in the last ten years and simultaneously internationalising their market.

> (Smith, 1989: 214)

Similarly, Shaiken *et al.* found little evidence of the emergence of 'crafticians' following the introduction of flexible technology. Their study of the impact of programmable technology in the US found instead that the changes taking place were making 'batch production work more like mass- than like craft-production' (1986: 181). What computer control offered management was the chance to extend assembly line practices, such as pacing of work and monitoring of performance, beyond mass production, since stand-alone machines could now be networked in integrated technology systems:

> The vision – however welcome – of a more broadly skilled work force emerging from work restructuring and the increased use of programmable technology holds more promise in theory than in practice in the US.

> (p. 182)

The narrower claims for the flexible firm have also been challenged. Evidence for the general development of a new employment model had not been well established, as was admitted later (Atkinson and Meager, 1986). Pollert's (1988) review of this evidence suggested that much of the change that had taken place – in part time employment, home working, freelancing, sub-contracting, and so on – could be explained by overall changes in employment patterns produced by shifts in the UK economy. The decline of manufacturing industry meant that a large number of full time, permanent jobs (occupied by men) disappeared. At the same time, growth in the service sector led to the employment of more women workers, a large proportion of whom were employed, as they traditionally had been, on part time contracts. This shift from full time to part time thus represents, not the adoption of a new employment model, but the redistribution of old practices. To the extent that a new form of thinking was involved, Pollert suggested (although tentatively), that it may have been a reflection of government policy – the Thatcher government creating the model, testing it out in the public sector, and then promoting its adoption in private enterprises.

These criticisms of the flexibility thesis raise questions about its direction and universality. They point to differences both between managerial words and actions, and in the processes which are producing change. All this may do little 'to upset or unseat those committed to the paradigm' (Smith, 1989: 218). The attractiveness of a theory may have little to do with its theoretical adequacy, and 'the term "flexibility" has become indelibly fixed as the solution to recession, heightened competition and uncertainty' (Pollert, 1988: 281). It may be wise to treat the grander claims of post-Fordism with scepticism; but behind the sweeping generalizations and rather simplistic theory there may well be an identification of major, if rather diverse, changes in contemporary production.

INTERNATIONAL COMPARISONS

Patterns of production differ widely and have changed significantly in this century. This makes it difficult to establish clear-cut similarities and differences between distinctive national developments. Even where apparently similar approaches to work have been adopted, differences in organizational and societal contexts may mean that the implementation of these approaches has been very different.

This can be found with what appears to be the most rigidly defined practice – Taylorism. Taylor himself, a notorious stickler for detail, frequently complained that his name was attached to a number of initiatives, even in the US, which he did not recognize as the true Taylor System. Littler (1982) pointed out important differences between the UK's adoption of Scientific Management – largely in the Depression years of the 1930s – and its US introduction in the growth years before the First World War. In the US it had been implemented by engineers under the banner of production efficiency and high wages; in the UK it had been introduced by accountants and aimed at cost reduction, labour shedding, and the breaking of work gang systems (especially the power of supervisors). The introduction of Scientific Management in the USSR, following the 1917 Revolution, was the centre of much political argument which was largely concerned with whether it was possible to construct a distinct Soviet form of production. The debate was resolved, following the intervention of Lenin, in favour of the approach adopted by Gastev (head of the Central Labour Institute), whose views were very similar to those of Taylor (Bailes, 1978; Sochor, 1981). Although Braverman (1974: 13) claimed that 'In practice, Soviet industrialization imitated the capitalist model . . . and the Soviet Union settled down to an organization of labour, differing only in detail from that of capitalist countries', it can be argued that its implementation in the USSR (in the context of an economy with a much less developed industrial system and fewer craft workers) did not generate a widespread deskilling of the work force. Again, although Fordism has undoubtedly been influential, its precise form may have varied in application. By the early 1920s even Ford had abandoned the English School, and the Sociology Department (renamed Personnel) had become less active. Other manufacturers, in attempts to emulate Ford's achievements, may have adopted a much misunderstood version of 'Fordism' (Williams *et al.*, 1992). In the UK, the introduction of a high, fixed daily wage was strongly resisted by a number of car companies, and their employers' federations, and piecework systems were continued up to the 1970s (Lewchuk, 1983).

The industrial psychology theories of human relations were greeted less enthusiastically in the UK than in the US (Rose, 1975), although Mayo himself was appointed as industrial adviser to the UK government after the Second World War. A number of companies in the UK and other European countries claimed an interest in the job enrichment schemes of Herzberg but how closely this rhetoric was related to actual practice is uncertain. In Scandinavia more wide-reaching production developments (such as those advocated by Emery and Thorsrud) have received much more attention (see Gyllenhammar, 1977, for a one-sided account of the changes introduced by the former president of Volvo). In the USSR the relaxation of the ban on (bourgeois) sociology following the death of Stalin led to the emergence of Soviet writings which drew on, and mirrored, US management texts in their emphasis on the social and psychological dimensions of work (Yanovitch, 1977), but, again, it is difficult to say how much of this was transmitted into actual management practice. There is certainly little evidence of it in Haraszti's (1977) detailed account of piecework in Hungary. All this suggests that it is difficult even to produce reliable descriptions of production practices in different societies, before we begin to analyse how and why they developed.

Enterprises in Germany

German enterprises differ from their UK and US counterparts in terms of patterns of both capital and management. Thus the control and organization of production are located in different social structures and processes. There are also different conditions created by the state. One of the most important of these is the co-determination system. As part of the reconstruction of German industry following the Second World War, legislation was enacted which required enterprises (first in the iron and steel industry, then more widely) to set up works councils and supervisory boards. These bodies enabled worker representatives to discuss and express their views on managements' strategic and operational intentions and practices. In addition, the Works Constitution Act placed restrictions on em- ployers' power to hire and fire workers. These developments led Lane (1988) to argue that industrial relations in Germany are 'predominantly cooperative', with managers seeking agreement both through works councils and in their dealings with industry-based unions.

Although Taylorist strategies have been implemented in some parts of German industry, they have not penetrated as deeply as in the UK and US; instead there remains a large pool of craft workers with high skill levels (Lane, 1988). Many of these are to be found in Germany's small and medium-sized specialist enterprises in the *Handwerk* (artisan) sector of the economy, which employed 20 per cent of West German workers in the 1970s. Craft workers are also employed in the larger mass-production enterprises, where in the 1970s they constituted 40 per cent of the manufacturing work force (Sorge and Maurice, 1990). Germany has developed an extensive vocational education and training infrastructure to support such skilled work, provided, at national level, by the federal government, and supplemented by enterprises' own schemes. Such craft workers constitute a core work force which have enjoyed highly skilled, relatively well paid, secure jobs – although economic difficulties following reunification are threatening this position. These workers exercise more discretion in their work than is usual in Britain, which results from management strategies emphasizing 'responsible autonomy' rather than 'direct control'. In implementing CNC machine-tool technology, managers have generally given responsibility for editing to machinists, thus enhancing their skills (Sorge *et al.*, 1983). Managerial responses to technical and market change in recent years have led to a reorganization of training to provide a range of skills enabling workers to be switched between products and processes. This may be seen as the creation of functional flexibility through the polyvalence of workers.

This rather rosy picture of employment practices in Germany can be exaggerated, and the evidence which Lane used to support her argument was strongest for indigenous male workers. Outside the skilled pool there were large numbers of women and immigrant/migrant workers who did not enjoy the same advantages. Nevertheless, German industry may be seen as having a more extensive commitment to a 'craft paradigm' than the UK and US. This was identified by Piore and Sabel as one of the key factors facilitating the development of flexible specialization in German enterprises.

These production patterns are the outcome of a number of influences in German economy and society. Having industrialized later than the UK, and with closer competitor countries than the US, the German economy developed in more specialized ways and tended to focus upon competing on quality in particular markets, rather than on cost competition across a full range of mass-production industries. Later industrialization may also be associated with the development of industry-based structures of unionism which contrast with the more complex pattern of the UK. In Britain unions have organized around recruitment from particular crafts, and from particular industries, and on the basis of general membership. In addition, white collar unions or sections have achieved separate negotiating rights. Whereas many UK managements bargain with a collection of unions, which often have conflicting interests, German employers typically deal with a single union. Since World War II statutory regulation of employment relationships has constrained managerial strategies aimed at labour shedding, whilst the education and training infrastructure has facilitated retraining to create 'versatile workers' (Piore and Sabel, 1984: 275). This has shaped the way German managers and workers have approached the adoption of new technology and responded to changing markets. Other influences have been the availability of long term capital from banks (guided by their own technological advisers) and a relatively high level of technical expertise among specialist managers.

Enterprises in Japan

The difficulty of international comparison is even more strongly demonstrated in studies of Japan. Most of the information available to Western observers concerns the large combines and core firms of industrial groupings. These constitute about 15 per cent of the Japanese work force and our knowledge of work in contractor and other smaller enterprises is sparse. Even within large enterprises, much of our knowledge is heavily influenced by the particular case of Toyota (Wood, 1991). This narrow empirical base is not remedied by studies of Japanese firms operating in the UK and US, since existing practices are selectively exported from Japan, new practices are created, and the societal contexts differ. Nevertheless some broad patterns may be identified.

Much discussion of production in Japanese enterprises emphasizes the lack of individual job demarcation (e.g. Kumazawa and Yamada, 1989; Storey, 1991; Wood, 1991). Here the notion of polyvalence seems broader than that applied to German production in that employees may be moved between a great variety of jobs and functions, and boundaries between different kinds of work – such as production/maintenance, or manual/non-manual – are blurred. The worker is generally seen as an employee of the enterprise rather than as a member of any specific occupation. The identification of workers with their enterprise is reinforced by a system of 'lifelong employment' in which moves between enterprises are discouraged. This is sometimes seen as a cradle-to-the-grave welfare employment strategy, but that is rather too simplistic a view. The strategy generally applies only to men, since women are expected to leave the enterprise on marriage. New recruits have to serve a period of probation before being accepted into the core work force, and after the age of fifty pressure is increasingly put on people to maintain productivity or take early retirement. The strategy may have been a particular feature of the decades following the Second World War when firms had a relatively youthful labour force and were expanding rapidly. More recently factors such as an aging work force, the adoption of labour-eliminating technology, and increased international competition may have put a strain on permanent employment practices. Nevertheless, the relative security of core workers in the large enterprises does seem to have facilitated flexible employment practices.

This is reinforced by two further factors. First the organization of labour in single, enterprise-based unions. Second, the emphasis on teamwork which developed from earlier systems of internal contract which were replaced in the

1910s and 1920s (Littler, 1982). Whilst Taylor's ideas were partially adopted in Japanese production (millions of translated copies of his work were sold) they were mainly applied to job analysis and the construction of standardized procedures, rather than as a means of breaking up work gangs and creating individual incentive payment schemes. The traditional work organization forms of gang bosses (*oyakata*) and their hired-out followers (*kokata*) were adapted to modern capitalist production. The skills of the work team were aligned with the interests of management through practices such as Quality Circles which:

> are a vehicle for systematically mining workers' knowledge and involvement in diagnosis and problem-solving in a way that directly contradicts the Taylorist dictum that workers are not paid to think.
>
> (Thompson, 1989: 222)

Although there are elements of Taylorism in the development of Japanese production systems, there are also elements of paternalistic management in attempts to bind employees in long term and broad-ranging relationships with the enterprise. With some over-simplification, we might characterize the life of a male permanent production worker in a large Japanese enterprise (let us call it XYZ) as: working in a team under a senior team leader assembling XYZ cars; living in an XYZ dormitory (if single) or apartment (if married); saving a high proportion of his earnings with the XYZ bank; insuring with the XYZ finance company; planning to buy an XYZ hi-fi system; and spending his evenings drinking beer produced by the XYZ brewery. The overall impression is a high degree of attachment to the enterprise, implying a kind of 'clan' loyalty.

This view of the clan has led some Western observers to portray the Japanese enterprise as a family (with the hidden assumption that families are happy). Kamata's (1982) fascinating, but stomach-churning, diary of his seven months on and around the Toyota assembly lines in the early 1970s conveyed a very different picture. His feelings about the experience can be gauged from the original Japanese title of his book, which translates as 'Toyota: Factory of Despair' (but was changed for publication in the US market). For Kamata, Toyota was an arena of intense work pressure, injury and death, union corruption, management domination, and worker subservience. When he returned to the plant at the end of the 1970s the only change he noted was that the assembly lines had been speeded up and the pace of work was even faster. He remained astonished that such a production system not only survived but appeared to be accepted as normal by Toyota workers.

This last point should remind us of the problem of inter-societal comparisons. The technology and production operations of the Toyota plant were familiar enough to Western observers and the kind of work Kamata described was reminiscent of that reported in UK (e.g. Beynon, 1973) and US (e.g. Chinoy, 1955) car assembly. However, the meaning it has for workers in other societies may be different, and explanations typically draw on 'cultural' characteristics to account for this. Despite any such cultural differences, many Western management writers have sought to identify particular Japanese management practices and examine the prospects of importing them into UK and US enterprises (Pascale and Athos, 1981; Voss and Robinson, 1987; Lubben, 1988; Oliver and Wilkinson, 1987; Gilbert, 1989; Im and Lee, 1989; Inman and Mehra, 1990; Cobb, 1991; Zipkin, 1991). The most important of these practices are the 'just in time' (JIT) and *kaizen* (continual improvement) systems, which seem to have developed at Toyota in the 1950s and 1960s and then spread, perhaps in modified form, to other Japanese enterprises.

JIT relies upon components being 'pulled' into production when they are required, rather than stocks of materials being 'pushed' through the plant. For example, minimal levels of components are maintained in assembly areas and when they run low a plate or card (*kanban*) is sent back down the line to manufacturing sections, where it acts as an instruction for a batch delivery. This prompts the manufacture of a further batch of components. Hence stocks are kept low and delivery is just in time to be used in assembly. Such a system depends on smooth operation to ensure that parts are reliable, since there are no alternative parts available to substitute for faulty deliveries. Hence emphasis is placed on: Total Quality Control (TQC), with the development of Quality Circles drawn from work teams, the planning of maintenance to achieve Total Preventative Maintenance (TPM), and the use of calculative techniques such as Statistical Process Control (SPC). Perhaps the most spectacular of the practices is *jidoka*, where assembly lines are stopped when a faulty component is discovered and the attention of production managers and workers is focused on identifying and solving the problem before production restarts.

The *kaizen* system of continual improvement, which appears to have been imported from the US by an American management consultant, Deming (Hodgson, 1987), is aimed not only at achieving levels of quality that can maintain this type of production system, but also at systematic cost reduction so that, for example, Sony requires its supply companies to reduce component prices by 10 per cent for each year of product life, and then reduces the number of components in its three-yearly redesign of television chassis (Williams *et al.*, 1991). In this way costs are markedly reduced in the design phase of the product cycle and continue to shrink during production. This cost reduction drive is extended through the supply chains into the contractor and sub-contractor firms, who are also required to provide JIT delivery.

These production systems depend upon a versatile labour force which can be switched rapidly in the short term, and can cope with step-changes in the medium term. Kumazawa and Yamada (1989: 8) argued that the 'most consistent feature of so-called Japanese-style management lies in its enormously flexible structure in which a large-scale enterprise deploys and redeploys its manpower resources', and Piore and Sabel (1984) concluded that Japan was very well placed to take the path of flexible specialization.

Comparisons with the UK and US

The development of production in Germany and Japan shows some broad contrasts with the UK and US. In Germany the spread of mass production has been less extensive, and in Japan there has been more emphasis on flexible arrangements within mass-production industries. The notion of polyvalence of labour seems more applicable in relation to the retraining of workers (Germany) and versatile employees (Japan). Taylorism and Fordism, although they have been influential in these countries, have not been central management control strategies in employment relations. In the last two decades there has been less overt conflict in industrial relations, and managers have concentrated more on increasing competitiveness through technological innovation (especially in Germany) and on quality-led production improvements (especially in Japan). Such differences may be related to historical and cultural differences such as the persistence of a 'craft paradigm' in Germany, and the moulding of a 'clan identity' in Japanese enterprises.

Such contrasts may easily be exaggerated and misinterpreted. Polyvalence need not necessarily mean 'multi-skilled' and may apply only to a particular section of the work force. As Nichols pointed out, many 'German employers have found themselves a vulnerable and disadvantaged work force' (1986: 120) from the ranks of migrant workers. Its conditions of work may be judged from accident rates in the car industry, where 'in West German press shops over ten times as many arms, legs, hands, and feet were amputated as in Britain' (1986: 119). Similarly, the competitive advantages gained by the core Japanese enterprises may rest upon 'an underworld of tens of thousands of small suppliers' (1986: 112) which have the conditions of sweatshops. Even in the advantaged core areas, where we find indigenous male workers, the patterns which have developed since World War II may now be under challenge as Germany seeks to deal with the industrial and economic consequences of reunification, and Japan with increasing competition from other South East Asian economies.

THE DEBATE ON PRODUCTION

Much of the early writing on production was aimed at identifying and/or prescribing its form, focusing on one determining factor. This factor was variously identified as technology (Blauner), the maximization of efficiency (as in Taylorism and Fordism), the psychology of human nature (Mayo, Herzberg) or participation (Emery and Thorsrud), or the drive for control over labour (Braverman). In the last decade or so the debate has become much more fragmented. This has occurred as researchers have identified a number of different production practices which relate to differences in managerial intentions and actions, and in worker subjectivities and reactions. Hence practices are seen as the outcome of struggles within management and labour and between them. These struggles takes place in the context of different markets – for capital, labour, and products – which present different and varying opportunities and constraints. All this is located within different societal contexts and is influenced by (among other things) the role of the state, educational and legal institutions, and the organization of capital and labour. More broadly, production practices reflect class formations in different societies; their racial and gender patterns; and the nature and treatment of their immigrant populations. Patterns of production reflect different societal histories, such as the timing of industrialization – early (e.g. UK), middle (e.g. Scandinavia) or late (e.g. Korea) – and the existing economic, political, legal, social and cultural structures of the industrializing country.

All this produces a complex, perhaps chaotic, picture of enterprises where it is impossible to specify any one best way of organizing the production of goods and services. The outcome may be a disabling confusion of ideas, made more perplexing by the rapidity of change. However, there are two emerging strands in the debate which may provide a means of reformulating theories of production. The first is the notion of *globalization*. This points to the way increasing international competition may create greater similarities between countries through the spread of particular technologies and management practices. The process is facilitated by the development of multinational corporations operating in world markets. Until the 1970s this was largely a phenomenon associated with giant US corporations, but the rise of joint ventures between Japanese and US/European companies may lead to the development of global enterprises, creating a new international division of labour. The second strand is *strategy*. This suggests that enterprises are not simply buffeted about by external conditions, nor are production systems the outcome of the interplay of innumerable factors. Instead, capitalist enterprises are seen as having purposes relating to capital accumulation which are interpreted, mediated, and pursued by executives and managers. Whatever the complexity of the issues involved, people do choose particular paths to follow and, in doing so, shape and reshape systems of production.

REVIEW

Short questions

What is meant by 'the division of labour'? How did Blauner define 'technology' and what model did he present of the stages of its development in production? What did he mean by 'alienation' and how did he see technology influencing it? What predictions did Blauner make about the future development of technology and its influence on workers in more automated industries? What problems did Taylor identify in late nineteenth century industry and how did he propose they should be tackled? What were the key engineering and management factors in Ford's development of assembly line production in his Highland Park plant? What are the similarities and differences in Taylorist and Fordist production? In what ways did Human Relations and Neo-Human Relations writers attack the 'efficiency' approaches of Taylor and Ford? What new kinds of job design practices did they advocate?

What distinction is made between 'labour power' and 'labour'? What does Braverman identify as the key management practice of the twentieth century? What was its impact on workers? What criticisms have been made of Braverman's use of the term 'skill'? What different forms of 'control' have been identified? How does an emphasis on 'consent' inform the debate? What is meant by 'subjectivity' and what is its significance? How does Edwards explain the stages of control and their effect on labour markets? Why did Bosquet think that managers were forced to abandon Taylorism? How did Storey see the 'frontier of control' in the 1970s? What two features of 'the employer offensive' are identified by Hyman and Elger? What alternative to confrontational industrial relations did other writers identify?

What social choices emerge from studies of the adoption and use of NC machines? What impacts have been identified in the introduction of computer technologies into offices? What management strategies does Child find in technological innovation? Why do Rose and Jones disagree with this? What key features of job redesign are noted by Kelly? What do Piore and Sabel mean by 'flexible specialization' and why do they think it was becoming increasingly important in the 1980s? What changes in employment are suggested by Atkinson's 'flexible firm' model? Why do some argue that flexibility is a myth? What key differences in production have been identified in German and Japanese enterprises?

Discussion points

Are different forms of production the result of different management strategies? Are manufacturing enterprises undergoing a transformation at the end of the twentieth century which is as profound as the rise of the factory system (at the end of the eighteenth) and the modern corporation (at the end of the nineteenth)?

7

ACCOUNTING AND THE LABOUR PROCESS

Accounting has a widespread influence on production in UK and US enterprises through costing systems, budgeting, variance analysis, investment appraisal, and other techniques. This chapter is concerned with the relationship between theories of work/workers and management accounting; and with claims that the emergence of a new manufacturing environment in the 1990s requires fundamental change to existing practices.

ACCOUNTING AND LABOUR

Until recently there have been few studies of the relationship between accounting and work/workers even though labour is a central component of both *cost accounting* (now usually narrowly defined as stock valuation for external reporting purposes) and *management accounting* (concerned with information for management decisions and control). Labour is often treated as a commodity used in production, differing only in degree from other commodities. For example, whereas for materials there may be a lengthy time lag from acquisition to sales revenue,

> In the case of labour there is normally a much shorter time lag from the time of payment for this resource until reimbursement of the sales revenue, and replacement cost and acquisition cost of labour are likely to be the same.
>
> (Drury, 1992: 58)

However, there is a qualitative difference between labour and other factors of production. What is purchased is not labour but labour power (the potential to work) and this cannot be separated from its suppliers. Whereas materials may be passive elements in production, labour is an active force in production, and accounting systems have developed in response to this.

193

Accounting, efficiency and Scientific Management

The rise of standard costing

Most authors draw strong connections between Scientific Management and the development of cost accounting in the twentieth century (Miller and O'Leary, 1987; Hopper and Armstrong, 1991). Before Taylor, job times were often based on historical data – the performance traditionally achieved – and in some cases on actual measurement of the work done. Taylor's contribution was to extend such measurements through work study. In some cases he constructed new ways of working by combining the fastest elements from different workers into a new task. In others, he simplified tasks so that each worker performed a restricted range of operations. His evangelistic publicizing of his approach gained widespread, though not universal, popularity among managers in the US, and later in the UK and other European countries. The notion that management could accurately determine the amount of labour time which would be required to complete each element of work was boosted by the work of Ford's engineers in the Highland Park plant who designed fragmented assembly tasks to fit the rhythm of the line – the pacing of work through technology.

Whether from records of previous performance, through study of current practices, or by specification of newly designed tasks, the outcome was the setting of *standard times*. Developments since these early approaches have refined work study so that every physical movement involved in the making of a product (and also in many office activities) has been identified and measured to fractions of a second. Elements of work have been minutely categorized into a taxonomy of human motion – such as 'reach', 'grasp', 'move', 'position', 'release'. Each of these elements is timed and then summed to produce the standard task time (see Box 7.1). The creation of such detailed classifications has made the development of synthetic times possible, so that work study practitioners may no longer time actual working practices but will look up the appropriate allowances in 'tables of value'.

The construction of standard times became the basis for the creation of *standard costs* by linking workers' wages to the achievement of standard performance. In some cases this was based on a direct piece-rate system in which the worker was paid a fixed amount for each completed unit of work at a rate determined by the standard time. Taylor was opposed to such systems on the grounds that they allowed workers partial control over the amount of production – they could set a target for wages and then produce only the quantity required to reach that level. Managers were likely to react by cutting the piece rate in order to force workers to produce more. Such practices were deplored by Taylor as arbitrary and unscientific. He proposed instead a 'differential piece-rate system' where managers would determine (scientifically) the precise quantity of work to be done and then pay a fixed ('fair') wage to those who completed it. The operation of this pay system was shown most clearly in his work on lathe

Box 7.1

Work measurement

Examples of elemental motion in the Methods–Time Measurement system:

Reach. There are five kinds of Reach. *Reach A* is where the hand moves to a fixed location. This is analysed in terms of the hand's acceleration, constant velocity, and deceleration stages. The standard time for a *Reach A* of five inches is 6.5 tmu* and for ten inches, 8.7 tmu.

Move. When the hand travels carrying an object this is a Move. There are three kinds of Move. *Move B* is where the hand takes the object to an approximate location. Allowance has to be made for the weight of the object as well as the distance travelled. The basic time for a five-inch *Move B* is 8.0 tmu when the object weighs up to 2.5 lb (or 1 kg). Heavier objects require the time to be scaled up by using a multiplication factor and the addition of a constant time increment to take account of the dynamic and static components of *Move B*.

Tables of value. Times for all the MTM elemental motions are available in Tables of Value.

* tmu = time measurement unit = 0.00001 hour = approximately one-thirtieth of a second.

Source: simplified from Whitmore (1987)

---

operators (see Box 7.2). Only those producing the 'correct' number of pieces would achieve the 'fair' rate of $3.50 per day.

In this respect, Taylor's system was similar to Ford's later '$5 Day' policy, where workers received this wage only if they carried out all their tasks in the time allowed. In another respect, Taylor's approach differed. Ford was continually pushing to increase production – most notably by speeding up the line. Such was Taylor's commitment to the notion of scientific study that he argued that the amount of production determined for a day's work could not, or ought not to, be exceeded – this would be injurious to the health of workers and the short term benefits would be offset by a longer term fall in production. When he discovered that after six months of the operation of his system at Bethlehem Steel production had exceeded targets by 0.5 per cent, he concluded that his original analysis had been slightly flawed and resolved to pursue greater precision. It seems unlikely that many managers, however much they were attracted by the notion of a science of work, would have shared Taylor's concern about overproduction.

Whether through true piece rates, fixed time-wage rates, or continually tightening time-wage rates, the development of work study provided the basis for

Box 7.2

Taylor's differential rate of piecework

This case concerns the production of steel forgings in Midvale Steelworks in 1884. Before Taylor's intervention production was four or five units per worker per day at 50 cents a piece. Taylor claimed that it was possible to turn out ten pieces per day and installed a payment system which paid 35 cents per piece when this target was achieved (but only 25 cents before that).

No. of forgings	Price per forging (cents)	Daily wage ($)
Production before Taylor		
4	50	2.00
5	50	2.50
Production under the Taylor system		
5	25	1.25
6	25	1.50
7	25	1.75
8	25	2.00
9	25	2.25
10	35	3.50

Source: adapted from Taylor (1911)

---

constructing *standard labour costs* per unit of production. Once these were added to *standard material costs* – 'based on product specifications derived from an intensive study of the input of quantity necessary for each operation' (Drury, 1992: 512) – two of the basic elements of standard product cost were in place. The third element – *overhead standards* – was also influenced by Scientific Management. Taylor's dictum that all possible brainwork should be removed from the shop-floor and located in the office created a new division of manual and mental labour, and those companies adopting his practices experienced greater direct labour productivity, but also a massive growth in indirect 'white-collar' over-head. The drawing of clear distinctions between operators and maintenance workers also narrowed the category of direct labour. Thus a central component of cost accounting – the identification of direct and indirect labour costs – can be seen to be influenced by the particular form of the social organization of labour.

The operation of standard costing systems

Scientific Management and standard costing spread in US, and later in UK, enterprises. Such systems are seen as powerful tools in the achievement of productive efficiency. Comparisons of actual performance with standard are provided through *labour efficiency variances*. In conventional textbook treatments such variances are held to derive from particular departures from production norms. For example,

> the use of inferior quality materials, different grades of labour, failure to maintain machinery in proper condition, the introduction of new equipment or tools and changes in the production process . . . poor production scheduling by the planning department, or a change in quality control standards.
>
> (Drury, 1992: 522)

Social analysis of the practices of Scientific Management suggests that the difficulties are much deeper and more systematic than this.

The original measurements are by no means as certain as the 'scientific' tag is meant to imply. Work study practitioners are aware that workers may alter their pace when they are being observed. They deal with this through the technique of 'rating'. The observer, having taken detailed timings to the nearest thirtieth of a second, scales them down (or up) to reflect whether the worker is thought to have been working more slowly (or faster) than normal. The official textbook of the Institute of Management Services (formerly the Institute of Practitioners in Work Study, Organisation and Methods) advised its students that:

> Rating is a purely subjective assessment of the rate of working . . . and the observer can expect no assistance from any form of instrument when making his judgment . . . the observer must compare the performance of the worker in carrying out each element of the job with a preconceived mental standard. Thus the basic time determined through the application of this factor is dependent upon the competence of the observer to perform this comparison, and on his ability to retain the mental image of the standard pace.
>
> (Whitmore, 1987: 48)

Quite apart from prompting scepticism about whether this process of mental imaging can sit comfortably with claims to scientific accuracy, it raises questions about the skill of work study practitioners in observing a wide range of different work – especially where that work is highly skilled. In one case I know, craft operators in an engineering factory urged management to set a time of thirty-three hours for one complex machining operation. When the allowed time was set at thirty hours by the work study department, I asked a worker representative whether he was disappointed. 'Not really. It actually only takes three hours!' Taylor's early work had promulgated a myth of the science of work, but the apparent accuracy of his predictions of output was probably the result of his power to direct the activities of labour – overcoming resistance to his system by dismissing unco-operative workers. As his methods spread, the adopting enterprises had to deal with the growing power of organized labour. In the US, Taylorites in the rapidly expanding economy of the 1910s were able to persuade workers that they would benefit from the introduction of Scientific Management through increased wages brought about by improved efficiency. In 1925 relations were sufficiently harmonious for a speaker from the Taylor Society to be given the opportunity of addressing the annual conference of the federation of US unions. In the UK, on the other hand, Taylorist practices were introduced in the Great Depression of the 1930s as a cost-cutting, labour-reducing policy and were greeted with considerable resentment both by workers and by their supervisors/ gang bosses (Littler, 1982). In both societies the existence of organized labour meant that, to varying degrees, time-wage rates were open to negotiation and struggle. Management was not always in a position to impose its 'scientific' timings on workers. Indeed, in the UK the rise of the shop steward movement (of non-official, volunteer union representatives) was closely associated with regular (monthly, weekly, even daily) confrontations with work study departments over job timings.

Standard times became subject to dispute and negotiation rather than the strict accuracy of the stopwatch coupled with the dubious subjectivity of 'rating'. This is reflected in standard times through the addition of 'allowances' to the basic, elemental times of the individual motions. There are two especially interesting allowances. The first is for 'biological needs [which] must invariably be satisfied, as a consequence of which all workers are awarded an allowance for "personal needs"' (Whitmore, 1987: 287). In addition, longer times to compensate for fatigue or especially dirty work are permitted. The measurement of such personal time is clearly difficult but work study practitioners are advised that it should be 'adequate'. The second kind of allowance is more certainly beyond the science of work study. Whitmore warned apprentice practitioners that their results would 'almost certainly be challenged' (p. 39) and that there would be pressure to compromise the basic times. On this he was insistent, 'Work study must guard against attempts to adulterate the time values for the purposes of appeasement' (p. 39). But, as he recognized, this might lead to deadlock between managers and workers and pressure for compromise. The solution adopted was ingenious. The pretence of scientific accuracy is maintained by refusing to change the basic times but permitting the award of an additional 'policy allowance' at managerial discretion which will resolve the political problems. The application of these devices – together with a bonus allowance (for 'motivation'), unoccupied time allowance, learner allowance, change-over allowance, and – as a final resort – contingency allowance means that the final standard time is a long way from the so-precisely measured elemental motions which are then altered by a 'purely subjective' rating factor. Standard times are not an objective statement of the length of normal human effort required to produce a unit of work; they are socially constructed expectations and are influenced by the changing balance of power between management and labour.

Once they have been established, there are also problems in implementing the standards. Though Taylor was able to punish non-compliance with dismissal, managers faced with organized labour, especially in tight labour markets, have found this more difficult (Friedman, 1977). Even in Ford's non-unionized Highland Park workers reacted to the line-pacing of work with 'skippies' – not fitting parts to one car in every so many (Gartman, 1979) – and non-compliance was still a problem in the company's Liverpool plant in the 1960s (Beynon, 1973). Ultimately both 'scientific' and 'technical' control are dependent upon managers having broader power over workers (Linhart, 1981). In the UK, car manufacturers (or their employers' federations) were uncertain about their ability to achieve such general power and most rejected the fixed wage policy of Ford until the end of the 1960s, preferring instead a traditional piece-rate system (Lewchuk, 1983). In the US, Roy (1952, 1953, 1955, 1959) detailed ways in which operators in a batch engineering factory resisted the standardized working which management attempted to impose. They took it easy on jobs where the timings were tight ('goldbricking') because they knew they would be unable to achieve the necessary rate. Where timings were loose they limited the amount they produced ('quota restriction') – fearing that management would change the rates – or built up 'kitties' of unreported work so they could work slower later. In these ways they attempted to control their pay and the rhythm of work.

Relations between managers and workers under Scientific Management are not always antagonistic. When Burawoy (1979) re-studied Roy's factory some thirty years later, many of the work study practices were essentially the same. But broader changes in employment relations meant that their impact was quite different. The operation of an internal labour market meant that workers who had some seniority could bid for jobs that were advertised within the company. Thus they could escape overbearing supervisors and piece-rate tasks on which it was difficult to make a good wage. This weakened the conflict with managers over job timings and, by playing the game of 'making out' against the rates, workers came to consent to the system.

Thus the creation and implementation of standard times are far more problematic than is suggested by the identification of exceptional departures from production norms. Standard times and costs are the numerical expression of expectations of output which depend upon relations between managers and workers which are affected by social factors – the state of the labour market, the organization of labour, the practices of management, and the responses of unions. Standard costing reflects the tensions endemic in the Taylorist and Fordist production systems which it measures and reports.

Accounting and Human Relations

By the 1970s many writers were identifying a reaction against Scientific Management. It might be expected that the adoption of industrial psychology approaches would have an important impact on accounting systems. The logical grounds for this expectation are strong. The basis of standard times was the performance of individual workers, whereas some industrial psychologists stressed group working and worker participation in determining working practices. Here it would be impossible to trace costs to individual elements of production – they would be invisible within the work group. In many cases this would mean that direct labour costs could not be assigned to particular products or processes. The job enrichment approach required job redesign where production tasks were supplemented by maintenance, quality control, self-supervising, and recording activities previously carried out by non-productive employees. This would imply a significant redrawing of the boundaries between direct and indirect labour. If the 1970s was a period of 'de-Taylorization' then changes in standard costing systems might have reflected this. In practice, however, there was little indication of such a shift. Although accounting textbooks occasionally made vague references to a need for workers to be motivated and suggested that there was more to this than pay incentives, motivation was not treated as a basis for redesigning accounting systems. Similarly there was little sign of new approaches in research studies.

One exception was Malmberg's (1980) study of the impact of job reform on accounting systems in a Swedish company. Production was organized into nine work groups and accountants responded by designing a new accounting system. Once the price of the product was established it was apportioned to each group. If they could produce more efficiently than calculated the group would register a 'profit', and each group was treated as a 'profit centre' which would 'buy' and 'sell' to other groups as internal 'customers' and 'suppliers'. Profit could be made by beating material standards (less waste) or labour standards (less time). Financial reports on each of the groups were produced eight times a year. These were discussed at meetings of the nine group supervisors with finance and production department personnel. The supervisors communicated the outcome of this discussion to their groups. Malmberg's discussion of the benefits of this system focused on psychological aspects, where 'Greater responsibility and his participation in decisions and plans for his working group, provide a worker with some positive motivation and increase his satisfaction at work' (1980: 86). With a rather different emphasis, one of the supervisors was quoted as stressing increased worker knowledge of the accounting system, and thus 'correct' handling of documents, as a key outcome. He saw the regular accounting reports as important since the 'workers know that these figures are financial realities' (p. 86).

This suggests that whatever the claimed increase in psychological satisfaction (no evidence was given) there were other significant changes in the impact of the accounting monitoring and control system. The so-called 'financial realities' were constructed from comparisons of actual performance with a pre-calculated standard manufacturing cost which included materials and labour (over which workers had some control) and a number of overhead items (over which they did not). The application of terms such as 'profit centre', 'customer', 'supplier' to work groups was an extension of similar usage for divisions and departments and the notion of 'autonomous work groups' was translated into 'autonomous companies'. The outcome was that 'many more workers became conscious of, and involved in, the ways in which their own work influenced the financial results'

(p. 81). It appears that the new accounting system was implicated in attempts to change workers' conception of themselves from producers of products to producers of profit. Just as Ford's English School had attempted to shape workers to production, here the accounting system was directed at reconstructing work groups as financial entities. Instead of variance analysis being used by managers as a means of monitoring and controlling the performance of workers against standards, workers themselves were encouraged to devise ways of beating standards for the reward of a symbolic 'profit'. Although Malmberg used the Human Relations concept of 'motivation', the case might more appropriately be viewed using labour process concepts of 'control' and 'consent'.

Accounting, control and consent

Control

An early accounting study using a labour process approach was that of the UK National Coal Board (Berry et al., 1985b; Hopper et al., 1987). This adopted Edwards's (1979) scheme of simple, technical, and bureaucratic control. The *simple* (direct) supervision of miners underground had always been difficult, for physical reasons and because of worker resistance, and the information available to (above-ground) managers was inadequate or unsatisfactory for control through instructions and disciplinary procedures. Management had traditionally relied upon *bureaucratic* control in the form of wage payment systems. But again there were difficulties here, and the standard costing system introduced in the 1950s was abandoned as a failure which, according to the 1958 NCB Annual Report, resulted from lack of accurate data on production. By the early 1980s management hoped it might be able to resolve some of its difficulties through *technical* control with the introduction of a computerized Mine Operating System (MINOS). This extensive computer network linked face-cutting machines and conveyors underground to a management information system on the surface. Hopper et al. regarded such expectations as optimistic, since data were channelled through control rooms where they were interpreted and presented as information, and many of the control room operators were active trade unionists. The control room itself became a site of struggle and resistance to management control. Thus the forms of control which Edwards had found to be important in US manufacturing industry were problematic in mining, and a mix of them was used. Miners' role in the construction and communication of information caused managerial difficulties, and miners' detailed knowledge of coal-getting meant they were able to resist management's monitoring and control with counter-arguments.

In this context the NCB began to develop increasing reliance on *financial control*. In the 1980s, the intervention of accounting into the management of the NCB began at the highest levels and then filtered down to area management (see Chapter 5). At the top financial information dominated, but at area level physical factors of geology, machinery, and mine layout were seen as more important, and information on these was carefully scrutinized in the belief that 'If you get production right, then finance falls into place [and] finance and accounting must not get in the way of managing' (Hopper *et al.*, 1987: 120). Although the financial targets were discussed at area level this appears to have been a rather ritualistic procedure. Accountants were centrally located at headquarters whilst collieries had only accounting clerks. This situation was characterized as 'loose coupling', since different parts of the control system were relatively detached from each other. The effects were: different managerial issues (such as geological, technical, market, and financial uncertainties) were kept separate; bad news in one sector did not lower morale elsewhere; and ambiguity quietened some intra-managerial conflict. The powerful mining engineers in middle management, who were antagonistic to emphasis on finance and markets, were kept away from discussion of these issues. Hence decisions about the future of the industry could be taken without arousing their opposition.

The accounting system did, however, have a broader impact: 'Although miners and most mining engineers and general managers in the NCB tended to avoid using financial information, they had internalized the logic that profit and loss were the absolute measures of performance – the bottom line' (Hopper *et al.*, 1987: 126). Thus when headquarters deemed twenty pits to be 'uneconomic', the accounting numbers, which had previously been ignored at colliery level, were accepted as an expression of the essential purpose of mining – profitability. Although the precise specification of profit and loss was contestable (see Box 5.3), it was not contested by miners or mining engineers. At the coal-face and in control rooms miners had resisted controls based on physical information and had been relatively successful in maintaining their independence. Financial control, using accounting information, presented a different challenge. This did not prevent the subsequent strike of 1984–85, but the apparent certainty of the accounting information caused considerable difficulty for miners in presenting their case.

Compliance, consent and the accounting subject

Adopting a rather different approach, Knights and Collinson (1987) put even greater emphasis on the ideological power of accounting. Their study of a UK heavy vehicle manufacturer in the early 1980s contrasted two forms of management communication with workers. The company had been taken over by a US multinational in 1972, and from 1978 onwards workers received a glossy in-house magazine which promised them they would be fully informed about corporate developments and there would be an informal style of cooperation between managers and workers, who would be on first name terms. All this would improve productivity and increase wages. This Human Relations approach was dismissed by the workers as a 'load of Yankee hypnosis' and, rather than being persuaded, they felt insulted by such an obvious attempt to manipulate their thinking.

In contrast with this psychological approach the use of accounting information was more effective – from a managerial viewpoint. In what might be seen as *soft accounting*, a 1979 edition of the magazine published 'a plain man's guide' to the company's finances. This contained a financial report (simplified and illustrated) which conveyed the message that wages and salaries constituted the second largest cost to the company (after payments to suppliers) whilst obscuring the profits made by shareholders. This information was accompanied by an editorial which stressed the difficult market conditions which the company faced, and implied a need for wage restraint. This message was quite different from the earlier (Human Relations) optimism and was presented to workers at the time of the annual round of wage negotiations. The message of warning in the magazine was soon fulfilled. In 1981 the work force was required to accept short-time working and a redundancy programme affecting 40 per cent of their jobs. In 1982 the US parent announced that it intended to sell the company, and in 1983 a 'feasibility study' was presented to union representatives which proposed further cuts, including the closure of one division. Here *hard accounting* was important. A 'financial audit' was presented in conventional format, with no explanatory commentary or graphics, which led to the conclusion that 'we have no alternative but to close [the division]'. Faced with these accounts – the bottom line – the work force did not resist, despite their deep distrust of management, and in a short time they were unemployed.

Knights and Collinson offered a number of explanations of why workers who had rejected the information of the Human Relations approach nevertheless accepted the financial audit. At one level the sheer technicality of accounting was crucial – workers and their representatives lacked the knowledge and skills required to challenge the company's accounts. But this was reinforced by deeper factors. First, the bad news of the audit confirmed workers' own experience of poor performance – indeed they had often complained bitterly about managerial incompetence and inefficiency. Second, 'the hard, impersonal and fixed character of mathematical representations [coincided] with the shopfloor's respect for the practical and straightforward world of production' (1987: 466). Third, the redundancy payments offered workers short term financial independence and the chance of escape from their dependence on management. The authors chose to interpret these explanations in terms of a 'macho' shopfloor culture. The men rejected the 'femininity' of Human Relations and its caring, sharing style. But the hard, practical, tough expression of managerial power through the clear-cut assertions of accounting corresponded with their own conceptions of working class masculinity. Thus there was a cultural respect for accounting which made it impossible to resist its message.

Whatever the merits of this particular interpretation, the study did highlight the role of accounting in attempts to shape the thinking of workers. In my own study of six large enterprises in 1979–80, this role was clearly recognized by accountants. In discussing Employee Accounting finance managers stressed its use in attempting to overcome resistance. 'If people don't understand what you're trying to do they may resist with a certain amount of teeth', 'They've got to be properly briefed', and 'It's an attempt to confront trade union pressure . . . it gives [management] a chance to talk to the individual . . . in a way it's a propaganda exercise' (Jones, 1990: 282–3). Whether such exercises are successful is less clear. Although managers may seek to persuade workers using hard accounting 'facts', workers may not accept them as factual statements. As many accountants are aware, they are often suspected of 'fiddling the figures' and 'cooking the books' to make the numbers prove whatever they want them to prove. Workers, too, have some notion of 'creative accounting'. Accountants are aware that manual workers see them as unproductive 'pen-pushers' who earn contempt rather than cultural respect. Even if accounting's 'masculinity' is thought to rest in its hard numbers, it is difficult to picture accountants as 'macho' figures.

The importance of accounting in achieving compliance may rest not so much on consent as on the difficulty of mobilizing dissent. Workers, confronted with a technical discipline which recreates the physical world of production in an abstract form which is alien to them, may find it difficult to retrace the steps from symbolic presentation to shopfloor reality. Accounting, at the same time that it makes some aspects of production visible, systematically obscures others. In Miller and O'Leary's (1987) view the way accounting creates visibility has led to 'the construction of the governable person'. Twentieth century developments in accounting have enabled people to be viewed, measured, and supervised in ways they had not been before. Accounting was part of a much broader project of standardizing people into the 'normal' person. Where once it had been enough to treat illness or punish crime, the aim began to be to create physical and mental health, and law-abiding citizens. The change, which at first may seem superficial, entailed a new way of thinking about people as 'subjects' – to be studied, shaped, and organized. Accounting moved from dealing with dishonesty, through stewardship, to an active ambition to create efficiency. Through their concern with waste and inefficiency, accountants created ways in which workers could be measured and compared – first against each other, then against abstract standards. Budgeting provided the basis for treating managers in the same way. Thus accounting had provided a calculative apparatus which encircled the person (whether worker or manager), enabling supervisors not only to 'know' the person (in terms of their contribution to efficiency and profit) and to intervene in their actions, but also to shift responsibility on to that person by holding them accountable for their measured performance. People had become subjects to be counted, accounted for, and accountable. If people did not become totally obedient employees they at least became governable through accounting regimes.

The power of accounting

All this points to the power of accounting in the management of the labour process. There is a danger that this power can be exaggerated. In studying difficulties which workers face in struggling with accounting information it is possible to present it as an irresistible force – a management control which succeeds where other controls have failed. If managers have been forced to amend or abandon Scientific Management, then 'scientific accounting' can be relied upon to take its place. This would be to ignore the tensions and contradictions which are present in any form of social relations in production. Balances of knowledge and power – both within management, and between management and labour – are dynamic, and any 'solution' is likely to contain the seeds of the next 'problem'. Similarly, a stress on the ways in which accounting makes people accountable may assume too readily that they become the 'subjects' which they are treated as – that they are socially constructed into the phenomena which are measured. This would be to ignore other social and non-social forces which influence human beings – and the ways in which people may actively shape themselves.

In addition to the danger of exaggerating the power of accounting over labour, there is also a problem in giving too simplistic an account of its development. It may be that certain aspects of accounting systems are the deliberate result of creating and refining means of controlling labour. But some aspects may be unintended consequences, and others may have been created through responses to changes which go beyond the immediate issues of the labour process. The next section deals with discussions of accounting change which emphasize markets and technology as key factors in innovation.

ACCOUNTING AND THE NEW MANUFACTURING ENVIRONMENT

If there was little sign of change in accounting practice in relation to production in the 1970s, the next decade saw an upsurge of interest in new developments, and the 1990s have been seen as a time when innovation in accounting is urgently required. This situation has arisen not from changing academic theories of work and workers but from broader social, economic, and technological change.

Johnson and Kaplan's (1987) history of the lost relevance of management accounting was linked with more immediate concern with the challenges facing US enterprises in the 1980s. The long term development of multi-product divisions was accelerated by contemporary changes in *consumer markets*. Following an analysis similar to that of Piore and Sabel (1984), markets were seen to be increasingly fragmented and volatile so that 'Today product lines and marketing channels have proliferated' (Cooper and Kaplan, 1988: 96). Such market changes led to new demands on *production systems*, where mass production was being replaced by low-volume batch runs of a greater product mix. In order to satisfy the demands of rapidly changing markets, managers needed to reduce lead times (from product design to sales) and throughput times (from raw materials to finished products). To achieve this, companies needed to grasp the opportunities offered by the growing range of new technology – especially computer-based innovations – which eventually promise Computer Integrated Manufacture –

(CIM) (Kaplan, 1986). These changes were made more urgent by the increase in international competition – especially from Japan. The success of Japanese companies was attributed to excellence in production systems with their emphasis on JIT and quality. Managers in US and UK enterprises were urged to adopt such approaches by learning 'the art of Japanese management' (Pascale and Athos, 1981, title). Not only must companies adapt to the new conditions, they must promote efficiency in all their operations to become 'world class' manufacturers at the end of the twentieth century.

The case against conventional accounting

In the face of this dramatic need for improvement, management accounting (already seen as having lost its relevance) was now portrayed as a positive handicap to innovating managers – especially in relation to Advanced Manufacturing Technology (AMT). Conventional accounting was widely attacked for its investment appraisals and costing systems.

Investment appraisal

Conventional practice was criticized for the measurements, techniques and criteria applied to investments. In relation to *measurements*, management accountants were portrayed as fixated on direct labour costs, with reductions here as the key (sometimes sole) indicator of the benefits of investment in AMT. But previous technological innovation had already reduced direct labour to a small element in production. For example, direct labour may represent only 3–5 per cent of product costs in many electronics products (Hunt *et al.*, 1985). This meant that innovators found it difficult to justify further investment on the basis of direct labour costs alone. However, supporters of AMT claimed that the real benefits lay elsewhere. Improvements in quality would lead to reductions in scrap, waste, rework, disruption, warranty claims, after-sales servicing, quality control, and machine down time (Primrose, 1988). Improved quality, coupled with JIT scheduling, would lead to lower stock levels, offering considerable inventory savings. This, together with the greater productivity of new machines, would reduce the demand for factory floor space (Kaplan, 1986). In addition to these specific benefits, advocates of AMT argued that it would provide flexible production and, when all the components were linked in computer networks, it held the promise of integrated systems from design through production to sales. Investment in AMT would enable managers, engineers, and workers to learn about the new technology, alerting them to future innovations, and thus they would be well placed to take advantage of future developments. By failing to take all these vital factors into account, management accountants were providing companies with an inadequate picture of the benefits of AMT.

Conventional investment appraisal *techniques* were also attacked. For many years academics have advocated the use of Discounted Cash Flow (DCF) as the superior method – specifically where the outcome is represented in terms of Net Present Value (NPV). This technique recognizes the time value of money – £1 received today being worth more than £1 received in the future – so that the benefits of long term projects can be evaluated against the current cost of capital. Uncertainty of cash flow predictions can be explored through 'sensitivity analysis' of the effect of changing assumptions, and riskiness can be incorporated by varying the discount rate. This sophisticated appraisal technique is recommended as the sound approach to investment decisions (Kaplan, 1986; Primrose and Leonard, 1986). Despite these arguments many companies continued to use the simpler, and strongly criticized, pay-back (PB) method (Pike, 1983; Woods *et al.*, 1984). Here the decisive factor is the length of time before enhanced cash flow will cover the cost of the investment. Even when companies adopted DCF (Pike and Wolfe, 1988) they were reluctant to give up PB even if some academics regarded it as 'a dead loss' (Jones and Dugdale, 1994). In the US, where DCF seems to be more widely used, there have been fears that managers will abandon it (Kaplan, 1986). Where it is used there are criticisms that it is often applied incorrectly, since practitioners are insufficiently skilled in its more refined techniques (Dugdale, 1990).

The third area of attack focused on the *criteria* management accountants typically apply. Their DCF assumptions may take an exaggerated view of the cost of capital. 'It may surprise managers to know that the real cost of capital may be in the neighbourhood of 8% . . . Since many US companies use hurdle rates of 15% or higher' (Kaplan, 1986: 88, 87). This gives rise to over-ambitious targets for AMT investment. Similarly, where PB is used the target periods are often two to three years (Dugdale and Jones, 1991) so failing to encompass the long term benefits of AMT. Further, the desirability of investment is often compared with a *status quo* position – assuming that production will continue at current levels if no investment is made – when a more reasonable assumption would be that business is likely to decline (Kaplan, 1986).

Conventional accounting was thus accused of providing 'wrong' or 'inadequate' information which deters managers from investing in AMT or leads to them 'investing in the wrong technologies for the wrong reasons' (Primrose, 1988: 355). Accounting is portrayed as a crucial (sometimes the sole) element in investment decisions and then its failings are cited as a powerful handicap to managers struggling to innovate.

Costing systems

Conventional accounting was also attacked for its continued use of outdated costing systems inappropriate to modern production. Again this criticism centred on the use of direct labour as the key benchmark for costs and the base against which overheads are 'recovered'. Standard costing systems, once appropriate for high labour input mass production, had become obsolete. For example, in one company 'the continual effort to prepare standard labor costs and then variances from these standards had little potential impact upon overall cost control' (Hunt *et al.*, 1985: 60). Apart from the waste of accountants' (expensive) time, this meant that more important aspects of production were marginalized or ignored.

Flexible production frequently increases the importance of set-up time before machines can be productive, and machine maintenance becomes a key to smooth JIT production. In conventional accounting these may be treated as indirect labour costs and become obscured among many other items of overhead or recovered against an arbitrary and inappropriate base. If information on set-up and breakdowns is not highlighted by cost systems managers are less likely to identify problems to which AMT may be a solution. Standard material costs include an allowance for scrap but this may imply an 'acceptable' level when TQM demands 'zero defects' (Brimson, 1988). The adoption of JIT systems can lead to a dramatic reduction of stock in which 'Tracing overhead through work-in-progress and finished goods inventory [provides] no useful information' (Hunt *et al.*, 1985: 61). The use of departments as budgetary units can cause difficulties when AMT produces integrated systems which cross departmental boundaries. For example, CAD/CAM may be purchased by the design department but the main benefits accrue to manufacturing departments through cost reductions in production because of improved product design (Currie, 1989a, b).

Thus standard costing systems have been attacked across the range of their elements – direct labour costs, material costs, variance analysis, overhead allocation, budgeting – and the entire rationale of the 'standard' has been criticized as inappropriate in the flexible, unstandardized world of modern production. This has two important implications. First, managers are not being provided with information which discloses problems in current production and helps them plan and implement improvements. Second, because standardized costs are applied to non-standard production, product costs become distorted and managers make inappropriate decisions about product pricing and product mix (Cooper and Kaplan, 1988). All this was seen as vital to the competitive position of enterprises and 'Failure to recognize the inadequacy of all existing cost accounting procedures . . . will terminate the current revival in [UK] manufacturing fortunes' (Waldron, 1988: 2). The subsequent world recession only increased the urgency with which this view was advanced.

New forms of accounting

Associated with this crescendo of complaint against conventional management accounting was a stream of advice from academics and management consultants on how the situation could be improved by adopting various new forms of accounting.

Investment appraisal for AMT

Apart from recommending the selection and proper application of DCF with more realistic criteria, accountants were urged to take a broader view of the benefits of AMT. Primrose argued that accountants should measure advantages of AMT which went far beyond direct labour costs, and they could do so, since 'Fortunately there should be no such thing as an intangible benefit because every benefit that can be identified, can be redefined, quantified and included in an investment appraisal' (Primrose, 1991: 42). This would enable accounting to be used as a 'scientific basis' for investment decisions. Other critics have been rather more restrained in their enthusiasm for the quantification of everything. Kaplan divided benefits into the tangible (including savings on inventory, floor space, and quality) and intangible (such as flexibility, shorter lead and throughput times, and learning about AMT). He advised accountants not to ignore these intangibles – nor to assign zero value to them – merely because they resisted quantification. 'Conservative accountants' might do this, since they 'prefer being precisely wrong to being vaguely right' (1986: 92). In difficult cases, having quantified all the benefits they reasonably could, innovative accountants should declare the extent to which the numbers fall short of financial targets and draw managers' attention to all the unquantified factors which might bridge the gap.

Both Primrose and Kaplan were worried that managers, faced with the news that they had been misled by conventional accounting, might react by rejecting all accounting information – throwing out 'science' and relying on 'faith'. Instead, they proposed, companies should adopt new forms of accounting which would provide 'better', or even 'correct', information. Both appeared to know, in advance of any calculations, that AMT would generally be beneficial to companies and hence accounting systems should be evaluated on their ability to establish, demonstrate, or legitimize this knowledge.

Activity Based Costing

Changes proposed for costing systems were more elaborate, and involved discarding accounting practices which had been initiated at the end of the nineteenth century and developed over the subsequent decades. The most influential and widespread of these new types of accounting was Activity Based Costing (ABC).

Johnson (1992b) traced the business roots of ABC to US General Electric in the early 1960s, and to later (apparently independent) developments in other US companies and management consultancies in the 1970s. These developments were later codified by academics and became known as ABC. Close attention to direct labour was found to distort product costs substantially because 'Virtually all of a company's activities exist to support the production and delivery of today's goods and services. They should therefore be considered product costs' (Cooper and Kaplan, 1988: 96). The cost of modern products is highly sensitive to the volume in which they are produced. Products made in small batches may take a small number of direct labour hours but require almost as much indirect labour as large batches – in design; purchasing, receiving and disbursing materials; production scheduling; set-up; sales; and other administrative/managerial activities. If this overhead is allocated on the basis of direct labour hours, then short-run products – with high margins – appear to be more profitable than is 'really' the case. In a dramatic example (see Box 7.3) Cooper and Kaplan demonstrated how the application of an ABC approach might revolutionize a company's view of its products. 'Management thought valve 3 was a cash cow. It might as well have mailed checks to its customers' (1988: 100).

The central aim of ABC is to trace costs from resources through activities to specific products. Typically this begins with interviewing departmental heads to find what their staff do, and what influences the time they spend doing it. For example, in an inventory control department the factor which determines work-load may not be the size of an order for materials, but the number of deliveries which are made. Here the significant accounting measurement would be 'unit cost per shipment', and products which generate many shipments ought to bear more of the inventory control support costs than those which are produced with fewer shipments. As ABC analysis proceeds, department by department, ac-countants attempt to determine the primary cause of each activity – its 'driver'. For example, in an engineering company the decision to produce a new drawing drives a number of other activities, which can be costed. Apart from the immedi-ate cost of drafting (say $95), the drawing sets in motion: inspection ($15), data-processing ($25), quality control ($80), stock-keeping ($20), and parts-ordering ($40) activities. With ABC, managers can see that the 'real' cost of all activities driven by 'new drawing' is $275 (Johnson, 1992b). Cooper and Kaplan argued that only two types of cost should be excluded from ABC – excess

Box 7.3

How ABC changes product profitability						
		Manufacturing overhead per unit ($)			Gross margin (%)	
Valve No.	Annual volume (units)	Old system	New system	% difference	Old system	New system
1	43,562	5.44	4.76	−12.5	41	46
2	500	6.15	12.86	+109.0	30	−24
3	53	7.30	77.44	+964.0	47	−258
4	**2,079**	**8.88**	**19.76**	**+123.0**	**26**	**−32**
5	5,670	7.58	15.17	+100.0	39	2
6	11,196	5.34	5.26	−1.5	41	41
7	423	5.92	4.39	−26.0	31	43

Source: Cooper and Kaplan (1988)

capacity and R&D for new products – but that, when all other activity drivers had been identified and measured, managers would be in a position to 'measure costs right: make the right decisions' (1988, title).

The typical outcome of an ABC analysis is that the new accounting information tells managers that their low-volume products are less profitable than they thought, because they have been 'undercosted'. But this should not lead them immediately to drop these products. If for various 'strategic' reasons it is decided to retain the lines, managers' attention should be focused on ways to reduce their production costs. Here ABC is likely to enhance the claims of new technology, 'since CIM is most efficient in high-variety, low-volume environments' (Cooper and Kaplan, 1988: 103). There may also be opportunities to redesign products so that they use standardized components. ABC should not lead to automatic decisions so much as 'help managers make better decisions about product design, pricing, marketing, and mix, and [encourage] continual operating improvements' (p. 103).

The presentation of ABC principles attracted rapid and widespread interest in academic and professional journals, in management consultancy within the giant accountancy houses, and in American and European manufacturing (and to a lesser extent service) industries. A UK survey found that 3 per cent of firms had implemented ABC, 9 per cent intended to, and 38 per cent were considering it (Drury *et al.*, 1992). ABC developed spin-offs such as Activity Based Budgeting and Activity Based Management and, by the early 1990s, was being hailed as a 'panacea' for all the ills of industry (Johnson, 1992b). The work of CAM-I (Computer Aided Manufacturing – International) publicized its message of the failure of conventional accounting and the promise of the new to a broader audience of engineers and managers (Jones, 1991).

Throughput accounting

Although ABC was the most celebrated, there were other new types of accounting initiated by a rejection of conventional practice. Throughput Accounting (TA) was inspired by the 'theory of constraints' – TOC (Goldratt, 1984). TOC is essentially concerned with maximizing the conversion of materials into products – *throughput*. In the early development of this approach the emphasis was on the identification of 'bottlenecks' – often, but not necessarily, focal machines – which were the key constraints on throughput. Companies should focus their attention on the management of these bottlenecks to ensure they are utilized to their maximum capacity. The assumption was that, if companies get production right, then financial benefits will follow. What is important is the rate at which products are made, and hence generate money. Later attention turned to market constraints, with an emphasis on the rate at which products are made and sold. These ideas have been refined and expounded through the work of the Goldratt Institute in the US and Europe.

After encountering Goldratt's early work, Waldron constructed TA. This proposed fundamental changes to the conceptual base of cost accounting (see Box 7.4). The TA attack on conventional accounting began with very different assumptions from those of ABC – 'Products are not profitable or unprofitable, businesses are' (Waldron, 1988: 1). If one product can make a contribution of £20 per unit but only ten can be made per day, then an alternative product which contributes only £10 per unit at a rate of thirty per day should be preferred. In the short term all costs are fixed, and what is important is the rate at which resources are applied to materials to produce sales. To reflect this, TA is centrally concerned with calculating the rate at which businesses earn money and focuses attention on maximizing the return per bottleneck hour – especially through the adoption of CIM.

These ideas were publicized by Galloway and Waldron (1988a, b; 1989a, b), advocated by their management consultancy firm, and have been adopted by some UK manufacturers (Darlington *et al.*, 1992). This proposed reform has, as yet, been less widely accepted than ABC – to which it is often hostile. In addition a rift has appeared between supporters of TOC and those of TA. The Goldratt Institute claims that TOC has been considerably developed from its earlier beginnings and that TA represents a narrow and distorted application of it. One UK associate of the institute has stated, 'There is no such thing as Throughput Accounting,' and advised his audience of management accountants to 'Forget about Throughput Accounting' (Lewis, 1993). This arcane wrangling about the

Box 7.4

Throughput Accounting	
Fundamental concepts of conventional cost accounting	*New principles of Throughput Accounting*
There are direct and indirect costs: direct costs are variable and indirect costs are fixed	Distinguishing between indirect and direct costs is no longer useful
Summing component costs to derive a product cost and subtracting the result from the sales price is a good way to determine relative product profitability	It is the rate at which the factory earns money that determines profitability, not the contribution of each product
Inventory is an asset and working on material increases its value	Inventory is not an asset. It is the product of unsynchronized manufacturing and stands between you and profit
Reducing component costs directly increases profit	Profit is a function of material cost, total factory cost and throughput

Source: Waldron (1988)

'true' application of TOC to accounting may have made managers uncertain about its relevance to their companies or inclined them to develop their own versions of accounting for throughput.

Accounting for cells

Although it has received less attention in academic journals, another development which seems important in a number of companies is accounting for work groups or cells. The construction of a work unit as a 'cell' is sometimes merely a convenient accounting device – for identifying and attributing costs – but it often results from a physical reorganization of machines and workers. The impetus for the latter comes from production engineering where a 'family' of operations is grouped together. With the adoption of AMT, this produces flexible manu- facturing cells (FMC). Each can then be treated separately for cost accounting purposes.

These changes – whether accounting- or engineering-led – are represented in accounting regimes which analyse each cell in terms of inputs from 'suppliers' and outputs to 'customers', which are often other cells within the company. The value added by each cell can be calculated and charged to the products which pass through. Companies differ in their methods of doing this, and even within one company different cells may be treated differently. The aim is not that account- ants should 'measure costs right' but that cell managers should gain a better understanding of those factors which affect costs. Thus no particular accounting technique is insisted upon. Instead managers are encouraged to explore a wide range of alternatives to standard costing – and to consider what can be learnt from them. Following currently fashionable jargon this is usually described as 'em- powerment' – providing cell supervisors with financial data and analytical tools which enable them to take responsibility for the cost of the activities they manage: they must 'own' their costs. Senior finance managers emphasize the role of accounting in creating a 'mind-set' in which cell leaders think 'as though they were shareholders in the business'. Much of this is reminiscent of Malmberg's description of work group accounting. But, a decade later, this is expressed in terms not of 'motivation and satisfaction' but of 'responsibility and accountability'.

Along with this there is frequently emphasis on 'de-layering' – stripping away unnecessary tiers of middle management – and reliance on an increased managerial role for cell supervisors. When cells are evaluated on criteria of success/failure, which become embedded in the accounting system – for example, by surcharging cells for late delivery to their internal customers – and when cell supervisors have absorbed an accounting frame of reference ('mind-set'), then these monitoring and control activities may require fewer middle managers to operate them. Accounting is intended to become the basis upon which cells create their own targets and measure their achievement. The point is not to measure costs more precisely, but to gain a better understanding of what causes them, and to drive them down. As one financial controller put it, when asked about the ABC

213

notion of costing being like firing arrows at a target which got nearer and nearer the bulls-eye, 'We prefer to use a bazooka and blast the whole target to bits.'

New accounting and manufacturing change

At the start of the 1990s conventional management accounting was under attack from many academics and management consultants, and there were some indications of companies changing their accounting systems. Is this a change which is necessary for, and capable of, revitalizing UK and US manufacturing enterprises?

Does accounting really handicap AMT?

The attack on conventional investment appeared to assume that accounting was the central (sometimes the sole) ingredient in investment decisions, and thus its shortcomings were a crucial handicap to AMT. In practice, decisions may not correspond with this view, and many writers have complained that the academic emphasis on refining techniques is misplaced (Haynes and Solomon, 1962; Ackerman, 1970; Hastie, 1974; King, 1975; Scapens et al., 1982). Practitioners place less emphasis on the role of accounting in AMT investment decisions (Jones and Dugdale, 1994). First, proposals originate outside accounting – they come from engineers and production managers – and are already filtered before formal appraisal begins. The origins of such proposals reflect managerial concern with increasing capacity to keep up with orders, or the updating of production technology. The economic viability of the proposals may well be assessed – either intuitively, or by simple calculations – before they come to the attention of accountants. Many projects with potentially high financial returns may well be rejected for non-financial reasons and never become formal proposals. Second, once submitted, proposals may not be judged solely on financial criteria. Financial information co-exists with market information, production information, and technology information, which all play their part in decision processes. The role of accounting is important in checking proposals out and giving an indication of the consequences of investment, but practitioners do not typically see it as determining decision outcomes (Jones and Dugdale, 1994).

Even in cases where accounting information is regarded as a vital component, the precise nature of measurements, techniques, and criteria may not have central significance for decisions. Measurement is often not the responsibility of accountants – rather, data are supplied by engineers or production managers. Aware of possible difficulties in establishing economic viability, they may exaggerate the benefits of AMT in 'spurious justifications' (Currie, 1989a, b). The remoteness of accountants from the new technology can make it difficult for them to detect such practices. If the 'real' benefits of AMT are not fully captured by accounting, this deficiency may be balanced by under-reporting of the 'real' costs – such as those of implementation and training (Currie, 1989c; Jones, 1991). Although current appraisal practices may be flawed, this does not necessarily bias investment away from AMT, since its costs and benefits may be easier to measure than other potential projects – such as management information systems, or the acquisition of land and buildings. Similarly, the selection of DCF or PB appears to have little practical impact on AMT decisions, and projects go ahead even with high hurdle rates or short pay-back criteria (Jones and Dugdale, 1994) and may even be accepted where the accounting information is negative (Black, 1983).

Overall, although the logical attack on conventional practice is strong, there is less support for the view that the practical outcomes handicap AMT investment. Japanese manufacturers, often cited as role models, continue to rely on conventional PB, centred on direct labour and requiring two- to three-year pay-back (Williams *et al.*, 1991; Jones *et al.*, 1993). There must therefore be some doubt whether adopting recommended practices will necessarily make any significant difference to AMT investment.

The end of conventional costing?

A persistent theme of critics has been the inappropriateness of standardized measures of materials and, more importantly, direct labour in the flexible environment of modern production. Nevertheless, recent surveys have found that standard costing is still extensively used in UK enterprises – even those which have introduced AMT and JIT (Puxty and Lyall, 1990; Drury and Dugdale, 1992). In part this may be explained by inertia. Costing systems in large enterprises are huge beasts which have been constructed over many years and fulfil a variety of functions (see Box 7.5). They may keep track of hundreds of products (or thousands) made up of tens of thousands of components (or hundreds of thousands). Inevitably errors creep into the system, with items being booked to the wrong accounting codes. Changes in particular elements of the system, perhaps for some specific short-lived purpose, may linger within computers, sporadically throwing up anomalies. Thus costing systems decay over time and must be regularly purged. All this implies that simply maintaining an existing system and providing routine information is a time-consuming task. The idea of abandoning it and creating a wholly new system is a daunting prospect for many companies.

There may be other reasons for the slowness of change. Some regard discussion of post-Fordism as exaggerated and suggest that much 'flexibility' is a myth. Many companies may be concerned with developing global mass markets for products based on standardized components rather than pursuing flexible specialization. Further, those companies which have been inclined to shift the balance of their production towards short-run, low-volume products may have been responding, not to changing markets, but to the information produced by conventional costing systems,

as many American and European manufacturers discovered in the 1970s and 1980s, when, using financial cost accounting information to measure

215

Box 7.5

Uses of costing systems

When making changes to its costing systems, accountants in one large manufacturing enterprise listed these as the most important uses:

- Sourcing decisions – make or buy?
- Investment decisions – do we buy new plant and machinery?
- Bidding decisions – what price shall we bid at?
- Manufacturing strategy – how shall we make the product?
- Control of product costs – where can we make savings?
- Allocation of resources – what should departmental budgets be?
- Rationalization – should sites and departments be reorganized?
- Behaviour of costs – what makes costs vary and change?

> product costs, they erroneously assumed that they could improve their company's profitability by abandoning *overcosted* commodity-type product lines and by proliferating *undercosted* varieties of newer 'high-tech' lines. In fact, that strategy usually depressed earnings and, in several cases, generated a 'death spiral' that led companies to the edge of bankruptcy.
>
> (Johnson, 1992b: 29)

Ironically, in producing 'better' information ABC typically shows the low-volume lines to be less profitable and may incline managers to drop them and return to their 'core business' in mass production/markets.

The claim that direct labour is no longer a significant proportion of product cost is also an artefact constructed by accounting. At each stage in production labour costs are incurred and become embedded in materials transferred to the next stage. Thus while labour costs may appear low to the manager of any particular stage (or department, or cell) the total contribution of labour to the final product is still high. The emphasis on compartmentalizing each stage as a 'profit centre' or 'mini-business' obscures this. However, even when labour costs appear low, this does not mean that managers regard them as unimportant. In highly competitive markets, where firms world-wide have access to the same technologies and techniques, price ranges are narrow and even marginal reductions in costs can be important. As one manager, asked whether he could be relaxed about manufacturing costs, put it, 'Oh no. No, no. No . . . in this business 50 cents counts' (Dugdale & Jones, 1993). The production of goods and services remains fundamentally a labour process, and labour costs still matter.

Perhaps companies' interest in ABC is a matter less of the declining importance of direct labour than of a growing focus on indirect labour costs. From the early 1980s enterprises have been expressing concern not only about 'white-collar' office overhead, but also about 'managerial fat', hence the drive to 'de-layering'. Hopper and Armstrong argued that this overhead grew in large enterprises up to the 1970s as a consequence of strong needs to control an organized and powerful work force. The pressure for change in the 1980s came from a combination of the challenge to US enterprises from foreign firms invading their markets, and the potential to re-establish management power over workers (and hence costs) in conditions of slack labour markets and political attacks on unionism. In this different climate 'the bureaucratic and costly apparatus of control in large core conglomerates, which had emerged in more benign economic conditions than the past fifteen years or so, is increasingly being questioned' (1991: 434).

ABC focuses on measuring indirect labour activities through interviews which give a general indication of workload, which 'we cannot estimate to four significant digits' (Cooper and Kaplan, 1988: 98). Such diffidence did not constrain work study practitioners, armed with their time measurement units, who also detected increasing enterprise concern with the measurement and control of indirect work (Whitmore, 1987). What distinguishes ABC from Scientific Management in the office is its less precise attempts at measurement and its accounting expression of this. Its outcome may well be the same – the reduction of costs by the reorganization and intensification of office work. Many companies adopting ABC seem content to undertake the analysis of duties, but do not proceed to implement new cost information systems based on this (Lyne, 1993). Here accountants appear to be undertaking tasks which, in a previous generation, were the preserve of work study engineers. That this will boost corporate performance without the use of new accounting systems is not surprising, since 'One time savings – sometimes referred to as "low hanging fruit" – await any rational attempt to reorganize work' (Johnson, 1992b: 35).

Overall, changes taking place in accounting systems may be less revolutionary than the advocates of new accounting claim. This view was expressed by the UK management accountancy profession in a response (*Evolution not Revolution*) to the American critics of its existing knowledge and skills:

> Evidence of the benefits of new accounting techniques and the continued benefits of some conventional techniques is only beginning to emerge. No general crisis has been identified within the management accounting profession *vis-à-vis* a changing manufacturing environment and therefore no radical reforms are recommended at this stage.
>
> (Bromwich and Bhimani, 1989: 3)

Accounting change and manufacturing performance

Whether seen as revolution or evolution, there was a widespread feeling that some important accounting changes were taking place in the 1990s. Whilst the accountancy profession continued to emphasize the importance of its existing and potential contribution to business success, some critics challenged the centrality of accounting to the management of enterprises.

Perhaps the most significant of these critics was Johnson – because of his joint authorship of *Relevance Lost*, which had inspired much of the furore over conventional accounting in the first place. His critique began with ABC. 'As someone who helped put the activity-based concept in motion, I feel compelled to warn people that I believe it has gone too far. It should be redirected and slowed down, if not stopped altogether' (Johnson, 1992b: 26). But his attack went much deeper than this. Not only was ABC unsuitable for strategic decisions and the management and control of operations, but all accounting information was of dubious value. What had emerged was 'a new competitive environment – call it the global economy – in which accounting information is not capable of guiding companies toward competitiveness and long term profitability' (p. 31). Instead companies should be concerned with information on customer satisfaction, and should manage their production systems following the ideas of Deming (1986). These, widely applied in Japan, were based on a 'philosophy' of quality – and required a new paradigm. Reliance on accounting had led to 'top-down control' when what was required now was 'bottom-up empowerment' (Johnson, 1992a, title). Empowerment 'happens when everyone's work is guided by and aligned to a common vision that company leaders shape and project by their own example' (quoted in Jayson, 1992: 31) and depends upon cooperation within enterprises rather than competition between departments, cells, profit centres, or mini-businesses. Accountants might have a role to play in this, but not the dominant position they had occupied in the past.

The argument that devising new forms of accounting is an inappropriate response to the competitive challenge of the 1990s gains support from studies of Japanese enterprises. Here there is little sign of interest in the kinds of new accounting proposed by UK and US academics and management consultants. Differences between Japanese and Western enterprises do not lie in the detail of their accounting systems, but in the relationship between accounting and other forms of information, and between accountants and other managers. Accounting information is not accorded such a privileged voice, nor are accountants so highly placed in managerial hierarchies. Instead engineering voices are stronger, and 'accountants' are more broadly educated/trained and incorporated into 'team management' (Williams *et al.*, 1991; Jones *et al.*, 1993). Managing by the numbers is not an issue merely because the numbers may be faulty and need to be replaced with 'better' or 'correct' numbers. It suggests over-reliance on finance and financial control in managing production, and far from addressing this issue 'much current literature (and management consultancy) tends to reinforce accounting as a central managerial function' (Jones *et al.*, 1993: 133). If UK and US enterprises have been outpaced by German and Japanese competition over recent years the problem may not be that conventional accounting has technical failings, but that accountants (and their modes of rationality) occupy such powerful positions. The solution therefore would not be to invent ever more sophisticated accounting forms, but to rethink reliance upon financial information and control, and the privileged position of accountancy, in UK and US enterprises at the end of the twentieth century.

ACCOUNTING AND THE DEBATE ON PRODUCTION

Management accounting in the 1970s and early 1980s showed little sign of the 'de-Taylorization' of industry, or of the 'psychological' approach which some social scientists had advocated and/or predicted. Instead the 'principles' of Scientific Management, as embedded in standard costing, continued to dominate accounting systems. The challenge to standard costing, when it came, was inspired more by concern about markets, technologies, and production systems than by theories of motivation and the nature of workers. Here accounting may have both responded to and fuelled the interest in post-Fordism.

Accounting research has emphasized its role in the control of labour. In direct control this is achieved through accounting specification of standards for production and the payment attached to this. In a more ideological manner, accounting has been portrayed as constructing the accountable and governable subject. A frequent theme has been the way in which accounting has increasingly been a vehicle for driving what some people like to call 'the discipline of the market' deep inside the enterprise – down to managers, supervisors, and even workers. Here the importance of accounting lies not merely in its technical calculations (though these have their own significance) but in its overall representation of the goals, requirements, and nature of production – production of products becoming more closely aligned with production of profit. Before 'empowering' lower-level employees to take 'responsibility' for their activities, managers attempt to ensure that their interests are 'aligned to a common vision'. In this accounting is important in constructing that vision, as well as holding people accountable for their pursuit of it.

In doing this accountancy has expanded its domain in production. The new accounting is concerned not only with the conventional role of supplying information, but also with the analysis of activities (ABC), the facilitating of throughput (TA), and the structuring of organizations (cell accounting). Accountants are entering territory which was once the preserve of work study/production scheduling engineers, or organization and methods/personnel staff.

None of this represents the necessary and inevitable rise of accounting's role in production. In German and Japanese manufacturing neither accounting nor accountants occupy such a dominant position as they do in UK and US enterprises. This has led some to see accountancy itself – not just the details of its current practice – as 'the problem'. However, such is the entrenched and central position which it occupies in our enterprises that it is unlikely to be displaced easily or quickly. And, whatever the merits of the new types of accounting, they have already become incorporated into textbooks, and a new generation of accountants and others on undergraduate, professional, and MBA programmes are being exposed to them. Despite Johnson's call for a 'profound shift' in business schools (Jayson, 1992), tomorrow's managers are still being influenced by today's accounting. Although much of the debate on production and the labour process has been uninterested in the role of accounting, the discussion in this chapter suggests that it has had a considerable impact – and is likely to continue to do so. Accounting not only reports on production, it also constructs images of the targets, achievements, problems, and solutions of production, and attempts to shape and control those who carry it out.

REVIEW

Short questions

What is the relationship between standard costing and Scientific Management? Why might variances between expected and actual standard labour costs emerge? What is implied in saying that standards are socially constructed? Why might the adoption of ideas from industrial psychology affect the applicability of standard costing systems? How do Hopper *et al.* think 'financial control' influenced engineers and miners in the NCB? Why do Knights and Collinson think accounting was seen as 'macho' in the vehicle manufacturing company and what were the implications of this? What do Miller and O'Leary mean by 'the governable person' and how does this relate to accounting?

What three features of investment appraisal have been attacked as handicapping investment in AMT? Why are conventional costing systems thought inappropriate in 'the new manufacturing environment'? How does ABC change managers' perceptions of costs? What key characteristics of conventional cost accounting are identified by Waldron and what alternatives does he propose? What roles does accounting play in the construction and 'empowerment' of production cells? What criticisms have been made of the view that accounting handicaps AMT? Why might companies be slow to adopt new forms of costing? Why does Johnson think accounting should become less important in enterprises at the end of the twentieth century?

Discussion points

Should accounting be seen as the ultimate means of gaining compliance in enterprises – controlling the parts that other management control systems cannot reach? Does the rise of a new manufacturing environment mean that conventional accounting should be replaced by new forms, or that 'managing by the numbers' should be abandoned? What is the potential of accounting in the 'empowerment' of employees?

Part IV

ACCOUNTING
Social analysis and social theory

8

SOCIAL ANALYSIS OF ACCOUNTING

This chapter provides an overview of the relationship between technical and social issues in accounting; considers how accountancy should respond to this; and suggests how accountants can be understood as social actors in social contexts. Throughout the book aspects of accounting theory and practice have been examined using various forms of social analysis. Rather than beginning with claims for the theoretical and methodological potential of 'the sociological perspective' I have preferred to explore substantive issues, drawing upon whatever insights were available and appeared appropriate. Here I wish to draw together some of the themes which have emerged.

'TECHNICAL' AND 'SOCIAL' IN ACCOUNTING

Many outsiders see accounting as a highly technical activity (and a very boring one) which is concerned with identifying, measuring, and reporting on financial issues – a form of economic calculation involving facts, numbers and arithmetic combined in a rigorously codified manner. Many accounting students probably encounter it as such in their early studies. Some would go further to argue that conventional textbooks portray accounting in this way – a view endorsed even in a text employing sociological perspectives:

> This text is not an attempt to study modern accounting. For one thing the focus would be too narrow . . . In addition this is what conventional accounting texts are about, the vast majority of which seem to get by successfully without needing to adopt anything other than a 'technical' accounting perspective.
>
> (Roslender, 1992: 4)

Accounting academics have been portrayed as typically viewing accounting 'as a factual and objective form of knowledge untainted by social values or ideology; accounting data is apparently an asocial product almost untouched by human hand' (Loft, 1986: 137). Outside academia, 'most accountants in practice would claim objectivity . . . many commentators and professionals still appear to consider

223

the setting of accounting standards as a purely technical activity' (Tricker, 1975: 1). The entire accountancy profession, with only a few exceptions, would appear to be steeped in this technical approach. Hopwood (1985a) reported on the activities of a committee set up by the (then) Social Science Research Council in the UK to explore alternative social approaches to accounting. The participants differed in their emphases, but generally their discussion of the conventional 'technical' approach to accounting characterized it in terms such as 'calculative', 'neutral', 'professional', 'uncritical', with a belief in 'progress' and 'efficiency'. It was this dominant view of accounting as objective/factual/neutral which they wished to challenge.

This identification of the vast majority of accountants as perceiving and/or portraying accounting as a solely technical activity is too simplistic. Within conventional textbooks and research what can be found is not the absence of social issues but particular kinds of social assumptions, theories, and analyses. These may be largely implicit, and under-explored, and not critically assessed but they are there nevertheless. Nor are practitioners convinced that their activities are purely objective/factual/neutral. They also recognize subjective aspects, are distrustful of the factual status of data, and stress that information must be provided to specific users who have particular purposes. The following section attempts to draw out the discussion of social aspects of accounting which appears in conventional texts and research.

Social context of accounting

The argument will be presented using the device of a 'black box' model. The assumption – for the moment – is that accounting practices are not in themselves social, and that social analysis can shed no light on this dark world. However, this closed box exists within a social context which may be examined through social analysis (see Box 8.1).

Behavioural implications

Probably the most widespread recognition of a connection between accounting and the wider social world concerns the *outputs* of the box, which are seen as

Box 8.1

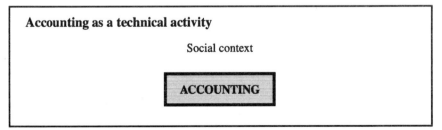

having 'behavioural implications'. Basic textbooks identify 'problems' which may be triggered by accounting information. Within enterprises, for example, 'budgets and performance reports can cause serious behavioural problems and can be harmful to motivation' (Drury, 1992: 16). In relations between the enterprise and wider society, 'Conventional financial reporting . . . may lead users of information to believe that maximization of profit is the sole aim of modern business enterprises when this is not so' (Gee, 1985: 111).

Of course not all consequences are 'problems', since the essential purpose of accounting is to 'help decision makers to make good decisions' (Drury, 1992: 3). Problems are therefore seen as *unintended consequences* of accounting practices. They arise through the improper application of accounting – 'used and interpreted with insufficient knowledge' (Drury, 1992: 16) – rather than intrinsic faults of the information. Attention is focused on outsiders – owners and managers – who must be educated by accountants to understand better the information from the black box (see Box 8.2).

Box 8.2

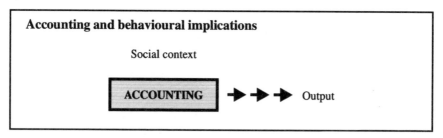

Accounting and behavioural implications

Social context

ACCOUNTING → → → Output

Social environment

Almost as readily conceded is that accounting is connected with its social environment through its *inputs*. 'From the outset . . . accounting behaved as a service responding to events rather than initiating change' (Jones, 1981: 22). Financial reporting, having been developed to serve joint stock companies, grew in importance with the rise of dispersed share ownership, and now must respond to the challenge of 'Green business'. Management accounting produced standard costs in response to Scientific Management, and must now adapt to a 'new manufacturing environment'. Accounting, it seems, is a cumulative outcome of social processes which are outside its own technical domain (see Box 8.3).

Thus, even in apparently 'technical' treatments of accounting, there is recognition of a wider social world of which accountants should be aware. This is hardly surprising, since accountancy claims to be a practical business discipline which is dedicated to responding to contemporary needs (inputs) in order to achieve desired ends (outputs). The point, even if obvious, is worth noting since it indicates that conventional textbooks do not ignore organizational and societal factors. They do, however, treat these either as unproblematic or as issues which

Box 8.3

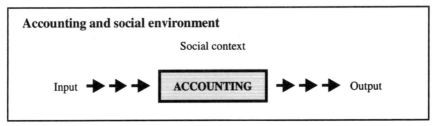

Accounting and social environment

Social context

Input ➡ ➡ ➡ ACCOUNTING ➡ ➡ ➡ Output

need not be explored, by declaring this 'is not a book on organizations or behavioural science, so we will not study alternative behavioural models here' (Horngren, 1977: 163). As Hopper *et al.* (1987) argued, this allows conventional textbooks to present a single view of enterprises and society – their needs, goals, problems, and solutions – in a commonsense way without critical analysis, or evidence, or any attempt to justify it. Whatever the preferred view, the reader is merely expected to accept it.

Social process

The addition of one further element to the model – *feedback* – can considerably enhance the power of social analysis. Outputs from accounting are evaluated and this can lead to changed input – revised requirements to which accounting must respond. This means that the notion of unintended consequences must be re-examined. If existing accounting practices produce harmful or undesirable effects, and this is recognized, then these practices may be changed so that the unintended consequences disappear. Often accountants do not change their practices; instead they respond to criticism by trying to deflect it. Having noted tension in the dual role of managerial accounting systems – as helpers and watchdogs – textbooks advocate emphasis on the assisting role of accounting information (Horngren, 1977; Drury, 1992). If annual reports are seen to mislead investors, then there are calls for the re-education of users so they no longer have an 'expectations gap' (Humphrey *et al.*, 1992) or for them to become more vigilant and cynical (Griffiths, 1986).

What if criticism is not quietened and feedback continues to signal a need for change? If accounting practices remain unaltered under these conditions this may imply endemic tensions which cannot be eliminated. Alternatively, it may be that the so-called unintended consequences were actually intended, but that this had been deliberately obscured. Both would show that 'unintended consequences' are more than simply unfortunate side effects of an otherwise harmonious system.

Closing the input–output loop through feedback (see Box 8.4) draws our attention to social processes in which 'the roles which accounting serves in organisations are created, shaped and changed by the processes of organisational

Box 8.4

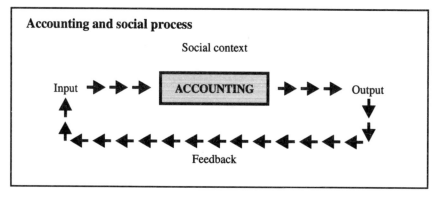

life' (Burchell *et al.*, 1980: 19). Both when accounting systems change, and when they do not, they are influenced by their social context.

So far we have embedded accounting in its social context through a model which, although simplistic, has allowed discussion of a number of issues. But the model has its limitations. It assumes the unambiguous existence of inputs (needs and wants) and outputs (problems and solutions), and that these exist outside accountancy. We now need to locate accountants in the social context.

Accountants in social context

We need to examine the relation between accountants and their social context in two ways – the influence that accountants have on that context; and the way the context influences the way accountants think and act (see Box 8.5).

Box 8.5

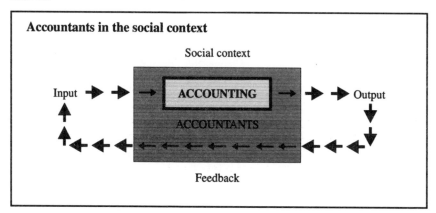

Accountants' influence on social context

The *output* of accounting is not merely a stream of technical information. It is interpreted by accountants and accompanied by advice. For example, the profession defines whether financial information is to be treated as 'true and fair' when it appears in annual reports. Similarly, information provided to management is filtered by the procedures of accountants.

> The transfer of too much information can cause 'information overload' which may result in the most important aspects of the message being lost, because it is buried in a mass of other information. The action of the receiver of the message would then be different from that which was intended by the originator of the message . . . The effectiveness of accounting information is determined by the manner in which it effects behaviour. In this sense, we may say that unless accounting information serves to produce the desired action, it has served no purpose at all.
>
> (Drury, 1992: 17)

Here Drury has reversed his usual chain of causality (information leads to decisions) to suggest that desired actions are identified first and then information is provided which promotes them. The accountant is no longer a mere gatherer of information, but has become an active participant in decision processes. Accountants filter information, promoting some views of the enterprise and suppressing others.

Similarly the *inputs* to accounting are filtered by accountants. Some inputs are eagerly sought, with accountants today claiming that they are the most appropriate group to deal with issues of 'corporate strategy' (Armstrong, 1993) and 'management control' (Emmanuel and Otley, 1985), just as in an earlier period they captured 'costing' and reformed it as 'cost accounting' (Armstrong, 1987a). In the last decade the giant international accounting houses have vastly increased their range of activities, providing all manner of 'management consultancy services'. This growth of inputs to accounting is not simply the result of increasing enterprise and societal needs for accounting information. It stems from the successful way that the accountancy profession, accounting firms, and accountants in enterprises have advanced claims that they – and not some other occupational group – should be the recipients of such inputs. Not all inputs are seized by accountants, however. Demands for social responsibility accounting were largely ignored by the profession, and so too were claims that accounting systems should fit Human Relations concepts of motivation. In some cases there are conflicts over whether inputs are acceptable, such as in the post-World War I argument about whether costing was a proper activity for accountants, which split the UK profession (Loft, 1986), and today in the debate over Green accounting (Owen, 1992). Thus what goes into and what comes out of the box is filtered by accountants who stand as its guardians.

This influence also extends to *feedback* – how the operation of accounting is

228

to be evaluated, and if necessary changed. Complaints about financial reporting and auditing practices are referred back to the profession itself to reconsider. Identification of conventional management accounting as inappropriate leads to accounting academics proposing new forms of accounting. Armstrong's (1987a) study of accounting in UK enterprises showed how accountants interpreted the economic crisis of the 1920s and reported it to managements together with their proposed solutions. After the Second World War it was again accountants who brought the news from the US that the solution of an earlier generation of accountants was now the problem and advocated new forms of accounting. Not only did their recommendations, in both periods, enhance the status of accounting, they simultaneously expanded the roles and career prospects of accountants in enterprises. There have also been claims that accountants have ignored or stifled investigation of unfavourable feedback. Johnson and Kaplan (1987) argued that some inputs can be contradictory, so that financial accounting's response to the need for reporting information led to the failure of management accounting to respond to management needs after the 1920s. Yet neither academics nor practitioners responded by creating new types of accounting until the 1980s. Thus, in their role as guardians of accounting accountants intervene in the evaluation of its practice and propose *revolution* (Glautier and Underdown, 1974; Johnson and Kaplan, 1987) or *evolution* (Bromwich and Bhimani, 1989) or defend the *status quo*. Few share the view of Johnson (1992a, b) that perhaps accountancy is inherently at fault because of its very nature and should be marginalized.

The development of accounting in the UK and US over this century has given it a prominent, if not dominant, position in enterprises. But it has spread far beyond this territory and, under the patronage of governments, become increasingly important in schools, universities, hospitals, prisons, and other social institutions. It has become a central element of governance in policy-making, planning, and regulation. 'Accounting has come to occupy an ever more significant position in the functioning of modern societies . . . No longer seen as a mere assembly of calculative routines, it now functions as a cohesive and influential mechanism for economic and social management' (Burchell *et al.*, 1980: 5, 6). Not only does accountancy influence the social context, it increasingly pervades it.

Accountants as social actors

If accountancy now pervades society the reverse has always been true – accountants themselves are deeply permeated by society. Emphasis on the technical aspects of accounting suggests that accountants are technicians who objectively perform measuring and calculating activities. This is implausible since, even in basic textbooks, there are references to requirements for subjective judgements, understanding of other people, and knowledge of social structures and processes inside and outside the enterprise. So we find in financial accounting that 'subjective opinions and estimates play an important part in historic cost accounting'

(Gee, 1985: 116); and in management accounting there is a need to recognize that 'the accounting system is only one of many control systems . . . a person can be affected by his family, religion, profession, company, department, and so forth. This point may be obvious but it is not trivial' (Horngren, 1977: 165).

Accountants' activities are thus influenced by their social experiences and skills, their membership and understanding of social groups, and their knowledge of social systems. Whilst this is recognized in textbooks, the insight is seldom pursued (Hopper *et al.*, 1987). Instead the boundary between the social world and the technical realm of accounting is maintained – constructing the black box model. The model has been helpful in identifying and organizing social themes in conventional textbooks and demonstrating that they do not 'get by successfully without needing to adopt anything other than a "technical" accounting perspective' (Roslender, 1992: 4). However, the model has now served its usefulness and will be abandoned. We need to explore how accounting itself is pervaded by society – both because influences from the social context do not stop at the boundary of accounting and because accountants, as social actors, carry society within themselves when they enter the realms of accounting. It is time to open the box.

Social construction of accounting

Although textbooks locate accounting in social context, its practices are usually presented in technical fashion. Yet, as we have seen throughout this book, the measurements, techniques, and criteria of accounting are deeply influenced by social factors.

Accounting data and information

The materials on which accountants work – the data to which techniques are applied – are products of the social world which accounting measures and reports. Dalton's (1959) study showed how information on maintenance costs was influenced by the social organization of production. Data on labour and materials used in maintenance and repair altered dramatically with a change of organization and produced startling divergences of 'actual' from 'estimated' costs. Roy's (1953, 1959) study of piecework disclosed 'kitty' practices where record sheets of completed work were retained by workers to cover periods when they wished to take it easy. This meant accountants received bogus data on work in progress. My own experience as a piece-rate worker was similar and taught me many techniques for 'fiddling'. But I also discovered that there were social limits to this. There were warnings from the supervisor that I was overdoing the fiddles – going beyond the 'normal' levels that were tolerated and even expected. In addition, if some products were required urgently my failure to turn in record sheets would result in worried visits of managers from 'upstairs'. If they discovered the undeclared products their further inquiries were likely to disturb the delicate balance of socially acceptable fiddling. Thus the data supplied to accountants from the shopfloor are neither facts of physical reality nor completely arbitrary numbers. Instead they are social constructions which emerge from a negotiated social order. So too are the data used to calculate expected performance as a basis for variance analysis. We have seen how figures for standard labour costs are derived from standard times on the basis of original timings multiplied by a subjective rating factor with the addition of various negotiated allowances. Again these figures are neither precise statements about physical time–effort performance, nor are they arbitrary. They reflect the social circumstances of their construction.

This social construction of data is not confined to the shopfloor. We have seen how engineers may manipulate data in support of new technology investment through 'spurious justifications' (Currie, 1989a) or supply accounting information to support proposals which have been generated for undisclosed social purposes (Wilkinson, 1983). Managers who are aware that their performance is being monitored through financial indicators 'tend consistently to distort the information they pass to their superiors which means senior managers are not informed of unfavourable items' (Drury, 1992: 603). In turn, senior managers may rely upon skilful accountants to construct data which show the enterprise in a preferred light – but not to such an extent that it will arouse the suspicions of financial analysts that the company is stepping too close to the boundary between acceptable 'creative accounting' and fraud.

Throughout the enterprise – from shopfloor to boardroom – data are constructed by interested parties operating within particular social conventions and forms of social organization. When accountants work on these data their raw materials are already social constructions of reality. Accountants, of course, are aware of this and although they deal with numbers the figures are 'not any old numbers' (Harper, 1988b, title). Accountants are suspicious of data not only because of their social construction, but also because they are subject to unintentional mistakes – clerical errors or 'bugs' in the computer. Therefore they check the numbers before beginning work on them. Given that not all the data can be verified, various judgements must be made about which to pursue. Is the data-provider reliable? Is some new product more hazardous to manufacture which might account for increased safety expenditure? Are the approaching Christmas holidays the reason for increased overtime working? Using broad knowledge of the company, accountants sift the numbers and attempt to confirm or change those that appear to be anomalies. This vital activity is so much part of the taken-for-granted world of accountants that it is often missing from descriptions of practice. From this data-set accountants construct their information. As we have seen, this is also a social process. It relies upon the subjective judgements of individual accountants and reflects their education, professional training, and work experiences. It is purposefully conducted in a social context and is influenced by the relationship between accountants and the users of information. It is also social because accounting's basic intellectual tools – its concepts – are particular representations of social reality.

231

Accounting concepts

We may distinguish between formal and informal concepts in accounting. By *formal* I mean the 'principles', 'assumptions', and 'fundamental concepts' which have been deliberately constructed by the profession. The 'accruals concept', for example, initially appears to be a technical statement that 'costs are recognized when they are incurred rather than when they are paid'. The application of this – what it means in practice – can involve accountants in very complex issues about the worlds they are reporting (see Box 8.6). What is to count (and to be counted) as a cost? A human life, a pending lawsuit, an ecological disaster?

This may be regarded as an extreme example, but in more routine, everyday judgements accountants regularly have to put particular interpretations on situations. In doing so they draw on *informal* concepts which have emerged from practice. Management accountants typically divide labour costs into 'direct' and 'indirect'. These terms may have been imported from organizational contexts where the adoption of Scientific Management practices produced a relatively clear division of labour. But is maintenance a direct cost? Is the training of direct labour to be included? Answers to these questions differ in different enterprises. In one company I know, accountants decided it was convenient to treat engineers

Box 8.6

The costs of Hooker Chemicals

In the 1930s Hooker Chemicals bought one mile of uncompleted canal in New York State and began using it as a dump for chemicals. In the early 1960s local people became aware of a high incidence of miscarriages and deaths, and families began to leave the area. House prices fell. By the 1970s the company had 'substantial clues' about problems and legal cases were pending against it. Then New York State and federal authorities set up an Emergency Relief Program for the area. In 1980 Occidental Petroleum, which now owned Hooker Chemicals, was charged by the Securities and Exchange Commission with 'failure to disclose' to shareholders hundreds of millions of dollars of 'potential liability' incurred under US environmental regulations.

The accruals concept requires costs to be included when they are incurred rather than when they are paid. When were these costs incurred? Chemical/environmental costs – from the 1930s. Medical/human costs – from the early 1960s. Housing costs – from the 1960s. Potential legal costs – from the 1970s.

How are accountants to decide this – and why do we trust them to do so?

Source: adapted from Tinker (1985)

---

as direct labour for their accounting purposes. They were then nervous of disclosing this, since they feared a backlash from the engineers, who might see categorization alongside manual workers as an insult to their professional status. Here a concept has been imported from production, transformed by accountants, and now may disturb its context through a new imagery.

The interrelationship between accounting concepts and the world they represent is dynamic. Accounting portrays the enterprise as being made up of 'costs', 'benefits', 'investments', 'expenditures', 'profit centres', 'contributions', 'overheads', and so on. This particular form of imagery – a distinctive construction of reality – affects thoughts and actions outside accounting. Managers of 'profitable' or 'efficient' departments may be seen as go-getters and be promoted. 'Uneconomic pits' are closed. The size of the office work force becomes a problem because 'indirect labour costs' are higher than those of competitors. Companies treated as 'going concerns' retain their investments and are granted loans. Accounting concepts reflect the social world in ways mediated by accountants as social actors and act back upon it.

Accounting rules

The way accountants apply their concepts to data is guided by a framework of rules. Again, these vary in their degree of formality. At the most formal end of the spectrum are rules which carry statutory force through Companies Acts and the profession's 'accounting standards'. The construction of these standards is a complex process involving many interested parties. For example, in the debate over inflation accounting in the UK in the 1970s, attempts to create a new standard led to extended political negotiation between different groups (Bryer and Brignall, 1985). Concern with historical cost accounting (HCA) led the profession to recommend a limited modification of current purchasing power (CPP). On the eve of its announcement the UK government set up an Inflation Accounting Committee of Inquiry which included representatives of the Confederation of British Industry and the Society of Investment Analysts as well as accountants. The profession was reluctantly required to move towards current cost accounting (CCA) despite much criticism from its members (Gee, 1985). Bryer and Brignall argued that the profession, unable to return to CPP since this had been publicly attacked by industry, responded to membership pressure by proposing a theoretically dubious 'gearing adjustment' to CCA. Thus the eventual rule, whilst a technical statement, was also a negotiated social order.

In a less formal sense, accounting rules are conventional procedures or techniques. They may have their origins in economic theory – such as 'discounted cash flow' – but the selection and use of the techniques are influenced by many personal, organizational, and societal factors. Indeed much accounting practice is 'conventional' in exactly this way – it is constituted by norms of action governed by social conventions.

Accounting world-views

At a deeper level we find a collection of broad assumptions about accounting that may be so embedded they are forgotten or treated as common sense (e.g. that accounting is to do with 'reporting', 'control', 'performance', 'decisions', 'profit') and, below this, fundamental world-views which orientate accountants' approach to accounting issues. Perhaps the most significant of these world-views is that of *efficiency*. If 'efficiency' is taken as a universal force, then accounting thought can be abstracted from the messy, experienced world – of social contexts and social actors – to a realm of pure reasoning. Here terms such as good/bad, appropriate/inappropriate, relevant/irrelevant would not represent particular values, but would be evaluated against an objective goal of maximizing efficiency. But:

> Just what is efficiency? At best it is a concept that can be subject to a wide variety of interpretations. Although it is possible to shape the world in the name of efficiency, there are very real problems in relating the generality of the concept to the specific operational procedures [of accounting], let alone their specific consequences in organizations, that can flow from its articulation and use. Of course that very ambiguity is a very positive factor in political discourse.
>
> (Hopwood, 1985b: 6)

Reference to efficiency can obscure political conflicts rather than remove them. The term means different things to different people. For *owners*, efficiency may be seen as the maximization of their wealth. *Workers* may see it as the highest reward (wages and other benefits) for the least expenditure of effort. *Customers* look for high quality against low cost in products, whilst *governments* seek to achieve and finance their policies. Even if efficiency is seen merely as an economic objective, it is difficult to see how *managers* (who have interests of their own) could distil all this into a single goal. *Environmentalists* add concern to voice the interests of nature – in terms of conservation, sustainability, and renewal – which are not expressed in purely economic terms. In the face of all of this, a desire to escape to an abstract world may be understandable but it is hardly plausible. Accounting practice is firmly established in a social world where it is:

> a means for resolving social conflict, a device for appraising the terms of exchange between social constituencies, and an institutional mechanism for arbitrating, evaluating and adjudicating social choices.
>
> (Tinker, 1985: 81)

Technical *versus* social?

Accounting can therefore be seen as a social activity not just because it exists in a social context and those who carry it out are social actors, but also because its procedures and mode of thought – data, concepts, rules, and world-view – are social constructions. To some, this may appear to be an argument for abandoning a 'technical' view of accounting and replacing it with a 'social' approach. This would be to retain a distinction which is invalid. Technical issues in accounting are social phenomena; the social world is created and transformed through technical developments. The point is not whether we should adopt a technical or a social view of accounting. Rather we need to explore how accounting can be understood as a 'socio-technical' activity. As Latour (1987) has argued – in relation to physical sciences and technologies – the more technical an activity is, simultaneously the more social it is. As debates become technically more complex they bring in more research and researchers, there are more appeals to other authorities to support propositions, more people are entangled in the arguments. The creation of technical facts is dependent on their social acceptance, and they continue to be 'facts' only if people act upon them – otherwise they slide out of existence.

The committee of academics exploring social approaches to accounting (mentioned above) never reported. This was not because its members could not decide whether accounting was technical or social; rather it was because they could not resolve 'disagreements on intertwining accounting with the social' (Hopwood, 1985a, subtitle) and what attitude accountants should adopt to this relationship. The crucial issue is how accountants, recognizing the socio-technical nature of their theories and practices, can and should think and act in the social world.

ACCOUNTING: NEUTRAL OR PARTISAN?

Some members of Hopwood's committee argued that accountants should distance themselves from the particularities of the social dimension of accounting.

> Accounting of itself cannot be the vehicle of social and political change although knowledge and understanding of financial data which accounting can produce may well be vitally important both to those who wish change and those who resist it: but accounting as a discipline cannot take sides although those who use it may well do so.
>
> (Quoted in Hopwood, 1985a)

This is essentially a moral claim that accounting, and by implication accountants, should inform social conflicts but not be part of them. For other members of the committee such a view was untenable because:

> the origins of specific accounts resided in the articulation of particular interests, in the creation of legitimacy for them and in the construction of a calculative and administrative apparatus which would further those interests.
>
> (Hopwood, 1985a: 367)

Here it would be impossible not to take sides, since all accounts must be particular – indeed there would be little point in creating them if they were not. This fundamental argument about whether accounting can and should be neutral, or whether it is inescapably partisan, has been debated by two champions – Solomons in the neutralist corner and Tinker in the partisan.

Representational faithfulness

Solomons sought to distinguish between accountants in their role as accountants and accountants in their role as citizens. As citizens they 'should be as much concerned to bring about desirable changes as anyone else' (1991a: 294). However, accountants as accountants should be neutral, or at least should strive to achieve the perfection of neutrality. Solomons built his argument through a number of analogies – 'I believe that accountants are like journalists. They should report the news. Not make it' (p. 287). He also likened accounting to a telephone representing the speaker's thoughts to the listener; a messenger bringing the news in ancient times; and, in his early work, to the practice of cartography (1978).

The analogy of map-making demonstrates Solomons's use of the notion of 'representational faithfulness'. The good map-maker continually attempts to refine and improve the representation (map) until it corresponds as accurately as possible to what it represents (the territory depicted). He argued that we judge such maps by how well they represent the facts – and not by the effects they produce. Analogously, accounting should strive to produce maps of economic reality, and should be judged on the accuracy of these maps, not upon their social consequences. Hence accountants can be neutral in respect of what they report, and the effects of reporting it.

This argument is notable for its appearance of simplicity and reasonableness. However, arguing through analogies is a risky activity, since, if they are taken seriously, analogies may rebound upon the analogist. I have in front of me an atlas (*Encyclopaedia Britannica*, 1963). It begins with a great many representations of the planet Earth. The content of these maps differs considerably. Apart from the more usual maps showing countries represented as political states, there are those showing population density, geological terrain, climatic regions, average temperatures, and much more. None of these is any more real than any of the others. How are we to judge them? Presumably on the basis of their usefulness to the user. If I wish to concentrate my marketing efforts I may be interested in population density. If I am planning my summer holiday I would like to know average August temperatures. Thus representations must be evaluated, at least in part, against their purpose.

The maps also differ in terms of the style or format of their presentation. They are constructed using different 'projections' – Mercator, Goode's Homolosine Equal-area, Eckert Equal-area, and others. If each has been constructed with the same technical rigour then each is an equally valid representation. Yet none of them is faithful in the sense that each represents a three-dimensional reality by a two-dimensional portrayal. No map can ever overcome this fundamental limitation. For that we would need to abandon maps and adopt globes (although these too have their limitations). The map-maker must recognize that maps are a fundamental distortion of reality and, instead of pursuing representational faithfulness to impossible ends, develop appropriate ways of using distortion. Or give up making maps.

If we consider another kind of map we may find that distortion, rather than being a problem, can be a solution. Take a road map. It shows cities as neat dark blobs connected by lines of different colours. Scaled up to the physical world these lines would represent roads several miles wide. In some respects an aerial photograph would be much higher on the scale of representational faithfulness. But it would not be a good road map. It is precisely because road maps distort reality that they have value.

I have taken Solomons's analogy of map-making seriously and explored it. If we return to his original concern to portray the neutrality of accounting in terms of its representational faithfulness we see the issue in a different way. The map analogy now suggests that accuracy, although not to be dismissed, is only one factor in evaluation. The appropriateness of content and format to the purposes of the constructors and users of maps is vital, and faithfulness to a 'real world' may be an impossible, and sometimes inappropriate, goal. Accounting inescapably produces particular distortions of the economic world. What is important is not to eliminate all distortion; rather, it is to recognize and consider those distortions which are constructed, and their purposes. Of course this discussion is itself a distortion. It has taken map-making as one analogy for accounting, when it could have chosen from scores of others. The purpose was to explore Solomons's ideas using the scheme he himself proposed. There are other approaches to this issue.

Practical reflexivity

If Solomons's approach was bluff common sense, Tinker's contribution was heavy with social theories and references – which his adversary considered 'philosophical obfuscation' (Solomons, 1991b: 311). He championed the cause of 'partisan' accounting with some reluctance, since he viewed his opponent as equally partisan – 'an evangelist'. The difference was that Tinker was prepared to acknowledge (indeed celebrate) bias, whereas Solomons attempted to deny (or purge) his own.

Tinker found the analogies – especially with map-making – a fascinating kind of myopia. 'Maps are never mere miniatures of the original; they are shaped by jingoistic, political, recreational, religious, economic, technical, and other interests – consciously intended and otherwise' (1991: 300). Looking again at my atlas, I find a map of 'Territorial Problem Areas and Status of Boundaries' (an unusual feature of atlases, which usually draw clear lines around 'nation states'). It identifies some territories as 'disputed', such as Machias Seal Island (claimed by Canada and the US) and Kashmir (claimed by India and Pakistan). However, Northern Ireland and the Basque region of Spain do not appear as geographical zones subject to dispute. Even when map-makers recognize that drawing their lines (boundaries) is a matter of social conflict, they have to decide which conflicts will be recognized and which not. The atlas also pictures a large, light-green mass, labelled YUGOSLAVIA. As I write, people in the territory this used to represent are being killed, while their 'leaders' – labelled Serbian, Croatian, and Moslem – are (quite literally) waving different maps at each other in 'peace talks'. For Tinker the notion of the map-maker as a neutral purveyor of information is as unrealistic as its use as an analogy for accounting.

He distinguished his 'practical reflexivity' approach from that of 'representational faithfulness' in three ways. First, it was not utopian – hoping that one day a 'true' picture might emerge – but was concerned with understanding the social circumstances in which various problems and distortions of accounting were brought into existence and maintained over time. These were to be seen not as spasmodic or anomalous mistakes, but as systematic products of the enterprises and societies on which accountants report. Second, his approach would not involve dedication to some abstract, and unobtainable, perfection of 'truth', but would recognize that ideas and actions are always embedded in the societies (places in time) from which they emerge and in which accountants are participants. This must always involve evaluations of truthfulness derived from contemporary (temporary and unstable) acceptance of truth-claims. Third, accountants would not be required to pretend to be split personalities – sometimes accountants-as-accountants, sometimes accountants-as-citizens. Instead they would acknowledge that they could do no other than be social actors and would recognize that their actions would reverberate around society. Ignoring this was no solution, since 'even "inaction" is a political act that inevitably changes/reproduces social relations' (Tinker, quoted in Jones, 1992: 253).

Rather than attempt to purge the technical domain of accounting of its pervasive social character – a hopeless and pointless task – practical reflexivity meant the development of social self-consciousness by accountants, who must seek to become people who recognize the social causes and effects of their actions and can critically evaluate their own role in shaping the world. This is an imperative not only from some altruistic sense of moral obligation to others, but also because accountants are enmeshed in the fragile social fabric. If accountants ignore, or are unwilling to fulfil, their moral responsibilities to others, then their positions of trust are in jeopardy. The warning to the accountancy profession is this – 'its social self-awareness of the contradictions which beset it is woefully inadequate; unless it acts expeditiously it may also suffer a spectacular martyrdom' (Tinker, 1991: 306).

Social creativity

These very different approaches to accounting and how it is to be done both recognize its social nature. 'It is unnecessary for Tinker to assert that accounting measures are "socially constructed and socially enactive". Of course they are' (Solomons, 1991b: 312). One seeks to deal with this by encouraging accountants to recognize and then strip away social influences – 'accountants being human, the avoidance of all bias may not always be achieved; but that should be the aim' (Solomons, 1991b: 311). The other identifies not 'bias' but 'social awareness' and seeks to open up investigation of how accountants can make choices which are 'socially reflective and critically self-conscious' (Tinker, 1991: 297).

Throughout the book there have been references to 'creative accounting'. In the light of this discussion the term itself appears problematic. As one of the leading critics put it, 'I know we all talk about "creative accounting" but this seems to suggest that there is a right method of accounting. This is not so' (Sikka, 1993, personal communication). All accounts are created. And they are created by social actors in social contexts. In this sense all accounting is socially creative activity. Disputes are not about whether accounting is social but about what kind of social activity it is, what kinds of social world it reflects/shapes, and what is to be done about this. If the discussion of this issue has been too long and pain-staking – and I suspect that some readers will have found it so – this is not because there is a choice to be made between a technical (or economic) view of account-ing and a social (or political) approach. Accounting academics, in their textbooks and research publications, recognize social dimensions to accounting. But often these are then ignored, restricted, marginalized, or trivialized. The discussion here has not sought to claim that accounting can be understood only as 'social'; but attempting to understand it as solely 'technical' is fruitless. 'Technical versus social' is a bogus dichotomy and we should be concerned with how accountants interrelate the two in their activities.

ACCOUNTANTS AS SOCIAL ACTORS IN SOCIAL CONTEXTS

The previous sections have mostly been concerned with academics' views of accounting. Their various theorizings on the social nature of the discipline may seem far removed from the immediate, everyday concerns of accountants in practice. Indeed, many 'critical' writers have seen their mission as the opening-up of a new social approach which practitioners lack. In this section I will argue that practitioners are well aware of social factors in accounting, and may well have a more sophisticated approach in their accommodation to them than many academics.

Understanding accountants

The approach adopted follows Weber's (1922) discussion of social action. He distinguished between *behaviour*, seen as responses to stimuli (e.g. reflex knee-jerks), and *action* – which applies to activities behind which lie the intentions of the actor. He also distinguished between action and *social action* – which takes into account the activities of other people. In order to understand action we need to explore the *meanings* which underlie it – we must interpret the observed actions in terms of their meaningfulness to the actor. Weber identified three broad categories of such action – 'traditional' (based on custom, convention, or habit), 'affective' (based on feelings or emotions), and 'rational' (where activity is the result of deliberate calculation). The last of these was becoming the dominant form in the twentieth century: most clearly demonstrated in business enterprises, where its purest expression was in accounting. The accountant, therefore, may be taken as the epitome of the rational actor. In what ways can accountants and accounting be understood as rational? Much accounting theory draws on a narrow definition of 'rational' decision-making influenced by neo-classical economics. This approach has been heavily criticized and 'administrative' or 'political' models have been suggested in its place. One of the limitations of this is that the models are treated as alternative and incompatible views of the world between which we have to choose. We may be able to combine the different views in a unified model of a broader rationality of decisions. This will be illustrated through a study of one particular practice – investment appraisal – examined through the perceptions of accountants who are involved with it.

In interviews with accountants (Dugdale and Jones, 1991; Jones and Dugdale, 1994) we found that even apparently simple questions, such as 'What investment appraisal technique do you use?', produced complex discussions involving many different kinds of explanation. Accountants were keen to explain not only what technique was used, but also why and how it was used. Each person made reference to the *technical* attributes of appraisals – Pay-back (PB) being simple, Net Present Value (NPV) more sophisticated and rigorous, taking into account the time-value of money. There was little disagreement over these attributes, which were presented as facts to be universally recognized. However these facts were evaluated differently. Some valued simplicity and hence preferred PB; some regarded rigour as the more important criterion and thus recommended NPV. These evaluations were related to *personal* explanations about techniques. One accountant had not used NPV for many years and thought the effort of re-learning it, and the danger of making mistakes in using it, would outweigh any claimed benefits of the technique; another, having recently qualified, felt she had been 'brainwashed' into using NPV because her lecturers had insisted upon it – she was 'a victim of my training'. They also referred to the acceptability of ac-counting information to users – generally other managers – in *social* explanations of techniques. In one case NPV was rejected because 'my managers wouldn't understand that'; in another, the company policy of sending managers on MBA courses meant they were familiar with many investment appraisal techniques. Whilst for accountants and financially informed managers NPV might be the collectively agreed 'best' method, it may not be socially acceptable to other groups such as engineers or non-accounting managers. In selecting techniques accountants consider all these issues. But their scope for discretion may be limited, as they explained in *political* explanations of techniques. One junior accountant, a supporter of NPV, had to supply accounting information which she regarded as 'irrelevant' when it was required by senior managers. Another, content to use PB, knew he would have to learn NPV if Head Office demanded it. Thus the selection of a particular technique is far more than a purely 'technical' question – and accounting practitioners are well aware of the fact. Their explanations of practice draw on many kinds of reasoning. All may be seen as rational – consciously thought through. There is the pure rationality of the calculations themselves; the practical rationality of working within your own knowledge and skill; the shared rationality of working in socially acceptable ways; and the self-interested rationality of recognizing the political power that others have over you.

From these different elements in explanations of practice I constructed a general framework for understanding accountants – a 'Socio-rational' model of action (Jones, 1992). *Objective rationality* applies to reasons which refer to 'factual' features of accounting – where the accountant assumes that the explanations he or she advances are capable of universal validation. They are usually concerned with the logic, rigour, certainty, and consistency of techniques. Their defining feature is that they are directed at the rationality of accounting itself. *Subjective rationality* applies to reasons which are particular to the individual accountant – although they can be explained to others. They reflect personal experience, knowledge, and skills which are unique to any one person. Their defining feature is that they are directed at the accountant as a rational actor. *Inter-subjective rationality* applies to reasons which are shared within a social group. They usually refer to practices which are socially acceptable either to other accountants or to managers. Their defining feature is that they are directed at the rationality of formal and informal rules in relation to the accounting profession and/or the enterprise. *Positional rationality* applies to reasons which refer to the position of accountants within the enterprise, what they wish to achieve, and their ability to do so. Their defining feature is that they are directed at the rational pursuit of interests conditioned by the power of the actor (see Box 8.7).

In these different forms of reasoning both the *means* and the *ends* of accounting are seen in various ways. Sometimes 'facts' are hard certainties about reality; sometimes they are those statements we agree about, even if others do not. Accounting may be seen at one moment as an objective calculation; at the next, as an expression of subjective judgement. Accountants may see themselves as following rules based on 'the laws of economics' whilst at the same time reflecting that they have internalized particular perceptions and values (socialization) and that various forces regulate their activities (social control). Thus the conduct of accounting practice – its means – are not viewed in a single light by practitioners. Nor are its purposes. Although textbooks may cite a single goal of the enterprise – usually the maximization of shareholder wealth – accountants in their lived experience of enterprises recognize that people differ in their personal goals, and that if one group identifies a target (say, accountants seeking cost reduction) then another group is likely to claim that the goal of the enterprise is better served by a different aim (say, engineers advocating investment in AMT). If the enterprise cannot satisfy all the goals of its individual and collective members the outcome will be a political solution in which several members compromise in a negotiated aim or where the most powerful interests dominate

Box 8.7

Socio-rational model

	Rationality			
	Objective	*Subjective*	*Inter-subjective*	*Positional*
Means				
Facts/ information	Universal reality	Individually constructed reality	Socially constructed reality	Politically constructed reality
Process	Pure calculation	Individual: perceptions and values	Social: perceptions and values	Political: interests
Source	Quasi-scientific laws	Individual experience and personality	Socialization Social control	Positions Power
Ends				
Goals	Single	Personal	Shared	Contested
Outcomes	Closed	Open	Intra-group closed/inter-group open	Politically closed

Source: Jones (1992)

the others. Immersed in this world, practitioners cannot rely solely on a 'technical' perspective on accounting. They may not spend much time theorizing on accounting-as-a-social-activity, but their everyday lives are a practical demonstration that it is one. They are aware that being a skilful social actor is as much a part of accounting as being a technical expert.

There are limits to understanding accountants as rational social actors. First, not all their acts may be rational – they may be driven by tradition, or emotion, or deep psychological motivations. Second, even if all individuals act rationally this does not imply that the collective outcome will be regarded as rational from anyone's point of view. Third, social action is understandable only by locating it in a social context – a world which is influenced by social actors but which exists outside them – and we need to explore the place of accountants in enterprises and society.

Locating accountants

In previous chapters we have looked at accounting's influence on capital, management, and labour, and relations between the three. We now need to locate accountants in this social structure.

Much discussion of accountancy stresses its *occupational organization* – the way in which a body of knowledge was created, delineated, and monopolized in the establishment of the profession (Armstrong, 1985, 1987a; Loft, 1986). In this process the patronage of capital and of the state is seen as a vital component (Johnson, 1977; Puxty *et al.*, 1987) relating to the roles of accounting in the production, realization and distribution of value by enterprises, and in the state's management of the economy (Berry *et al.*, 1985b; Neimark and Tinker, 1986; Lehman and Tinker, 1987). Here accountants' primary location would be as members of an occupation enjoying privileges established by their professional associations with the backing of powerful forces in society. This is important in understanding accountants, since it is reflected in their education and training, the development of knowledge and skills, and the structuring of demand for accounting services and their supply in labour markets. The profession constitutes a powerful reference group which creates and legitimizes the meanings which accountants attach to their practices.

Although this occupational organization is undoubtedly important, for accountants within enterprises their location in *corporate organization* is also relevant. Many accountants may have a relatively weak identification with their occupational group – seeing accountancy as the starting point of a managerial career. Many do not read their professional journals, do not attend conferences, and may see 'their' professional association as little more than the body which set examinations passed many years ago (Jones, 1992). For these people the enterprise itself may be more important both in shaping their views and in locating them in the social structure.

The identity of accountants may therefore have a twofold character: accountants-as-professionals and accountants-as-managers. Some writers have seen such dualism as causing a tension between professional and organizational values and principles (Scott, 1966; Friedson, 1971). In the case of accountants such conflict seems unlikely to be strong, because many of the organizational rules are constructed by individual accountants as 'management control', and because accountancy bodies present their members as 'business professionals' (ICAEW) or 'management professionals' (CIMA). However, different accountants occupy differing positions in relation to their occupation and enterprises. To explore this we need to examine what unites and what divides these 'accountants'.

To some extent, accountants share similarities in their selection, training, and career which produce *social closure* of the occupation in terms of gender, race, family and educational background. This may encourage the development of a unified world-view amongst themselves and unite them with other managers with similar characteristics and backgrounds. Operating against such unifying forces is the development of a *division of labour* within accountancy. Activities once undertaken by the nineteenth century 'bookkeeper' have become separated into two fairly distinct roles. On the one hand routine numerical processing (now conducted by 'accounting clerks'); on the other, interpreting, advising, and controlling duties (carried out by 'accountants'). This represents a process of

243

polarization in which a small elite distances itself from a larger number of lower-level employees (Armstrong, 1993). Members of the lower ranks are predominantly female and their prospects of career moves to higher levels may be diminishing (Crompton and Jones, 1984). Against this view, Roslender (1992) identified the emergence of a new intermediate stratum of 'senior accounting technicians' who supervise routine accounting activities. These, in the UK, may be members of quasi-professional bodies, such as the Association of Accounting Technicians. He found evidence that the large accounting houses were routinizing some accounting tasks so that they could be carried out by relatively inexpensive 'technicians' rather than by qualified 'professionals'. This may be a second stage of polarization in which the activities of those in the more senior positions are themselves subject to a division of labour whereby the more mechanical tasks are stripped away and allocated to those lower down the enterprise. One financial director told me, 'Although they like to think of themselves as professionals, 80 per cent of what my accountants do is routine. Therefore I can get rid of 80 per cent of my accountants so that those who are left concentrate on the 20 per cent of interpreting–advising work for which you really need qualified people.'

All of this suggests important social cleavages in 'the middle layers' (Braverman, 1974) – those who stand between capital and labour. This is further compounded by the instability of these middle layers in general. Class analysis of what is usually called 'the new middle class' (to distinguish it from the 'old' class of people running small businesses) has identified it with locations with mixed economic functions – both *functions of collective labour* and *global functions of capital* (Carchedi, 1977). On the one hand, the middle layers are involved with co-ordination-and-unity and thus make a contribution to productive labour. On the other hand, they are also involved in control-and-surveillance and thus act as agents of capital. Their location in the enterprise is not economically identified by ownership (although as individuals they may well hold capital) but by their employment of labour (though they themselves are also employees). They are controllers of labour but are themselves controlled by capital.

These ambiguities in the location of the middle layers – showing some features of capital and some of labour – have led to very different categorizations of their place in the social structure. Some have seen them as essentially agents of capital (e.g. Poulantzas, 1974), whilst others regard them as 'privileged wage labour' (e.g. Hopper *et al.*, 1987). Carchedi (1977) argued that they simultaneously performed economic functions of both capital and labour and thus had divided class interests; whilst Wright (1978) placed them between capital and labour as a class with distinct interests but which was liable to fragmentation – the upper edges joining the ranks of the capitalist class, the lower sinking into the working class.

The approach adopted in this book has been to identify 'management' as a distinct category, standing between capital and labour, which has its own distinctive interests. In part this was a matter of convenience in structuring interrelated debates into discrete chapters. But it also reflected my own experience within enterprises where, whatever the uncertainties and ambiguities of locating the middle layers in broader society, *the management* typically portrayed itself, and was seen by workers, as a unified and solid authority – a taken-for-granted reality of working life. This has been most evocatively expressed in relation to a Hungarian factory, but might apply to many other enterprises:

> THEY, THEM, THEIRS: I don't believe that anyone who has ever worked in a factory, or even had a relatively superficial discussion with workers, can be in any doubt about what these words mean. In every place of work, without any definition or specification, without any gestures, special tones of voice, winks of the eye or pointing of the finger, *them* means the same thing: the management, those who give the orders and take the decisions, employ labour and pay wages, the men and their agents who are in charge – who remain inaccessible even when they cross our field of vision . . . nowhere, except among factory workers, have I heard this absolute *them*, peremptory, exact and crystal clear.
>
> (Haraszti, 1977: 72)

This appearance of unity and solidity is only one aspect of management. There are social forces which are *centripetal* – encouraging cohesion among managers as a social category. But there are also *centrifugal* forces which tend to divide and fragment management. In locating accountants within the enterprise we find similarities (in their backgrounds, education, and training) leading to social closure – forming them as a distinct occupation collectively organized by their professional bodies. At the same time they are also divided by horizontal differentiation (e.g. between financial and management accountants) and vertical differentiation (e.g. between finance directors, accountants, accounting technicians, and accounts clerks). They may share knowledge and skill in accounting techniques, and use similar language, but their positions in enterprises, and their experience of change, are very different. For those at the upper edge of the occupation, developments in the twentieth century have generated many senior positions in the management of UK and US enterprises which have relied heavily on financial information and control. Those who occupy the lowest positions may carry out accounting tasks but they are not accorded the title 'accountant' and have been submerged in the ranks of general clerical workers. Of those between these extremes, many may already be experiencing routine, highly supervised work (Roslender, 1992) and others may feel the impact of the 'de-layering' of middle management.

The future of individuals in all these positions will be influenced by the general prospects of accounting within the enterprise. The central position achieved by accountancy in UK and US enterprises over this century is now being challenged in debates which identify: a concern with 'managing by numbers' (Ezzamel *et al.*, 1990); the importance of other management practices aimed at quality and customer satisfaction (Johnson, 1992a); and the lower position of accountants and lesser influence of accounting in other societies, especially Germany and Japan (Strange, 1991; Williams *et al.*, 1991; Currie, 1992; Jones *et al.*, 1993). Although accounting techniques are unlikely to be abandoned 'it seems likely that the influence of accounting has peaked' (Morgan and Willmott, 1993: 7).

Given the complexity of accountants as social actors, and of the social contexts in which they act, the future of accountancy cannot be predicted. Perhaps it is so deeply embedded in the enterprise that it will prove resistant to change; or perhaps it will find a new relevance in the twenty-first century. On the other hand, if the critics are correct the 'golden age' of accountancy may be nearly over. The outcome cannot be known now – it will be shaped by the social processes explored in this book.

9

SOCIAL THEORY IN ACCOUNTING

Earlier chapters have drawn on a number of studies which explored substantive issues in the relationship between accounting and the enterprise. In reporting this research I was not centrally concerned with the identification and evaluation of the underlying social theories which informed it. That is the aim of this chapter.

In the last decade a division of accounting research into two camps – 'conventional' and 'critical' – has become customary. In some ways the use of such labels is unhelpful, since (like all such distinctions) it can conceal as much as it reveals. Conventional research (or 'mainstream', or 'traditional') has many strands within it. Although much of it derives from economics, some approaches are more overtly social. Much, but not all, of it rests upon a belief that a highly mechanistic model of natural science research – 'positivism' – can be applied to accounting. Although large-scale statistical analysis, often based on questionnaire surveys, may be the norm, it is not the only form. Similarly, critical accounting research draws on a variety of different social theories, and focuses on a wide range of issues, and argument between these strands is often as heated as the debate with conventional approaches (Neimark, 1990). Although the greater emphasis on case studies or field research may be distinctive, there have been relatively few examples of these. The term 'critical' may be taken to mean academic scepticism – a requirement for argument and evidence – which is a feature of many kinds of research; or an active hostility to existing forms of accounting, which is not shared by all who are cited as representatives of the new accounting research (Morgan and Willmott, 1993). Nevertheless, there is sufficient which is distinctive about these two bodies of research to allow separate discussion of their roots in social theory.

The basis of social theory is the link between people and societies. This has been expressed in different ways at different times – from Marx's (1868) claim that people make their own history but cannot determine the conditions under which they do so, to Thomas's (1928) assertion that what people believe to be real is real in its consequences, to Mills's (1959) identification of 'the sociological imagination' which should connect 'personal troubles' with 'public issues'. In linking 'the person' with 'society' social theories differ in the emphasis they place on one or the other. This influences the focus of social analysis, the content and methods of research, and the kinds of explanation advanced. Some theories place emphasis on society and are concerned with the ways in which social systems, structures, and processes produce particular kinds of social beings, and delineate their opportunities and constraints. Other theories begin with the person and are concerned with the ways in which they create the societies in which they live, emphasizing the role of human agency and social interaction. Dawe (1970) found these approaches so distinct that he labelled them 'the two sociologies'. Occupying some middle ground there are theories which take particular social forms – groups, institutions, organizations, discourses – as the focus of study. But even in the more extreme examples of emphasis on the external reality of society, or alternatively the social construction of society through meanings, there is an implicit presence of the under-emphasized complementary view. Theories which deal with social systems contain assumptions about the ways it is possible for people to think and act. Theories which concentrate on interpreting people's meanings presuppose a society which sustains their existence. Much current sociological theory is concerned with ways in which these 'top-down' and 'bottom-up' approaches can be combined in social analysis – most notably in a long series of works by Giddens (e.g. 1973, 1984, 1992). In this book I have identified the issue as relating social action to social contexts. Accounting research, drawing on social theory, reflects the different emphases of these various theories.

CONVENTIONAL ACCOUNTING RESEARCH

Much accounting research draws upon economics for its theory and thus displays the dominant neo-classical, marginalist approach adopted in that discipline (Tinker, 1985). Of course, economics has its own social theories embedded within it, but rather than excavating these, I will concentrate on conventional research which has more overtly social themes. Identifying social theory in accounting research raises a problem we have met before. When a theory is so widely accepted that challenges or alternatives are not anticipated and/or recognized then writers may not specify the theoretical foundation of their work. Indeed they may not recognize that they use 'theory' at all but assume that it is 'common sense'. Thus in much work there are assumptions that accounting serves the needs of enterprises and adapts to changing environments, with little or no justification of this view. Where there is identification of the theoretical origins of the research this often draws upon organization theories – especially open systems and contingency theory (Emmanuel and Otley, 1985; Morgan and Willmott, 1993). Both were constructed in the 1960s. Open system theory was inspired by biological science and emphasized the way enterprises – viewed as organisms – respond to changes in their environment. It was refined by Lawrence and Lorsch (1967) to encompass the ways in which sub-units (e.g. departments) respond to their own sub-environments (e.g. consumer markets, technological developments) and interrelate with each other. Contingency theory was developed by Pugh and Hickson (1976) and Pugh and Hinings (1976), and attempted an elaborate taxonomy in which independent variables (such as size, ownership, technology, markets) were matched with key (dependent) variables in organization structures and processes.

What these have in common is their view of enterprises and sub-units within them as 'parts' which are to be analysed in relation to other parts which constitute the 'whole'. This is combined with the claim that 'different structures are appropriate in different circumstances', which leads to the conclusion that 'there is no universally appropriate AIS [accounting information system] that applies equally to all organizations in all circumstances' (Emmanuel and Otley, 1985: 41, 254). Whilst open systems and contingency theory may be 'the least sociological of organisation theories' (Morgan and Willmott, 1993: 8) they are quite overtly social theories and lead to particular forms of social analysis. They emphasize that accounting cannot be understood outside its social context and that it would be fruitless to construct some 'best' form of accounting and attempt to impose it on all organizations. No doubt this approach was helpful in opening up ways of studying accounting, and it 'has dominated behavioural management accounting research from about 1975' (Emmanuel and Otley, 1985: 41), although in the last few years other approaches have become more common (Roslender, 1992). However, even as it was being adopted in accounting research, it was being strongly criticized in its home territory of organization theory (Otley, 1980). The limitations and problems of the approach can be explored by examining the social theory in which it is rooted. Open systems and contingency theory themselves are particular variants of a much broader – and older – general social theory which has caused considerable controversy in social science – *functionalism*.

Origins and development of functionalism

In essence 'functionalism' applies to forms of social analysis in which social objects, events, processes or institutions are explained in terms of the way they fit with each other to maintain the social whole. Introduced by Spencer, it was developed by Durkheim (1895) into a powerful and influential social theory. Durkheim viewed the functioning of society through two analogies. Pre-industrial society was seen as *mechanistic* – each of the parts relating to others like components of a machine. We talk of the 'function' of the carburettor as mixing air and fuel for injection into the cylinders of an engine. For modern societies, he preferred an *organic* metaphor – all parts relating to each other like cells (or clusters of cells) in an organism. So we speak of the 'function' of the heart as pumping blood around the human body. The difference between the two models is that the former implies stable, fixed components with certain, unchanging purposes; the latter implies that parts have evolved over time and are in constant change as cells die and are replaced. Durkheim believed that his functionalist approach could provide a means of analyzing societies and explain how social institutions operated. But it could not explain why institutions came into existence – it was not a causal explanation.

Those who adopted Durkheim's ideas in the twentieth century tended to forget this reservation on causality in claiming that social phenomena exist because of the functions they fulfil – the parts being explained in terms of the needs they serve. What are these needs? In anthropology two answers to this question emerged. Malinowski (1944) focused on universal *biological needs* – food, shelter, warmth, etc. – and the secondary needs that stem from these. Thus in his study of islanders he explained the existence of 'magic' through the way belief in rituals and charms reduced fishermen's fear of the sea, and thus emboldened them to face its dangers, and so enabled them to catch fish. In this way magic ultimately functioned to serve biological needs. Radcliffe-Brown (1952) was more concerned with *social needs* – those of society as a whole – such as order, governance, education, defence. In every society social institutions could be found which carried out these essential functions. For anthropologists of the period functionalism may be seen as a liberating theory since it offered a means of analysing societies with which they were unfamiliar. Instead of greeting foreign customs as bizarre, uncivilized, peculiar, or irrational, they were able to push aside (partially) their ingrained prejudices (from their own societies) and explore foreign societies on those societies' own terms. The social analysis is largely descriptive – concentrating on tracing relationships – and may be termed *soft* functionalism (Lee and Newby, 1983). However, as functionalist theories were developed in sociology a cruder and more restrictive form emerged.

The rise of *hard* functionalism in American sociology was strongly influenced by Parsons (1937). He identified four fundamental needs which apply to every society and sub-unit of society and which constitute the social system. *Adaptation*: all social systems must adapt to their physical environment (e.g. through the economic sub-system of society). *Pattern maintenance*: all social systems need to recruit (or reproduce) new members and shape them to the existing system (e.g. through family and education sub-systems). *Goal attainment*: all social systems need to ensure that activities are directed towards the first two (e.g. through the political sub-system). *Integration*: all social sub-systems must fit together to constitute the whole. The approach asserted that 'society and the actions of its members *must* be viewed as a total system or even a set of systems' (Lee and Newby, 1983: 263).

The kind of social analysis which emerged can be seen in its most notorious example – Davis and Moore's (1945) 'functionalist theory of stratification'. They began with the observation that all societies display inequalities in the distribution of rewards (which they initially defined broadly, but then represented as money). If this is universal, they argued, then inequality must be a necessary and inevitable feature of social systems. The universal need was that all societies must ensure that the scarce supply of talented and skilled people occupy the most important positions. If they do not, then societies cannot survive. Unequal rewards provide incentives to individuals to develop their talents (willing to bear the 'sacrifice' of education and training), to seek important positions, and to carry out their duties conscientiously. The effect of this is to produce societies in which there are highly rewarded and lowly rewarded groups. This is an unintended consequence of the need for 'societal survival' and is inescapable (see Box 9.1).

Critique of functionalism

This explanation of the social structure had a strong commonsense appeal to many but was soon attacked on a broad front and with much passion. The scope and vigour of the attacks suggest that there is a lot at stake here, and we need to consider the limitations and problems of hard functionalism in some detail.

To begin with there were *empirical* challenges to Davis and Moore which questioned their description of the operation of society. Studies of education demonstrated that inequalities in society were barriers to the creation and mobilization of talented, skilled people – for example, yielding lower levels of achievement among those from poor families and some racial minorities, and handicapping female students in some subjects (especially engineering and science). In the case of some of the most highly rewarded members of society – entertainment and sporting stars, stock-market speculators, international drug dealers – it is far from clear that they occupy positions most important to society's survival. Nor is it certain that money is the driving force behind the aspirations of those who seek high office in the state, the Church, education, the military, and so on. Even if education is seen as merely a means of acquiring vocational skills, perhaps not all students regard their studies as a sacrifice to be endured only in return for lucrative later careers – some may even enjoy student life. These, and many other objec- tions, were aimed at the factual basis of Davis and Moore's arguments.

There were also strong reservations about the *conceptual* basis of the theory. Questions of 'talent' and 'skill' are not clear-cut and the identification of those attributes in individuals is itself shaped by social inequalities of class, gender, and race. Just how are we to identify 'important positions'? It cannot be on the basis of payment, since that is what the theory attempts to explain. If we hope to find some public consensus on this question we may find that some will nominate the

Box 9.1

Functionalist view of stratification

Scarce skills → Unequal rewards → Important positions

Unequal rewards → Social stratification

Important positions → Societal survival

Source: adapted from Davis and Moore (1945)

chiefs of government, industry, the Church, the health service, education, the military, and so on. But equally valid are lists which give priority to food providers (e.g. farmers and fishers), housing providers (e.g. bricklayers and joiners), warmth providers (e.g. coal miners and power workers), health providers (e.g. nurses and doctors), or disease preventers (e.g. refuse and sewerage workers). Is it possible for the attribution of importance to be separated from the personal values of the attributor? Davis and Moore's own answer to this was sketchy (in a footnote) and their original list of important positions was generally ignored in the subsequent debate – not least by themselves in their replies to critics.

There were further criticisms of the *explanatory* power of the theory. It may tell us something about the distribution of rewards between individuals (social differentiation) but it does not address the issue of how these become layered – like geological strata – into social classes (social stratification). It does not explain why different societies have very different forms and degrees of inequality, or how these become structured into castes, elites, professions, under-classes, or upper classes.

This is related to *logical* problems in the theory. Social phenomena exist, so the logic runs, to produce necessary consequences. For those who wish to construct causal explanations similar to those in natural science, this is an untenable position. Causality is generally assumed to depend upon 'a definite sequence in the relationship between cause and effect so that the cause must always occur before the event which is held to be its consequence', whereas functionalist explanations are 'in terms of what comes after and not what comes before' (Lee and Newby, 1983: 276). To argue that because *this* exists the effects are *that* is not to explain why it exists. The point may appear obvious but in complex functionalist analyses it is often obscured.

Finally, and generating the anger in attacks on Davis and Moore's theory, there were complaints about its *ideological* leanings. If the soft functionalism of anthropology had encouraged researchers to find ways of dealing with their prejudices in confronting unfamiliar societies, hard functionalism was seen as reinforcing existing social biases in familiar (home) society. Are you concerned about poverty in wealthy societies, unequal treatment of women and racial minorities, or the separation of the elected from the electorate? The answer from functionalism appeared to be that, since they exist, they must be necessary and inevitable features of modern society. To attempt to change any of them would not only be foolish (failing to comprehend social realities) but also positively anti-social, since it would threaten the survival of society. Thus functionalism was identified as an ideological means of legitimizing the *status quo* – part of a quintessentially conservative politics in which those enjoying high rewards could justify their position whilst simultaneously disregarding the claims of others. From this perspective the achievement of Davis and Moore was to take the familiar economics of supply and demand in labour markets and build upon them a grandiose – but fundamentally flawed – social justification.

These attacks were made on a particular variant of functionalism – of the hard kind – and highlighted empirical, conceptual, explanatory, logical, and ideological discontents with the approach. There have been attempts to recover a softer form of functionalism which would not be vulnerable to such criticisms. Most notably these came from Merton (1968). He abandoned the notion that all existing features of society are indispensable, with no alternatives, that they all fit neatly together, and that every feature makes a positive contribution. Instead he argued that some social phenomena are neutral in relation to the maintenance of society and others 'dysfunctional' – having harmful effects. Whilst this may free functionalism from the taint of conservative bias, it weakens any explanatory power which it may claim. Now social phenomena are seen to exist when they serve a positive function, and also when they do not – which means we have not explained why they exist. In addition, how do we know whether the effects are positive or not? The only solution offered appears to be 'applying purely arbitrary moral judgements' (Lee and Newby, 1983: 276).

The difficulty of reforming hard functionalism to make it a more plausible, and less offensive, social theory goes back to its Durkheimian roots and the question of causality – in particular it relates to issues of conflict and change in society. If we adopt the mechanistic analogy, the functioning of parts is seen as the outcome of intentional human action. Carburettors are designed by engineers following specific briefs of engine performance requirements. It quickly becomes apparent that many social institutions – our families, schools, leisure pursuits, religious organizations – are not the outcome of such deliberate design processes. Even institutions which may appear more machine-like – such as business enterprises – are socially constructed through the interactions of many people, rather than the product of some single guiding intelligence. Throughout this book we have seen how enterprises are arenas of conflict, struggle, and compromise. Similarly if we take the alternative organic metaphor there are fundamental difficulties in applying it to society. In biology the functioning of parts is seen as the outcome of extended historical processes of evolution in which genetic mutation through sexual reproduction creates many changes which then succeed and develop (or fail and disappear) in processes of 'natural selection'. Again, if we attempt to apply such a model to social systems – usually labelled 'Social Darwinism' – the analogy quickly breaks down. Societies and enterprises may be described as 'evolving' if the term is used in a very general manner, but they do not do so in a Darwinian sense through sexual reproduction and genetic mutation over hundreds of generations. In both models the concept of function may have been useful in describing how social systems operate, but they do not provide answers to questions about why they exist.

These criticisms suggest that functionalism is deeply flawed as a social theory. This is not to imply that all explanations employing a concept of 'function' must therefore be rejected. Identifying functions which social phenomena have in relation to other social phenomena remains an important element of social analysis. Even if, in sociology, 'Functionalism today is a very unfashionable school of thought . . . [its] language of terms and concepts [has] now slipped into general use' (Lee and Newby, 1983: 280, 264). Many who would not recognize themselves as functionalists use concepts of 'system', 'structure', 'integration', 'institution', 'norms' and 'roles' which reflect the functionalist tradition. However, for those seeking causal explanations functionalism can never be adequate. To deal with 'why?' questions we need theories of change which do not present society as consciously designed to achieve some specific goal/s, or as the inevitable result of the progress of history. We need explanations which recognize the complexity of social action within social contexts and the tensions and conflicts which are generated and reflected in it. These are issues to which functionalism does not provide answers.

Functionalism in conventional accounting research

Armed now with the hindsight of over a hundred years of debate about functionalism in sociology and anthropology, we can review its relatively recent contribution to accounting through conventional textbooks (e.g. Horngren, 1977; Drury, 1992) and in research through contingency theory (e.g. Hopwood, 1974; Gordon and Miller, 1976; Otley, 1980; Emmanuel and Otley, 1985). The limitations and problems of the underlying theory have been identified in its application in accounting. Hopper *et al.* (1987) argued that conventional textbooks assume a consensus in society and in enterprises so that goals are clear and agreed in a world characterized by order and harmony. Disputes over the distribution of rewards, and accounting's role in informing them, are marginalized or ignored in this approach. Management is portrayed as a 'neutral arbiter' of the running of the social system, with accounting providing a 'technical and neutral information service' continually improved as a result of 'progress'. Conflicts within systems – of management and accounting – are treated as 'anomalies' or 'defects' which can be resolved by reform of accounting practice (or of its presentation). In taking the social system of the enterprise for granted, and offering descriptions of its (usually) smooth functioning, this kind of approach displays the signal features of the functionalist approach – with all its attendant problems. These were recognized by some accounting researchers such as Hopwood, who moved on to very different social theories. Among those who remained convinced of the merits of contingency theory there was recognition of its limits. Emmanuel and Otley warned of uncritical acceptance of the theory and argued that 'to link specific contingent variables with specific features of [accounting information systems] design is currently unsubstantiated and may ultimately be fallacious' (1985: 254).

Despite attacks from critics and reservations among some of its adherents, the functionalist nature of much accounting research persists in works which seek to demonstrate how accounting serves the needs of enterprises and societies to assist their orderly functioning. For a period during the 1950s and 1960s functionalism 'provided the nearest thing to orthodoxy that has ever existed in sociology, certainly within the English-speaking world' (Lee and Newby, 1983: 261). The demolition of this orthodoxy, and the revitalization of sociology, was a difficult and controversial process and still leaves a residue of theoretical problems. By the start of the 1980s functionalism had achieved a similar orthodoxy in what was labelled 'behavioural accounting research'. This orthodoxy came under increasing attack from 'critical accountants' in the 1980s – and this, unsurprisingly, generated its own difficulties and controversies.

CRITICAL ACCOUNTING RESEARCH

In developing new approaches to accounting not based on functionalist perspectives researchers have drawn upon a wide range of other social theories. Much of this work is difficult to get to grips with, and some is ferociously reader-unfriendly. For those who are used to the lightweight theories of conventional approaches, critical research may 'be viewed simply as a way of giving accounting a touch of the exotic [or] as a publishing gimmick [in papers which give] a summary of yet another thinker so far unheard-of within accounting' (Miller *et al.*, 1991: 398). Morgan and Willmott identified the defining feature of this 'new accounting research' as the way in which it is 'self-consciously attentive to the social character of accounting theory and practice'(1993: 3). The range of these new approaches is enormous and cannot be dealt with in detail here. Much of it can be found in the journals – *Accounting Organizations and Society*; *Critical Perspectives on Accounting*; *Accounting Auditing and Accountability*; and *Advances in Public Interest Accounting* – although it is now beginning to have an impact in more conventional publications. Some key strands within this research can be identified.

Social constructionism

In reaction against the heavy emphasis on system and structure in conventional writings, some researchers explored the small-scale world of social action. Such approaches are usually labelled 'naturalism'. Accounting appears as meanings in subjective perceptions and interpretations of the social world, and as communication in interactions between people. Typically this work studies accounting in particular locations and portrays it as an interpretive/communicative activity which both reflects and shapes its organizational surroundings (e.g. Colville, 1981; Tomkins and Groves, 1983; Covaleski and Dirsmith, 1983, 1986).

The approach is drawn from *social constructionism*, which itself is derived from two older traditions. In European social theory *phenomenology* developed from Kant, through Wittgenstein and Husserl, to Schutz. In the US *interactionism* developed from James, through Mead, to Garfinkel and Goffman, and became 'a kind of official opposition to functionalism in American sociology' (Lee and Newby, 1983: 316). These two traditions were combined by Berger and Luckman

(1967) as a theory of 'the social construction of reality'. Knowledge is seen as inter-subjective – constructed of statements which are socially accepted as facts. Since our knowledge of the external world is socially constructed, our inner world – of the self – is inevitably a socialized phenomenon. People are active human agents who skilfully use their knowledge to pursue their ends. The social world is orderly only to the extent that we share the same knowledges, and that we reproduce order through social interaction. Berger and Luckman modelled the interrelationship of society (public knowledge) and individuals (active agents) as a continuing loop (see Box 9.2). The kinds of social explanation we advance depend on where we break into the loop – at one point human agents construct society, at another they are the constructions of that society.

This theory generates some strong methodological guidance for researchers. First, they should discover the meanings which local terms have for actors, rather than impose ready-made definitions on situations. Second, they should discover the social rules through which these terms are ordered (for example, whether they are central or peripheral). Third, they should study how terms and rules come together to create particular 'dramatic' settings, with their own plots and narratives, in which action takes place. Fourth, they should uncover the further set of social rules by which plots and narratives are created, justified, and transmitted to others.

Applied to accounting, this approach encourages researchers to be sensitive to ways in which accounting terms (e.g. 'direct labour costs', 'budgetary control', 'true and fair') have particular meanings in specific times/places rather than being universal phenomena. They are 'fragile products of circumscribed and tentatively negotiated meanings' (Hopper *et al.*, 1987: 442). It highlights the need to discover how accounting defines the organizational context of action by contributing a distinctive language to its plots and narratives – a particular presentation of goals and performances. This has produced studies of account ing-in-action which are rich in detail and insight, exploring different ways in which people understand and apply accounting, and how it shapes them and their social world.

Box 9.2

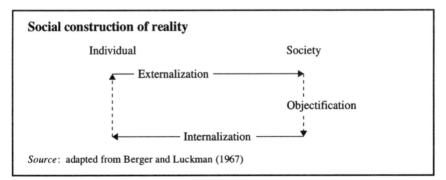

The approach has some limitations which reflect those of the phenomenology/interactionism tradition from which it springs. Of central concern is the issue of *relativism*, 'a philosophical doctrine which asserts that there is no way in which humans can escape the limiting, selective and relative effects of the conditions in which knowledge is produced' (Lee and Newby, 1983: 232). The most extreme version of social constructionism – *ethnomethodology* – asserts not merely that we socially construct reality, but that reality is no more or less than our social construction of it. What it is we perceive as 'real' is our 'reality'. There is no way in which humans can have absolute knowledge of any 'real world' which they may suppose to exist outside themselves, and hence there are no grounds for evaluating one relative statement against a different one. Researchers have no business trying to define what is 'really' real; they should concentrate on discovering and reporting only the meanings that reality has for those they are studying.

Not surprisingly, this rejection of a notion of an external reality which is separate from our perceptions of it has been unpalatable to many social theorists. It appears to abandon reason in human life and prevents us from asking whether action is rational in relation to its context. In rejecting functionalism's bold assertion that society is composed of social systems, social constructionism moved to another extreme – that we should be exclusively concerned with ways in which people accomplish a sense of reality (meanings) and should be agnostic about whether this is a rational response to the world (reality). The problem for social analysts is that if the world is full of such meanings we have no reasoned way of deciding which ones to study and report, nor any means of comparing one with another. Nor can we explain why particular constructions of reality exist (and not others) or why they change. This is highly frustrating for those who believe that the point of understanding the world is so that we may act in it and change it. Those opposed to the relativist position have seized eagerly on what they see as its fatal flaw. To assert that 'There can be no absolute statements' is, of course, to make an absolute statement which therefore, by its own logic, must be rejected. Its opponents hope that this ticking time-bomb within relativism will cause it to self-destruct whenever it appears in its different guises.

These concerns are reflected in commentaries on naturalism in accounting research. Whilst it generates rich pictures of accounting in action, it may end up by being a fundamentally uncritical activity, merely accepting and reporting the existing perspectives and values of accountants and others connected with accounting.

> Whilst naturalism may reveal alternative sets of meanings attributed to accounting . . . its insights are decoupled from an appreciation of wider processes of social change and conflict.
>
> (Hopper *et al.*, 1987: 444)

Theories of capitalist society

Many of those who wished to explore wider processes drew on classical sociology in the German tradition. Here the work of Weber would appear especially relevant to accounting. Although he associated the origins of capitalism with the beliefs and values of 'the Protestant ethic', his analysis of the development of capitalist society emphasized its rationalization. Like many nineteenth century writers he saw the modern world as one in which beliefs based on tradition and religion were being replaced by rational modes of thought. But whereas other writers saw this in terms of 'practical reasoning' – the common sense of people in an age of reason – Weber treated it as specific forms of thought which developed around clusters of human activity. The combination of a variety of elements – the emergence of autonomous private enterprises; the creation of free labour and free markets; the commercialization of economic life based on a monetary economy; and the increasing calculability of the technical conditions of production and administration – led to the increasing rationalization of society. The clearest development of this was in business enterprises, where it was expressed most particularly through their accounting regimes. Thus we would expect Weberian ideas to be widely employed in accounting research. Curiously this is not so. With only a few exceptions (e.g. Colignon and Covaleski, 1991), his work has largely been ignored.

The other key figure of this tradition of classical sociology, Marx, has been much more widely influential. Fundamental in Marx's work is the idea that a society's *mode of production* – the way in which it produces goods and services – conditions its social structure and processes, and the social consciousness of its members. The mode of production is seen as having two interrelated components: the means (or forces) of production (e.g. land, labour, buildings, machinery) and the social relations of production (e.g. landowner–tenant or employer–employee relations). Societies may be characterized as agrarian 'feudal' or 'Asiatic', and industrial 'capitalist' and 'socialist' types. Each has a different mode of production which produces distinctly different forms of society.

In capitalist society a fundamental feature is the circuit of capital (see Box 9.3). In the enterprise capital sets in motion an extended and continuing process. It begins by purchasing commodities such as land, buildings, materials, and labour power, which are combined to produce goods and services which have 'use value'. This is the moment of *production* of value. In capitalist economies the products are commodities which have 'exchange value' when they are sold in markets, which is the moment of *realization* of value. In successful enterprises the value realized is greater than the capital used up in the process. This 'surplus value' is then dispersed to the owners of the original capital (as 'profits') or retained within the enterprise to accelerate the next cycle ('ploughing back'). This is the moment of *distribution* of value. The driving force of the process is capital accumulation – the stock of value represented by capital increases on each circuit. Thus a key issue is: where does the increased value come from? For Marx, most

Box 9.3

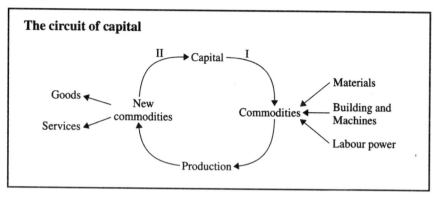

The circuit of capital

commodities bought by capital (at exchange value) give up their worth when they are applied in production (use value) and no value is added there. In the case of one special commodity what is bought is labour power and what is applied is labour. This crucial distinction, which we met earlier, means that what you buy and what you get are not the same. Marx argued that the value added by labour is greater than that returned to labour – workers produce more than is required for their own sustenance. This is the source of the 'surplus value' which is 'appropriated' by providers of capital who do not produce anything themselves.

On this economic 'base' stands a 'superstructure' of social relations. Capital and labour are not merely economic abstractions but are embodied in people who occupy economic positions as capitalists (the bourgeoisie) or industrial workers (the proletariat). As capitalist society develops these become progressively self-conscious social forces – the owning and the working classes – and struggles between them shape the development of society. Politics becomes an arena of class struggle between parties representing the interests of capital and labour, replacing earlier struggles between landowners and land workers. This process generates new ways of thinking about, and justifying, society, so that the ruling ideas of any age are the ideas of the ruling class. But of course they are only the ruling ideas, not the only ideas. The notion of 'relative autonomy' suggests that even if educational, scientific, literary, and artistic pursuits and institutions reflect the society from which they emerge, they are not totally determined by that society, and so may generate new ideas which are capable of changing it. For example, although schools may be set vocational tasks in preparing future workers and managers to fit into existing society, they also develop an ethos of personal development and critical awareness which has the potential of changing society. This is not an exceptional or abnormal feature of social life, since in society we find 'contradictions' – tensions inherent in the mode of production and its reproduction – which are the motor force of change. One such contradiction, as we saw earlier, is that management is concerned with both co-ordination-and-unity (since production is a social, collective activity) and with control-

and-surveillance (because capitalist production is based on private property and the individual appropriation of added value). This means that any managerial 'solution' can only be a temporary balance in private/social, individual/collective tensions, and contains the seeds of new forms of contradiction which, sooner or later, will emerge as the new 'problem'. If functionalism stressed stability and order, Marxian approaches are built upon conflict and change.

These concerns are reflected in accounting research which adopts Marxian perspectives (e.g. Cooper and Sherer, 1984; Tinker, 1985; Armstrong, 1985, 1987a, b, 1991, 1993; Hopper et al., 1986; Tinker and Neimark, 1987; Hopper and Armstrong, 1991). Much of it has adopted a narrow focus on the moment of production in studies of the way accounting is implicated in the contradictory processes of co-ordinating and controlling the labour process. Rather less attention has been paid to other moments in the circuit of capital where accounting is also important, since 'value has to be represented, distributed, and transferred, not only between corporations dealing with finance capital, but also to, and through, the state' (Hopper et al., 1987: 448). There have also been political economy approaches which locate accounting in the wider processes of the production and reproduction of capitalist societies and ways in which the state conditions the possibilities of continued cycles of capital accumulation.

Criticism of such approaches has focused on a key difficulty generally in Marxian analyses. Marx stated that the mode of production conditions the social structure. A crucial issue is what is meant by the term 'conditions'. In hard (or scientific) versions of Marxian analysis it is taken to mean 'causes' or 'determines', and thus the theory appears as crude materialism – the physical conditions of human life dictating our social relationships and our thoughts. This has led to some accounting researchers being attacked as 'Marxist functionalists' – a claim that they have merely replaced classical functionalism (accounting serving the interests of society) with a version which is equally mechanistic and portrays accounting as serving the interests of capital. In rejecting this view, it is claimed that Marx's own analyses of specific social formations show that it was not his intention and that the emphasis on a material base was merely a guiding thread in his studies. It is not clear whether 'Marx regards the base/superstructure distinction as absolutely crucial or merely a handy metaphor' (Lee and Newby, 1983: 116), and this ambiguity was hardly resolved by Engels's explanation, after Marx's death, that it applied only 'in the final analysis'. If we take a softer (or humanist) view of Marx's work we avoid the difficulties of economic determinism but we are left with theories which have less clear-cut explanatory power. If our social relations and ideas are not determined by the mode of production but only influenced by it, then what else influences them? Why should we assume that the influence of capitalist production is even the most important? Perhaps ideas have a much stronger influence on society than materialist explanations of accounting recognize. Overall, although important in challenging assumptions of order and stability, it too has problems in addressing the issues on which functionalism was attacked.

One attempt at an escape from these problems within the Marxist tradition was developed by the Frankfurt School of *critical theory* – Adorno, Horkheimer, Marcuse, and others. Recognizing the resilience of capitalism – its resistance to the revolutionary agenda of socialism – these theorists were essentially concerned with ways in which it reproduced itself over time, and they shifted the focus from economic issues to psychological and ideological dimensions of society. Their work began in Germany in the 1930s, where issues of relativism had a dangerous immediacy. Whilst they did not regard knowledge as absolute fact, they were faced with the rise of the absolutism of Hitler and Nazism, which they could not accept as simply another (relative) world-view. Many of them were Jewish and by 1933 most had fled, often to America. Their central concerns in social theory were the nature of modern knowledge and forms of authoritarianism in modern society.

For accounting research the most influential of this group has been a later member – Habermas. His work began with concerns similar to those of Weber – the increasing rationalization of European and North American societies. This development encompassed the increasing power of bureaucracies, the use of science as a means of domination and legitimation, and the substitution of technical inquiry for political debate. The result was a population, largely depoliticized, who had retreated from citizenship into privatized consumption. Taking an inter-subjective view of knowledge – that 'facts' are truth claims accepted by others – he drew a strong connection between ways of thinking and the social situations in which thought takes place. In order for 'reason' to develop there needed to be a free and open exchange of ideas in debates on society. The problem was that, in existing society, debates were structured and restricted by sectional interests which crippled people's striving for reason. Instead of constructive dialogue, society was stifled by authoritarian monologue. The solution would be to generate emancipatory discourse by constructing 'ideal speech situations' and hence change society.

Accounting researchers drawing on this tradition (e.g. Laughlin *et al.*, 1982; Laughlin and Puxty, 1983, 1984; Laughlin, 1987) have had two interests: to explore conventional accounts and demonstrate how the 'knowledge' they embody reflects sectional interests; and to imagine how new, emancipatory forms of accounting might emerge. By and large, their work has been more successful in achieving the former aim and it has been attacked for degenerating into a 'a methodological approach' (Roslender, 1992) which has forgotten its liberational project. In this it reflects a central problem in Habermas's work – the more strongly we argue that our present mode of thinking is invaded by existing society, then the less plausible it is to imagine ways in which we can begin to think in ways uncontaminated by that society, and therefore capable of transforming it.

Theories of postmodernity

A central concern with ideas and ways of thinking also emerged in the French tradition of social theory, especially in the work of Derrida, Foucault, and Lyotard, generating a loose collection of approaches termed *postmodernism*. One of the distinctive attributes of postmodernism is that it defies clear definition and delineation. For those who do not share its assumptions this is highly frustrating, but advocates argue that it is an essential feature of the attempt to create new ways of looking at, and talking about, the world. We may, however, identify some consistent themes. There is usually a concept of 'modern society' – a phenomenon addressed by theorists such as Durkheim, Marx, and Weber. This society may be highly structured, giving the appearance of a social system driven by great social forces and movements. However, in the second half of the twentieth century this was increasingly transformed into a new social formation – postmodern society. Postmodern society is characterized by fragmentation. At the level of the individual, the approach was influenced by Freud's analysis of the fragmented self – as 'id', 'ego', and 'super-ego'. People are seen to have many identities – as producers, consumers, sexual beings, family members, and so on. Thus postmodern society is characterized by social division, rather than unity, with many cross-cutting cleavages. Ideas developed in modern society, such as that there are functional relationships between parts of social wholes, or that change is driven by struggles between class interests, must be abandoned in postmodern society. Indeed, even the terms 'individual' and 'society' must now be deconstructed, showing them as particular European and North American intellectual inventions of the past few centuries. Thus the agenda of postmodernism is twofold: analysis of 'modernity', examining its nature and conditions of emergence and change; and explorations (and celebrations) of social differences in 'postmodernity'.

The writer from this tradition who has had the greatest impact on accounting research is Foucault, whose work was an extended study of modernity. What was the hallmark of 'the modern'? In Foucault's writing it increasingly became identified as modern knowledge of, and means of organizing and controlling, the human body. This is associated with the rise of the 'human sciences' in 'disciplinary society'. A key element in his analysis was the concept of 'discourse', which is a constellation of verbal/intellectual acts (e.g. writing papers, addressing conferences, selecting articles for publication), physical acts (e.g. conducting experiments, injecting patients), and technologies (e.g. techniques, documents, tools). By studying continuities and discontinuities in such discourses it is possible to see how the human sciences – medicine, psychiatry, criminology – developed, and how they became power/knowledge regimes. This involves 'genealogy' (e.g. finding when key concepts came into existence, and identifying the lineage of the discourse) and 'archaeology' (e.g. locating concepts in their material and discursive contexts). Foucault found strong similarities among the human sciences. Each defined human beings as objects of study, about which knowledge could be created. For example, having produced the concept of 'mad', psychiatrists began to study 'mad people' rather than souls possessed by demons. The human sciences developed social practices of 'the gaze' (processes of surveillance) and 'the examination' (processes of interrogation). The former was most clearly demonstrated in Bentham's prison design, where a central observation tower (the 'panopticon') allowed continuous observation of all prisoners. The latter is seen in doctors' diagnostic interviews with patients. These social practices create 'visibility' – they enable the study of the human object as defined in the discourse. They also generate a reconceptualization by the object so that he or she now becomes the subject of the discourse – we see ourselves as 'patients' or 'sane people'. When knowledge of the body is used to effect change in it (to 'reform' the criminal, 'cure' the ill, make the mad 'sane') we see how discipline in the sense of intellectual practice is linked with discipline in the sense of 'to shape' and 'control', and thus how power and knowledge are interrelated.

As Roslender noted, 'Even had he lived, Foucault probably would not have turned his attention to accounting' (1992: 149). Nevertheless, his influence on critical accounting research has been astonishingly widespread (e.g. Burchell *et al.*, 1985; Hoskin and Macve, 1986, 1988; Loft, 1986; Hopwood, 1987; Miller and O'Leary, 1987; Ezzamel *et al.*, 1990; Walsh and Stewart, 1993). In 1987 he was the ninth most cited writer in the leading accounting journals (Beattie and Ryan, 1989). Interest has focused on ways in which accounting creates visibility – bringing some issues into the light whilst obscuring others; how it does so through creating concepts (such as 'costs', 'benefits', 'performance') which attach to 'accounting entities' as objects for study; and how the disciplinary/disciplining discourse of accounting constructs subjects as 'governable persons'.

For critics of Foucauldian analysis, there are many problems in this approach, as in postmodernism in general. On occasions discourses appear to be presented as social phenomena which act in their right – creating and transforming themselves – quite separately from human interests and intentions. In providing detailed histories of discourses there is no attempt to evaluate them except in relation to their own criteria, since knowledge of the world is seen as inextricably intertwined with ways of knowing it. Further, it is argued that in studying discourses we generate new human science discourses which are also power/knowledge regimes, so that we can never escape discipline but merely generate new forms. If so, and if we have no means of evaluating different discourses against each other, then emancipation is a myth. We cannot distinguish between truth and falsity, and human reason does not provide a basis for changing the world in the name of truth, fairness, justice, beauty, or anything else. For critics, this is relativism gone berserk again. Behind its radical, debunking rhetoric Foucauldian accounting research has been accused of having a deeply conservative bias (Neimark, 1990). Its advocates hotly deny this and claim that deconstructing disciplinary regimes is a liberational act in its own right. However, it is far from clear how deconstruction can inform action and hence facilitate changing the world. Perhaps these criticisms are too harsh (or specific), since, as Morgan and

Willmott (1993) noted, the vast bulk of critical accounting, and not just its postmodernist tendency, remains enfortressed in academia and has made little impact on the wider world of accounting policy and practice.

Other developments

The three strands discussed above represent much of critical accounting research, but it has a very wide scope, bringing in many other theories from sociology, anthropology, psychology, and philosophy which cannot be covered here. However, two further recent developments should be noted.

The first is *environmentalism* (e.g. Gray, 1990b; Owen, 1992). Here social theory is only slowly emerging and there are struggles to create new ways of relating people, society, and nature. Postmodernists lumped together a number of disparate theorists (such as Durkheim, Marx, and Weber) as 'modernists' and argued that their classical sociological formulations must be abandoned. Perhaps we are now seeing the emergence of new social theories (say 'ultramodernism') in which modernists and postmodernists will be classified together as obsessed with the social world, with only a marginal concern with its relationship to the physical world. The aim would be to produce more adequate socio-physical theories. For the moment it is not clear what such theories might look like.

More firmly established in accounting debates is *feminism*. There is some dispute over whether feminism constitutes a social theory in its own right, or whether it is a set of gender-conscious versions of the theories discussed above – Marxist feminism, postmodernist feminism, and so on. In accounting, however, feminism has provided a distinctive contribution by focusing on what may be its most obvious aspect but which is so often ignored – that accounting is, very largely, created and practised by men (e.g. Burrell, 1987; Tinker and Neimark, 1987; Giancanelli *et al.*, 1990; Macintosh, 1990; Kirkham, 1992; Lehman,1992). Some of the early research was concerned with identifying and explaining gender inequality in the accountancy profession, particularly through historical studies. There have also been discussions about the way in which accounting systematically renders gender invisible in enterprises, or is combined with particular pictorial and narrative representations of women in annual reports. At a deeper level it has been argued that accounting itself is a gendered set of practices – that it is an expression of a masculine ethos, or mode of thought, and hence 'macho' (Knights and Collinson, 1987); or that it represents the 'yang' of life whilst repressing the 'yin' (Hines, 1992). Feminist accounting research is now a dynamic and rapidly growing field which promises to provide many new ways of understanding how accounting and gendered persons interact in gendered contexts.

SOCIAL THEORY AND SOCIAL ANALYSIS

Predictably, attempts to develop alternatives to the functionalist simplicities of conventional research have produced a body of work which is complex, difficult, and controversial. Those encountering it for the first time may be perplexed and inclined to dismiss it as irrelevant or unpractical. As proponents of each position identify the weaknesses and limitations of others, it can appear that the only consistent theme to emerge is that all social theory is fundamentally flawed, and that the project of creating social theories of accounting is impossible. As Lee and Newby confessed, 'We cannot offer any ready-made general solution to such difficulties' (1983: 322). They did, however, make three suggestions which may help us to come to terms with difficulties of social theory, and encourage us to continue the social analysis of accounting. First, social theory can offer a 'reasoned procedure' for analyzing and comparing social phenomena which is not 'available from common sense or ideological dogma' (p. 322). Second, that if this procedure differs between social theories what this 'really shows is that we cannot study everything at once' (p. 323). If, for the moment, we concentrate on social action, then we use approaches which are appropriate but which we will replace with others when, later, we turn our attention to social context. Third, that 'philosophical uncertainty need not prevent us from examining substantive problems' (p. 323). This last point appears crucial for those conducting social analyses and needs to be explored further.

Much of the discussion in this chapter has been concerned with *Theory* – grand, abstract, generalizing ways of theorizing the social world. Comparing one such Theory with another is one way of evaluating them; but it is not the only way. We can also assess a Theory through the specific theories generated by those who adopt it – how they describe and explain the particular phenomena in which we are interested. At this level I find two things of note. First, that issues in substantive explanations are far more readily accessible. This may be a matter of personal skill or taste, but I suspect that most readers will have experienced far less difficulty with particular theories of the nature of capital, management, and labour, than with the discussion of their underlying Theory in this chapter. Second, differences between each Theory often appear less definite and divisive when substantive statements are made about what is happening in enterprises and why. Accounting researchers drawing on very different traditions may find valuable insights in each other's work. Indeed for Willmott (forthcoming) it is high time to cut loose from 'a paradigm mentality' which seeks to pigeon-hole research on the basis of its fundamental assumptions about the nature of knowledge (epistemology) and reality (ontology).

This does not mean that all substantive theories are compatible; but it does suggest that the marked distinction between Theories at the abstract level are blurred when dealing with the concrete. We should also note that Theory itself comes from somewhere. In part it is built upon substantive social analyses either carried out by Theorists themselves, or interpreted from the work of others. Hence, to some degree, social analysis should be seen as the source of social theory as well as its application. Only in the most dogmatic approaches to research is the analysis generated a predetermined result of the theory adopted. Since no Theory can ever be perfect, none can be expected to be wholly adequate in explaining what is encountered in research. Hence theories may be combined or modified. There is a dynamic relationship between theory and analysis. Since we live in the social world we cannot ever study it as theoryless 'innocents'; but the construction of new theories demonstrates that study is not dictated by the initial theorizing.

Theory also develops through interaction with other Theory, by responding to the challenges of critics, and thus each is (to a degree) shaped by the set of theories with which it co-exists. Here the clear distinctions between Theories may be less evident in differences between Theorists. Weber attacked 'vulgar Marxists' (as did Marx) rather than Marx himself. Habermas drew on, and developed, the ideas of both Marx and Weber. Foucault made complimentary comments on the work of Habermas – which Miller (1987) curiously dismissed as merely an act of politeness. This last observation prompts the suggestion that perhaps the emergence of distinct camps in critical accounting is due as much to disciples' evangelistic proclamation of the great and unique qualities of their chosen Theorist as to any fundamental incompatibility of different social theories.

As a final observation on theory and analysis, it seems to me that the direction of much current social theory is highly cerebral, that it sees 'the mind' as driving 'the body', and that in explaining action it places 'thinking' before and above 'doing'. This is a perspective to which academics – who make a trade of theorizing – are particularly inclined. They are highly sensitive to theories, concepts, discourses, ideologies, and so on. Not surprisingly these often figure prominently in their studies and explanations of social phenomena. This may be to project their own consciousness on to others who do not share their preoccupation with the intellect and its thoughts. It is at least possible that people act first and think later; and that knowledge is reflective of experience. This, of course, would be to identify physical action in the real world as a source of social knowledge, concepts, and theories. In current social theory this view is likely to be regarded as an idiotic or ignorant heresy. Perhaps it is. Nevertheless I wished to raise it as an issue at the end of this difficult chapter which has generally accorded theory a privileged position. This is not to suggest a complete reversal in which theory is entirely a product of action and context; rather, I see a dynamic interrelationship where each influences the other. Social analysis combines various social theories with empirical observations. In doing so it is shaped by social theory, which informs the questions to be asked, the nature of interpretations, and the forms of explanation advanced. At the same time, acts of interpretation and explanation modify existing theories and give rise to new ones.

The same analysis may be applied to the relationship between accounting theories and practices. Textbooks often assume that there should be a relationship in which accounting practice is the outcome of accounting theory, and then researchers bemoan a gap between the two in which practice lags behind theory. However, the construction of accounting practice has influences outside accounting theory. It reflects the personal experiences and skills of its practitioners, their membership of corporate as well as professional groups, and their positions in enterprises. In many ways they inhabit different worlds from those of the academics who construct theory and their thinking is different (Jones and Dugdale, 1994). Accountants are social actors in social contexts who actively construct their accounting, rather than people who simply put accounting theory into practice. The ways they do this are shaped by their social situations, and by the social theories which influence their understanding of these situations. Changes in accounting practices and the adoption of different social theories may lead to the modification of existing accounting theories or the creation of new ones. It is this which I have explored in this book and which constitutes a social analysis of accounting and the enterprise.

Postscript

ACCOUNTING, ENTERPRISES AND SOCIETY

Most of this book has been concerned with ways in which social theories and analyses can inform our understanding of accounting in modern enterprises. In conclusion I wish to change the focus to look at how studies of accounting can enrich wider social research and change our understanding of enterprises and society. To a large extent accounting research has remained within its own intellectual terrain and has had little impact upon other disciplines, although this is slowly changing.

> For students of industrial sociology, organizational behaviour and . . . organization studies accounting has been virtually invisible. Quite simply accounting is understood to lie 'outside' their domain: accounting is regarded as a technical specialism which has little direct relevance for the behavioural study of industrial society or modern organizations.
>
> (Morgan and Willmott 1993: 7)

In short, accounting has been left for accountants to study. In some ways this is understandable, since for the non-accountant accounting presents a formidable facade of technicality, jargon, and mystique – the closed world of the black box. In addition, the privacy of accounting is protected by its image as a boring discipline and practice – a view embedded in, and reinforced by, jokes told by accountants and non-accountants alike. In the UK there are perhaps a couple of score of sociologists who have shown some interest in researching the territory, but most of them have been concerned with the nature of accountancy as a profession. Those who have attempted to go further and get to grips with the technicalities of the practice of accounting, and the everyday life of the accountant, number a mere handful – and they appear frequently throughout this book. Yet, despite its difficulties, the study of accounting is surely an important element in understanding modern enterprises and societies. The absence of such studies in broader social science severely limits and distorts the social theories and analyses which are generated.

A number of issues have emerged in the book which highlight the importance of studying accounting. In relation to *capital*, the most influential social theories in the debate on ownership and control now stress the role of financial control, where executives and managers are seen as constrained to pursue 'profit' through the application of accounting measures of financial performance. Yet the discussion of 'creative accounting' has shown that such measures are extremely slippery, open to manipulation by managers, and may leave owners floundering in a mass of dubious, and ambiguous 'information'. Financial accounting, it would appear, simply cannot bear the explanatory burden placed upon it in theories of impersonal capitalism. In theories of *management* there continues to be a view that accounting is essentially an expression of 'formal rationality' which is seen either as determining decisions, or as a technical gloss on real decision processes which are social or political. What this view fails to recognize is that accounting processes themselves absorb, obscure, transform, and recreate values so that they are not merely ideological facades which hide the politics of management – they are part of that politics. Recent studies have suggested that this politics may have shifted from bureaucratic control based on rules for action to pseudo-market control where accounting regimes reconstruct 'managers' as mini-entrepreneurs running their own mini-businesses within the enterprise. This entails, simultaneously, the construction of new forms of management control, and new conceptions of the subject who is to be controlled. Here accounting takes in the language of 'de-layering' and 'empowerment' which has emerged in contemporary managerial discussions of organization. In relation to *labour*, much discussion of the labour process simply fails to see the roles that accounting plays in measuring, reporting, and controlling work and workers. In the debate about de-Taylorization and new forms of work the legacy of Scientific Management in vast, complex systems of standard costing, connected with a wide range of enterprise decisions and activities, went largely unnoticed. Again, recent studies have suggested changes in which the ideological role of accounting has been important in attempts to incorporate workers more securely in the enterprise as self-conscious producers of profit.

In all this, the territory occupied by accountants in UK and US enterprises has been expanding. The giant accounting houses are present not only as auditors but as management consultants selling a vast range of financial and non-financial advice. Accountants are involved in investigating and measuring productive and administrative activities, in decisions on organizational structures and processes, and in communicating images of the nature and goals of enterprises in management briefing sessions and employee reports. They have become the most successful managerial specialism and occupy many of the senior and decisive positions. This is not an inevitable outcome of the essentially economic nature of enterprise. Studies in Germany and Japan have shown it is not a universal, but a specific social formation which needs to be explored. Indeed, there are currently voices – even a few within accountancy – which claim that many of the crucial problems of UK and US enterprises stem precisely from their particular reliance on accounting.

The emphasis in this book has been on enterprises – business organizations, privately owned, producing goods and services traded in market places – but the influence of accounting goes much further. Increasingly accounting has become a paradigm for administration and management, adopted in schools, universities, hospitals, prisons and elsewhere. It has been implicated in processes by which pupils, students, patients, prisoners, and others have been reconceptualized as customers, consumers, and clients. Those employed in these organizations have become providers (sometimes 'sellers') of educational, health, and custodial services. More people, in more places, and more often, are being counted, accounted for, and held accountable through the medium of accounting. Increasingly it pervades modern life.

Of course, it is possible to exaggerate the importance of accounting. This is especially likely to be the case in a book devoted to the analysis of accounting and directed at students of accounting. Accounting is not everything; nor is it everywhere. It is not the most important phenomenon in modern life. However, exaggeration of the influence of accounting is not the most pressing problem in relation to wider social science. Here accounting has generally appeared in marginal, fragmented, and often ill-informed ways. If this book has put too much stress on accounting, and has made excessively bold claims for its place in modern enterprises and societies, then at least it may stimulate broader discussion of accounting issues. This book was never intended as a comprehensive social analysis of accounting – merely as a vehicle to enable more people to enter current debates. I hope that readers will have been able to tolerate the limitations, omissions, distortions, misunderstandings, ambiguities, and other difficulties in my treatment of issues. Further, I hope that at least some will be stimulated to explore the debates more deeply, and then to contribute to them.

BIBLIOGRAPHY

Aaronovitch, S. (1955) *Monopoly: A Study of British Monopoly Capitalism*, London, Lawrence & Wishart.

Aaronovitch, S. (1961) *The Ruling Class*, London, Lawrence & Wishart.

Abell, P. (1982), 'On the structure of the democratic firm', in Dunkerley, D. and Salaman, G. (eds) *The International Yearbook of Organization Studies: 1981*, London, Routledge & Kegan Paul.

Ackerman, R. W. (1970), 'Influence of integration and diversity in the investment process', *Administrative Science Quarterly*, September, pp. 341–352.

Adams, R. (1992), 'Why is the environment of interest to accountants and accountancy bodies?', in Owen, D. (ed.) *Green Reporting: Accountancy and the Challenge of the Nineties*, London, Chapman & Hall.

Albrow, M. (1970), *Bureaucracy*, London, Pall Mall Press and Macmillan.

Ansari, S. and Euske, K. J. (1987), 'Rational, rationalizing and reifying uses of accounting data in organizations', *Accounting, Organizations and Society*, vol. 12, no. 6, pp. 549–570.

Argyris, C. (1964), *Integrating the Individual and the Organization*, New York, Wiley.

Armstrong, P. (1985), 'Changing managerial control strategies: the role of competition between accounting and other organisational professions', *Accounting, Organizations and Society*, vol. 10, no. 2, pp. 129–148.

Armstrong, P. (1987a) 'The rise of accounting controls in British capitalist enterprises', *Accounting, Organizations and Society*, vol. 12, no. 5, pp. 415–436.

Armstrong, P. (1987b), 'Engineers, management and trust', *Work, Employment and Society*, vol. 4, pp. 1–28.

Armstrong, P. (1991), 'Contradiction and social dynamics in the capitalist agency relationship', *Accounting, Organizations and Society*, vol. 16, no. 1, pp. 1–25.

Armstrong, P. (1993), 'Professional knowledge and social mobility: post-war changes in the knowledge-base of management accounting', *Work, Employment and Society*, vol. 7, no. 1, pp. 1–21.

ASSC (1975), *The Corporate Report*, London, Accounting Standards Steering Committee.

Atkinson, A. B. (1972), *Unequal Shares: Wealth in Britain*, London, Allen Lane.

Atkinson, J. (1984), 'Manpower strategies for flexible organisations', *Personnel Management*, August, pp. 28–31.

Atkinson, J. and Meager, N. (1986), 'Is "flexibility" just a flash in the pan?', *Personnel Management*, September, pp. 26–29.

Bailes, K. E. (1978), *Technology and Society Under Lenin and Stalin: Origins of Soviet Technical Intelligentsia, 1917–1941*, Princeton, Princeton University Press.

Baran, B. (1988), 'Office automation and women's work: the technological transformation of the insurance industry', in Pahl, R. E. (ed.) *On Work*, Oxford, Blackwell.

271

Baran, P. A. and Sweezy, P. M. (1966), *Monopoly Capital*, New York, Monthly Review Press.

Baritz, L. (1960), *The Servants of Power*, Middleton, Wesleyan University Press.

Barnard, C. (1938), *The Functions of the Executive*, Cambridge, Mass., Harvard University Press.

Barwise, P., Marsh, P. R. and Wensley, R. (1989), 'Must finance and strategy clash?', *Harvard Business Review*, September–October, pp. 85–90.

Baumol, W. J. (1959), *Business Behaviour, Value and Growth*, New York, Macmillan.

Beattie, V. A. and Ryan, R. J. (1989), 'Performance indices and related measures of journal reputation in accounting', *British Accounting Review*, vol. 21, no. 3, pp. 267–278.

Becker, H. (1967), 'Whose side are we on?', *Social Problems*, vol. 14, no. 3, pp. 239–247.

Benjamin, C. (1991), 'Dynamism and efficiency: the power of the corporate family', *Guardian*, 18 February 1991.

Bennis, W. (1966), *Changing Organizations*, New York, McGraw-Hill.

Benson, I. and Lloyd, J. (1983), *New Technology and Industrial Change*, London, Kogan Page.

Benston, G. J. (1982), 'Accounting and corporate accountability', *Accounting, Organizations and Society*, pp. 87–105.

Berger, P. and Luckman, T. (1967), *The Social Construction of Reality*, London, Allen Lane.

Berle, A. A. (1960), *Power Without Property*, New York, Harcourt Brace.

Berle, A. A. and Means, G. C. (1932, reprinted 1968), *The Modern Corporation and Private Property*, New York, Macmillan.

Berry, A. J., Cooper, D., Hopper, T. and Lowe, E. A. (1985a), 'NCB accounts: a mine of misinformation?', *Accountancy*, January, pp. 10–12.

Berry, A. J., Capps, T., Cooper, D., Ferguson, P., Hopper, T. and Lowe, E. A. (1985b), 'Management control in an area of the NCB: rationales of accounting practices in a public enterprise', *Accounting, Organizations and Society*, vol. 10, no. 1, pp. 3–28.

Beynon, H. (1973), *Working for Ford*, Harmondsworth, Penguin.

Black, S. P. (1983), 'Numerically controlled machine tools in a heavy manufacturing and assembly plant', in Buchanan, D. A. and Boddy, D. (eds) *Organisations in the Computer Age*, Aldershot, Gower.

Blauner, R. (1964), *Alienation and Freedom*, Chicago, University of Chicago Press.

Blaza, A. J. (1992), 'Environmental management in practice', in Owen, D. (ed.) *Green Reporting: Accountancy and the Challenge of the Nineties*, London, Chapman & Hall.

Bosquet, M. (1972), 'The "prison factory"', *New Left Review*, vol. 73, May, pp. 23–33.

Bourn, M. and Ezzamel, M. (1986), 'Organizational culture in hospitals in the National Health Service', *Financial Accountability and Management*, vol. 2, no. 3, pp. 203–225.

Braverman, H. (1974), *Labor and Monopoly Capital: The Degradation of Work in the Twentieth Century*, New York, Monthly Review Press.

Brimson, J. A. (1988), 'CAM-I cost management systems project', in Capettini, R. and Clancy D. K. (eds) *Cost Accounting, Robotics and the New Manufacturing Environment*, New York, American Accounting Association.

Bromwich, M. and Bhimani, A. (1989), *Management Accounting: Evolution not Revolution*, London, CIMA.

Brown, G. (1977), *Sabotage: A Study in Industrial Conflict*, Nottingham, Spokesman Books.

Bryer, R. A. and Brignall, T. J. (1985), 'The demystification of inflation accounting: a case study in divestment from UK manufacturing industry', *Interdisciplinary Perspectives in Accounting Conference*, University of Manchester, July.

Buck, J. (1992), 'Green awareness: an opportunity for business', in Owen, D. (ed.) *Green Reporting: Accountancy and the Challenge of the Nineties*, London, Chapman & Hall.

Burawoy, M. (1979), *Manufacturing Consent: Changes in the Labor Process Under Monopoly Capitalism*, Chicago, University of Chicago Press.

Burch, P. H. (1972), *The Managerial Revolution Reassessed*, Lexington, Mass., Lexington Books.

Burchell, S., Clubb, C., Hopwood, A., Hughes, J. and Nahapiet, J. (1980), 'The roles of accounting in organizations and society', *Accounting, Organizations and Society*, vol. 5, no. 1, pp. 5–27.

Burns, T. and Stalker, G. (1961), *The Management of Innovation*, London, Tavistock.

Burrell, G. (1987), 'No accounting for sexuality', *Accounting, Organizations and Society*, vol. 12, no. 1, pp. 89–101.

Carchedi, G. (1977), *On the Economic Identification of Social Classes*, London, Routledge & Kegan Paul.

Carey, A. (1967), 'The Hawthorne studies: a radical criticism', *American Sociological Review*, vol. 32, no. 3, pp. 403–416.

Carr-Saunders, A. M. (1928), 'Professionalization in historical perspective', in Vollmer, H. M. and Mills, D. L. (1966), *Professionalization*, Englewood Cliffs, Prentice-Hall.

Chandler, A. D. (1962), *Strategy and Structure*, Cambridge, Mass., MIT Press.

Chandler, A. D. (1977), *The Visible Hand: The Managerial Revolution in American Business*, Cambridge, Mass., Harvard University Press.

Chevalier, J. M. (1969), 'The problem of control in large American corporations', *Anti-Trust Bulletin*, vol. 14, pp. 163–180.

Child, J. (1972), 'Organisational structure, environment, and performance: the role of strategic choice', *Sociology*, vol. 6, no. 1, pp. 1–22.

Child, J. (1985a), 'Managerial strategies, new technology and the labour process', in Knights, D., Willmott, H. and Colinson, D. (eds) *Job Redesign: Critical Perspectives on the Labour Process*, London, Gower.

Child, J. (1985b), 'The introduction of new technologies: managerial initiatives and union responses in British banks', *Industrial Relations Journal*, autumn, pp. 19–33.

Child, J. (1986), 'Technology and work: an outline of theory and research in Western social sciences', in Grootings, P. (ed.) *Technology and Work: East–West Comparison*, Beckenham, Croom Helm.

Chinoy, E. (1955), *Automobile Workers and the American Dream*, New York, Doubleday.

Cicourel, A. (1968), *The Social Organization of Juvenile Justice*, New York, Wiley.

Clawson, D. (1980), *Bureaucracy and the Labor Process: The Transformation of US Industry, 1860–1920*, New York, Monthly Review Press.

Clegg, S. R. and Higgins, W. (1990), 'Against the current: organizations, sociology, and socialism', *Organisation Studies*, vol. 8, no. 3, pp. 201–222.

Cobb, I. (1991), 'Understanding and working with JIT', *Management Accounting*, vol. 69, no. 2, pp. 44–46.

Cockburn, C. (1983), *Brothers: Male Dominance and Technological Change*, London, Pluto.

Cohen, M. D., March, J. G. and Olsen, J. P. (1972), 'A garbage can model of organizational choice', *Administrative Science Quarterly*, March, pp. 1–25.

Colignon, R. and Covaleski, M. (1991), 'A Weberian framework in the study of accounting', *Accounting, Organizations and Society*, vol. 16, no. 2, pp. 141–158.

Collard, R. (1989), *Total Quality: Success Through People*, London, Institute of Personnel Management.

Colville, I. (1981), 'Reconstructing "Behavioural Accounting"', *Accounting, Organizations and Society*, vol. 6, no. 2, pp. 119–132.

Cooley, M. (1980), *Architect or Bee? The Human/Technology Relationship*, Slough, Langley Technical Services.

Cooley, M. (1981), 'The Taylorisation of intellectual work', in Levidow, L. and Young, B. (eds) *Science, Technology and the Labour Process*, London, CSE Books.

Coombs, R. (1985), 'Automation, management strategies and labour process change', in Knights, D., Willmott, H. and Colinson, D. (eds) *Job Redesign: Critical Perspectives on the Labour Process*, London, Gower.

Cooper, D. J. (1975), 'Rationality and investment appraisal', *Accounting and Business Research*, summer, pp. 198–202.

Cooper, D. J. and Sherer, M. J. (1984), 'The value of corporate accounting reports: arguments for a political economy of accounting', *Accounting, Organizations and Society*, vol. 5, no. 3/4, pp. 207–232.

Cooper, R. and Kaplan, R. S. (1988), 'Measure costs right: make the right decisions', *Harvard Business Review*, September–October, pp. 86–103.

Coriat, B. (1980), 'The restructuring of the assemby line: a new economy of time and control', *Capital and Class*, no. 11, pp. 34–43.

Cotgrove, S., Dunham, J. and Vamplew, C. (1971), *The Nylon Spinners: A Case Study in Productivity and Job Enlargement*, London, Allen & Unwin.

Council for Economic Development (1971), *Social Responsibilities of Business Corporations*, New York, CED.

Covaleski, M. A. and Dirsmith, M. W. (1983), 'Budgeting as a means of control and loose coupling', *Accounting, Organizations and Society*, vol. 8, no. 4, pp. 323–340.

Covaleski, M. A. and Dirsmith, M. W. (1986), 'The budgetary process of power and politics', *Accounting, Organizations and Society*, vol. 11, no. 3, pp. 193–214.

Crompton, R. and Jones, G. (1984), *White-Collar Proletariat: Deskilling and Gender in Clerical Work*, London, Macmillan.

Crowe, R. (1992), 'Green issues and the investor: inadequacies of current reporting practice and some suggestions for change', in Owen, D. (ed.) *Green Reporting: Accountancy and the Challenge of the Nineties*, London, Chapman & Hall.

Crump, L. (1989), 'Japanese managers, Western workers: cross-cultural training as development issues', *Management Development*, vol. 8, no. 4, pp. 48–55.

Currie, W. L. (1989a), 'The science of justifying new technology to top management', *MBA Review*, vol. 1, no. 1, spring.

Currie, W. L. (1989b), 'The art of justifying new technology to top management', *Omega, The Journal of Management Science*, vol. 17, no. 5, pp. 409–418.

Currie, W. L. (1989c), *Managerial Strategies for New Technology*, Aldershot, Gower.

Currie, W. L. (1992), *The Strategic Management of AMT in the UK, USA, Germany and Japan*, London, CIMA.

Cyert, R. M. and March, J. G. (1965), *A Behavioural Theory of the Firm*, Englewood Cliffs, Prentice-Hall.

Dahl, R. A. (1970), *After the Revolution*, New Haven, Yale University Press.

Dahrendorf, R. (1959), *Class and Class Conflict in an Industrial Society*, London, Routledge & Kegan Paul.

Dalton, M. (1959), *Men Who Manage*, New York, Wiley.

Damodaran, L. (1980), 'Word processing: occupational and organizational effects', *Management Information Services*, June, pp. 14–23.

Daniels, A. K. (1971), 'How free should professions be?', in Freidson, E. (ed.) *The Professions and their Prospects*, London, Sage.

Darlington, J., Innes, J., Mitchell, F. and Woodward, J. (1992), 'Throughput accounting: the Garrett Automotive experience', *Management Accounting (UK)*, April, pp. 32–38.

Davis, K. and Moore, W. E. (1945), 'Some principles of stratification', *American Sociological Review*, vol. 10, no. 2, pp. 242–49.

Dawe, A. (1970), 'The two sociologies', *British Journal of Sociology*, vol. 21, pp. 207–218.

de Vroey, M. (1975a), 'The separation of ownership and control in large corporations', *Review of Radical Political Economics*, vol. 7, no. 2, pp. 1–10.

de Vroey, M. (1975b), 'The owners' interventions in decision-making in large corporations', *European Economic Review*, vol 6, pp. 1–15.

BIBLIOGRAPHY

Deming, W. E. (1986), *Out of the Crisis: Quality, Productivity and Competitive Position*, Cambridge, Cambridge University Press.

Dent, J. (1990), 'Strategy, organization and control: some possibilities for accounting research', *Accounting, Organizations and Society*, vol. 15, no. 1/2, pp. 3–25.

Dent, J. F., Ezzamel, M. A. and Bourn, M. (1984), 'Reflections on research in management accounting and its relationship to practice', in Hopwood, A. G. and Schrender, H. (eds) *European Contributions to Accounting Research*, Amsterdam, Free University Press.

Diamond Report (1975) *Royal Commission on the Distribution of Income and Wealth*, London, HMSO.

Dierkes, M. and Bauer, R. A. (1973) *Corporate Social Accounting*, New York, Praeger.

Dore, R. (1989), 'Where we are now: musings of an evolutionist', *Work, Employment and Society*, vol. 3, no. 4, pp. 425–446.

Downing, H. (1980), 'Word processors and the oppression of women', in Forester, T. (ed.) *The Microelectronic Revolution*, Oxford, Blackwell.

Drucker, P. (1964), 'Control, controls and management', in Bonini C. P., Jaedicke R. K. and Wagner, H. M. (1964) *Management Control: New Directions in Basic Research*, New York, Wiley.

Drury, C. (1992), *Management and Cost Accounting*, Wokingham, Van Nostrand Reinhold.

Drury, C. and Dugdale, D. (1992), 'Surveys of management accounting practice', in Drury, C. (ed.) *Management Accounting Handbook*, Oxford, Butterworth Heinemann.

Drury, C., Braund, S., Osborne, P. and Tayles, M. (1993), *A Survey of Management Accounting Practices in UK Manufacturing Companies*, London, ACCA.

Dubin, R. (1956), 'Industrial workers' worlds: a study of the central life interests of industrial workers', *Social Problems*, no. 3, pp. 135–147.

Dugdale, D. (1990), 'Is there a "correct" method of investment appraisal?', *Management Accounting (UK)*, October pp. 36–38.

Dugdale, D. and Jones, T. C. (1991), 'Discordant voices: accountants' views of investment appraisal', *Management Accounting (UK)*, November, pp. 54–56, 59.

Dugdale, D. and Jones, T. C. (1993), 'Investment decisions and the social construction of trust', *Interdisciplinary Approaches to Accounting Workshop*, Manchester Conference Centre, January.

Dugdale, D. and Jones, T. C. (1994), 'Finance, strategy and trust in investment appraisal', *Management Accounting (UK)*, April, pp. 52–56.

Durkheim, E. (1893: reprinted 1964), *The Division of Labour in Society*, London, Macmillan.

Durkheim, E. (1895: reprinted 1964), *The Rules of Sociological Method*, London, Collier-Macmillan.

Edwards, R. C. (1979), *Contested Terrain: The Transformation of Work in the Twentieth Century*, London, Heinemann.

Emery, F. E. (1977), 'The assembly line: its logic and our future', in Emery, F. E. (ed.) (1981) *Systems Thinking: Volume Two*, Harmondsworth, Penguin.

Emery, F. E. and Thorsrud, E. (1969), *Form and Content in Industrial Democracy*, London, Tavistock.

Emery, F. E. and Thorsrud, E. (1976), *Democracy at Work*, Leiden, Martinus Nijhoff.

Emmanuel, C. R. and Otley, D. T. (1985), *Accounting for Management Control*, Wokingham, Van Nostrand Reinhold.

Esland, G. (1976), *Professions and Professionalism*, Milton Keynes, Open University Press.

Estes, R. (1976), *Corporate Social Accounting*, New York, Wiley.

Ezzamel, M. and Hilton, K. (1980a), 'Divisionalization in British industry: a preliminary study', *Accounting and Business Research*, spring, pp. 197–214.

Ezzamel, M. and Hilton, K. (1980b), 'Can divisional discretion be measured?', *Journal of Business Finance and Accounting*, summer, pp. 311–329.

Ezzamel, M., Hoskin, K. W. and Macve, R. H. (1990), 'Managing it all by numbers: a review of Johnson and Kaplan's *Relevance Lost*', *Accounting and Business Research*, vol. 20, no. 7/8, pp. 153–166.

Fama, E. (1980), 'Agency problems and the theory of the firm', *Journal of Political Economy*, vol. 88, no. 2, pp. 288–307.

Fayol, H. (1914: translation 1949), *General and Industrial Management*, London, Pitman.

Filsner, G. and Cooper, M. (1992), 'The environment: a question of profit – the ordinary investor and environmental issues in accounting', in Owen, D. (ed.) *Green Reporting: Accountancy and the Challenge of the Nineties*, London, Chapman & Hall.

Flanders, A. (1970), *Management and Unions*, London, Faber.

Flint, D. (1980), *The Impact of Change on the Accounting Profession*, Edinburgh, ICA Scotland.

Florence, P. S. (1947), 'The statistical analysis of joint stock company control', *Statistical Journal*, part 1.

Florence, P. S. (1953), *The Logic of British and American Industry*, London, Routledge & Kegan Paul.

Florence, P. S. (1961), *Ownership, Control, and Success of Large Companies*, London, Sweet & Maxwell.

Follet, M. P. (1924), *Creative Experience*, London, Longman & Green.

Fox, A. (1974), *Beyond Contract: Work, Power and Trust Relations*, London, Faber.

Fransman, M. (1988), 'The Japanese system and the acquisition, assimilation and further development of technological knowledge: organisational form, markets and government', in Elliot, B. (ed.) *Technology and Social Process*, Edinburgh, Edinburgh University Press.

Freidson, E. (1970), *Profession of Medicine*, New York, Dodd Mead.

Freidson, E. (1971), 'Professions and the occupational principle', in Freidson, E. (ed.) *The Professions and their Prospects*, London, Sage.

Freidson, E. (1973), 'Professionalisation and the organisation of middle-class labour in post-industrial society', in Halmos, P. (ed.) *Professsionalisation and Social Change*, Sociological Review Monograph no. 20, Keele, University of Keele.

Friedman, A. (1977), *Industry and Labour: Class Struggle at Work and Monopoly Capitalism*, London, Macmillan.

Galbraith, J. K. (1967), *The New Industrial State*, London, Hamish Hamilton.

Gallie, D. (1978), *In Search of the New Working Class*, Cambridge, Cambridge University Press.

Galloway, D. and Waldron, D. (1988a), 'Throughput Accounting – 1: the need for a new language for manufacturing', *Management Accounting (UK)*, November, pp. 34–35.

Galloway, D. and Waldron, D. (1988b), 'Throughput Accounting – 2: ranking products profitably', *Management Accounting (UK)*, December, pp. 34–35.

Galloway, D. and Waldron, D. (1989a), 'Throughput Accounting – 3: a better way to control labour costs', *Management Accounting (UK)*, January, pp. 32–33.

Galloway, D. and Waldron, D. (1989b), 'Throughput Accounting – 4: moving on to complex products', *Management Accounting (UK)*, February, pp. 40–41.

Gambling, T. (1978), *Beyond the Conventions of Accounting*, London, Macmillan.

Gartman, D. (1979), 'Origins of the assembly line and capitalist control of work at Ford', in Zimbalist, A. (ed.) *Case Studies on the Labour Process*, New York and London, Monthly Review Press.

Geddes, M. (1992), 'The social audit movement', in Owen, D. (ed.) *Green Reporting: Accountancy and the Challenge of the Nineties*, London, Chapman & Hall.

Gee, P. (1985), *Spicer and Pegler's Book-keeping and Accounts* (19th edition), London, Butterworth.

Giancanelli, P., Gallhofer, S., Humphrey, C. and Kirkham, L. (1990), 'Gender and accountancy: some evidence from the UK', *Critical Perspectives on Accounting*, vol. 1, no. 2, pp. 117–144.

Giddens, A. (1973), *The Class Structure of the Advanced Societies*, London, Hutchinson.

Giddens, A. (1984), *The Constitution of Society*, Cambridge, Polity.

Giddens, A. (1992), *The Transformation of Intimacy: Love, Sexuality and Eroticism in Modern Societies*, Cambridge, Polity.

Gilbert, J. P. (1989), 'The state of JIT implementation and development in the USA', *International Journal of Production Research*, vol. 28, no. 6, pp. 1099–1109.

Glautier, M. W. E. and Underdown, B. (1974), *Accounting in a Changing Environment*, London, Pitman.

Glenn, E. K. and Feldberg, R. L. (1979), 'Proletarianizing office work', in Zimbalist, A. (ed.) *Case Studies on the Labour Process*, New York and London, Monthly Review Press.

Goldman, P. and Van Houten, D. (1980), 'Managerial strategy in turn-of-the-century American industry', in Dunkerley, D. and Salaman, G. (eds) *The International Yearbook of Organisational Studies: 1979*, London, Routledge & Kegan Paul.

Goldratt, E. (1984), *The Goal*, London, Gower.

Goldsmith, R. W. and Parmalee, R. C. (1940), *The Distribution of Ownership in the 200 Largest Non-Financial Corporations*, Monographs of the Temporary National Economic Committee, no. 29, Washington, D.C., US Senate.

Goldthorpe, J. H., Lockwood, D., Bechhofer, F. and Platt, J. (1968a), *The Affluent Worker: Industrial Attitudes and Behaviour*, Cambridge, Cambridge University Press.

Goldthorpe, J. H., Lockwood, D., Bechhofer, F. and Platt, J. (1968b), *The Affluent Worker: Political Attitudes and Behaviour*, Cambridge, Cambridge University Press.

Goldthorpe, J. H., Lockwood, D., Bechhofer, F. and Platt, J. (1969), *The Affluent Worker in the Class Structure*, Cambridge, Cambridge University Press.

Goode, W. (1961), '"Professions" and "non-professions"', in Vollmer, H. M. and Mills, D. L. (eds) (1966) *Professionalization*, Englewood Cliffs, Prentice-Hall.

Gordon, L. A. and Miller, D. (1976), 'A contingency framework for the design of accounting information systems', *Accounting, Organizations and Society*, vol. 1, no. 1, pp. 59–70.

Gordon, R. A. (1945), *Business Leadership in Large Corporations*, Washington, D.C., Brookings Institution.

Gouldner, A. W. (1954), *Patterns of Industrial Bureaucracy*, New York, Free Press.

Gouldner, A. W. (1957), 'Cosmopolitans and locals', *Administrative Science Quarterly*, vol. 2, no. 4, pp. 281–366.

Gray, R. D. (1990a), 'The accountant's task as a friend to the earth', *Accountancy*, June, pp. 65–68.

Gray, R. D. (1990b), *The Greening of Accountancy: The Profession after Pearce*, London, Certified Accountants Publications.

Gray, R. D., Owen, D. and Maunders, K. (1987), *Corporate Social Reporting: Accounting and Accountability*, London, Prentice-Hall.

Greenwood, E. (1957), 'Attributes of a profession', *Social Work*, vol. 2, no. 3, pp. 44–55.

Griffiths, I. (1986), *Creative Accounting: How to Make your Profits what you Want them to be*, London, Waterstone.

Gulick, L. H. and Urwick, L. (eds) (1937), *Papers on the Science of Administration*, New York, Columbia University Press.

Gyllenhammar, P. G. (1977), *People at Work*, London, Addison-Wesley.

Hall, R. H. (1968), 'Professionalization and bureaucratization', *American Sociological Review*, vol. 32, no. 1, pp. 92–105.

Hammond, T. A. (1991), 'The marginalization of African-American public accountants 1900–1965', *Third Interdisciplinary Perspectives on Accounting Conference*, University of Manchester, July.

277

Handy, C. (1985), *Understanding Organizations*, Harmondsworth, Penguin.

Haraszti, M. (1977), *Worker in a Workers' State: Piece-rates in Hungary*, London, Pelican.

Harman, C. (1979), *Is a Machine After Your Job?*, London, Socialist Workers' Publications.

Harper, R. (1988a), 'The fate of idealism in accounting', *Second Interdisciplinary Perspectives on Accounting Conference*, University of Manchester, July.

Harper, R. (1988b), 'Not any old numbers: an examination of practical reasoning in an accountancy environment', *Journal of Interdisciplinary Economics*, vol. 2, no. 4, pp. 297–306.

Harrison, B. (1985), 'Pitfalls of academic accounting', *Accountancy*, January, p. 13.

Harrison, R. (1972a), 'How to describe your organization', *Harvard Business Review*, September–October.

Harrison, R. (1972b), 'When power conflicts trigger team spirit', *European Business*, spring.

Harte, G. and Owen, D. (1992), 'Current trends in the reporting of green issues in the annual reports of United Kingdom countries', in Owen, D. (ed.) *Green Reporting: Accountancy and the Challenge of the Nineties*, London, Chapman & Hall.

Hastie, K. L. (1974), 'One businessman's view of capital budgeting', *Financial Management*, winter, pp. 36–44.

Haynes, W. W. and Solomon, M. B., Jnr. (1962), 'A misplaced emphasis in capital budgeting', *Quarterly Review of Economics and Business*, February, pp. 39–46.

Herman, E. S. (1981), *Corporate Control, Corporate Power*, Cambridge, Cambridge University Press.

Herzberg, F. (1968), 'One more time: how do you motivate employees?', *Harvard Business Review*, January–February, pp. 53–62.

Hilferding, R. (1910: reprinted 1981), *Finance Capital*, London, Routledge & Kegan Paul.

Hines, R. D. (1988), 'Financial accounting: in communicating reality we construct reality', *Accounting, Organizations and Society*, vol. 13, no. 3, pp. 251–261.

Hines, R. (1992), 'Accounting: filling the negative space', *Accounting, Organizations and Society*, vol. 17, no. 3/4, pp. 313–341.

Hiromoto, R. (1988), 'Another hidden edge: Japanese management accounting', *Harvard Business Review*, July/August, pp. 22–26.

Hodgson, A. (1987), 'Deming's never-ending road to quality', *Personnel Management*, July, pp. 40–44.

Hofstede, G. (1980), *Culture's Consequences*, Beverly Hills, Sage.

Hopper, T. and Armstrong, P. (1991), 'Cost accounting, controlling labour and the rise of the conglomerates', *Accounting, Organizations and Society*, vol. 16, no. 5/6, pp. 405–438.

Hopper, T., Cooper, D., Lowe, A., Capps, T. and Mouritsen, J. (1986), 'Management control and worker resistance in the National Coal Board: financial controls in the labour process', in Knights, D. and Willmott, H. C. (eds) *Managing the Labour Process*, London, Macmillan.

Hopper, T., Storey, J. and Willmott, R. (1987), 'Accounting for accounting: towards the development of a dialectic view', *Accounting, Organizations and Society*, vol. 12, no. 5, pp. 437–456.

Hopwood, A. G. (1972), 'An empirical study of the role of accounting data in performance evaluation', *Journal of Accounting Research*, vol. 10, supplement, pp. 156–182.

Hopwood, A. G. (1974), *Accounting and Human Behaviour*, Englewood Cliffs, Prentice-Hall.

Hopwood, A. G. (1983), 'On trying to study accounting in the contexts in which it operates', *Accounting, Organizations and Society*, vol. 8, no. 2/3, pp. 287–305.

Hopwood, A. G. (1985a), 'The tale of a committee that never reported: disagreements on intertwining accounting with the social', *Accounting, Organizations and Society*, vol. 10, no. 3, pp. 361–377.

Hopwood, A. G. (1985b), 'Accounting and the domain of the public: some observations on current developments', *Price Waterhouse Public Lecture on Accounting*, University of Leeds, November.

Hopwood, A. G. (1987), 'The archaeology of accounting systems', *Accounting, Organizations and Society*, vol. 12, no. 3, pp. 207–234.

Horngren, C. T. (1977), *Cost Accounting: A Managerial Emphasis*, London, Prentice-Hall.

Hoskin, K. W. (1993), 'Education and the genesis of disciplinarity: the unexpected reversal', in Messer-Davidow, E., Shumway, D. R. and Sylvan, D. J. (eds) *Knowledges: Historical and Critical Studies in Disciplinarity*, London, University Press of Virginia.

Hoskin, K. W. and Macve, R. H. (1986) 'Accounting and the examination: a genealogy of disciplinary power', *Accounting, Organizations and Society*, vol. 11/12, no. 2, pp. 105–136.

Hoskin, K. W. and Macve, R. H. (1988), 'The genesis of accountability: the West Point connection', *Accounting, Organizations and Society*, vol. 13, no. 1, pp. 37–73.

Hughes, T. P. (1983), *Networks of Power: Electric Supply Systems in the US, England and Germany, 1980–1930*, Baltimore, Johns Hopkins University Press.

Hughes, T. P. (1988), 'The seamless web: technology, science, et cetera, et cetera', in Elliot, B. (ed.) *Technology and Social Process*, Edinburgh, Edinburgh University Press.

Humphrey, C., Turley, S. and Moizer, P. (1991), 'Protecting against detection: the case of auditors and fraud?', *Third Interdisciplinary Perspectives on Accounting Conference*, University of Manchester, July.

Humphrey, C., Moizer, P. and Turley, S. (1992), 'The audit expectations gap – plus ça change, plus c'est la même chose', *Critical Perspectives on Accounting*, vol. 3, no. 2, pp. 109–136.

Hunt, R., Garrett, L. and Merz, C. M. (1985), 'Direct labor costs not always relevant at Hewlett-Packard', *Management Accounting (US)*, February, pp. 58–62.

Hyman, R. and Elger, T. (1981), 'Job controls, the employer offensive and alternative strategies', *Capital and Class*, vol. 15, autumn, pp. 115–145.

Im, J. H. and Lee, S. M. (1989), 'Implementation of Just-in-Time systems in US manufacturing firms', *International Journal of Operations and Production Management*, vol. 9, pp. 5–14.

Inman, R. A. and Mehra, S. (1990), 'The transferability of Just-in-Time concepts to American small businesses', *Interfaces*, vol. 20, no. 2, pp. 30–37.

Jamous, H. and Peloille, B. (1970), 'Professions or self-perpetuating systems? Changes in the French university-hospital system', in Jackson, J. A. (ed.) *Professions and Professionalization*, Cambridge, Cambridge University Press.

Jayson, S. (1992), 'Focus on people – not costs', *Management Accounting (US)*, September, pp. 28–33.

Jenkins, D. (1974), *Job Power*, London, Heinemann.

Jensen, M. C. and Mecklin, W. H. (1976), 'Theory of the firm: managerial behaviour, agency costs and ownership structure', *Journal of Financial Economics*, vol. 3, no. 4, pp. 305–360.

Johnson, H. T. (1992a), *Relevance Regained: From Top-down Control to Bottom-up Empowerment*, New York, Free Press.

Johnson, H. T. (1992b), 'It's time to stop overselling Activity-Based concepts: start focusing on customer satisfaction instead', *Management Accounting (US)*, September, pp. 26–35.

Johnson, H. T. and Kaplan, R. S. (1987), *Relevance Lost: The Rise and Fall of Management Accounting*, Boston, Mass., Harvard Business School Press.

Johnson, T. (1977), 'The professions in the class structure', in Scase, R. (ed.) *Industrial Society: Class, Cleavage and Control*, London, Allen & Unwin.

Johnson, T. (1980), 'Work and power', in Esland, G. and Salaman, G. (eds) *The Politics of Work and Occupations*, Milton Keynes, Open University Press.

Jones, B. (1982), 'Destruction or redistribution of engineering skills: the case of numerical control', in Wood, S. (ed.) *The Degradation of Work? Deskilling and the Labour Process*, London, Hutchinson.

Jones, B. (1988), 'Work and flexible automation in Britain: a review of developments and possibilities', *Work, Employment and Society*, vol. 2, no. 2.

Jones, E. (1981), *Accounting and the British Economy 1840–1980: The Evolution of Ernst and Whinney*, London, Batsford.

Jones, T. C. (1988), *Accounting, Information and Decisions*, Occasional Papers in Sociology, no. 6, Department of Economics and Social Science, Bristol Polytechnic.

Jones, T. C. (1990), 'Corporate social accounting and the capitalist enterprise', in Cooper, D. and Hopper, T. (eds) *Critical Accounts*, London, Macmillan.

Jones, T. C. (1991), 'Designer accounts: of machinations, myths and machines', *Third Interdisciplinary Perspectives on Accounting Conference*, University of Manchester, July.

Jones, T. C. (1992), 'Understanding management accountants: the rationality of social action', *Critical Perspectives on Accounting*, vol. 3, no. 3, pp. 225–257.

Jones, T. C. and Dugdale, D. (1994), 'Academic and practitioner rationality: the case of investment appraisal', *British Accounting Review*, vol. 26, no. 1, pp. 3–25.

Jones, T. C. and Dugdale, D. (forthcoming), 'Manufacturing accountability', in Berry, A., Broadbent, J. and Otley, D. (eds) *Managerial Control: Theories, Issues and Practices*, London, Macmillan.

Jones, T. C., Currie, W. L. and Dugdale, D. (1993), 'Accounting and technology in Britain and Japan: learning from field research', *Management Accounting Research*, vol. 4, no. 2, pp. 109–137.

Kamata, S. (1982), *Japan in the Passing Lane*, London, Pantheon.

Kaplan, R. S. (1984), 'The evolution of management accounting', *Accounting Review*, vol. 59, no. 3, pp. 390–418.

Kaplan, R. S. (1986), 'Must CIM be justified by faith alone?', *Harvard Business Review*, March–April, pp. 87–93.

Kaplan, R. S. (1987), 'Regaining relevance', in Capettini R. and Clancy D. K. (eds) *Cost Accounting Robotics and the New Manufacturing Environment*, New York, American Accounting Association.

Kelly, J. (1982), *Scientific Management, Job Design and Work Performance*, London, Academic Press.

Kerr, C., Dunlop, J. T., Harbison, F. H., and Myers, C. A. (1960), *Industrialism and Industrial Man*, London, Heinemann.

Kharbanda, O. and Stallworthy, E. (1991), 'Let's learn from Japan', *Management Accounting (UK)*, March, pp. 26–33.

King, P. (1975), 'Is the emphasis of capital budgeting misplaced?', *Journal of Business Finance and Accounting*, spring, pp. 69–82.

Kirkham, L. (1992), 'Integrating herstory in history in accounting', *Accounting, Organizations and Society*, vol. 17, no. 3/4, pp. 287–298.

Knights, D. and Collinson, D. (1987), 'Disciplining the shopfloor: a comparison of the disciplinary effects of managerial psychology and financial accounting', *Accounting, Organizations and Society*, vol. 12, no. 5, pp. 457–477.

Kotz, D. M. (1978), *Bank Control of Large Corporations in the United States*, Berkeley, University of California Press.

Kumazawa, M. and Yamada, J. (1989), 'Jobs and skills under the lifelong Nenko employment practice', in Wood, S. (ed.) *The Transformation of Work?*, London, Unwin Hyman.

Lane, C. (1988), 'Industrial change in Europe: the pursuit of flexible specialisation in Britain and Germany', *Work, Employment and Society*, vol. 2, no. 2, pp. 141–168.

Lane, C. (1989), *Management and Labour in Europe: The Industrial Enterprise in Germany, Britain and France*, London, Edward Elgar.

Larner, R. J. (1966), 'Ownership and control in the 200 largest non-financial corporations: 1929 and 1963', *American Economic Review*, vol. 56, pp. 777–787.

Larner, R. J. (1970), *Management Control and the Large Corporation*, New York, Dunellen.

Larson, M. S. (1977), *The Rise of Professionalism: A Sociological Analysis*, Berkeley, University of California Press.

Latour, B. (1987), *Science in Action: How to Follow Scientists and Engineers Through Society*, Milton Keynes, Open University Press.

Latour, B. (1988), 'The Prince for machines as well as for machinations', in Elliot, B. (ed.) *Technology and Social Process*, Edinburgh, Edinburgh University Press.

Laughlin, R. C. (1987), 'Accounting systems in organizational contexts: a case for critical theory', *Accounting, Organizations and Society*, vol. 12, no. 5, pp. 479–502.

Laughlin, R. C. and Puxty, A. G. (1983), 'Accounting regulation: an alternative perspective', *Journal of Business Finance and Accounting*, vol. 10, no. 3, pp. 451–479.

Laughlin, R. C. and Puxty, A. G. (1984), 'Accounting regulation: a reply', *Journal of Business Finance and Accounting*, vol. 11, no. 4, pp. 593–596.

Laughlin, R. C., Lowe, E. A. and Puxty, A. G. (1982), 'Towards a value-neutral positive science of accounting: a comment', *Journal of Business Finance and Accounting*, vol. 9, no. 4, pp. 567–571.

Lawrence, P. R. and Lorsch, J. W. (1967), 'Differentiation and integration in complex organizations', *Administrative Science Quarterly*, June, pp. 1–48.

Lee, D. and Newby, H. (1983), *The Problem of Sociology*, London, Hutchinson.

Leggatt, T. (1970), 'Teaching as a profession', in Jackson, J. A. (ed.) *Professions and Professionalization*, Cambridge, Cambridge University Press.

Lehman, C. R. (1992), '"Herstory" in accounting: the first eighty years', *Accounting, Organizations and Society*, vol. 17, no. 3/4, pp. 261–285.

Lehman, C. R. and Tinker, T. (1987), 'The "real" cultural significance of accounts', *Accounting, Organizations and Society*, vol. 12, no. 5, pp. 503–522.

Lenin, V. I. (1917: reprinted 1966), *Imperialism: The Highest Stage of Capitalism*, Moscow, Progress Press.

Lester, K. (1992), 'Protecting the environment: a new managerial responsibility', in Owen, D. (ed.) *Green Reporting: Accountancy and the Challenge of the Nineties*, London, Chapman & Hall.

Lewchuk, W. (1983), 'Fordism and British motor car employers, 1896–1932', in Gospel, H. F. and Littler, C. R. (eds) *Managerial Strategies and Industrial Relations*, London, Heinemann.

Lewis, D. (1993), 'The Theory of Constraints in accounting', *Chartered Institute of Management Accounting Meeting*, Swindon, November.

Lindblom, C. E. (1968), *The Policy-Making Process*, New York, Prentice-Hall.

Linhart, C. (1981), *The Assembly Line*, London, John Calder.

Littler, C. R. (1978), 'Understanding Taylorism', *British Journal of Sociology*, vol. 29, no. 2, pp. 185–207.

Littler, C. R. (1982), *The Development of the Labour Process in Capitalist Societies: A Comparative Analysis of Work Organisation in Britain, the USA, and Japan*, London, Heinemann.

Littler, C. R. and Salaman, G. (1984), *Class at Work*, London, Batsford.

Loft, A. (1986), 'Towards a critical understanding of accounting: the case of cost accounting in the UK, 1914–1925', *Accounting, Organizations and Society*, vol. 11, no. 2, pp. 137–170.

London Stock Exchange (1991), *Stock Exchange Quarterly* (summer), London International Stock Exchange of the United Kingdom and the Republic of Ireland.

BIBLIOGRAPHY

Lubben, R. (1988), *Just-in-Time Manufacturing*, New York, McGraw-Hill.
Lundberg, F. (1937), *America's Sixty Families*, New York, Vanguard.
Lundberg, F. (1969), *The Rich and the Super-Rich*, London, Nelson.
Lupton, C. and Wilson, C. (1959), 'The social background of "Top decision makers"', in Urry, J. and Wakeford, J. (eds) (1974) *Power in Britain*, London, Heinemann.
Lyne, S. (1993), 'An evaluation of the roles of Activity-Based accounting information', *Management Accounting Research Group Conference*, University of Aston, September.
Lynn, M. (1991), 'Can the environment survive the recession?', *Accountancy*, September, pp. 76–77.
McGregor, D. (1960), *The Human Side of Enterprises*, New York, McGraw-Hill.
Macintosh, N. (1990), 'Annual reports in an ideological role: a critical theory analysis', in Cooper, D. J. and Hopper, T. M. (eds) *Critical Accounts*, London, Macmillan.
McKendrick, N. (1970), 'Josiah Wedgwood and cost accounting in the industrial revolution', *Economic History Review*, vol. 23, no. 1, pp. 45–67.
Malinowski, B. (1944), *A Scientific Theory of Culture*, Chapel Hill, University of Carolina Press.
Mallet, S. (1975), *The New Working Class*, Nottingham, Spokesman Books.
Malmberg, A. (1980), 'The impact of job reform on accounting systems', in Kanawaty, G. (ed.) *International Labour Organization*, 2nd edition, pp. 79–94.
March, J. G. (1987), 'Ambiguity and accounting: the elusive link between information and decision making', *Accounting, Organizations and Society*, vol. 12, no. 2, pp. 153–168.
Marglin, S. (1974), 'The origins and functions of hierarchy in capitalist production', in Nichols, T. (ed.) (1980) *Capital and Labour: Studies in the Capitalist Labour Process*, London, Fontana.
Marris, R. (1964), *The Economic Theory of 'Managerial' Capitalism*, London, Macmillan.
Marris, R. (1972), 'Why economics needs a theory of the firm', *Economic Journal*, March special issue, pp. 321–352.
Marx, K. (1868: reprinted 1976), *Capital: Volume One*, Harmondsworth, Penguin.
Marx, K. (1894: reprinted 1967), *Capital: Volume Three*, New York, International Publishers.
Maskell, B. (1989), 'Performance measurement for world class manufacturing', Part III, *Management Accounting*, vol. 7, no. 9, pp. 36–41.
Maslow, A. H. (1958), *Motivation and Personality*, New York, Harper & Row.
Maunders, K. T. (1981), 'Employee reporting', in Lee, T. A. (ed.) *Developments in Financial Reporting*, Oxford, Philip Allen.
Maurice, M., Sorge, A. and Warner, M. (1980), 'Societal differences in organizing manufacturing units', *Organization Studies*, vol. 1, no. 1, pp. 59–86.
Mayo, E. (1933), *The Human Problems of an Industrial Civilization*, Cambridge, Mass., Harvard University Press.
Mayo, E. (1945), *The Social Problems of an Industrial Civilization*, New York, Macmillan.
Melrose-Woodman, J. and Kverndal, I. (1976), *Towards Social Responsibility: Company Codes and Ethics of Practice*, Management Survey no. 28, London, British Institute of Management.
Merton, R. K. (1968), *Social Theory and Social Structure*, New York, Free Press.
Meyer, S. (1980), 'Adapting the immigrant to the line: Americanization in the Ford factory, 1914–1921', *Journal of Social History*, vol. 14, no. 1, pp. 67–81.
Miliband, R. (1969), *The State in Capitalist Society*, London, Weidenfeld & Nicolson.
Miller, P. (1987), *Domination and Power*, London, Routledge & Kegan Paul.
Miller, P. and O'Leary, T. (1987), 'Accounting and the construction of the governable person', *Accounting, Organizations and Society*, vol. 12, no. 3, pp. 235–265.
Miller, P., Hopper, T. and Laughlin, R. (1991), 'The new accounting history: an introduction', *Accounting, Organizations and Society*, vol. 16, no. 5/6, pp. 395–403.
Mills, C. W. (1940), 'Situated actions and vocabularies of motive', *American Sociological Review*, vol. 5, no. 6, pp. 904–913.

BIBLIOGRAPHY

Mills, C. W. (1959), *The Sociological Imagination*, New York, Oxford University Press.

Mills, R. W. (1988), 'Pricing decisions in UK manufacturing and service companies', *Management Accounting (UK)*, November, pp. 38–39.

Mitchell, A., Puxty, A. G., Sikka, P. and Willmott, H. (1991), *Accounting for Change: Proposals for Reform of Audit and Accounting*, Discussion Paper no. 7, London, Fabian Society.

Mitchell, A., Puxty, A. G., Sikka, P., and Willmott, H. (1993), *A Better Future for Auditing*, London, University of East London.

Mokken, R. J. and Stokman F. N. (1974), 'Interlocking directorates between large corporations', *European Consortium for Political Research Conference*, Strasbourg.

Monsen, R. J. (1973), 'Is social accounting a mirage?', in Dierkes, M. and Bauer, A. A. (eds) *Corporate Social Accounting*, New York, Praeger.

Moore, W. E. (1970), *The Professions: Roles and Rules*, New York, Russell Sage.

Morgan, G. (1986), *Images of Organisation*, Beverly Hills, Sage.

Morgan, G. and Willmott, H. (1993), 'The "new" accounting research: on making accounting more visible', *Accounting, Auditing and Accountability Journal*, vol. 6, no. 4, pp. 3–36.

Morgan, J. and Luck, M. (1973), *Managing Capital Investment*, Rugby, Mantec.

Morgan, M. and Weerakoon, P. (1989), *Japanese Management Accounting: Its Contribution to the Japanese Economic Miracle*, Harmondsworth, Penguin.

Moyes, J. (1988), 'The dangers of JIT', *Management Accounting (UK)*, February, pp. 22–24.

Muir, R. (1910), *Peers and Bureaucrats*, London, Constable.

Munro, R. J. B. and Hatherley, D. J. (1993), 'Accountability and the new commercial agenda', *Critical Perspectives on Accounting*, vol. 4, no. 4, pp. 369–395.

Neimark, M. (1990), 'The king is dead. Long live the king', *Critical Perspectives on Accounting*, vol. 1, no. 1, pp. 103–114.

Neimark, M. and Tinker, T. (1986), 'The social construction of management control systems', *Accounting, Organizations and Society*, vol. 11, no. 4/5, pp. 369–395.

Nelson, D. (1975), *Managers and Workers*, Madison, University of Wisconsin Press.

Nichols, T. (1969), *Ownership, Control and Ideology*, London, Allen & Unwin.

Nichols, T. (1975), 'The "socialism" of management: some comments on the new "human relations"', *Sociological Review*, vol. 23, no. 2, pp. 245–265.

Nichols, T. (1986), *The British Worker Question: A New Look at Workers and Productivity in Manufacturing*, London, Routledge & Kegan Paul.

Nichols, T. and Armstrong, P. (1976), *Workers Divided: A Study in Shopfloor Politics*, London, Fontana.

Nichols, T. and Beynon, H. (1977), *Living With Capitalism*, London, Routledge.

Noble, D. F. (1979), 'Social choice in machine design: the case of automatically controlled machine tools', in Zimbalist, A. (ed.) *Case Studies on the Labour Process*, London, Monthly Review Press.

Nyman, S. and Silberston, A. (1978), 'The ownership and control of industry', *Oxford Economic Papers*, vol. 30, no. 1, pp. 74–101.

Oliver, N. and Wilkinson, B. (1987), 'Just-in-time, just-too-soon?', *Industrial Society Magazine*, September.

Oliver, N. and Wilkinson, B. (1988), *The Japanization of British Industry*, Oxford, Blackwell.

Oppenheimer, M. (1973), 'The proletarianisation of the professional', in Halmos, P. (ed.) *Professionalisation and Social Change*, Sociological Review Monograph no. 20, Keele, University of Keele.

Otley, D. T. (1980), 'The contingency theory of management accounting: achievements and prognosis', *Accounting, Organizations and Society*, vol. 5, no. 4, pp. 194–208.

Ouchi, W. G. (1980), 'Markets, bureaucracies and clans', *Administrative Science Quarterly*, vol. 25, pp. 129–141.

Owen, D. (1981), 'Why accountants can't afford to turn their backs on social reporting', *Accountancy*, January, pp. 44–45.

Owen, D. (1982), 'Social accountability: a role for accountants', *Accountants Record*, July, pp. 4–6.

Owen, D. (1992), 'The implications of current trends in green awareness for the accounting function: an introductory analysis', in Owen, D. (ed.) *Green Reporting: Accountancy and the Challenge of the Nineties*, London, Chapman and Hall.

Pahl, R. E. and Winkler, J. (1974), 'The economic elite: theory and practice' in Stanworth, P. and Giddens, A. (eds) *Elite and Power in British Society*, Cambridge, Cambridge University Press.

Parker, L. D. (1986), 'Polemical themes in social accounting: a scenario for standard setting', *Advances in Public Interest Accounting*, vol. 1, pp. 67–93.

Parkin, F. (1979), *Marxism and Class Theory: A Bourgeois Critique*, London, Tavistock.

Parsons, T. (1937: reprinted 1969), *The Structure of Social Action*, New York, Free Press.

Pascale, R. and Athos, A. (1981), *The Art of Japanese Management*, Harmondsworth, Penguin.

Pavalko, R. M. (1971), *Sociology of Occupations and Professions*, Itasca, Peacock.

Perks, R. W. and Gray, R. H. (1979), 'Beware of social accounting', *Management Accounting*, December, pp. 22–23.

Perks, R. W. and Gray, R. H. (1981), 'What is social accounting?', *Management Accounting*, July–August, p. 29.

Perrow, C. (1970a), *Organisational Analysis: A Sociological View*, London, Tavistock.

Perrow, C. (1970b), 'Departmental power', in Zald, M. N. (ed.) *Power in Organizations*, Nashville, Vanderbilt Press.

Perrow, C. (1972), *Complex Organizations: A Critical Essay*, Glenview, Scott Foresman.

Peters, T. J. and Waterman, R. H. (1982), *In Search of Excellence: Lessons from America's Best Run Companies*, New York, Harper & Row.

Pfeffer, J. (1981), *Power in Organizations*, London, Pitman.

Pike, R. H. (1983), 'Review of recent trends in formal capital budgeting processes', *Accounting and Business Research*, summer, pp. 201–208.

Pike, R. (1988a), 'The capital budgeting revolution', *Management Accounting (UK)*, vol. 66, no. 9, pp. 28–30.

Pike, R. H. (1988b), 'An empirical study of the adoption of sophisticated capital budgeting practices and decision-making effectiveness', *Accounting and Business Research*, autumn, pp. 341–351.

Pike, R. H. and Wolfe, M. B. (1988), '*Capital Budgeting for the 1990's*, London, CIMA.

Piore, M. J. and Sabel, C. F. (1984), *The Second Industrial Divide: Prospects for Prosperity*, New York, Basic Books.

Pollard, S. (1965), *The Genesis of Modern Management*, London, Edward Arnold.

Pollard, S. (1984), *The Wasting of the British Economy*, London, Croom Helm.

Pollert, A. (1981), *Girls, Wives, Factory Lives*, London, Macmillan.

Pollert, A. (1988), 'The "flexible firm": fixation or fact?', *Work, Employment and Society*, vol. 2, no. 3, pp. 281–316.

Poulantzas, N. (1974), *Classes in Contemporary Capitalism*, London, New Left Books.

Primrose, P. L. (1988), 'The motivation for manufacturing investment', in Worthington, B. (ed.) *Advances in Manufacturing Technology* III: *Proceedings of the Fourth National Conference on Production Research*, London, Kogan Page.

Primrose, P. (1991), 'The appliance of science', *Manufacturing Engineer*, November, pp. 42–43.

Primrose, P. L. and Leonard, R. (1987), 'The relationship between costing systems and AMT investment', in McGoldrick, P. F. (ed.) *Advances in Manufacturing Technology* II: *Proceedings of the Third National Conference on Production Research*, London, Kogan Page.

Pugh, D. S. and Hickson, D. J. (1976), *Organisational Structure in its Context: The Aston Programme* I, Farnborough, Saxon House.

Pugh, D. S. and Hinings, C. R. (eds) (1976), *Organisational Structure – Extensions and Replications: The Aston Programme* II, Farnborough, Saxon House.

Puxty, A. G. (1986), 'Social accounting as immanent legitimation: a critique of technicist ideology', *Advances in Public Interest Accounting*, vol. 1, pp. 95–111.

Puxty, A. G. and Lyall, D. (1990), 'Cost control: the managers' perspective', *Management Accounting (UK)*, December, pp. 46–47.

Puxty, A. G., Willmott, H. C., Cooper, D. J. and Lowe, T. (1987), 'Modes of regulation in advanced capitalism: locating accountancy in four countries', *Accounting, Organizations and Society*, vol. 12, no. 3, pp. 273–291.

Radcliffe-Brown, A. (1952), *Structure and Function in Primitive Society*, London, Oxford University Press.

Ramanathan, K. V. (1976), 'Toward a theory of social accounting', *Accounting Review*, vol. 51, no. 3, pp. 516–28.

Ramsay, H. (1990), *1992: The Year of the Multinational?*, Papers in Industrial Relations, Coventry, University of Warwick.

Reader, W. J. (1966), *Professional Men: The Rise of the Professional Classes in Nineteenth Century England*, London, Weidenfeld & Nicolson.

Renner, K. (1904: translated 1949), *The Institutions of Private Law and their Social Function*, London, Routledge & Kegan Paul.

Rice, A. K. (1958), *Productivity and Social Organisation*, London, Tavistock.

Roberts, J. and Scapens, R. W. (1985), 'Accounting systems and systems of accountability – understanding accounting practices in their organizational contexts', *Accounting, Organizations and Society*, vol. 10, no. 4, pp. 443–456.

Roethlisberger, F. J. and Dickson, W. (1939), *Management and the Worker*, Cambridge, Mass., Harvard University Press.

Rose, M. (1975), *Industrial Behaviour*, London, Allen Lane.

Rose, M. and Jones, B. (1985), 'Managerial strategy and trade union responses in work reorganisation schemes at enterprise level', in Knights, D., Willmott, H. and Collinson, D. (eds) *Job Redesign: Critical Perspectives on the Labour Process*, London, Gower.

Rosenbrock, H. (1979), *The Re-direction of Technology*, Research paper, London, Council for Science and Society.

Rosenbrock, H. (1985), 'Engineers and the work people do', in Littler, C. R. (ed.) *The Experience of Work*, Aldershot, Gower.

Roslender, R. (1992), *Sociological Perspectives on Modern Accountancy*, London, Routledge.

Roth, J. A. (1974), 'Professionalism: the sociologist's decoy', *Sociology of Work and Occupations*, vol. 1, no. 1, pp. 6–23.

Roy, D. (1952), 'Quota restriction and goldbricking in a machine shop', *American Journal of Sociology*, vol. 57, pp. 427–442.

Roy, D. (1953), 'Work satisfaction and social reward in quota achievement: an analysis of piecework incentive', *American Sociological Review*, vol. 18, p 507–514.

Roy, D. (1955), 'Efficiency and "the fix": informed relations in a piecework machine shop', *American Journal of Sociology*, vol. 60, pp. 255–266.

Roy, D. (1960), 'Banana time: job satisfaction and informal interaction', *Human Organizations*, vol. 18, pp. 158–168.

Russell, J. (1978), 'The coming of the line: the Ford Highland Park plant, 1910–1914', *Radical America*, vol. 12, no. 1, pp. 29–45.

Sabel, C. F. (1982), *Work and Politics*, Cambridge, Cambridge University Press.

Sakuri, M. (1990), 'The influence of factory automation on management accounting practices: a study of Japanese companies', in Kaplan, R. (ed.) *Measures for Manufacturing Excellence*, Boston, Mass., Harvard Business School Press.

Salaman, G. (1979), *Work Organizations: Resistance and Control*, London, Longman.

Salaman, G. (1981), *Class and the Corporation*, London, Fontana.

Scapens, R. W. (1988), 'Management accounting – researching practice: a review of the practice of research', *Annual Conference of the Accounting Association of Australia and New Zealand*, Canberra, Australian National University, August.

Scapens, R. W. (1990), 'Researching management accounting practice: the role of case study methods', *British Accounting Review*, vol. 22, no. 3, pp. 259–281.

Scapens, R. W. and Arnold, J. A. (1986), 'Economics and management accounting research', in Bromwich, M. and Hopwood, A. G. (eds) *Research and Current Issues in Management Accounting*, London, Pitman.

Scapens R. W., Sale, J. T. and Tikkas, P. A. (1982), *Financial Control and Divisional Capital Investment*, London, CIMA.

Scarborough, P., Nanni, A. J., Jnr. and Sukarai, M. (1991), 'Japanese management accounting practices and the effects of assembly and process automation', *Management Accounting Research*, vol. 2, no. 1, pp. 27–46

Schumpeter, J. A. (1919: reprinted 1950), *Capitalism, Socialism and Democracy*, New York, Harper & Row.

Scott, J. P. (1982), *The Upper Classes*, London, Macmillan.

Scott, J. P. (1985), *Corporations, Classes and Capitalism*, second edition, London, Hutchinson.

Scott, J. P. (1986), 'The debate on ownership and control', *Social Studies Review*, pp. 24–29.

Scott, W. G. (1966), 'Professionals in bureaucracies: areas of conflict', in Vollmer, H. M. and Mills, D. L. (eds) *Professionalization*, Englewood Cliffs, Prentice Hall.

Scott, W. G. (1967), *Organisation Theory*, Homewood, Irwin.

Shaiken, H. (1979), 'The numerical control of work, workers and automation in the computer age', *Radical America*, vol. 13, no. 6, pp. 29–45.

Shaiken, H. (1984), *Work Transformed: Automation and Labour in the Computer Age*, New York, Holt Rinehart & Winston.

Shaiken, H., Herzenberg, S. and Kuhn, S. (1986), 'The work process under more flexible production', *Industrial Relations (US)*, vol. 23, no. 2, pp. 167–183.

Shapiro. S. P. (1987), 'The social control of impersonal trust', *American Journal of Sociology*, vol. 93, no. 3, pp. 623–658.

Shocker, A. D. and Sethi, S. P. (1974), 'An approach to incorporating social references in developing corporate action strategies' in Sethi, S. P. (ed.) *The Unstable Ground: Corporate Social Policy in a Dynamic Society*, Los Angeles, Melville.

Sikka, P. and Willmott, H. (1991), 'Illuminating the state-profession relationship: some evidence', *Third Interdisciplinary Perspectives on Accounting Conference*, University of Manchester, July.

Simon, H. A. (1945), *Administrative Behaviour*, New York, Macmillan.

Simon, H. A. (1976), *Administrative Behaviour*, third edition, New York, Free Press.

Smith, A. (1776: reprinted 1974), *The Wealth of Nations*, Harmondsworth, Penguin.

Smith, C. (1989), 'Flexible specialization, automation and mass production', *Work, Employment and Society*, vol. 3, no. 2, pp. 203–220.

Smith, E. O. (1983), *The West German Economy*, London, Croom Helm.

Sochor, Z. A. (1981), 'Soviet Taylorism revisited', *Soviet Studies*, vol. 33, no. 2, pp. 246–264.

Solomons, D. (1978), 'The politicization of accounting', *Journal of Accountancy*, November, pp. 213–225.

Solomons, D. (1991a), 'Accounting and social change: a neutralist view', *Accounting, Organizations and Society*, vol. 16, no. 3, pp. 287–95.

Solomons, D. (1991b), 'A rejoinder', *Accounting, Organizations and Society*, vol. 16, no. 3, pp. 311–312.

Sorge, A. and Maurice, M. (1990), 'Machine tool manufacturers in France and Germany', *International Journal of Human Resource Management*, vol. 1, no. 2, pp. 141–172.

Sorge, A., Hartmann, G., Warner, M. and Nicholas, I. (1983), *Microelectronics and Manpower in Manufacturing: Applications of Computer Numerical Control in Great Britain and West Germany*, Aldershot, Gower.

Stewart, A., Prandy, K. and Blackburn, R. (1980), *Social Stratification and Occupations*, London, Macmillan.

Storey, J. (1980), *The Challenge to Management Control*, London, Kogan Page.

Storey, J. (1991), 'Do the Japanese make better managers?', *Personnel Management*, August, pp. 24–28.

Strange, N. (1991), 'Management accounting and competitive advantage: a comparison of British and German management accounting', *Management Accounting Research Conference*, University of Aston, September.

Suzuki, N. (1989), 'The attributes of Japanese CEOs: can they be trained?', *Journal of Management Development*, vol. 8, no. 4, pp. 5–11.

Sweeting, R. C., Bright, J., Davies, R. E. and Downes, C. A. (1991), 'Manufacturing accounting practices and techniques', *British Accounting Association Conference*, University of Salford, April.

Sweezy, P. A. (1956), *The Theory of Capitalist Development*, New York, Monthly Review Press.

Taylor, F. W. (1903, 1911, 1912: reprinted 1947), *Scientific Management*, New York, Harper & Brothers.

Thomas, W. I. (1928), *The Child in America*, New York, Knopf.

Thompson, E. P. (1967), 'Time, work-discipline and industrial capitalism', *Past and Present*, no. 38, pp. 56–97.

Thompson, G. (1982), 'The firm as a "dispersed" social agency', *Economy and Society*, vol. 11, pp. 233–50.

Thompson, P. (1989), *The Nature of Work*, second edition, Basingstoke, Macmillan.

Tinker, A. M. (1985), *Paper Prophets: A Social Critique of Accounting*, Eastbourne, Holt Rinehart & Winston.

Tinker, A. M. (1991), 'The accountant as partisan', *Accounting, Organizations and Society*, vol. 16, no. 3, pp. 297–310.

Tinker, A. M. and Neimark, M. (1987), 'The role of annual reports in gender and class contradictions at General Motors, 1917–1976', *Accounting, Organizations and Society*, vol. 12, no. 1, pp. 71–88.

Tomkins, C. and Groves, R. (1983), 'The everyday accountant and researching his reality', *Accounting, Organizations and Society*, vol. 8, no. 4, pp. 389–406.

Tricker, R. I. (1975), *Research in Accountancy – a Strategy for Further Work*, London, Social Science Research Council.

Trist, E. L. and Bamforth, K. W. (1951), 'Some social and psychological consequences of the longwall method of coal getting', *Human Relations*, vol. 4, no. 1, pp. 3–38.

Trist, E. L., Higgin, G. W., Murray, H. and Pollack, A. B. (1963), *Organizational Choice*, London, Tavistock.

Tyson, T. (1990), 'Accounting for labor in the early nineteenth century: the US arms making experience', *Accounting Historians Journal*, vol. 17, no. 1, pp. 47–59.

Tyson, T. (1993), 'Keeping the record straight: Foucauldian revisionism and nineteenth century US cost accounting history', *Accounting, Auditing and Accountability Journal*, vol. 16, no. 2, pp. 4–16.

Urwick, L. F. (1928), 'Principles of direction and control', in Lee, J. (ed.) *Dictionary of Industrial Administration*, London, Pitman.

Urwick, L. F. (1947), *The Elements of Administration*, London, Pitman.

Vancil, R. F. (1979), *Decentralization: Ambiguity by Design*, Homewood, Irwin.

Voss, C. A. and Robinson, S. J. (1987), 'Applications of Just-in-Time manufacturing techniques in the UK', *International Journal of Operations and Production Management*, vol. 7, no. 4, pp. 46–52.

Waldron, D. (1988), 'Accounting for CIM: the new yardsticks', *EMAP Business and Computing Supplement*, February, pp. 1–2.

Walker, R. G. (1984), *'A True and Fair View' and the Reporting Obligations of Directors and Auditors*, Canberra, Australian Government Publishing Services.

Walsh, E. J. and Stewart, R. E. (1993), 'Accounting and the construction of institutions: the case of a factory', *Accounting, Organizations and Society*, vol. 18, no. 7/8, pp. 783–800.

Walton, P. (1991), *The True and Fair View: A Shifting Concept*, London, Chartered Association of Certified Accountants.

Watts, R. L. and Zimmerman, J. L. (1986), *Positive Accounting Theory*, New York, Prentice-Hall.

Weber, M. (1922: translated 1968), *Economy and Society*, New York: Bedminster Press.

Webster, J. (1986), 'Word processing and the secretarial labour process', in Purcell, K., Wood, S., Waton, A. and Allen, S. (eds) *The Changing Experience of Employment*, London, Macmillan.

Westergaard, J. and Resler, H. R. (1975), *Class in a Capitalist Society: A Study of Contemporary Britain*, London, Heinemann.

Wheelwright, E. L. and Miskelly, J. (1967), *Anatomy of Australian Manufacturing Industry*, Sydney, Law Book Company.

Whitehead, T. N. (1938), *The Industrial Worker*, London, Oxford University Press.

Whitmore, D. A. (1987), *Work Measurement*, second edition, London, Heinemann.

Wicks, C. (1992), 'Business and the environmental movement', in Owen, D. (ed.) *Green Reporting: Accountancy and the Challenge of the Nineties*, London, Chapman & Hall.

Wilensky, H. L. (1964), 'The professionalisation of everyone?', *American Journal of Sociology*, vol. 70, no. 2, pp. 135–158.

Wilkinson, B. (1983), *The Shopfloor Politics of New Technology*, London, Heineman.

Williams, K., Williams, J. and Thomas, D. (1983), *Why are the British Bad at Manufacturing?*, London, Routledge & Kegan Paul.

Williams, K., Haslam, C. and Williams, J. (1991), 'The Western problematic against the Japanese application', *Third Interdisciplinary Perspectives on Accounting Conference*, Manchester, July.

Williams, K., Haslam, C. and Williams, J. (1992), 'Ford versus "Fordism": the beginning of mass production?', *Work, Employment and Society*, vol. 6, no. 1, pp. 517–555.

Williams, R., Jnr (1959), *American Society*, New York, Knopf.

Williamson, J. H. (1966), 'Profit, growth and sales maximisation', *Economica*, vol. 33, no. 129, pp. 1–16.

Williamson, O. E. (1975), *Markets and Hierarchies: Analysis and Antitrust Implications*, New York, Free Press.

Willis, P. (1977), *Learning to Labour*, Farnborough, Saxon House.

Willmott, H. (forthcoming), 'Beyond the paradigm mentality', *Organization Studies*.

Winner, L. (1980), 'Do artefacts have politics?', *Daedalus*, summer, pp. 121–136.

Wood, S. (1991), 'Japanization and/or Toyotaism?', *Work, Employment and Society*, vol. 5, no. 4, pp. 567–600.

Woods, M., Pokorny, M., Lintner, V. and Blinkhorn, M. (1984), 'Investment appraisal in the mechanical engineering industry', *Management Accounting (UK)*, vol. 62, no. 10, pp. 36–37.

Woods, M., Pokorny, M., Lintner, V. and Blinkhorn, M. (1985), 'Appraising investment in new technology: the approach in practice', *Management Accounting (UK)*, vol. 63, no. 10, pp. 36–37.

Woodward, J. (1958), *Management and Technology*, London, HMSO.

Wright, E. O. (1978), *Class, Crisis and the State*, London, New Left Books.

288

BIBLIOGRAPHY

Wrong, D. (1961), 'The oversocialized concept of man in modern sociology', *American Sociological Review*, vol. 26, April, pp. 183–193.

Yanovitch, M. (1977), *Social and Economic Inequality in the Soviet Union*, London, Martin Robertson.

Yoshikawa, T., Innes, J. and Mitchell, F. (1989), 'Japanese management accounting: a comparative survey', *Management Accounting*, vol. 68, no. 11, pp. 20–23.

Zeitlin, M. (1974), 'Corporate ownership and control: the large corporation and the capitalist class', *American Journal of Sociology*, vol. 73, pp. 1073–1119.

Zipkin, P. H. (1991), 'Does manufacturing need a JIT revolution?', *Harvard Business Review*, January–February, pp. 40–50.

NAME INDEX

Aaronovitch, S. 47
Abell, P. 115
ACCA *see* Chartered Association of Certified Accountants
Accounting Auditing and Accountability 255
Accounting Organizations and Society 255
Ackerman, R.W. 214
Adams, R. 65
Adorno, Theodor 261
Advances in Public Interest Accounting 255
Albrow, M. 99
Anaconda 45
Andersen 75
Argyris, C. 157
Arkwright, Sir Richard 9, 11, 26
Armstrong, P. 24, 26, 30, 109, 112, 114, 125, 126, 137, 142, 228, 229, 243, 244, 260
Atkinson, J. 50, 180–1, 182, 192; and Meager, N. 183
Austria 112

Babbage, Charles 14, 32
Bailes, K.E. 184
Baran, B. 176
Baran, P.A. and Sweezy, P.M. 47
Baritz, L. 107
Barnard, C. 90
Baumol, W.J. 41
Beattie, V.A. and Ryan, R.J. 263
Belgium 52, 112, 147
Benjamin, C. 53, 54
Bennis, W. 115
Benson, I. and Lloyd, J. 54

Benston, G.J. 61
Bentham, Jeremy 263
Berger, P. and Luckman, T. 255–6
Berle, A.A. 39; and Means, G.C. 38–40, 41–2, 44, 45, 46, 56, 61, 87
Berry, A.J. *et al.* 131, 132, 201, 243, 333
Bethlehem Steel Works 156, 195
Beynon, H. 163, 166, 188
Bhopal 64
Black, S.P. 172
Blackburn Mail 16
Blauner, R. 148–9, 160, 169, 190, 191
Blaza, A.J. 65
Bosquet, M. 158, 167
BP 164
Braverman, H. 14, 160–2, 164, 169–70, 172, 173–4, 176–7, 184, 190, 192, 244
Brimson, J.A. 208
British Institute of Management 65
British Leyland 168
British Nuclear Fuels 63
British Steel 168
Bromwich, M. and Bhimani, A. 217, 229
Brown, G. 166
Bryer, R.A. and Brignall, AT.J. 233
Buck, J. 65
Burawoy, M. 102, 163, 199
Burch, P.H. 46, 47
Burchell, G. *et al.* 121, 122, 142, 227, 229, 263
Burns, T. and Stalker, G. 93, 94
Burrell, G. 264
Business Week 46

Cadbury family 48
Cadbury, Sir Adrian 183
Cadbury-Schweppes 183

SUBJECT INDEX